WAYNE PUBLIC LIBRARY
MAIN LIBRARY
461 Valley Road
Wayne, NJ 07470

NOV

W9-BPP-795

NOV 0 5 2018

WAYNE PUBLIC LIBRARY
MAIN LIBRARY
461 Valley Road
Wayne, NJ 07470

REFERENCE

WAYNE PUBLIC LIBRARY
MAIN LIBRARY
461 Valley Road
Wayne, NJ 07470

NOV 0 5 2018

CRITICAL INSIGHTS

Civil Rights Literature, Past & Present

REFERENCE

WAYNE PUBLIC LIBRARY
MAIN LIBRARY
461 Valley Road
Wayne NJ 07470

NOV 0 3 1976

CRITICAL INSIGHTS

Civil Rights Literature, Past & Present

Editor

Christopher Allen Varlack

University of Maryland, Baltimore County

SALEM PRESS

A Division of EBSCO Information Services, Inc.

Ipswich, Massachusetts

GREY HOUSE PUBLISHING

Copyright © 2017 by Grey House Publishing, Inc.

*Credit: Saeed Jones, excerpts from "Jasper, 1998" and "Prelude to Bruise"
from Prelude to Bruise. Copyright © 2014 by Saeed Jones. Reprinted with the
permission of The Permissions Company, Inc. on behalf of Coffee House Press,
www.coffeehousepress.org.*

All rights reserved. No part of this work may be used or reproduced in any manner
whatsoever or transmitted in any form or by any means, electronic or mechanical,
including photocopy, recording, or any information storage and retrieval system,
without written permission from the copyright owner. For information, contact
Grey House Publishing/Salem Press, 4919 Route 22, PO Box 56, Amenia, NY
12501.

∞ The paper used in these volumes conforms to the American National Standard
for Permanence of Paper for Printed Library Materials, Z39.48-1992 (R2009).

Library of Congress Cataloging-in-Publication Data
(Prepared by The Donohue Group, Inc.)

Names: Varlack, Christopher Allen, editor.
Title: Civil rights literature, past & present / editor, Christopher Allen Varlack,
University of Maryland, Baltimore County.
Other Titles: Critical insights.
Description: [First edition]. | Ipswich, Massachusetts : Salem Press, a division
of EBSCO Information Services, Inc. ; Amenia, NY : Grey House Publishing,
[2017] | Includes bibliographical references and index.
Identifiers: ISBN 978-1-68217-268-1 (hardcover)
Subjects: LCSH: Civil rights in literature. | Civil rights movements in literature.
| American literature--20th century--History and criticism. | American literature-
-21st century--History and criticism. | Civil rights movements--United States-
-History--20th century. | Civil rights movements--United States--History--21st
century.
Classification: LCC PS228.C55 C58 2017 | DDC 810.9/35873--dc23

PRINTED IN THE UNITED STATES OF AMERICA

Contents

Critical Contexts

Critical Readings

Resources

Dedication

In "Letter from Birmingham Jail," Martin Luther King, Jr. wrote that "[w]e had no alternative except to prepare for direct action, whereby we would present our very bodies as a means of laying our case before the conscience of the local and the national community" (291). The road for equal rights and opportunities across history in the United States is therefore covered with the bodies of those who have lost their lives and sacrificed in order to obtain the freedoms and equality so vital to the American dream. *Critical Insights: Civil Rights Literature, Past & Present* is dedicated to all those who have lost their lives in this ongoing struggle and who challenged the barriers of race, gender, orientation, class, and religion that often continue to divide this nation today. Their courage and their legacy are preserved, in part, in the pages of this text.

About This Volume

Christopher Allen Varlack

From its flawed notion of "separate but equal" after the *Plessy v. Ferguson* decision to the rampant violence against black bodies throughout the nineteenth and twentieth centuries, the United States faced a clear racial divide perpetuated by its Jim Crow culture and the overarching disenfranchisement of blacks. In response, on August 28, 1963, noted American orator and civil rights activist Dr. Martin Luther King Jr. delivered his iconic "I Have a Dream" speech on the Lincoln Memorial, urging radical social and political change in a society marred by a rich history of segregation and discrimination. Since then, we have recognized this speech as a symbol of the enduring struggle for equal civil rights and the pursuit of the core values upon which the United States is based. Issues of race, however, are only part of the civil rights debate still taking place nationwide. While the 2015 *Cambridge Companion to American Civil Rights Literature* offers an updated examination of works such as King's, effectively bringing the discussion of the Civil Rights Movement and its seminal texts into the twenty-first century, its study has not gone far enough, leaving behind vital conversations about gender, sexual orientation, and class that are part of the "inescapable network of mutuality" (King 290) in the United States. This edited volume, *Critical Insights: Civil Rights Literature, Past & Present*, attempts to expand the conversation by calling attention to the diverse range of civil rights issues at the heart of American literature across genre and across time.

Though the field of scholarship surrounding the African-American Freedom Struggle is certainly quite extensive, few works available today interrogate the sociopolitical impulse in the breadth of African-American literature like Kavon Franklin's "Free Speech and Racial Rhetoric: African-American Writers on Race in the United States." Tracing the overarching cultural and political critique of works from Jupiter Hammon to Ta-Nehisi Coates' 2015 *Between the World and Me*, Franklin asserts the inherent value of these literary records in helping us to make sense of the civil rights struggle today. Like Franklin, Jessie LaFrance Dunbar, in "Inadequate Conception of Human Complexity," focuses on the intersection of key works in American literature, stressing the ways in which Ralph Ellison's works, including *Invisible Man*, not only challenge the 1959 study produced by Stanley Elkins but also the very notion that slavery irrevocably damaged the larger black community. Carol Bunch Davis' essay, "'Be Loyal to Yourselves': Jim Crow, Black Cultural Nationalism, and US Cultural Memory in Ossie Davis' *Purlie Victorious*," continues to review key works of the Civil Rights Movement by interrogating Davis' critique of segregation as well as his call for self-affirmation among a people who, despite the long history of slavery and prejudice, refuse to remain oppressed. The final of this critical contexts section, "Haunting America: Racial Identity and Otherness in Civic Society" by Mary K. Ryan, offers a comparative perspective of works by Ralph Ellison, Kiese Laymon, and Toni Morrison to discuss the ways in which the invisibility of blacks speaks to the need for an aggressive civil rights campaign even in the twenty-first century. Together, these works provide the necessary framework for understanding the African-American struggle for civil rights we most commonly think of in American history.

In its endeavor to explore the key themes and directions of civil rights literature, *Critical Insights: Civil Rights Literature, Past & Present* then engages fifteen additional critical readings essays across five sections, the first titled, "United, We Shall Overcome": Literature of the Civil Rights Era and Beyond. Essays in this section cover key works from the 1950s through the 1970s that call attention to the issues of discrimination, prejudice, and non-violent direct action so vital to the Civil Rights Movement. For instance, in "Unpacking Notions of Citizenship through James Baldwin's *Another Country*," Hope Jackson examines the concept of citizenship at work in one of Baldwin's most celebrated texts, complicated by the color of the protagonist's skin in a society where *black* and *American* are often seen as diametrically opposed. Through this essay, Jackson highlights the hypocrisy of American inclusivity that necessitates civil rights action such as today's Black Lives Matter campaign. Seeking to expand our knowledge of nonviolent direct action past King's more Christian interpretation, in "'On Revolution and Equilibrium': Barbara Deming's Secular Nonviolence," Sheila Murphy probes Deming's secular construction and the insights that it offers for protests movements deeper into the twenty-first century. The final essay, "'[B]ut yesterday morning came the worst news': Margaret Walker Alexander's *Prophets for a New Day* by Seretha D. Williams, looks at the ways in which Walker recasts the slain leaders of the Civil Rights Movement, from Martin Luther King Jr. to Medgar Evers, as Old Testament prophets. In the end, this section speaks to the central themes and values of the Civil Rights Movement as a widespread effort to enact social change across the United States.

The following section, entitled "Women of the World Unite": Womanhood, Civil Rights, and the Politics of Identity, focuses on the under-examined role of women activists, thinkers, and writers well beyond the Civil Rights Movement. In his essay, "The Mothers' Tragedy: Loss of a Child in the Works of Gwendolyn Brooks, Dudley Randall, and Michael Harper," for instance, Eric J. Sterling examines the suffering of black mothers in African-American literature and the longstanding impact of violence against black bodies through events such as the Sixteenth Street Baptist Church Bombing and the murder of Emmett Till. In "Alice Walker and Claudia Rankine: Reclaiming the Ocularity of the Self," Margaret Cox explores the work of two renowned figures in more contemporary black literature with an emphasis on the ways in which their works have actively encouraged the African-American community to reject externally constructed notions of identity and reclaim what she terms "the ocularity of the self." The final essay in this section also interrogates the works of Alice Walker, though placing emphasis on her largely under-examined short fiction. In "'Crooning [the] Lullabies [of] Ghosts': Reclamation and Witness as Socio-Political Protest in the Short Fiction of Alice Walker," Christopher Allen Varlack asserts that the storytelling tradition itself plays an integral role in the civil rights struggle, as the black men and women who serve as keepers of the African-American tale inherently rebel against a system of white supremacy that would rather those stories of violence and oppression disappear. With its emphasis on the role of women in this larger struggle for equal rights, this section proposes that the Women's Liberation Movement and the long Civil Rights Movement are essentially intertwined.

The third section, "I Am Gay, Straight, Bi . . . A Person": Representations of the LGBTQ Rights Movement, begins to probe another under-examined sector of the civil rights struggle in American literature: the Gay Rights Movement still ongoing today. Addressing the notion of queer metronormativity and the limitations it places on a more expansive definition of queer expression or politics, in his essay, "The City and The Country: Queer Utopian Spaces in John Rechy's *City of Night* and Patricia Highsmith's *Price of Salt*," Derrick King explores the city and country in conversation as crucial to the utopian vision that LGBT+ literature often anticipates. This essay is followed by "B(l)ack up on the Shelf: The Erasure of Black Queerness in Martin Luther King Jr.'s Why We Can't Wait." Here Robert LaRue seeks to trace the erasure of Bayard Rustin from King's iconic work as part of a widespread silencing of black homosexual voices, not as an indication of the homophobia within the black community but rather as a reflection on the movement's attempt to appeal to the white public in terms that it could best understand. Concluding this section, Tasia Milton's "Writing Civil Rights after James Byrd, after Matthew Shepard" explores Saeed Jones' collection Prelude to Bruise and the trauma experienced by the gay and black communities alike in a nation that, at times, seemed determined to eradicate cultural difference. Like Dunbar's earlier work in this collection, Milton interrogates the experience of trauma while also asserting the possibility that its victims are not defined nor deformed by it.

Because issues of class and the socioeconomic hierarchy across the United States reflect a more contemporary civil rights debate projected on the national stage, the fourth section of this collection is entitled, "We Are the 99%": Economic Mobility and Class Stratification in the Civil Rights Debate. Leonard A.

Steverson, in "'The Process of Becoming Nobody': Reflections on E. Franklin Frazier's *Black Bourgeoisie: The Rise of a New Middle Class*," offers an insightful look at Franklin's controversial exposé on the black middle class, recognizing the study as vital for the sociological concepts that it produced and for providing an in-depth analysis of race and class essential in American discourse. In "Toward a More Inclusive America: Jesse Jackson's 1984 and 1988 Democratic National Convention Discourse," however, Enrico Beltramini focuses on how this socioeconomic divide surfaced in political conversations of the 1980s as Jesse Jackson maintained an aggressive campaign for president of the United States built on a core promise of uplifting the working class. In these speeches, Jackson expanded upon Fred Hampton's notion of the Rainbow Coalition that is at the heart of this edited volume, as illustrated by the cover image; Beltramini's work is therefore a much needed part of the dialogue this collection unearths as it highlights the importance of all disadvantaged groups in the fight for social change. Kaila Philo, in her essay, "Agency, Activism, and the Black Domestic Worker in Kathryn Stockett's *The Help* and Delores Phillips' *The Darkest Child*," concludes this section with an intensive look at the plight of black domestic workers in texts by black and white authors alike. While Stockett's novel advances the controversial white savior trope, Phillips' offers a new perspective—one in which the black female protagonists are unafraid of voicing their disenfranchisement with both a social and economic system that limits their opportunities for advancement.

The final section, From "The New Jim Crow" to #BlackLivesMatter: Contemporary Civil Rights Literature, attempts to link civil rights discourse of the nineteenth and twentieth centuries with efforts of the present day. In "Staging MLK in the Age of Colorblindness: *The Good Negro* and *The Mountaintop*," for instance, Andrew Sargent examines two contemporary plays that seek to challenge the oversimplified version of Dr. Martin Luther King Jr. that has long dominated the public memory of the Civil Rights Movement. By probing the works of Tracey Scott Wilson and Katori Hall, Sargent thus calls attention to King's full humanity as well as the integral role of those who fought alongside him in shaping his vision of brighter days. In Corrie Claiborne's "What Happens When Death Becomes a Poem?: Understanding the Place of Mourning in Civil Rights Literature," she draws a connection between the literature of the early Civil Rights Era and the wealth of literature in constant production today as a form of remembrance and protest against the violence blacks have faced, from Trayvon Martin to Sandra Bland. Like Claiborne, in "Social Media Meets Social Justice: The Role of the Hashtag in the Contemporary Conversation on Race," Deborah F. Kadiri also examines the contemporary historical moment and role of both texts and technology in changing the nature of this conversation. Positing the hashtag as a new genre one day capable of overcoming the limitations of civil rights activism past, Kadiri suggests that a new wave of civil rights literature is emerging to combat the invisibility of black lives by foregrounding those conversations in the highly visible space of social media. Together, these essays will change how we conceptualize civil rights literature, past and present, by highlighting the diversity of tactics authors now use to engage that important debate.

This volume concludes with an extensive chronology, outlining the histories of the civil rights debate across race, gender, and orientation while also attempting to situate the key works of civil rights literature produced. Because past studies have heavily focused on the Civil Rights Movement at the expense of the Women's Liberation Movement and the Gay Rights Movement at large, the inclusion of this chronology is one of the highlights of this volume. In its effort to push the boundaries of critical thought regarding civil rights literature, *Critical Insights: Civil Rights Literature, Past & Present*, we believe, is a valuable and much-needed contribution to today's scholarship and seeks to connect the examples left behind by activists decades before to a more diverse and contemporary range of civil rights texts, including new media in constant production today. Ultimately, this project should serve as a starting place for the much deeper conversations that thinkers from Martin Luther King Jr. to Harvey Milk contend must happen in this new day and age, for there are other civil rights issues not discussed within its pages (the overwhelming mistreatment of Native Americans, the rising debate over gender identity, and the need for equal access to resources and opportunities for disabled citizens, etc.) that must also be explored. In the words of Harvey Milk, "Unless you have dialogue, unless you open the wall of dialogue, you can never reach to change people's opinion" (168). This, we hope, can be just the beginning of such a conversation.

Works Cited

King, Martin Luther, Jr. "Letter from Birmingham Jail." *A Testament of Hope: The Essential Writings and Speeches of Martin Luther King, Jr.* Ed. James M. Washington. New York: HarperCollins, 1986. 289-302.

Milk, Harvey. "The Hope Speech." *Great Speeches of the 20th Century.* Ed. Bob Blaisdell. Mineola, NY: Dover, 2011. 167-171.

"Caught in an Inescapable Network of Mutuality": The Intersection of Race, Gender, and Orientation in American Civil Rights Literature_____

Christopher Allen Varlack

From the Revolutionary War (1775–1783) and the struggle for independence from British monarchial oppression to the ongoing tension amidst an ever-evolving Black Lives Matter sociopolitical campaign (2013–present), the American people have been embroiled in a continual fight for civil rights that has ravaged the nation, leaving millions battered from the battlefield to city streets, all in pursuit of the core values that comprise the American Dream: life, liberty, and the pursuit of happiness for all. During this journey, the blood of slaves and soldiers ran like rivers "ancient as the world and older than the flow of human blood in human veins" (Hughes 23), slaking the thirst of growing lands we now know as the United States. Leaders of the emerging Women's Rights Movement, from Susan B. Anthony to Lucretia Mott to Julia Ward Howe, tackled headfirst an American patriarchal system that effectively relegated women to second-class status, denying them the right to vote, to own property outside of marriage, and to make decisions about their own bodies, among a number of other issues (pay inequity, domestic violence, etc.)—all concerns that are still quite prevalent in the twenty-first century. Discontent with the pervasive racial hierarchy and the notions of white supremacy that limited opportunity for black men and women, Martin Luther King Jr., Malcom X, Medgar Evers, and others marched, too, "present[ing their] very bodies as a means of laying [their] case before the conscience of the local and national community" (King 291). Meanwhile, San Francisco City Supervisor Harvey Milk stood alongside gay and lesbian activists at a time of rampant homophobia and institutionalized prejudice against the LGBTQ community, rallying against a culture that rendered them invisible.

As we see in these examples, US history is largely defined by a consistent fight against the forces of oppression that disparaged difference, engaging in that dangerous practice of cultural Othering and widespread discrimination on the basis of race, gender, sexual orientation, religion, and ability. This history is evident in the sting of the whip—that tradition of chattel slavery that literally denied the nation's blacks their freedom and humanity. It is evident from Stonewall Inn in Manhattan to the Pulse gay nightclub in Orlando, where gunman Omar Mateen shot and killed dozens of gay and lesbian residents in 2016, continuing a trend of violence against homosexual bodies. And it is evident in the rise of hate crimes against people of Middle Eastern descent post-9/11, such as the murder of Balbir Singh Sodhi in Mesa, Arizona, attacked by Frank Silva Roque—just one in a long line of bigoted men and women enacting violence against "towelheads" (qtd. in Lewin) in a society that even today ostracizes non-white individuals. Most importantly, however, it is evident in the literature left behind by both writers and activists, who recorded not only the history of violence and discrimination faced by minority peoples, but also the individual and group efforts to combat that oppression. Recognizing, as King once declared, that "we are caught in an inescapable network of mutuality" (290), these authors refused to remain silent or be silenced, using their words to assert the value of marginalized communities, thus leaving us an important lesson as we continue this fight into the twenty-first century: we must speak up in order to rise.

"While There is Actually No Negro Problem, There is Definitely a Caucasian Problem": American Civil Rights Literature and the Racial Mountain

For many, the fight for civil rights in the United States has largely centered on the issues of ethnicity and race, as the historical mistreatment of Native Americans, African Americans, and other people of color seems to suggest. From the advent of chattel slavery to the forced relocation of Native Americans from their native lands to the institutionalization of racism with the Jim Crow Age, a racial fissure emerged that divided the United States—a direct consequence, according to noted essayist and satirist George Schuyler, of the myth of the Negro problem. In his 1944 essay, "The Caucasian Problem,"

Schuyler argues that this fiction "is written into the laws, accepted by organized religion; it permeates our literature, distorts our thinking and is deeply imbedded in our customs and institutions" (37) dating back to days well before the *Plessy v. Ferguson* decision that legalized racial segregation across the United States. The notion of the Brute Negro, for instance, was predicated upon fears of racial miscegenation post-Reconstruction and the perception of a rising black threat to the white-dominated power structure of the South. As a result, the rise of the sharecropping system, the founding of the Ku Klux Klan in Tennessee, the development of black codes to disenfranchise black voters, the policy of "separate but equal," and the creation of what Michelle Alexander terms "the New Jim Crow" through mass incarceration of blacks were all some of the many strategies employed historically to not only handle the Negro problem but also to keep the color line in place.

Early African-American civil rights literature thus finds its roots in the slave narratives of figures such as Henry Bibb and Frederick Douglass, who catalogued the trials of their enslavement in order to call attention to the degradation of the American people at large. Such narratives were integral to exposing the ills of slavery, particularly in the face of a growing body of pro-slavery literature and fiction that presented the contended slave and wretched freedman stereotypes so popular across the United States. It was not until the Harlem Renaissance (1920s–1940s), however, when the life and culture of the African-American community took center stage, that the literature produced by black authors began to have its most lasting impact, championed by leaders such as Alain Locke, who called for a truly radical transformation in the conceptualization of the American Negro. In his 1925 essay, "Enter the New Negro," for example, Locke argued that "the Old Negro had long become more of a myth than a man" (631). For generations, after all, he trotted in the minds of American thinkers—some intangible object to be sensibly "argued about, condemned or defended, to be 'kept down,' or 'in his place,' or 'helped up,' to be worried with or worried over, harassed or patronized, a social bogey or a social burden" for the white American man (631). Those same perceptions inevitably translated into the Negro American mindset, the thinking Negro, as Locke often identified him, conditioned to "focus his attention on controversial issues, to see himself in the distorted perspective of a social problem" (631)—a constant, unavoidable concern. The death of the Old Negro and his social-burden mentality was thus a principal goal perpetuated in many Harlem Renaissance works.

Literature of this time was also heavily concerned with civil rights violations as well as the cultural disdain toward African-American people—a central theme in the poetry, essays, and short fiction of the era. Perhaps one of the most renowned and heavily anthologized works, Countee Cullen's "Incident" acknowledges these issues by describing a childhood encounter in Baltimore where he was called a nigger by a young white boy on the bus and thus received his first taste of the racial divide dominant in the American city. Unlike "Heritage" and some of his other poetic works, this poem was noticeably less introspective, less concerned with the conflicting values circulating in the African-American mind. Instead, the poem appeared more concerned with providing a portrait of the American cultural landscape as experienced by this Negro child. And because the experience ultimately had a lingering effect on his mind, he ended with that lasting impression he wanted to resound in the American reader: "Of all the things that happened there / That's all that I remember" (ll. 11-12). In doing so, Cullen diverged from the individual racial experience, directly expressing "the sense of group and its common experiences" by using his personal encounters with race and the racial divide as a platform from which to illustrate the more universal (Locke, "The Message" 69). The poem, after all, transcends the individual incident and the young racist boy on the bus. Instead, the poem takes on a greater significance, demonstrating the lasting effect of racial disparity on the Negro American mind and the depth that racist prejudice pervaded as even the youngest of children were already taught to see blacks as inferior.

The speeches and essays of the Civil Rights Movement then offered the next wave in the emerging civil rights discourse related specifically to issues of race. Composed in 1953, "Stranger in the Village" by James Baldwin, for instance, sought to challenge this notion of white supremacy that had long defined the American social and political infrastructure. Asserting that "[t]his world is white no longer, and it will never be white again" (175), Baldwin interrogated the refusal to accept the new role that blacks would play in twentieth-century American life, having risen from their past positions as the downtrodden slave and the genteel servant to help realize the multicultural mosaic that comprised the American Dream. Building upon Locke's conception of the New Negro, here he asserts that "[t]he time has come to realize that the interracial drama acted out on the American continent has not only created a new black man, it has created a new white man, too. . . . I am not, really, a stranger any longer for any American alive" (175). For American society to continue to operate under the principles of Jim Crow and white supremacy is, therefore, detrimental to the nation as a whole, for "[p]eople who shut their eyes to reality simply invite their own destruction, and anyone who insists on remaining in a state of innocence long after that innocence is dead turns himself into a monster" (175). By foregrounding these often unspoken realities, like so many other noted black writers and activists of his time, Baldwin projected an image of a United States unable, for much longer, to resist this impending change, for the cries of oppression and the demand for equality were far too loud to ignore.

"Stigmatized as 'Odd' and 'Unfeminine'": American Civil Rights Literature and the Gender Mountain

The struggle for equitable rights, however, is not restricted to the African-American Civil Rights Movement of the 1950s and 60s, for race has been only one barrier to equal opportunities in the United States. Gender has long since been a dividing line as well, particularly under a social and political system that was patriarchal in nature and not only denied women the right to vote but also trapped them in the controversial cult of domesticity—the nineteenth-century notion that a woman's place was in the home. By restricting women to the role of caretaker or homemaker, American society inherently devalued the contribution of women to American life, stigmatizing women eager to work outside of the home. As Shirley Chisholm notes in her

1969 address to the House of Representatives, "[W]omen that do not conform to the system, who try to break with the accepted patterns, are stigmatized as 'odd' and 'unfeminine'"—the type of seemingly unruly and uncontrollable women who found themselves in mental institutions throughout the nineteenth and twentieth centuries. Even Rosie the Riveter, after all, was expected to lay down her tools at the end of World War II when the soldiers fighting on the frontlines finally returned to their jobs and their homes, a freshly-cooked meal supposedly awaiting them at the dinner table.

The Women's Liberation Movement, however, was a cornerstone in the American fight for increased rights for all and attempted to challenge these outdated societal expectations not only by redefining the role of women outside of the home but also by demanding an equal stake in shaping the social and political climate of the United States. In her July 1837 *Letters on the Equality of the Sexes*, for instance, Sarah Grimké dared to "ventur[e] on nearly untrodden ground" and to "advance arguments in opposition to a corrupt public opinion" by suggesting that God created women and men equal and that the patriarchal interpretation of the Bible was in fact a "perverted interpretation of Holy Writ" (3). Rejecting religious discourse that asserted a gender hierarchy dating back to the days of Adam and Eve, Grimké instead envisioned man and woman with equal dominion over the land. In her December 17, 1849 speech, "Discourse on Woman," Lucretia Mott builds upon this fundamental critique, arguing that "[t]here is nothing of greater importance to the well-being of society at large—of man as well as woman—than the true and proper position of woman" (3) and that "[w]oman is claiming for herself stronger and more profitable food" (4). In a society where women were denied the right to vote and were afforded little (if any) protections against domestic or sexual abuse, these early critiques were just as dangerous as they were groundbreaking, refusing to accept the role of women as the mules of a male-dominated world.

As the fight for increased civil rights advanced, activists of a constantly evolving women's liberation movement were forced to tackle headfirst the consistent double standards that so many women faced when characterized as bad mothers and bad wives for venturing outside of the family home (a perceived threat to the nuclear family values that had become so sacred to early American life) and asserting a less restrictive sexual identity, often outside of marriage. In 1963, feminist and activist Betty Friedan brought this discussion to the forefront with her seminal work, *The Feminine Mystique.* In her opening chapter, for instance, Friedan proclaims that:

> [t]he problem lay buried, unspoken, for many years in the minds of American women. It was a strange stirring, a sense of dissatisfaction, a yearning that women suffered in the middle of the twentieth century in the United States. Each suburban wife struggled with it alone . . . . [S]he was afraid to ask even of herself the silent question—'Is this all?'" (57)

Though the dream of being a mother and a housewife is certainly an ideal for some women, in this passage, Friedan calls attention to the ways in which that expectation, for others, is far more oppressive. These women, who were taught "that truly feminine women do not want careers, higher education, political rights," were cast off as merely "neurotic, unfeminine, unhappy women who wanted to be poets, physicians, or presidents" (Friedan 57). Under this system, their ambitions were stifled and their dreams deferred for the sake of tradition until the rise of the sexual revolution, during which more and more women traded in their house gowns for the newly invented knee-high boots and miniskirts.

For Friedan, this shift represented a longstanding obligation to "no longer ignore that voice within women that says: 'I want something more than my husband and my children and my home'" (78). Though this certainly manifested in a need for unobstructed sexual exploration (still an issue today with the stigma surrounding female sexual promiscuity), for others, it manifested in a push for equal opportunity in the social, economic, and political sectors of American life. This notion is perhaps best articulated in Hillary Clinton's address to the UN Fourth World Conference on Women on September 5, 1995. Hosted in Beijing, China, the conference saw a diverse gathering of women from across the globe who were eager to celebrate the accomplishments of women in the twentieth century but also the actions necessary to keep moving forward, to break the glass ceiling hanging dangerously low over women's heads. Like the progenitors of the Women's Liberation Movement before her, Clinton argued that discrimination was detrimental for all and not just in the United States. "As long as discrimination and inequities remain so commonplace . . .," she remarked, "as long as girls are valued less, fed less, fed last, overworked, underpaid, not schooled, subjected to violence in and outside their homes—the potential of the human family to create a peaceful, prosperous world will not be realized." Only when women are afforded the opportunities to stand on equal ground with their male counterparts could the world truly thrive. This world, after all, is strictly patriarchal no longer, so the notion of female inferiority could not truly persist unfettered ever again.

"A Green Light to All Who Feel Disenfranchised, A Green Light to Move Forward": American Civil Rights Literature and the Sexual Mountain

Emerging in the early 1900s, the Gay Rights Movement shared similar roots with the Civil Rights Movement and the Women's Liberation Movement before it. Characterized as deviant and abominations in this largely conservative society, members of the LGBTQ community were not only restricted from equal access to the freedoms and opportunities that were at the foundation of the American Dream but were also silenced, restricted from free expression of a core part of their identities. Homosexuality and bisexuality, in fact, were still characterized as mental illnesses—a fact made all the more apparent with the rising belief in conversion or reparative therapy: a form of pseudoscience including methods as extreme as chemical castration and electro-shock therapy to recondition one's sexual orientation toward the established societal norm. The development of the Mattachine Society in 1951 and the Daughters of Bilitis in 1956 thus marked a potential turning point in American history as gay rights organizations began to emerge across the nation to upend the widespread misconceptions of the gay and lesbian community while calling attention to the need for a new norm: a culture of acceptance and equality. This platform inherently shaped the civil rights literature to emerge throughout the twentieth and twenty-first centuries, particularly the speeches of gay rights activists not interested in a "don't ask, don't tell" cultural ideology but rather in a culture built upon equal opportunity for all, a culture built upon mutual respect.

Delivered on the steps of San Francisco City Hall on June 25, 1978, Harvey Milk's "The Hope Speech" is a seminal speech of the Gay Rights Movement aimed at accomplishing this core goal of evoking an American conversation about the rights of the LGBTQ community in a nation arguably close-minded and homophobic. During this speech, delivered just a few months before his assassination, Milk first outlined the pervasive mistreatment of the community he had come to represent both politically and personally, acknowledging that "[g]ay people have been slandered nationwide. We've been tarred and we've been brushed with the picture of pornography. In Dade County, we were accused of child molestation" (170). For Milk, however, and the people gathered to celebrate California Gay Freedom Day, addressing these myths and the destructive stereotypes that they engendered was just part of the mission of the twentieth century, for much of American history was steeped in a tradition of oppression and discrimination that could not be resolved without a concerted effort to heal its contaminated roots. Milk therefore called for an open dialogue on gay rights—one that would challenge the image of the deviant homosexual corrupting the innocence of America's youth—but more importantly the election of LGBTQ leaders to local and national offices in order to give "a green light to all who feel disenfranchised" and to usher in a new era of "hope to a nation that has given up" (171). In these words, Milk thus reflected a vision for America at large—a vision reflected from King's notion of an "inescapable network of mutuality" (290) to Jesse Jackson's later campaign for what he termed the "Rainbow Coalition" to bridge the fissures that so heavily divided the United States.

Though many writers and activists answered Milk's call for a resounding conversation that would shake the very norms that inhibited equality and the widespread achievement of the elusive American Dream, it is Elizabeth Toledo's April 25, 2000 speech, "Life, Liberty, and the Pursuit of Happiness: The GLBT Movement at a Crossroads," that most strongly tackles the unresolved issues of civil rights inequities for the gay community after Milk's death. Presenting to the National Press Club, Toledo argues that the advancements of the African-American Civil Rights Movement were not as widespread as many imagined. "In fact," she asserts, "the legal reality is that those of us in same sex relationships have not been fully protected from discrimination in housing, jobs, family law, education—virtually every aspect of our lives is subject to discrimination" (Toledo 121). It was not until 2003, after all, that the US Supreme Court overturned the nation's existing sodomy laws with the *Lawrence v. Texas* case, effectively decriminalizing same-sex sexual activity and challenging the notion of homosexuality as fundamentally deviant behavior. Likewise, it was not until 2010 that the US Senate repealed the controversial "Don't Ask, Don't Tell" policy that put sexual identity and the desire to serve one's country at odds for LGBTQ service people. As a result, Toledo maintains, "[w]e are under open assault by those who would deny us basic human rights" (122).

For Milk and Toledo, however, both held hope that this open assault would one day reach its end, though the radical cultural and political transformation needed was "depend[ent] upon our ability to build strong political infrastructure and organize on the state and local level" (Toledo 122). Recognizing this too, Elizabeth Birch, Director of the Human Rights Campaign, stood before the Democratic National Convention on August 15, 2000 and delivered a speech that would help shape the Democratic Party platform and the direction of the United States' civil rights struggle today. Here Birch proclaims that "[w]ise leadership never takes refuge in silence," like Milk before her, effectively urging the nation's political leaders to engage in an open conversation about gay rights and to no longer allow this sector of society, too long dejected and distressed, to battle issues such as AIDS and homophobic violence "virtually alone in the face of a stony, silent government" (124). Calling then for the election of Al Gore as president of the United States, Birch argued for a new tradition to emerge—one not defined by its "silent apathy in the face of hatred" but rather by its "simple equality—the equal right to work, raise a family, serve our country in every way and be free from the shackles of brutality and hate" (124). Until such a change could occur, the American family would remain fractured and the devastating tradition of silence would certainly continue, shifting across new groups (the transgender community, Muslims, and immigrants, etc.), each targeted for discrimination and disenfranchisement from the American Dream.

American Civil Rights Literature and the Class Hierarchy

More recently, however, the conversation of civil rights has moved beyond issues of race, gender, and sexual orientation to also include debate over the pervasive class hierarchy at work in the United States. Though class structure has always been a concern, with the nation arguably built on the backs of the downtrodden and poor, such conversations have not taken center stage in the mainstream American political and cultural discourse since the days of Jesse Jackson's pleas for the working poor or discussions of tenement living in Jacob Riis' 1890 *How the Other Half Lives: Studies of the Tenements of New York*. Because the American dream is built upon the notion that an individual, through hard work and determination and even the pursuit of a college degree, can rise above a meager upbringing, the stagnation of the working class and the rise in populations far below the poverty line reveal the startling truth about the American class hierarchy: the notion of an American Dream was merely an unfulfilled promise without the resources and policies in place to promote the uplift of communities generally underserved and underrepresented in the twentieth and twenty-first centuries.

Modern political leaders, such as 2016 Democratic Party candidate Bernie Sanders, have played an integral role in unearthing these conversations, highlighting the ways in which wealth is concentrated in a small percentage of the population and how the controversial practices put in place by large corporations leave many Americans unable to support themselves and their families as a result of a minimum wage inconsistent with the cost of living. In the 2016 election cycle, this issue became a cornerstone of the Sanders debate, calling attention to the reality that:

> the top one percent of the people on this planet own more wealth than the bottom ninety-nine percent, while the wealthiest sixty people— sixty people—own more than the bottom half—3 ½ billion people. At a time when so few have so much, and so many have so little, we must reject the foundations of this contemporary economy as immoral.

His words, to the Pontifical Academy of Social Sciences, however, are not new, reflecting an earlier civil rights struggle to provide increased economic opportunity and advancement for the working poor. John F. Kennedy, for instance, argued in his 1962 address to the Economic Club of New York that the United States should "not accept an unemployment rate of five percent or more, such as we have had for 60 out of the last 61 months. There is no need for us to be satisfied with a rate of growth that keeps good men out of work and good capacity out of use." Tackling what he perceived as a general complacency with the economic progress of the 1950s and 60s, Kennedy argued that the United States was producing below capacity, simultaneously failing to tap into the 30 to 40 billion dollars that he believed the nation was capable of producing and failing to provide jobs for the unemployed class reliant on struggling welfare programs to make ends meet. Under his perspective, economic growth should not deter efforts to uplift the lower class, "[f]or on the strength of our free economy rests the hope of all free nations. We shall not fail that hope—for free men and free nations must prosper and they must prevail."

Aligned with Kennedy's thinking, Dr. Martin Luther King Jr. developed his own economic plan to reduce American poverty amidst the "Poor People's Campaign," advocating for a universal basic income—what senior associate editor for *The Atlantic*, Jordan Weissmann, aptly describes as "an idea that, while light-years beyond the realm of mainstream political conversation today, had actually come into vogue in the late 1960s." Though much of King's activism centered on the issues of race and the mistreatment of African-American people in both social and judicial sectors, King was also heavily concerned with the development of a socioeconomic plan to move the nation forward, recognizing that equality extends beyond just the color of one's skin. Eager to find a seat at the proverbial table for all, he came to understand that true change in the twentieth century could not solely be conceptualized as young black children and young white children holding hands in the creation of a more united United States. It must also entail the coming together of people across class lines so that the central fractures that had, for far too long, separated the American people could be mended and so that the content of one's character would be the only necessary dividing line at the forefront of the American consciousness. King's plan thus envisioned a United States that thrives in its mutuality rather than a not-so-united United States struggling to become the land of opportunity that its founding fathers hoped it would be.

"Together . . . We Will Rise": The Legacy of American Civil Rights Literature

As these texts reveal, the United States (and the world at large) is far from the post-racial, colorblind society that some scholars have claimed it to be. Particularly in this multicultural world still heavily shaped by its perpetual conflicts of difference, the markers of race, gender, and sexual orientation are some of the most prominent dividing lines that threaten to tear humanity apart. For that reason, the pursuit of civil rights may never truly end—a fact that makes civil rights literature all the more vital as a reminder of the journey we have taken and of the unfulfilled goals (of life, liberty, and the pursuit of happiness for all) that we still must fight to achieve. By returning to past works, such as Martin Luther King Jr.'s infamous "Letter from Birmingham Jail" and Shirley Chisolm's "Equal Rights for Women" speech, we can then begin the daunting process of building a better America—one that embraces that "inescapable network of mutuality" (King 290), enabling us to finally stand together and rise.

At the same time, we must also look forward at the works of civil rights discourse in constant production today, for their assessment of the racial, gender, and sexual landscape can give us much needed fuel to deconstruct emerging walls, whether symbolic or physical. "This is our history—," after all, declared Senator Cory Booker in his speech at the 2016 Democratic National Convention, "knowing that liberty is not secure until it's secure for all." But knowing is no longer enough. From now on, we must begin to speak up; we must "declare that we are a nation of interdependence and that in America love always trumps hate. [We must] declare so that generations yet unborn can hear us: we are the United States of America; our best days are ahead of us. And together . . . we will rise" (Booker).

Works Cited

Alexander, Michelle. *The New Jim Crow: Mass Incarceration in the Age of Colorblindness.* New York: The New P, 2012.

Baldwin, James. "Stranger in the Village." *Notes of a Native Son.* Boston: Beacon P, 1984. 159-175.

Birch, Elizabeth. "First Convention Speech by a Gay Organization's Leader." 2000. Daley 123-125.

Booker, Cory. Democratic National Convention. Wells Fargo Center, Philadelphia, PA. 26 July 2016.

Chisholm, Shirley. "Equal Rights for Women." House of Representatives, Washington, DC. 21 May 1969.

Clinton, Hillary. "Women's Rights are Human Rights." UN Fourth World Conference on Women. Beijing, China. 5 Sept. 1995.

Cullen, Countee. "Incident." *The Portable Harlem Renaissance Reader.* Ed. David Levering Lewis. New York: Penguin, 1994. 234.

Daley, James, ed. *Great Speeches on Gay Rights.* Mineola, NY: Dover, 2010.

Friedan, Betty. *The Feminine Mystique.* 1963. New York: Norton, 1997.

Grimké, Sarah. *Letters on the Equality of the Sexes, and the Condition of Woman.* 11 July 1837. Charleston: BiblioBazaar, 2008.

Hughes, Langston. "The Negro Speaks of Rivers." *The Collected Poems of Langston Hughes.* Ed. Arnold Rampersad & David Roessel. New York: Vintage, 1995.

Kennedy, John F. "Address to the Economic Club of New York." Economic Club of New York. Waldorf Astoria Hotel, New York, NY. 14 Dec. 1962.

King, Martin Luther, Jr. "Letter from Birmingham Jail." *A Testament of Hope: The Essential Writings and Speeches of Martin Luther King, Jr.* Ed. James M. Washington. New York: HarperCollins, 1986. 289-302.

Lewin, Tamar. "Sikh Owner of Gas Station is Fatally Shot in Rampage." *New York Times* 16 Sept. 2001.

Locke, Alain. "Enter the New Negro." *Survey Graphic* 6.60 (1925): 631-634.

—. "The Message of The Negro Poets." *The Works of Alain Locke.* Ed. Charles Molesworth. Oxford: Oxford UP, 2012. 68-78.

Milk, Harvey. "The Hope Speech." *Great Speeches of the 20th Century.* Ed. Bob Blaisdell. Mineola, NY: Dover, 2011. 167-171.

Mott, Lucretia. "Discourse on Woman." The Assembly Buildings, Philadelphia, PA. 17 Dec. 1849.

Sanders, Bernie. "The Urgency of a Moral Economy: Reflection on the 25th Anniversary of Centesimus Annus." The Pontifical Academy of Social Sciences, Vatican City, Italy. 15 Apr. 2016.

Schuyler, George. "The Caucasian Problem." 1944. *Rac[e]ing to the Right: Selected Essays of George Schuyler.* Ed. Jeffrey B. Leak. Knoxville: U of Tennessee P, 2001. 37-50.

Toledo, Elizabeth. "Life, Liberty, and the Pursuit of Happiness: The GLBT Movement at a Crossroads." 2000. Daley 119-122.

Weismann, Jordan. "Martin Luther King's Economic Dream: A Guaranteed Income for All Americans." *The Atlantic.* The Atlantic Monthly Group, 28 Aug. 2013. Web. 15 Dec. 2016.

CRITICAL
CONTEXTS

Free Speech and Racial Rhetoric: African-American Writers on Race in the United States_____

Kavon Franklin

The Civil Rights Movement encompasses more than just Martin Luther King Jr.'s dream and Rosa Parks' refusal to give up her seat on a bus; it predates the 1950s, and it goes beyond Birmingham and "Bull" Connor. Although the modern Civil Rights Era is usually dated as beginning with the *Brown v. Board of Education* decision in 1954 and ending with the passage of the Voting Rights Act in 1965, the freedom struggle in fact goes back to the earliest days of Africans in the Americas circa 1570, almost fifty years before the first shipment of human cargo from Africa landed in Jamestown. During that time, an enslaved man named Yanga escaped from a plantation in Veracruz, Mexico, and fled to the highlands to form a *palenque*, or maroon community, which even Spanish troops could not bring to heel. By the mid-seventeenth century, black men and women in the British colonies had begun filing "freedom suits" and occasionally winning, as in the cases of Elizabeth Key in 1656 and Elizabeth Freeman, Quock Walker, and others in the 1700s.

When Freeman and Walker won their cases in 1781, the first African-American authors had emerged, and by the 1800s, black writer-activists were unambiguously and unabashedly denouncing slavery and the subjugation of blacks who were free in name only. The work from this period anticipated much of the black cultural thought that was to come later. Without it, the gains made in the 1950s and 60s would have been impossible, and a black president would have certainly been out of the question. Of course, the two terms of President Barack Obama did not solve racism any more than the legislation passed in the 60s did. As such, though many often teach the Civil Rights Movement as if it has a beginning, middle, and end, in fact—human nature being what it is—the struggle for civil rights will never stop, continuing today in the many campaigns for equality along the lines of race, gender, sexual orientation, religion, and more.

Cultural moods, after all, can shift wildly and then back again. One CNN commentator, David Gergen, said Republican presidential candidate Donald Trump had, through his rhetoric and rallies, "unleashed spirits in this country," which is just the right word: *unleashed*—not *created*—for when it comes to race relations, there has always been a great deal of hatred, anger, hurt, and fear bubbling under the surface when not bubbling over the top. African-American writers, public intellectuals, and musicians have been on the forefront of exposing it, even in the face of hostility from a general public tired of hearing about America's original sin: the enslavement, exploitation, and brainwashing of African and African-American people. In other words, the "white racial resentment" (Bouie) and "ethno-nationalism" (Clift) discussed so much lately does not surprise many in the black community, especially social critics and agitators who have faced it for so long.

This is why learning history and learning from history is so important. The books, pamphlets, articles, and speeches left behind by authors including Frederick Douglass, Ida B. Wells, W. E. B. Du Bois, and others are treasures and should be treated as such. The work they did is timeless and not meant to be relegated solely as African-American history. It is American history. In some cases— to paraphrase William Faulkner—its implications today are so widespread that it cannot yet be considered history at all.

"The Light Broke in By Degrees": Early African-American and Antebellum Literature

There is a paucity of literature from African Americans before the 1800s, even with a broad definition of that term that includes poetry, letters, narratives, and sermons. In 1760, for instance, Jupiter Hammon, a slave, was the first African-American writer to have work published. His poem, "An Evening Thought: Salvation by Christ, with Penitential Cries," was solely focused on converting sinners to Christ. Likewise, one of the other "firsts" in black literature did not mention slavery at all. Lucy Terry was just a teenager when she wrote "Bars Fight" in 1746 (published in 1885) about a massacre of whites by Native Americans in Deerfield, Massachusetts. It was such a hit that it was memorized by locals and eventually transcribed and printed long after the original manuscript had been lost. Due to that piece, Terry is thought to be the first black poet of a widely circulated work, though Phillis Wheatley is the first black person writing in the English language to have a book published. Her 1773 collection *Poems on Various Subjects, Religious and Moral* brought her to the attention of notable figures in Europe and North America, most remarkably George Washington, who expressed admiration, and Thomas Jefferson, who showed contempt.

Wheatley was highly touted around the time of the book's release but fell into obscurity toward the end of her short life. Her literary reputation took a hit when many of the black writers of the early and mid-twentieth century claimed that she was an imitative poet and a simpering supporter of slavery in works such as "On Being Brought from Africa to America"—a poem that she wrote when she was about fourteen years old. It contains the lines, "'Twas Mercy brought me from my pagan land/Taught my benighted soul to understand" (ll. 1-2). In *Home* (1966), Amiri Baraka, then known as LeRoi Jones, describes Wheatley's work as "ludicrous" and derides the poet for her detachment from "black voices" and black culture (qtd. in Gates, "Mister..."). In *The Militant Black Writer* (1969), Stephen Henderson claims that Wheatley's work reflects "the old self-hatred that one hears in the *Dozens* and in the blues," and in that same year, poet Dudley Randall compared her to a "favored house slave and a curiosity" (qtd. in Gates, "Mister..."). In more recent times, however, several scholars, such as Julian D. Mason and Carole A. Parks, have come to Wheatley's defense, challenging the contention that her work was overly imitative or somehow endorses or romanticizes slavery. Together, they argue that her poems are subversive and that her personal correspondence proves she detested the institution that bound so many slaves.

Hammon, Terry, and Wheatley were all slaves at one point—Hammon remained one for life—but they did not author slave narratives. When they were writing in the 1700s, most of those were written (or relayed) by whites, as in the case of Ayuba Suleiman Diallo's story written by Thomas Bluett in 1734, the 1760 narrative of Briton Hammon, and the 1772 narrative of "African Prince" James Albert Ukawsaw Gronniosaw. The fact that whites penned these texts might account for why they lack the bite of later narratives by people who had actually been in bondage. For instance, Diallo's memoir (as related by Bluett) has a detached air about it. In fact, Bluett editorializes that slavery might have been a good thing for Diallo and his people. In his view, Diallo should be appreciative of his time around Westerners for giving him knowledge "to a Degree which he could never have arrived at in his own Country" (59). The condescension shown by Bluett is nowhere to be found in narratives actually written by those who were enslaved. The works of Frederick Douglass, Henry Bibb, or William Grimes in contrast lift the lid off the physical punishment, sexual exploitation, and intellectual and emotional starvation suffered by slaves.

The other extant documents "by" African Americans from this time are the last statements of black men such as "Jeffrey," "Pomp," and "Arthur" before their executions. Typically, in these "confessions" the condemned men claim they were "treated very kindly" by their owners and urge other slaves "to avoid Desertion from their Masters, Drunkenness and Lewdness" ("The Life, and Dying Speech of Arthur"). It was only with *The Interesting Narrative of the Life of Olaudah Equiano, or Gustavus Vassa, the African* in 1789 that the unvarnished truths about the slave trade begin to be told.[1] Equiano's book provides "the only substantial description of the Middle Passage from the slave's viewpoint" (Gates, *Life* 42). In the narrative, he writes about the suffocating conditions in the area of the ship where he and other Africans were housed. "The shrieks of the women, and the groans of the dying, rendered the whole a scene of horror almost inconceivable" (Equiano 79), he writes, painting a much more vivid picture than anything in James Albert Ukawsaw Gronniosaw's slave narrative, supposedly dedicated to the Countess of Huntingdon. In the account of Gronniosaw's bondage, there is much more emphasis on his deliverance from idolatry than the misery endured aboard the vessel that took him out of Africa.

As illuminating as Equiano's narrative is, the anti-slavery movement required more stoking than any one man's tale could provide. As the nineteenth century progressed, newspapers became vitally important in the fight for justice. For instance, *Freedom's Journal*, the first black-owned and operated weekly newspaper, was founded in 1827 to provide a platform for abolitionist rhetoric. Edited by Samuel Cornish and John Russworm, the newspaper made a name for itself for its stance against colonization (the repatriation of American blacks to Africa) and as a rare place to find stories with African Americans discussed in a positive light. Their goal was to bestow dignity to a black public that had constantly been attacked and accused of various vices and crimes by the mainstream white press.

The paper folded in 1829, but in that same year, the African-American community received another champion. In particular, David Walker wrote and serialized the first text written by an African American that can properly be called radical, militant, or pro-black. Walker's "Appeal to the Coloured Citizens of the World" set black literature on a new path. In the four-part treatise, he called for the slaves to free themselves instead of waiting for a change of heart from their white oppressors, whom he refers to as an "unjust, jealous, unmerciful, avaricious and blood-thirsty set of beings, always seeking after power and authority" (20). Needless to say, this material was not publicly available; in fact, historians believed it may have been smuggled in the coat linings of black sailors as they headed south. When it was discovered by whites, there was so much outrage that black seamen were temporarily banned from disembarking for fear that they would smuggle it to communities where literate black troublemakers could share it with slaves.

Their fears were not entirely unfounded. Nat Turner's 1831 slaughter of whites in Virginia was exactly the type of event that slaveholders and their sympathizers feared would happen once blacks were allowed to read and write. There had already been two thwarted uprisings in the 1800s—the slave Gabriel's 1800 attempt and the planned 1822 rebellion by Denmark Vesey—so black abolitionists were facing serious risks when they spoke on behalf of their people. This makes Maria W. Miller Stewart even more amazing. As an African-American woman, she was doubly cursed in the eyes of society, but she insisted on having her voice heard, becoming the first black woman to venture into political writing and oratory. Stewart receives very little attention in history textbooks, which often allot one spot for a black woman of this era—usually Sojourner Truth whose "Ain't I a Woman?" is much in dispute. As early as 1831, however, Stewart was advocating for abolition and women's rights before influential groups, such as the New England Anti-Slavery Society in Boston, began decrying bondage and life spent in "mean, servile labor" for free black people (par. 6). In the same speech, she says, "I am a true born American; your blood flows in my veins" (par. 6),[2] calling attention to the newfound role of blacks in American society not just as a result of miscegenation but also because of the increased activism by blacks that would eventually reshape the society itself.

In any case, such critiques were a frequent occurrence in speeches by abolitionists, such as Frederick Douglass, who became a titan of the movement after *Narrative of the Life of Frederick Douglass* was published in 1845. Douglass used his fame to spread the message that black people—men, women, slave, and free— are human beings, not chattel, and thus are entitled to dignity and freedom. His very existence was positive proof that an African heritage, or even a life in bondage, did not render one hopelessly vulgar, violent, and uneducated. This was fresh information for pro-slavery factions like those in Douglass' native Maryland. Speaking before packed crowds, Douglass denounced his home state as a place where men and women were "reared for the market, just as horses, sheep, and swine" ("Reception"). Henry Bibb was another influential figure—an escaped slave who fled to Canada where he founded *The Voice of the Fugitive* newspaper in 1851. Bibb, whose *Narrative of the Life and Adventures of Henry Bibb* was published in 1849, also pledged to "contend for the natural equality of the human family, without regard to color, which is but fading matter" (204).[3]

Like David Walker and others of his time, there are also African Americans who argue black people should not wait for the approval and love of whites and should not seek permission to make up their own minds. These ideas, however, are not new. Henry

Highland Garnet advanced these ideas in a speech read at the 1843 National Negro Convention in Buffalo, New York, that was quickly disavowed by many of the convention's organizers. In this speech, Garnet says it is better for enslaved men to "die immediately" than live in bondage. The enslaved, he says, should follow the lessons of Gabriel, Denmark Vesey, and Nat Turner whom he called patriots. Although they had been killed for their actions, he lauds them for being "noble and brave" and concludes the speech with a soon-to-be famous declaration: "Let your motto be resistance!" (Garnet). Likewise, Willis Hodges, writing in his *Ram's Horn* newspaper in 1849, notes, "We do not tell you to murder the slaveholders, but we do advise you to refuse longer to work without pay." It is better, he claims, to "die, rather than bequeath a state of slavery to your posterity" (Hodges). And at the State Convention of Massachusetts Negroes in 1858, prominent African-American abolitionist Charles Lenox Remond declares the time for "twaddling and temporizing" to be over and asks to see "black men stand up for and by themselves."

Most importantly, Remond also expresses contempt for blacks who flee to more hospitable countries instead of staying at home and fighting to make America live up to her founding principles. Such figures included Martin Delany, a one-time co-publisher of Douglass' first anti-slavery newspaper, the *North Star*. Delany, considered one of the fathers of black nationalism, was also an advocate of African Americans leaving the United States to settle in places such as Liberia. "We love our country," Delany writes in *The Condition, Elevation, Emigration, and Destiny of the Colored People of the United States* (1852), "but she does not love us" (ch. 23). He was not the last leader of a back-to-Africa movement, however. In the 1920s, Jamaican-born Marcus Garvey, founder of the United Negro Improvement Association (UNIA), was the loudest champion of blacks heading out of the United States so they might have a chance at liberty and prosperity. One of the flyers for the UNIA's African Redemption Fund claimed that the association was going to raise four billion dollars "from the Negro people all over the world, to set Africa Free and to set the race free industrially, socially and politically" (Garvey). But there were many who did not think they should head "home" to find justice; in their minds, they were already home in America even if they were treated as unwelcomed guests.

To Be Free: Literature of the Reconstruction Era

Reconstruction (1865–ca. 1877) was therefore a promising time for the black community, helping former slaves finally envision a home in the United States. The slaves were emancipated and assisted by the Freedmen's Bureau with the transition into freedom, several educational opportunities were available to black people, and a number of black men were elected to Congress, some of whom, such as Rep. Jefferson Long (R-Georgia) and Rep. Josiah T. Walls (R-Florida), had been slaves before the Civil War. The promise America seemed to have made to her dark children was broken, however, when Reconstruction ended. There are numerous reasons given to explain its demise. President Andrew Johnson was about as poor a leader for blacks as Jefferson Davis would have been, funding for the Freedmen's Bureau dried up, the Freedmen's Bank went bust, there was an economic panic in 1873, federal troops who had once protected black citizens were withdrawn from the South, and many formerly sympathetic whites came down with race fatigue. As a result, much of the South was returned to white Democratic control and a culture of legalized segregation called Jim Crow emerged that would keep black people in physical and figurative chains for decades.

Booker T. Washington became arguably the most famous black man of his era precisely because he avoided making inflammatory statements in light of the discrimination against blacks. As the president of the Tuskegee Institute, he wielded great power and amassed numerous enemies, mainly other African Americans who were irritated by his calls for blacks to focus on earning a living—no matter how humble—instead of trying to gain equal status with white intellectuals and power brokers. Washington's views, as expressed in his 1895 "Atlanta Compromise" and his 1901 autobiography *Up from Slavery*, are quite different from those of W. E. B. Du Bois, a Harvard-educated scholar, who—early on in his career—advanced the notion of the most advanced or "Talented Tenth" of African

Americans leading their people out of emotional, educational, and cultural wilderness. Washington also had a foe in William Monroe Trotter who mocked his claims in person and in the pages of his *Boston Guardian.*

In 1905, Trotter, Du Bois, and twenty-seven other men formed the Niagara Movement, a forerunner to the National Association for the Advancement of Colored People (NAACP) of which Du Bois would be involved for decades. Eventually, Du Bois' views changed from the class-consciousness of his younger days to the Communism of his later years, but throughout it all, he remained a powerful voice for African Americans. In 1901, for instance, Du Bois was one of the founders and the first editor of *The Crisis*, a publication of the NAACP. Another major achievement was the publication of *The Souls of Black Folk* in 1903, which is, in many ways, as relevant now as it was during its publication due to Du Bois' dissection of white supremacy and the conflict it creates within African Americans. One of the treasures of the book is Du Bois' rumination on the concept of double consciousness, best described as "a conflicted, dichotomized identity" of being both black and American "where the former identity labeled one a 'problem' to be ignored, pitied, or stigmatized and the latter identity served as a constant reminder of a legacy of oppression and station to be esteemed but never reached" (Barnes).

Women writers and activists also played an integral role in advocating for change for the African-American community. For example, journalist Ida B. Wells exposed the unrelenting racism and violence, namely lynching. Wells was so outspoken that she had to leave Memphis after publishing articles in *Free Speech* and pamphlets such as *The Red Record* (1896), scoffing at the myth that lynched black men were killed for raping white women. Another charter member of the NAACP, Mary Church Terrell, like Maria W. Miller Stewart, advocated for "colored women with ambition and aspiration" who were "handicapped on account of their sex" and "mocked on account of their race" (8). And Anna Julia Cooper was also concerned with cultivating the minds of young black women. Cooper, who was born a slave, went on to earn a bachelor's degree from Oberlin College in 1884, so she understood the importance of education. In a collection of her essays, *A Voice from the South* (1892), she beseeched men to support her cause and not "drop back into sixteenth century logic" on the subject of women's education (Cooper).

During this time, a precursor to the artistic and cultural movement known as the Harlem Renaissance, Cooper goes on to claim that only through the efforts of black women can the "regeneration" and "re-training of the race" begin (28). From her view, black women played an integral role as intellectuals in the twentieth century, even though the New Negro intellectual emerging at the time was predominantly envisioned male. In spite of her declarations, however, women continued to be sidelined in the civil rights efforts of the day. The Niagara Movement, spearheaded by Du Bois and Trotter, first met in 1905 and, soon after, hit a rough patch when the two men disagreed over whether women should be allowed to join. Du Bois was in favor; Trotter was opposed. Du Bois—like Douglass before him—was more broadminded in his views regarding the equality of women than many other men of his time—men who were firmly entrenched in the view that domestic issues, not politics, were the sphere of women and who, in this way, proved sexism could be as pernicious to the souls of black folks as racism.

Rise and Shine: Literature of the Harlem Renaissance Era

The Jim Crow laws that were making life very difficult for African Americans at the end of the nineteenth century continued on into the twentieth, but one newspaper, more than any other, was dedicated to decrying them—the *Chicago Defender*. Founded by Robert S. Abbott in 1905, it would become "the nation's most influential black weekly newspaper by the advent of World War I" ("The Chicago Defender") and cover everything from the rise of Marcus Garvey to the creation of the Brotherhood of the Sleeping Car Porters and the horrors of the Red Summer of 1919. The paper's editorials also urged black southerners to move to the North for a chance at a better life. Many heeded the advice, and during the Great Migration, particularly during the 1910s to the 1930s, the African-American population in Chicago, Detroit, and New York City grew about 40 percent ("Great

Migration"). In particular, Harlem, which would give its name and essence to the Harlem Renaissance or New Negro Movement, went from a white community in the late 1800s to one with more than 75,000 blacks in 1920 (Hine, Hine, & Harrold 369). This community would become emblematic of the best that blacks had to offer, a place where African Americans were applauded for their wit, intellect, and urbanity.

During this period, some of the most potent literature, art, music, and dance to ever come from African Americans was created and devoured by a receptive public. There had been black writers and visual artists before, but the work of the Harlem Renaissance—the very imagery of Harlem—planted itself in the imagination of a black audience eager to see itself reflected with accuracy or at least dignity. During this period, for instance, the poetry of Langston Hughes and Sterling A. Brown celebrated the joys of African-American life and lamented the cruelty and violence so common in blighted neighborhoods. The essays of Marita Bonner explored what it was like to be "Young—a Woman—and Colored." Wallace Thurman lampooned shadeism in *The Blacker the Berry* (1928), while George A. Schuyler ridiculed the foolishness of white supremacist thought in *Black No More* (1931). As we see, the output that came out of the Harlem Renaissance was not, by and large, an imitation of the works of white Americans; it was distinctly black.

Just as Eubie Blake and Noble Sissle revolutionized theatre with *Shuffle Along* in 1921, so, too, did Jean Toomer, Langston Hughes, Countee Cullen, and other key Harlem Renaissance figures alter perceptions of what it meant to be black artists. Writers like Sterling Brown created dialect-heavy poems, while others simply avoided it. Some believed there was such a thing as distinctly black art; others, like George Schuyler, scoffed at the idea. Then there were people who changed positions during their lifetimes, like the fair-skinned Jean Toomer whose *Cane* (1923) is usually cited as the first novel of the Harlem Renaissance, though it is really a collection of sketches, poems, and stories. Toomer, the grandson of prominent Louisiana politician P. B. S. Pinchback, later walked away from the movement and apparently the concept of blackness itself, but *Cane* remains noteworthy for its empathetic, knowing treatment of poor, rural black life in the Jim Crow South.

Other major novels of the era include Jessie Redmon Fauset's *Plum Bun* (1928), which deals with the issue of passing—a common theme also taken up in Nella Larsen's *Passing* (1929). In both works, light-skinned black Americans, limited in their opportunities, seek to shed their racial identities and pursue new opportunities (such as economic stability, education, and love) as white women. The notion of passing, however, is taken to another level in Schuyler's *Black No More*. It is a fantastical novel in which a cure for blackness is created, which exposes the phony race pride of many black leaders and the fragility of the notion of racial purity. *Black No More* is unjustly neglected, possibly because of Schuyler's political conservatism, but it is a blistering satire and along with Langston Hughes' *Not Without Laughter* (1930) is one of the most important novels of the Harlem Renaissance.

Despite his work in many mediums, Hughes is, of course, best known for his poetry. His verses, often criticized for being too straightforward, have withstood time because they resonate with a vast swath of readers. "The Negro Speaks of Rivers," "America," "Mother to Son," and "I, Too" are just some of the poems he wrote during the Harlem Renaissance that dealt with the fear, hope, love, and bitterness of those imprisoned by skin color or poverty. Of course, there were other writers who rivaled Hughes for prominence in the 1920s and 30s, namely poet Countee Cullen, who is now often discussed as someone who downplayed his blackness in his work, thanks to sentiments expressed in "To Certain Critics," where he made it clear he would not limit himself to dissections of the "race problem." Cullen did, however, write several poems such as "Incident" and "The Shroud of Color" in which he directly addressed the lingering effects of racism or the need to rise above discrimination.

While the Harlem Renaissance was renowned for its cultural production, many have argued that it yielded little change in the socio-racial landscape of the United States. This concern continued into the 1940s. Though this decade brought other victories as well, like President Harry Truman abolishing segregation in the armed forces with his Executive Order 9981 (signed July 26, 1948), the lives of many African Americans did not improve in the ways that so many white people's did after the end of World War II. Discrimination in housing, employment, and schooling continued. Many blacks wondered why they had fought for a country that did not regard them as citizens, and some were finally ready to push for the rights that had been promised to them but were never delivered.

The Second Reconstruction: Literature of the Civil Rights Movement and Beyond

The modern Civil Rights Era of the 1950s and 60s is also a justifiably lauded period during which a number of heroes and heroines would emerge, including attorney Thurgood Marshall, seamstress Rosa Parks, Pullman car porter E. D. Nixon, and a trio of famous pastors: Martin Luther King Jr., Ralph Abernathy, and Fred Shuttlesworth. A series of marches, sit-ins, and boycotts were launched, which showed that a sizable segment of the African-American population was unified enough to fight against homegrown terrorism and economic exploitation. It is Martin Luther King Jr., however, who gets the most glory, perhaps because he is considered the most eloquent writer of the movement. A learned man, King peppered his works with allusions and quotations from ancient philosophers as in "Letter from Birmingham Jail" (1963), which references the Apostle Paul, Martin Luther, and Thomas Jefferson among others. He also warns the clergyman to whom the letter is addressed that victims of oppression will eventually fight back.

Likewise, James Baldwin focused his attentions on saving America's soul from its racist self, though his work did not always present such an optimistic view as King's. He was present at several of the historic civil rights marches but rejected the notion that he was a civil rights leader; nevertheless, he was profoundly adept at examining, writing about, and speaking about the ways that the American Dream was a nightmare for many blacks (Daniels). James Baldwin's *The Fire Next Time* (1963) was composed of two essays. The first laments white supremacy but warns that the fates of white

Americans and black Americans are inextricably linked and that there will be no solution to racial conflicts without the participation of both groups. In the second essay, Baldwin addresses his early religious life before musing on the concept of freedom, stating that most people, despite claims to the contrary, simply do not want it.

Malcolm X, a one-time Nation of Islam minister, was also a magnetic speaker. Although he, too, mocked the term *civil rights* and the notion of passivity in the face of violence, he was active in the fight against racist oppression and had the telling-it-like-it-is quality of Baldwin, which earned him as much admiration as it did enmity. His "Ballot or the Bullet" delivered at the Cory Methodist Church in Cleveland, Ohio, on April 3, 1964 is a searing indictment of Uncle Sam, and his *Autobiography of Malcolm X* is still widely read as a foundational text for many of the black writers and intellectuals growing up in the Black Power Movement and beyond (including President Barack Obama). Author Kevin Powell, for example, describes reading *The Autobiography of Malcolm X* and being amazed that, although he had attended highly touted schools, he had never heard of this man who would become his first male role model. Malcolm X was a hero to many who admired his independent spirit and fiery delivery. They could relate to the pain of losing a father to racism after Rev. Earl Little was murdered by white supremacists angered by his Garveyite beliefs and losing a mother to mental illness after she was unable to provide for her children in the wake of her husband's death. Malcolm's story is the story of so many African Americans trapped in a racist society and in their own colonized minds, but unlike so many others, he was able to course correct, discovering books, Islam, and eventually himself, so it is no wonder young people, particularly those searching for examples of strong, self-possessed black men, continue to look to him for inspiration.

Eldridge Cleaver's *Soul on Ice* (1968) was another seminal document of the Black Power era, presenting America with an account of the injustices associated with black life by the man who would go on to become the Minister of Information for the Black Panthers. Other important books from this period include 1970's

The Prison Letters of George Jackson, which made a celebrity out of "Soledad Brother" Jackson nearly a year before he was shot dead by a guard during a melee, and *Revolutionary Suicide* (1973) by Black Panther leader Huey P. Newton. These works laid the groundwork for conversations on race that continue today through nonfiction works such as Harriet Wilson's *Medical Apartheid* (2007), Michelle Alexander's *The New Jim Crow* (2010), Bryan Stevenson's *Just Mercy* (2014), and Ta-Nehisi Coates' *Between the World and Me* (2015). There are also many conversations about race on C-SPAN, social media, and twenty-four-hour cable news networks today, particularly after the latest shooting of unarmed black men. Still, despite these national conversations, there is a sense that whatever movement exists is floundering, evident through the frequent question, "Where are our leaders?"

Ultimately, this question can be answered a number of ways. One theory is that there are people who are doing big things in their communities but who do not get the attention they warrant because the public is more interested in reality stars. Some people claim there simply are no dynamic leaders, while others reject the notion that leaders are even necessary. There is, however, a treasure trove of knowledge left behind by African Americans going back more than two centuries that we cannot forget. Some of the best and brightest Americans in history spent their lives and in some cases gave their lives to improve social conditions for black people. They wrote novels, poems, essays, articles, songs, sermons, and chants, and from this material there is more than enough to inspire this generation and all others to follow to speak, march, boycott, and make the world they wish to see—with or without leaders.

Notes

1. Since the 1990s, there has been debate among scholars over certain aspects of Equiano's tale, namely his claim to have been born in Africa, but his book remains an important one and was very influential "at a time when whites in Europe and the United States had just begun to question the institution" of slavery (Gates, *Life* 43).

2. Considering the history of miscegenation in the United States, Stewart might have been speaking literally in this statement. After all, miscegenation

was fairly common during slavery. In *Incidents in the Life of a Slave Girl* (1861), Harriet Jacobs, writing under the pseudonym Linda Brett, describes the persistence with which her master pursued her. She claims she escaped his clutches, but many owners succeeded in sexually exploiting their slaves. Frederick Douglass, William Grimes, Jermain Loguen, Henry Bibb, and many other abolitionists were the offspring of white fathers and enslaved women. Stewart's thinly veiled remark was a reminder that even people with two African-Americans parents, as she had, could and often did share ancestors with white people.

3. In a way, the statements of Douglass and Bibb echo the phrase "Black Lives Matter," which came into vogue after a spate of killings of black men—often by law enforcement officers—beginning in the early 2010s (or at least that is when renewed attention began). As in the 1800s, there are people who lack a basic human empathy for black people, especially lower-class or "ghetto" blacks, whom they seem to view as a separate species. After the killings of Michael Brown, Trayvon Martin, and too many others, social and traditional media were hosts to a chorus of voices, mostly white, who felt the young men got what they deserved and were, as Melissa Harris-Perry put it when she was still a host on MSNBC, guilty of their own murders. Many African Americans were stunned (and stung) to discover that their otherwise nice, normal white friends, colleagues, and neighbors did not see young black people as people but as problems and predators.

Works Cited

Barnes, Sandra. "A Sociological Examination of W.E.B. Du Bois' *The Souls of Black Folk.*" *North Star* 7.2 (2003): 1-6.

Bibb, Henry. *Narrative of the Life and Adventures of Henry Bibb.* New York: Author, 1849.

Documenting the American South. 1998. University Library, U of North Carolina at Chapel Hill, 2004. Web. 13 Dec. 2016.

Bluett, Thomas. *Some Memoirs of the Life of Job, the Son of Solomon, the High Priest of Boonda in Africa; Who was a Slave About Two Years in Maryland; and Afterwards Being Brought to England, was Set Free, and Sent to His Native Land in the Year 1734. Documenting the American South.* 1998. University Library, U of North Carolina at Chapel Hill, 2004. Web. 13 Dec. 2016.

Bouie, Jamelle. "How Trump Happened." *Slate.* The Slate Group. 13 Mar. 2016. Web. 13 Dec. 2016.

"The Chicago Defender." *PBS.org.* Public Broadcasting Service, n.d. Web. 18 Dec. 2016.

Clift, Eleanor. "Pat Buchanan: Donald Trump Stole My Playbook." *The Daily Beast*. The Daily Beast Co LLC, 31 May 2016. Web. 13 Dec. 2016.

Cooper, Anna Julia. *A Voice from the South*. Xenia, OH: Aldine, 1892. *Documenting the American South*. 1998. University Library, U of North Carolina at Chapel Hill, 2004. Web. 13 Dec. 2016.

Daniels, Lee A. "James Baldwin, Eloquent Writer in Behalf of Civil Rights, Is Dead." *New York Times*. New York Times Company, 2 Dec. 1987. Web. 13 Dec. 2016.

Delany, Martin. *The Condition, Elevation, Emigration, and Destiny of the Colored People of the United States*. 1852. *Project Gutenberg*. Web. 13 Dec. 2016.

Douglass, Frederick. "Reception Speech. At Finsbury Chapel, Moorfields, England, May 12, 1846 & Dr Campbell's Reply." *Lit2Go*. Florida Center for Instructional Technology, U of South Florida, 2016. Web. 13 Dec. 2016.

Equiano, Olaudah. *The Interesting Narrative of the Life of Olaudah Equiano, or Gustavus Vassa, the African. Written by Himself. Vol. I. Documenting the American South*. 1998. University Library, U of North Carolina at Chapel Hill, 2004. Web. 13 Dec. 2016.

Garnet, Henry Highland. "An Address to the Slaves of the United States of America, Buffalo, N.Y., 1843." *Digital Commons*. U of Nebraska-Lincoln, n.d. Web. 13 Dec. 2016.

Garvey, Marcus. "Aims and Objects of Movement for Solution of Negro Problem." 1924. *National Humanities Center Resource Toolbox: The Making of African American Identity*. National Humanities Center, n.d. Web. 13 Dec. 2016.

Gates, Henry L., Jr. *Life Upon These Shores: Looking at African American History, 1513–2008*. New York: Alfred A. Knopf, 2011.

_____. "Mister Jefferson and the Trials of Phillis Wheatley." *2002 Jefferson Lecture*. National Endowment for the Humanites, n.d. Web. 26 Aug. 2016.

Gergen, David. "Trump Rally Postponed, Protesters Clash; Trump: I Don't Want People Hurt; Trump Protesters Marching In the Streets of Chicago." *Anderson Cooper 360°*. CNN, 11 Mar. 2016. Web. 13 Dec. 2016.

"Great Migration: The African-American Exodus North." *Fresh Air*. Natl. Public Radio, 13 Sept. 2010.

Hine, Darlene Clark, William C. Hine, & Stanley Harrold. *African American: A Concise History*. 5th ed. Upper Saddle River, NJ: Pearson, 2014.

Hodges, Willis. "Slaves of the South, Now Is Your Time!" 1849. [*The Ram's Horn*.]

National Humanities Center Resource Toolbox: The Making of African American Identity. National Humanities Center, n.d. Web. 13 Dec. 2016.

"The Life, and Dying Speech of Arthur, a Negro Man; Who Was Executed at Worchester, October 20, 1768. For a Rape Committed on the Body of One

Deborah Metcalfe." Boston, 1768. *Documenting the American South*. 1998. University Library, U of North Carolina at Chapel Hill. Web. 18 Dec. 2016.

Remond, Charles L. "Convention of the Colored Citizens of Massachusetts, August 1, 1858." *ColoredConventions*. University of Delaware, n.d. Web. 13 Dec. 2016.

Stewart, Maria W. Miller. "Lecture Delivered at Franklin Hall." Boston, 21 Sept. 1832. *Voices of Democracy: The U.S. Oratory Project* 1 (2006). Web. 18 Dec. 2016.

Terrell, Mary Church. "The Progress of Colored Women." National American Woman Suffrage Association, Washington, DC, 1898. *Antislavery Literature Project*. Web. 18 Dec. 2016.

Walker, David. *Walker's Appeal, in Four Articles; Together with a Preamble, to the Coloured Citizens of the World, but in Particular, and Very Expressly, to Those of the United States of America, Written in Boston, State of Massachusetts, September 28, 1829*. Boston: Author, 1829. *Documenting the American South*. 1998. University Library, U of North Carolina at Chapel Hill. Web. 18 Dec. 2016.

Wheatley, Phillis. "On being brought from Africa to America." *Poem on Various Subjects, Religious and Moral*. London, 1773. *American Verse Project*. Web. 18 Dec. 2016.

Inadequate Conception of Human Complexity: Ellison Revises Elkins

Jessie LaFrance Dunbar

> Contrary to some, I feel that our experience as a people involves
> a great deal of heroism. From one perspective slavery was horrible
> and brutalizing. . . . And the Negro writer is tempted to agree. "Yes,
> God damn it, wasn't that a horrible thing!" And he sometimes agrees
> to the next step, which holds that slaves had very little humanity
> because slavery destroyed it for them and their descendants. That's
> what Stanley Elkins' "Sambo"[1] argument implies. But despite the
> historical past and the injustices of the present . . . I have to affirm
> my forefathers and I must affirm my parents or be reduced in my
> own mind to a white man's inadequate—even if unprejudiced—
> conception of human complexity. (Ellison, *Conversations* 119)

There are two striking observations historian Stanley Elkins
makes in his lengthy rejoinder to the onslaught of negative critical
attention paid his 1959 monograph, *Slavery: A Problem in American
Institutional and Intellectual Life.*[2] Published in the December 1975
edition of *Commentary* magazine, Elkins' "The Slavery Debate"
outlines the discursive shift from what sociologists and historians
like himself termed the "damage" theory—the notion that black
people were inexorably altered by the experience and legacy of
slavery—to the "resistance" theory, aptly summarized in the above
statement, which was advanced primarily by black scholars and
activists in the 1960s and 70s. Strikingly, Elkins observes that the
"crest of the 'damage' cycle . . . coincided almost perfectly with
a state of mind regarding race relations whose dominant concern
was integration and civil rights" ("The Slavery Debate" 41). One
important implication of Elkins' claim is that the damage cycle was
an important and useful contribution to the discursive terrain of
black equality. Elkins, and other scholars with similar approaches
to writing about African-American history, believed that they
were encouraging government intervention on behalf of black
communities that had been irreparably damaged by slavery and its
aftermath. Though Elkins' damage claim was a hotly debated topic,

most scholars and activists would agree that the legacy of slavery did, in fact, necessitate the Civil Rights Movement, though the dominant narrative of the movement tends to replace the root causes of inequality with its symptoms: segregation being the primary goal of the dominant narrative.

Equally striking is Elkins' intimation that he considered his most formidable opponent to be Ralph Waldo Ellison—a novelist as well as literary and cultural critic who demanded a "new vision of the American black experience" that did not simply "appeal to the white conscience" ("The Slavery Debate" 43). After all, Ellison was invoking the work of writers from earlier generations. James Weldon Johnson, for instance, enticed white readers by promising that his novel, *Autobiography of an Ex-Colored Man* (1912), would provide them an initiation into the freemasonry of the black race as he drew aside the veil separating black thought about white communities from black action toward white communities. More notable, even, was the protest novel, exemplified by Richard Wright's wildly successful *Native Son* (1940). The protagonist, Bigger Thomas, personifies the frustrations felt by black people limited by Jim Crow laws. Novelist and essayist James Baldwin, like Ellison, was also opposed to protesting inequality by appealing to the consciences of white America. Rather, both Baldwin and Ellison were of the mind that black people were equal to whites, whether white Americans acknowledged it or not.

Despite the pervasiveness of these ideas, to Elkins at least, Ellison was one of the most outspoken supporters of the resistance theory and a leader championing the notion that the resilience and creativity of African-American people is the basis of a black culture by which the larger American society has been shaped. While Elkins and other scholars of his ilk were attempting to derail the move toward two Americas by offering scholarly explanations for the seeming disparity between oppressed black and free white people, Ellison thus rejected the notion of any chasm between the two cultures, arguing that the dominant culture is black culture and the reverse.

Elkins' 1975 defense of his seminal work grapples successfully with Ellison's argument that black culture is more than "three hundred years [of] simply . . . *reacting*" to white dominance (Ellison, "An American Dilemma" 339) but overlooks the transculturation argument altogether. The oversight is underscored by Elkins' invocation of Daniel Patrick Moynihan's 1965 report on the Negro family, which he describes as unconstrained and shocking prose meant to persuade inside policymakers that "a massive federal commitment to rebuilding the economic life of black communities" was imperative both for Negro and American prosperity ("The Slavery Debate" 42). That a major component of Elkins' defense of the report, and by extension his own research, is that it was not intended for mass public consumption—more specifically, it was not written with "touchy persons watching over [Moynihan's] shoulder" ("The Slavery Debate" 42)—bolsters Ellison's and other black scholars' assertion that white people wanted to define what was good for their fellow black citizens.

This type of Othering perpetuated a myth that black people were resigned to the futile exercise of attempting to cross boundaries from the margins into "mainstream" America when, as Ellison observed, black people helped create the mainstream ("Transcript of the American Academy" 409). Indeed, Ellison asserts in his 1970 essay "What America Would be Like Without Blacks" that "whenever the nation grows weary of the struggle toward the ideal of American democratic equality," its citizens view everything having to do with black Americans as inextricably linked to their racially imposed status (580).[3] If, in fact, they resisted this urge, they might "become aware of the fact that for all the harsh reality of the social and economic injustices visited upon [Negroes], these injustices have failed to keep Negroes clear of the cultural mainstream; Negro Americans are, in fact, one of its major tributaries" (580).

Still, the public discourse continued to focus primarily on both the "Negro Question" and "Negro Problems." In 1965, the Department of Labor released a document composed by Daniel Patrick Moynihan, who was the Secretary of Labor under President Lyndon B. Johnson. *The Negro Family: The Case for National*

Action, now known simply as The Moynihan Report, pared down the problems in the black community to one fundamental issue: the dissolution of the African-American family unit. According to Moynihan's study, nearly twenty-five percent of all black households were headed by women, twenty-five percent of all black children were born out of wedlock, and the percentage of blacks dependent on government assistance was on the rise (9). One section in particular touched a nerve in the black academy. Chapter three, entitled "The Roots of the Problem," discusses the impact of slavery on the African-American psyche and relies heavily on Elkins' infamous monograph, concurring with the historian's assessments of black dependency and lack of culture. Elkins privileged the concept of black acculturation in his 1959 thesis when he concluded that captivity so dramatically shifted the slaves' worldview that they were left without culture or the faculties to survive independently. Bondsmen and women, according to his research, were consigned to a perpetual state of childish docility:

> Much of his past had been annihilated; nearly every prior connection had been severed. Not that he had really "forgotten" all these things— his family and kinship arrangements, his language, the tribal religion, the taboos, the name he had once borne, and so on—but none of it any longer carried much meaning. The old values, the sanctions, the standard, already unreal, could no longer furnish him guides for conduct, for adjusting to the expectations of a complete new life. (Elkins, *Slavery* 101)

> Old values, thus set aside, could be replaced by new ones. It was a process made possible by "infantile regression"—regression to a previous condition of childlike dependency in which parental prohibitions once more became all-powerful and in which parental judgments might once more be internalized . . . It is no wonder that their obedience became unquestioning, that they did not revolt, that they could not "hate" their master. (117, 122)

The suggestion that black Americans were a people without a past lends itself to the idea that slavery simultaneously stripped people of African descent of culture and replaced it with slave culture.

Moreover, there is also a troubling supposition that American culture developed alongside slavery without being impacted at all by the enslaved or free black populations. The concept of acculturation, however, had been dismissed as early as 1940 with the publication of Cuban anthropologist Fernando Ortiz's important monograph, *Cuban Counterpoint.* Among the most important arguments Ortiz advanced is that cultural exchanges are never unidirectional. Thus, it would have been impossible for people of African descent to have simply been transformed by American culture without making their own contributions to the developing culture.

Heavily reliant upon Elkins' findings, The Moynihan Report catalyzed a decade-long campaign to prove the strength and worth of African-American men, and, by extension, the black family. By late summer 1965, it had been leaked to the press just in time for news sources to use it to explain the causes of the Watts Riots in California. On August 27, 1965, John Herbers of the *New York Times* wrote, "Still unpublished in its entirety and still officially confidential, the [Moynihan] report has come in for new attention since the Los Angeles riots, for it pinpoints the causes of discontent in the Negro ghettos and says the new crisis in race relations is much more severe than is generally believed" (13). Because civil rights activists such as Dr. Martin Luther King Jr., Roy Wilkins, and Whitney Young had approved President Johnson's well-received commencement speech on June 4, 1965, at Howard University, influenced by and largely based on Moynihan's publication, no one had forecast the storm of fury that would result from the report itself.

What is more, the controversial report brought even more negative attention to

Elkins' research, making *Slavery: A Problem in American Institutional and Intellectual Life* a prime target for up-and-coming historians and other "black spokesmen" who Elkins suggests were Ellison-inspired ("The Slavery Debate" 44). For example, in 1970, historian Willie Lee Rose argued that the black father's discounted influence in the slave community was the result of Eurocentric, patriarchal views like Elkins' and Moynihan's. John Blassingame debunked the myth of this Sambo persona in *The Slave Community*

(1972), and Herbert Gutman's 1976 publication *The Black Family in Slavery and Freedom, 1750–1925* spoke directly to the Moynihan report, taking an almost militant stance in favor of the adaptive capacities of American slaves. The objective of their research was to disprove the theory that the developing trend of fatherless households in black communities of the 1960s and 70s dated back to slavery. Gutman logically concluded that if the "tangle of pathology" (29) to which Moynihan referred was pervasive in the black community, it would have to have been more concentrated in urban black communities just after the Civil War than it was in the 1960s, but it was not. In addition to their direct refutations of Elkins' thesis, these texts adapted the Boasian theory of cultural relativism[4] to advance the resistance theory.

As Elkins observes in "The Slavery Debate," Ellison had made similar claims as early as 1944 in his review of the lauded *An American Dilemma: The Negro Problem and Modern Democracy* (1944)—a study of American race relations authored by Swedish economist Gunnar Myrdal. In it, Ellison emphasizes a perennial blind spot of white scholars from that generation, writing:

> Myrdal sees Negro culture and personality simply as the product of a "social pathology". Thus he assumes that "it is to the advantage of American Negroes as individuals and as a group to become assimilated into American culture, to acquire the traits held in esteem by the dominant white Americans" . . . [A]side from implying that Negro culture is not also American, [Myrdal] assumes that Negroes should desire nothing better than what whites consider highest. . . . It does not occur to Myrdal that many of the Negro cultural manifestations which he considers reflective might also embody a *rejection* of what he considers "higher value". There is a dualism at work here. It is only partially true that Negroes turn away from white patterns because they are refused participation. There is nothing like distance to create objectivity, and exclusion gives rise to counter values. ("An American Dilemma" 339-40)

While these thoughtful excerpts lead Elkins to concede that Ellison "carried his point" on black culture, Elkins pivots, offering a response to the resistance theory. Elkins held that culture, as developed under an institution such as slavery, is not acquired without a price ("Slavery Debate" 54). Elkins quotes from this and other hard-hitting Ellison prose publications with no mention of Ellison's National Book Award-winning novel, *Invisible Man* (1952), which is problematic as it specifically traces a black male protagonist's psychological journey toward the development of the very counter values Ellison mentions in his 1944 review.

A bildungsroman first-person narrative, the novel moves its unnamed protagonist from the South to the North, from racial oblivion to racial consciousness, and from invisibility to visibility (though this final pairing frequently occurs simultaneously). More broadly, the novel synthesizes "mid-twentieth century African American racial consciousness with America's ... cultural aspirations and accomplishments" (Bland 52), rendering the work universal in its exploration of the existential crisis of identity formation. It is also, as Ellison biographer Lawrence Jackson notes, the means by which "Ellison had moved from being an embattled social critic, a position he had occupied during most of the years he wrote *Invisible Man,* to being a symbol of America's willingness to accept talented blacks" (*Emergence of Genius* ix). The novel is also one of the most protracted and convincing arguments Ellison makes against Elkins' theories of Sambo, psychic shock, and the meaninglessness of black origins in closed systems of oppression.

The same manner in which slavery haunts the dominant narrative of civil rights without overt invocation, the spirit of Sambo is present throughout the novel and begins with the invisible man's confession of the shame he previously felt for having been a descendant of slaves:

> I am not ashamed of my grandparents for having been slaves. I am only ashamed of myself for having at one time been ashamed. About eighty-five years ago they were told that they were free, united with others of our country in everything pertaining to the common good, and, in everything social, separate like the fingers of the hand. And they believed it. They exulted in it. They stayed in their place, worked hard, and brought up my father to do the same. But my grandfather is

the one. He was an odd old guy, my grandfather, and I am told I take after him. "I want you to overcome 'em with yeses, undermine 'em with grins, agree 'em to death and destruction, let 'em swoller you till they vomit or bust wide open." (Ellison, *Invisible Man* 16)

There is an obvious tension between the persona of the invisible man's rage-filled grandfather, who outwardly adopts many of the characteristics of the Sambo archetype, and Elkins' historical referent who is "docile but irresponsible, loyal but lazy, humble but chronically given to lying and stealing" and whose "relationship with his master was one of utter dependence and childlike attachment" (*Slavery* 82). However, the grandfather's docility is a sham; his true personality exists behind what sociologist W. E. B. Du Bois called "the veil."[5] For much of the narrative the invisible man is thus preoccupied with largely futile attempts to decipher the meaning of his grandfather's final words, for he, like Sambo, has been raised by his own parents to be obedient and content, and, most importantly, he has been taught to assimilate to the dominant white culture. It is not until the novel's end that he is satisfied to interpret "yessing" them to death as "affirm[ing] the principle on which the country was built and not the men . . . who did the violence" because the principle was greater than the men and all the methods used to corrupt its name (Ellison, *Invisible Man* 574).

The three theories of personalities that Elkins employs to explain the development and ubiquity of the Sambo persona are instructive in deciphering the argument that Ellison is making in the novel about docility, paternalism, and role-playing. The Freudian suggests that personality development in children varies directly with the child's relationship to the father, Sullivan's theory of "significant others" broadens the Freudian theory to include any individuals who hold power over the developing child, and role theory links personality to the different roles one can play (Elkins 115-133). Elkins' implication here is that bondsmen had little room for development of variegated personality types within the context of the abusive paternalistic relationship between master and slave. That Sambo can only exist in a paternalistic system is evident in Elkins' historical treatment. That white paternalism is a romantic idea that has no place in conversations about the horrors of slavery or in the practice of achieving civil liberties is thus an important motif in Ellison's novel.[6]

Sambo's presence in *Invisible Man* is complemented by the pervasiveness of condescending, selectively blind, and deceitful white father figures throughout the novel. Characterizing his hefty monetary donations to the invisible man's college as "first-hand organizing of human life" (Ellison 42), Mr. Norton is not unlike the nameless college Founder, "the cold Father symbol," whose campus statue is frozen with outstretched hands in a gesture of either lifting or lowering a veil from or onto the eyes of a kneeling slave (36). Young Mr. Emerson fancies himself Huck Finn to the invisible man's Jim (not unlike Stanley Elkins claiming the title of abolitionist) in his feverish and poorly executed attempts to advise the protagonist of what is best for him. And Jack, leader of a communist organization, asserts that the function of "The Brotherhood" is "not to ask [the Harlem community] what they think, but to tell them" (473).

Though each of these men might have been considered progressive and even well-meaning in the contemporary historical moment, they recall the apologist (paternalist) literature generated by white plantation owners in response to the damning testimonies of ex-slaves.[7] Put another way, their actions were precipitated less by good will and more by guilt and a desire to establish or preserve reputations as people on the right side of history. Thus, when the veteran "doctor," arguably the most astute and self-actualized character in the novel, offers the invisible man two pieces of advice, "Be your own father" and "Leave the Mr. Nortons alone" (Ellison, *Invisible* 156), it is clear that Ellison seeks to dismantle the notion of white paternalism and the Sambo monolith.

The invisible man's final confrontation with Brother Jack provides a perfect example of Ellison's refutation of the infantile and docile Sambo archetype. When Brother Jack scolds the invisible man for organizing a memorial for an ex-member, Tod Clifton (who is slain in an altercation with police for illegally selling Sambo dolls), Jack describes the crowd of mourners and demonstrators as "raw materials to be shaped to our program" and Clifton as "infantile" (Ellison, *Invisible* 473). The protagonist's developing awareness that he is not unlike Clifton's Sambo dolls transforms his obedience and loyalty into rage. "'Who are you, anyway,'" he asks, "'the great white father . . . Wouldn't it be better if they called you Marse Jack?'" (473). To this point, Jack had attempted to acculturate the invisible man, relieving him of his identity and providing him a new name and a script that would advance their agenda, often to the protagonist's own detriment. When the invisible man ponders whether he will strangle Brother Jack, it becomes obvious that the acculturation process did not take, for, as the invisible man advises, "though I had seldom used my capacities for anger and indignation, I had no doubt that I possessed them" (237). Thus, Ellison's reading of Sambo is less aligned with Elkins' assertion that Sambo was a stock character molded through the tyranny of their plantation fathers and more in line with that of historian Eugene Genovese who observes that "Sambo . . . was Sambo only up to the moment that the psychological balance was jarred from within or without; he might then well have become Nat Turner" (71).

Invisible Man also anticipates and refutes Elkins' argument that African connections had been severed through a series of shocks, rendering black American slaves and their progeny a people without a past.[8] The psychic shock theory had gained some traction throughout the first half of the twentieth century, perhaps most notably when sociologist E. Franklin Frazier gestured toward black amnesia in his 1939 monograph *The Negro Family in the United States* and entered into a heated public debate with anthropologist Melville Herskovitz, who outlined African continuums in African-American culture in *The Myth of the Negro Past* (1941). Ellison was familiar with both Frazier's[9] and Herskovitz's scholarship and was likely entering into conversation with them before Elkins joined the discussion in 1959.

Interestingly, after undergoing electric (psychic) shock therapy, the invisible man, experiences a rebirth into black culture, replete with the "distinct wail of female pain" (Ellison, *Invisible Man* 235), loss of language, new white overalls, blurred vision, and a metaphorical umbilical cord "attached to the stomach node" (243).

Instead of severing the invisible man's ties to his black southern roots, the procedure seems to amplify those connections. For instance, while he was once ashamed to eat pork chops, grits, and biscuits under the white gaze in a New York restaurant, the reborn protagonist leaves the medical facility and is struck by the nostalgic odor of baked yams, which he buys and eats with his bare hands as he walks the city streets. Though he began his psychological journey as an accommodationist, pandering to white audiences as he did during the Battle Royal, the procedure transforms the once amiable fellow into a resentful man who feels the urge to speak out against racial and economic injustice. Finally, he abandons his all-consuming belief in the righteousness of the American democratic experiment to become a radical mouthpiece for the Communist party.

The similarities between the invisible man's electric shock transformation and Frazier's and Elkins' psychic shock theories should not be overlooked. The inference is that no process is jarring enough to divorce a person from his racial or regional culture, as evidenced by the invisible man's unapologetic southern blackness after electroshock therapy. He further explores this thesis in a 1970 *TIME* article. Ellison pointedly states that the American language, like the nation itself, began by "merging the sounds of many tongues," much of which are "derived from the timbre of the African voice and listening habits of the African ear" ("What America Would Be" 581). Ellison enters a decade-old debate on African continuums in American culture in this scene and clearly comes down on the side of anthropologist Melville Herskovitz rather than that of Frazier and Elkins.

Yet, for all the sociopolitical contraventions in *Invisible Man*, it is Ellison's prose writing that Elkins credits with making a "deep impression" not only on him but upon the black intellectuals who would join Ellison in the battle to undercut Elkins' Sambo thesis. Their success was palpable. By the 1980s, Elkins "moved from an emphasis on damaged Sambo to a call for a model balancing servility and creativity" (Rose xi), thereby shifting the focus of slave researchers from rewriting and revising history to resurrecting the texts of ignored and forgotten slave authors.

By opening "The Slavery Debate" with Ellison's 1944 redress of black stereotyping, Elkins supports the thesis Jacquelyn Dowd Hall would advance in her influential essay, "The Long Civil Rights Movement and the Political Uses of the Past." According to Hall, the dominant narrative of the Civil Rights Movement has focused largely on what Bayard Rustin has termed the "classical" era of the struggle, beginning with the 1954 *Brown v. Board of Education* decision and closing with the Voting Rights Act in 1965. Such a narrative recognizes Dr. Martin Luther King Jr. as the story's hero with the contents of "I Have a Dream" functioning as the very definition of integration and equality. In so doing, the complexity of a movement that focused on dismantling institutionalized impediments to equality has been co-opted by color-blind discourses, respectability politics, and regional recriminations. In fact, what Hall convincingly argues is that the "truer story" of the long Civil Rights Movement finds its origins in "the liberal and radical milieu of the late 1930s . . . accelerated during World War II, [and] stretched far beyond the South" (1234).

It is therefore important to recognize that there were also "heroes" like Ellison who did not subscribe to respectability politics and who did not view integration as a club to which African-American people demanded access. Ellison rejected any approbation of his eloquence and literary successes as tethered to his race. His genius was part of a nationalist identity. Thus, when literary critic Ken Warren asked "whether or not we ought to continue to count Ellison as a Negro or black writer" and William Faulkner asserted that Ellison "managed to stay away from being first a Negro; he is still first a writer" (qtd. in Jackson, "Politics of Integration" 171), Ellison succeeded, not in becoming raceless but in forcing the issue of nationhood over race. Ellison's position was thus central to the civil rights discourse because American identity is sufficiently complex to permit space for diversity of thought and human complexity. Ellison's quarrel with Elkins therefore created a synergy between the seemingly opposed ideas that slavery shaped American identity but was not the bedrock of black American culture. Rather, "the Negro American . . . is the product of the synthesis of his blood mixture, his social experience, and what he has made of his predicament" (Ellison, "If the Twain" 574). The black American experience, Ellison argues, is emblematic of American democracy with its "stringent testing and the possibility of its greatest human freedom" ("What America Would Be" 584). That Ralph Ellison, an African-American man, forced "the beleaguered Elkins," a formidable white historian, to "conced[e] the validity of Ellison's case" (Elkins, "The Slavery Debate" 44) is equally symbolic in its destruction of the foundation upon which "the myth of white superiority rests" (Ellison, "If the Twain" 572).

Notes

1. Elkins characterizes the Sambo as "the typical plantation slave" whose "behavior was full of infantile silliness and his talk inflated with childish exaggeration" (*Slavery* 82). For Elkins, "it was indeed this childlike quality that was the very key to his being" (82).

2. In 1918, Ulrich B. Phillips published *American Negro Slavery*, a monograph that identifies slaves as docile, dependent, and closely resembling the Sambo character that pervaded American literature and theater at the turn of the century. Kenneth M. Stampp's *The Peculiar Institution* (1956) echoed these views of the personalities of enslaved men and women but disagreed with Phillips' argument that the ills of slavery were wildly exaggerated. Though Elkins criticizes Phillips' and Stampp's presentations of black personages on the plantation, his own conclusions are so similar that they suggest he explains rather than refutes his predecessor's views. Elkins argues that the American slave system superseded the severity of Latin American slavery, since the former stripped its chattel of their African identity and independence— two factors that contributed to the development of the ubiquitous Sambo personality. As such, Elkins—whose conclusions represent a synthesis of historical ideas—became the target of a critical backlash from scholars interested in revising the recorded history of American slavery, many of whom were African American. From the 1970s forward, these historians reread the same primary texts that Phillips, Stampp, and Elkins analyzed but included the slave narratives that their predecessors had disregarded. Their goal was to remove "the haze of romance" from these historical analyses in order to present the "truth" about slavery.

3. This is not unlike the present political moment in which there has been sociological evidence to support the notion that black children are perceived as older, therefore more dangerous and less in need of protection, than their white counterparts. See Phillip Atiba Goff et al., "The Essence of Innocence:

Consequences of Dehumanizing Black Children" (2014). There has also been a disproportionate number of police killings of unarmed black people, which has been explained by implicit bias against black people based on racial stereotypes.

4. In the early part of the twentieth century, Franz Boas developed a theory that in order to fully comprehend a person's beliefs and motivations, they must be understood within the context of his or her culture. For example, one cannot understand African-American culture by viewing it through the lens of Eurocentric ideals.

5. Du Bois uses the metaphor of the veil to describe what he calls double consciousness. According to Du Bois, double consciousness is a condition that affects marginalized people who are forced to measure themselves against the values and ideals of the dominant culture. The veil metaphor is therefore vital, as it was adapted by many African-American novelists, including James Weldon Johnson, Ann Petry, Richard Wright, and Toni Morrison.

6. Financial gain was the impetus for American slavery. Anti-black and white paternalist rhetoric were advanced in an effort to diminish the barbarity of the institution. The myth of white paternalist behavior toward docile, childlike slaves has nothing to do with why the African slave trade began and provides little credible information about the horrors of the institution, its effect on the enslaved, or the motivations of plantation owners, overseers, and slavers.

7. One of the most popular of the proslavery novels was William Gilmore Simms's *The Sword and the Distaff* (1852). Like most apologist novels, Simms's work featured a kind, patriarchal master and a pure and genteel mistress guiding their childlike slaves toward Christianity.

8. According to Elkins, the first shock was the shock of capture, the second shock was the long march to the sea, the next was sale to the European slavers followed by the Middle Passage journey, and the final shock in the process of enslavement came with the Negro's introduction to the West Indies (*Slavery* 99-100).

9. In a 1965 interview for *Harper's Magazine*, Ellison remarked, on the impact of sociologists such as Frazier, "If a Negro writer is going to listen to sociologists who tell us that Negro life is thus and so in keeping with certain sociological theories, he is in trouble because he will have abandoned the task before he begins" ("A Very Stern Discipline" 726).

Works Cited

Bland, Sterling Lecater, Jr. "Being Ralph Ellison: Remaking the Black Public Intellectual in the Age of Civil Rights." *American Studies* 54.3 (2015): 51-62.

Callahan, John F., ed. *The Collected Essays of Ralph Ellison.* New York: The Modern Library, 1995.

Elkins, Stanley M. *Slavery: A Problem in American Institutional and Intellectual Life.* Chicago: U of Chicago P, 1968.

_____. "The Slavery Debate." *Commentary* 60.6 (1975): 40-54.

Ellison, Ralph. "An American Dilemma." Callahan 328-340.

_____. "A Very Stern Discipline." Callahan 726-754.

_____. *Conversations with Ralph Ellison.* Ed. Peggy Whitman Prenshaw. Jackson: UP of Mississippi, 1995.

_____. "If the Twain Shall Meet." Callahan 563-577.

_____. *Invisible Man.* New York: Vintage Books, 1990.

_____. "What American Would Be Like Without Blacks." Callahan 577-584.

Genovese, Eugene D. "Rebelliousness and Docility in the Negro Slave: A Critique of the Elkins Thesis." *The Debate Over Slavery: Stanley Elkins and His Critics.* Ed. Ann J. Lane. Chicago: U of Illinois P, 1971.

Hall, Jacquelyn Dowd. "The Long Civil Rights Movement and the Political Uses of the Past." *The Journal of American History* 91.4 (2005): 1233-1263.

Herbers, John. "Report Focuses on Negro Family." *New York Times* 27 Aug. 1965: 13.

Jackson, Lawrence P. *Ralph Ellison: Emergence of Genius.* New York: Wiley, 2002.

_____. "Ralph Ellison's Politics of Integration." *A Historical Guide to Ralph Ellison.* Ed. Steven C. Tracy. New York: Oxford UP, 2004. 171-206.

Moynihan, Daniel Patrick. *The Negro Family: The Case for National Action.* Washington, DC: Office of Policy Planning and Research, United States Department of Labor, 1965.

Rose, Willie Lee. Preface. *Slavery and Freedom.* Ed. William H. Freehling. New York: Oxford UP, 1982.

"Be Loyal to Yourselves": Jim Crow Segregation, Black Cultural Nationalism, and US Cultural Memory in Ossie Davis' *Purlie Victorious*_____

Carol Bunch Davis

> I have a specific reason for writing a play like *Purlie Victorious* in the manner in which it was written. My intent was to have a handbook of consolation, information and struggle, which my people and their friends could use to understand, explain the situation in which they found themselves, and point the way toward a possible solution.
>
> Ossie Davis, "The Wonderful World of Law and Order"

In the statement above, playwright, director, activist and actor Ossie Davis offers his reflection on *Purlie Victorious* (1961) after its staging in the midst of the African-American Freedom Struggle's so-called "heroic era," which prompts questions about the significance of its representations. How did the play enable audiences to gain a deeper understanding of Jim Crow segregation? What explanation for segregation did it offer? Finally, what potential solution to the daily indignity of Jim Crow segregation's practice during the African-American Freedom Struggle did it propose?

Purlie Victorious offers a farcical satire of segregation set in the recent past on a rural plantation in Southern Georgia and traces self-proclaimed preacher Purlie Victorious Judson's and other sharecroppers' efforts to reclaim their church, Big Bethel, from Ol' Cap'n Cotchipee in order to "preach freedom in the cotton patch" (Davis, *Comedy* 16). Described as "a man consumed with that divine impatience, without which nothing truly good, or truly bad, or even truly ridiculous, is ever accomplished in this world—with rhetoric and flourish to match" (6), Purlie left the plantation after a beating from Cotchipee during his youth. Returning there twenty years later to claim a five-hundred-dollar inheritance to purchase the church, he brings an Alabama maid, Lutiebelle Jenkins, to stand in for his recently deceased Cousin Bee, who is the rightful heir. After discovering Lutiebelle's identity, Cotchipee refuses to give her the money, but in another farcical turn, Charlie, Cotchipee's "integrationist" son and bookkeeper, secretly signs the church deed over to Purlie. Following Charlie's revelation, the congregation—Missy, Gitlow, and Idealla—invites Charlie to become the first member of the newly integrated "Big Bethel, Church of the New Freedom for all Mankind" (79). The play's final scene offers Purlie's eulogy for Cotchipee, who, as a son of the Confederacy, died from the shock of Charlie's "betrayal."

As a satire, *Purlie Victorious* necessarily exposes and discredits Jim Crow segregation's folly as it critiques its spatial and social logic throughout the play. Yet Davis also proposes important interventions in cultural memory's master narrative of the Freedom Struggle era through iterations of black nationalism[1] and "negro-to-black conversion" narratives[2] that guide the play's dramatic structure. Cultural memory—or the media, institutions, and practices that construct a master narrative of the Freedom Struggle era—typically begins with the *Brown v. Board of Education* Supreme Court decision in 1954, followed by the Montgomery Bus Boycott in 1955. The March on Washington in 1963 and the passage of the Voting Rights Act of 1965 mark the timeline's apex. Finally, the emergence of black nationalism and Black Aesthetic/Arts cultural production in 1966 put alongside Student Nonviolent Coordinating Committee (SNCC) activist Stokely Carmichael's calls for Black Power the same year purportedly offer evidence of the heroic era's demise.

Yet *Purlie Victorious* intervenes in both the master narrative's chronology and its insistence on an opposition between the "heroic era" and Black Aesthetic/Arts cultural production and expression. As historian James Smethurst argues, it accomplishes this by situating black cultural nationalism within the play as "an ideological stance . . . that casts a specific 'minority group' as a nation with a particular, if often disputed, national culture [and] stems from a concept of liberation and self-determination" (17) and by casting the representations of its key characters—Purlie, Lutiebelle, Idealla, and Gitlow—within a black cultural nationalist conversion narrative crucial to the characters' arc and the play's dramatic structure. Further, by framing black cultural nationalism as a continuation of black Christianity, *Purlie Victorious* refuses cultural memory's prevailing narrative that situates them as mutually exclusive and offers an iteration of black southern identity that challenges representations of black southerners inundating both the mainstream and African-American press. In its exploration and critique of segregation's aesthetics, *Purlie Victorious* not only consoles those who are impacted by its spatial and social logic, but it also exposes and denaturalizes their operations on the Georgia plantation where the play is set in order to inform, to understand, to explain, and ultimately to offer solutions to racial segregation's sociopolitical impacts on and outcomes for black southerners.

In addition to this critique of segregation through its allusions to black cultural nationalism, the play turns to and enacts three conventions that literary critics Brian Norman and Piper Kendrix Williams assign to a segregation narrative tradition. First, such narratives trace racial cartographies where "race infuses the landscape" and "Jim Crow and other kinds of segregation are naturalized" (Norman & Williams 5-6). Second, such works include the spatialization of fear that dramatizes "the fear and consequences related to marking, crossing, or not crossing lines of segregation" (5-6). Finally, segregation narratives detail scenes of cross-racial contact that "underscore the effects and basic injustices—from petty to fatal—of segregated societies" (5-6). While *Purlie Victorious* deploys each segregation narrative convention in its representations, it also stages an interruption of those conventions by drawing upon the ideological framework of black cultural nationalism.

Satire and the Politics of Respectability

While *Purlie Victorious* engages segregation's and black cultural nationalism's aesthetics, the play also satirizes a Civil Rights Movement strategy underwriting many of the Freedom Struggle era's protests—the politics of respectability and civility within racial uplift ideology. Racial uplift ideology describes a social and political strategy employed in the era of de jure segregation during the late nineteenth and early twentieth century that charged black middle-class spokespeople and leaders with refuting the pervasive stereotypical representations of African Americans widely circulating in US culture. Presenting themselves as living rebuttals to those images, this select group of African Americans cultivated images of civility and respectability that depended on class stratification among African Americans as well as a narrative of upward mobility that would aid in "reforming the character and managing the behavior of the black masses" ("Racial Uplift") steadily streaming into northern industrial cities from the south during the Great Migration.

But racial uplift ideology's focus on representing black homes and family life within the parameters of respectability and civility continued through the Freedom Struggle era, during which such images played a key role in enacting the protests of the period. Calling on participants to offer a solemn and stoic demeanor and to wear their Sunday best as they engaged in nonviolent direct action protests, organizers and leaders warned that outbursts of emotion or violence in reaction to what they might encounter could undermine efforts toward full citizenship. Such markers of respectability offered proof that African Americans were prepared for full citizenship and were worthy of inclusion in the American body politic. Yet, despite respectability and civility's prominence in the Civil Rights Movement's so-called "heroic era," *Purlie Victorious* eschews that strategy as the play engages both satire and gallows humor to explore representations of black identity in the Jim Crow South. Through its satirical reading of segregation's spatial logic and iconography as well as its engagement with black cultural nationalism, *Purlie Victorious* interrogates the notions of white supremacy underwriting Jim Crow segregation and racial uplift ideology's sometimes narrow representational strategies deployed to counter white supremacy.

As the play strategically deploys stereotypically black southern figures, including the country preacher, the Mammy, the country ingénue, and the Uncle Tom, it situates them within a conversion narrative that yokes black Christianity and black cultural nationalism.[3] Historian William L. Van Deburg argues that black cultural nationalism's compelling possibilities and implications when it develops from black Christianity during the Freedom

Struggle era are instructive, observing that "[b]y refusing to allow whites to define their existence, black Christians could now claim the biblical promise of freedom. . . . [T]hey no longer would be ashamed to accept themselves as they were. They would be reborn into blackness" (79). The play's refusal to read black Christianity and black cultural nationalism as mutually exclusive enables it to both transform the figures' standard meanings through its satirical representation of them as well as illuminate "the economic, political, and social situations" of African Americans in the south in their deployment (Carr 19).

Consequently, Davis' play wrests segregation's symbols and iconography in the South, or what the play calls "the cottonpatch," away from their origins in minstrelsy and presses them into black cultural nationalism's service.[4] Put alongside its engagement of the segregation narrative tradition, specifically the synergy between black Christianity and black cultural nationalism represented in the play, it consequently complicates our reading of black southerners, southern iconography, and the African-American Freedom Struggle's historiography. *Purlie Victorious*' narrative and representational play with both segregation's and black cultural nationalism's aesthetics—as well as its critique of racial uplift ideology embedded in such narrative play—thus offer an iteration of African-American subjectivity beyond segregation's aesthetics and resonates with post-black discourse.

Prefiguring Post-blackness
Generally, post-black discourse describes black cultural production and cultural criticism that turns away from proscriptive aesthetic criteria that seeks to impose a singular or fixed notion of what constitutes African-American cultural products or cultural production. Three recurring themes help to establish post-black discourse's overriding representational concerns: a rejection of racial uplift ideology; a refusal to accept 1960s-era Black Aesthetic artistic criteria as well as a willingness to lampoon or satirize those strictures; and finally, an embrace of wide-ranging cultural genealogies. While much of post-black discourse critiques the tendency of Freedom-

Struggle-era cultural production to narrowly define black identity and rely upon W. E. B. Du Bois' notion of double consciousness, or a sense of "always looking at one's self through the eyes of others" (3), *Purlie Victorious* marks an early gesture toward the post-black text's play and improvisation with its representations. Literary critic Bertram Ashe locates the key difference between post-black, or what he and some other critics call post-soul texts, and their predecessors in the post-black artist's "relationship to the idea of freedom" (619) because post-black texts refuse the opposition between collective struggle and artistic freedom that is not present in earlier periods of cultural production, like the Freedom Struggle era. In short, the absence of an organized struggle for collective freedom in the post-black era shifts from an emphasis on a fixed, collective black identity to the post-soul period's explorations of such constructions. Yet *Purlie Victorious*, which was written and staged between 1954 and 1961, during the earliest years of the Civil Rights Era, engages in precisely those explorations.

Mapping Race and Space in the Cottonpatch

Beginning with its description of the farmhouse in which much of the play's action is set, *Purlie Victorious* traces segregation's aesthetics throughout its three acts and illustrates the ways in which race infuses the play's South Georgia landscape. The stage direction indicates that the home's antiquated interior is "threadbare but warm hearted, shabby but clean" and is equipped with "long strips of gunny-sacking hanging down to serve as a door" as well as a "large rough-hewn table with three homemade chairs" and an "old dresser," which stands against a wall (Davis, *Comedy* 5). A door leads directly to the cotton field where the play's black characters work, and the field's perpetual visibility through the wooden window, "which opens outward on hinges" (5), offers a constant reminder of the South's segregated terrain. Linking the segregated plantation to what actor Ruby Dee called "the insidious economic underpinnings of racism" (Davis, "Wonderful" 105), Purlie describes Cotchipee's home as a "big white house, perched on top of [a] hill with [them] two windows looking down at us like eyeballs" and asserts that "everything and everybody, he owns!" (Davis, *Comedy* 8-9).

Moreover, segregation's aesthetics clothe the characters themselves. Purlie wears a "claw hammer coat, which though far from new, does not fit him too badly," while Lutiebelle, who has been employed by "Miz Emmylou" as a maid, dons a "dowdy, but well-intentioned" coat "with [a] stingy strip of rabbit fur around the neck" and "flat-heeled and plain white shoes, such as a good servant girl in the white folks' kitchen who knows her place" wears (Davis, *Comedy* 6). Similarly, Purlie's sister-in-law Missy wears "a ragged old straw hat, a big house apron over her faded gingham, and low-cut, dragged-out tennis shoes on her feet" (9), and all three but Missy and Lutiebelle in particular offer a stark contrast to the many images of SNCC members who had initiated nonviolent, direct-action sit-ins at lunch counters in Nashville, Tennessee; Greensboro, North Carolina; and other cities across the South in 1960, just a year before the play's debut.

However, as historian Tanisha C. Ford points out, by 1961, when the SNCC began its campaigns in the rural South, the women working on those campaigns adopted changes to their dress that coincided with the organization's employment of the word *revolutionary* to describe its members and aims (637). While their shift from Sunday-best dress to denim work shirts, pants, and overalls had practical motivations—they were much easier to care for in the often inhospitable locales to which they traveled—the shift also marked a desire to "celebrate" the clothing of African-American sharecroppers as well as to demonstrate their willingness to transgress intra-racial class lines and their political alliance with the people they hoped to help organize and empower to vote (Ford 637-638). In short, Ford frames the significance of organizers' dress as an alternate mode of activism. From that vantage, the play's detailing of the characters' attire takes on another dimension of meaning, as it defies the representational politics of respectability that enforced a Sunday-best dress code. Ultimately, as the play sketches a racial geography that outlines "where certain bodies belong and the various sociolegal codes that attend such geographic inscriptions" (Norman & Williams 4), it also denaturalizes the representational politics of respectability.

The fear associated with transgressing racial boundaries reinscribes Jim Crow segregation's racial geography in the play. In one example, Purlie discusses his plans for Lutiebelle's impersonation with his sister-in-law Missy and his brother Gitlow. Trying to convince Gitlow to go along with his plan and tell Cotchipee that the inheritance belongs to Lutiebelle, Purlie argues that Lutiebelle is "just the size—just the type—just the style" to fool Cotchipee, yet Gitlow counters that she is "just the girl to get us all in jail—the answer is no!" (Davis, *Comedy* 13). The fear associated with transgressing racial boundaries similarly informs Lutiebelle's uncertainty about Purlie's plan. Admitting to Purlie her anxiety about going "up that hill" and "pretend[ing] in front of white folks," she also reveals that the "big talking" about whites she did on the train is easily done "from the proper distance" (23-24). Yet even in this admission, Lutiebelle reveals that some of her fear resides in her reticence to transgress intra-racial class lines.

Ultimately, Lutiebelle worries how she, as a maid who has "never been near a college" (Davis, *Comedy* 24), might pass as Cousin Bee, who was a college student. When Purlie contends that "college ain't so much where you been as how you talk when you get back," he then asks her where is her race pride, and she replies, "Oh, I'm a great one for race pride, sir, believe me—it's just that I don't need it much in my line of work! Miz Emmylou sez—" (24). Yet as Lutiebelle echoes Miz Emmylou's warnings about transgressing racial boundaries, Purlie interrupts her, challenging her to critically read her former employers' assertions through the lens of black cultural nationalism's ideologies, particularly its interrogation of dominant beauty standards:

> PURLIE: Damn Miz Emmylou! Does her blond hair and blue eyes make her any more of a woman in the eyes of her men folks than your black hair and brown eyes in mine?
>
> LUTIEBELLE: No sir!

PURLIE: Is her lily-white skin any more money-under-the-mattress than your fine fair brown? And if so, why does she spend half her life at the beach trying to get a suntan?

LUTIEBELLE: I never thought of that!

PURLIE: There's a whole lotta things about the Negro question you ain't thought of. The South is split like a fat man's underpants; and somebody besides the Supreme Court has gotta make a stand for the everlasting glory of our people!

LUTIEBELLE: Yessir! (Davis, *Comedy* 24-25)

Purlie couches his intervention in gendered beauty standards that might appear to delimit Lutiebelle's contribution to and participation in challenging racial boundaries. However, his focus on such standards alludes to sociologist Maxine Leeds Craig's insights on how racial identity shaped beauty standards during the Freedom Struggle era. She contends that "black women and white women stood in different locations in relation to the institutions that established and perpetuated national beauty ideals," and because beauty contests, media advertising, and other entities either ignored black women or developed images that reinforced white dominant beauty standards, "black women had to contest their wholesale definition as non-beauties" (Craig 5). Craig's assertions illuminate Purlie's efforts to redirect Lutiebelle's focus on Miss Emmylou as they emphasize the significance of black women's beauty in broader efforts to build racial pride as a path to empowerment. In effect, Purlie encourages Lutiebelle to challenge the standard definition of beauty as part of a larger black cultural project. As Craig observes, African-American women's beauty was part of the "symbolic repertoire" used to assert race pride as part of a broader cultural awakening (5).

These early scenes develop the scaffold for the play's key scenes of cross-racial contact that set its civil rights master narrative intervention in motion. Moreover, they turn on satirical representations of the Uncle Tom and the "backwoods" ingénue. Critic Darryl Dickson Carr observes that some black aestheticians rejected satire as a useful mode of representation because the objects of ridicule often include "the black community itself, which directly contradicts their calls for racial unity" (123). However, as it deploys such figures, *Purlie Victorious* situates the representations within a conversion narrative, which echoes cultural nationalism's calls for the recovery of a national culture "that is linked to an already existing folk or popular culture" (Smethurst 17). In short, Purlie's trickster figure-as-country preacher facilitates the folk figures' conversion to black cultural nationalism and enables them to recognize what he calls "a native land in neither time nor place—a native land in every Negro face" (Davis, *Comedy* 81).

Purlie's brother Gitlow offers a compelling example. While he serves as the Uncle Tom figure through his "deputy-for-the-Colored" (Davis, *Comedy* 13) role on the plantation, he demonstrates that he is receptive to conversion through his dissemblance with Cotchipee early in the play's first act. The play details a confrontation between Cotchipee and his son, Charlie, beginning with a discussion about the commissary's exploitive practices and ending with Charlie's support pledge for the Supreme Court's 1954 *Brown v. Board of Education* decision. Afterward, Cotchipee asks Gitlow to sing Stephen Foster's parlor song "Old Black Joe"—a direct reference to minstrelsy and the origins of the stereotypical figures the play satirizes. He complies, but when Cotchipee observes that "he lives for the day" that Gitlow will sing the song over his grave, Gitlow responds, "Me too, 'ol Cap'n, me, too!" (38). As Gitlow anticipates Cotchipee's demise, he also interrupts the ideology informing the archetypical Uncle Tom figure that prioritizes his white master's well-being above his own. In effect, Gitlow's double entendre cues his preparedness for a cultural awakening because he prioritizes his own welfare over Cotchipee's.

Purlie then paves the way for his conversion in Act Two by reflecting on their status within Jim Crow's repressive economic and social hierarchy. Purlie points out to Gitlow, Lutiebelle, and Missy that "a man the color of [Cotchipee's] face . . . can live by the sweat of a man the color of mine!" and observes that while Cotchipee lives on "the fat of the land . . . and never hit a lick . . . our fine young men serve at his table; and our fine young women serve in his bed!" (Davis, *Comedy* 71). This call to action, which "stirred Gitlow deep" (73), mobilizes his conversion in the third act and is instantiated as he refuses Cotchipee's order to arrest Purlie. Rejecting the deputy-for-the-Colored designation, Gitlow grabs Cotchipee's gun, twirls it beyond his reach, and finally signifies on "Old Black Joe," the song that had earlier comforted Cotchipee. Repeating its refrain with what the stage direction describes as "a brand new meaning," Gitlow tells Cotchipee, "Gone are the days" (77).

The play's "country" ingénue, Lutiebelle, similarly responds to Purlie's call to action. In the first act, Lutiebelle cites Miss Emmylou to authenticate every opinion she offers. As the stage directions suggest, Lutiebelle is afraid to take the final leap "into self-confident womanhood . . . because no one has ever told her it is no longer necessary to be white in order to be virtuous, charming or beautiful" (Davis, *Comedy* 7). Punctuating all of her observations with "Miz Emmylou sez" lends legitimacy to Lutiebelle's opinions, and it is an impulse that Purlie troubles throughout the first act. In one example, after he apologizes for the long distance they have walked from the train station to the farmhouse, Lutiebelle asserts that "walking's good for you, Miz Emmylou sez" (7). In his signifying response, Purlie astutely observes that "Miz Emmylou can afford to say that: Miz Emmylou got a car. While all the transportation we got in the world is tied up in second hand shoe leather" (7). Once again denaturalizing Jim Crow's economic and social hierarchies, Purlie underscores how Miz Emmylou's assessments fail to address Lutiebelle's lived realities. In that sense, Purlie's signifying responses within the sermon mark African-American Christianity and black cultural nationalism's intersection.

This intersection comes into focus when Lutiebelle, like Gitlow, is reborn into blackness. In Act Three, Lutiebelle steps self-possessed—and without Miz Emmylou's narrative stage whispers—into self-confident womanhood. This enables her to tell Cotchipee, after he accuses Purlie of stealing the inheritance, that "stealing ain't all that black and white" (Davis, *Comedy* 75). She is also able to set her own efforts toward denaturalizing Jim Crow into motion, as she asks him, "Who kept me in slavery from 1619 to 1863, working me to the bone without no social security?" (75).

In effect, Purlie's "preaching freedom in the cotton patch" (Davis, *Comedy* 16) means he catalyzes the community to articulate their own critiques of its segregation's aesthetics to serve their self-advocacy and to practice their own iterations of freedom. Framing his blend of black cultural nationalism and black Christianity as an attempt to "make Civil Rights from Civil Wrongs; and bring that ol' Civil War to a fair and just conclusion" (25), his admonitions to Missy, Gitlow, and Lutiebelle enable them to engage that process. Put alongside his earlier assertions that full citizenship for African Americans in the South cannot be won entirely through legislation and jurisprudence—or, as he tells Lutiebelle, "the South is split like a fat man's underwear; and somebody beside [*sic*] the Supreme Court has got to make a stand for the everlasting glory of our people" (25)— Purlie's engagement with the community illustrates the significance of being "reborn" into blackness for the play's characters.

Purlie Victorious in Cultural Memory

Despite these interventions, cultural memory—or the institutions, media, and practices that frame a collective history for the nation—narrowly circumscribe the meanings in the play's reviews at its debut as they reject the alternate meanings its representations offer. In an anonymous *Time* magazine review, Davis is critiqued for "people[ing] a Broadway stage with Negro characters that the N.A.A.C.P. has long claimed do not exist" ("Uncle Tom" 88-89). The review continues, scorning both the characters and, significantly, the play's black cultural self-affirmation. The critic writes:

> Unacceptable as real Negroes, the play's characters live a fantasy life that Playwright Davis presents as gorged with self-pity and filled with a lust for revenge over past wrongs. Under the surface laughter lies chauvinism: "I find, in being black, a thing of beauty. . . a native land in every Negro face!" Substitute the word white and any playwright would be howled down as a racist. ("Uncle Tom" 88-89)

The review also draws on the Walter Lee Younger character in Hansberry's *A Raisin in the Sun* to interpret Purlie Victorious Judson, suggesting that both Judson and Younger are "frustrated" and "overambitious" but that Younger has, in effect, learned from his experience. The reviewer writes, "*Raisin*'s hero grew to recognize that in race relations, as in life, there are no shortcuts, and he courageously set his face toward self-discipline, hard work and fair play" ("Uncle Tom" 88-89). The anonymous *TIME* review illustrates how aesthetic criteria for African-American playwrights was confined by "the ghosts of previous representations, performances and historical events occurring in that historical moment" (Davis, *Prefiguring* 15) as well as how black self-affirmations were framed as anti-white racism.

Following the same trajectory, Susan M. Black argues in *Theater Arts* that the play "is based on the assumption that there is a humorous side to the racial problem" and asserts that "maybe there is but Mr. Davis hasn't found it, possibly because he was looking in the wrong direction. . . . [L]ines like. . . . 'being colored can be a lot of fun sometimes when ain't nobody looking' are never going to set me rolling in the aisles" (12). Similarly, critic Robert Brustein, who engaged in a widely publicized debate with the late playwright August Wilson about the racial politics of American theatre thirty years later, asserts in *The New Republic* that Davis has "set back inter-racial harmony. . . by about fourteen years. . . . [T]he author has replaced white stereotypes of Negroes with Negro ones; but I must say that the hate and violence seething under the shut-my-mouf benevolence of the cardboard caricatures really gave me a start" (22). These reviews reflect critics' refusal to engage representations of African-American identity beyond its extant boundaries. They instead elect to police those boundaries and to impose a narrow rubric of meaning that derives largely from a monolithic notion of blackness and its representation.[5]

Critic Bertram Ashe argues that post-soul cultural producers differ from those of earlier eras because post-soul cultural producers' "ideological bottom line was the African American struggle for freedom" (619). Yet *Purlie Victorious* broadens freedom's ideological bottom line through its explorations of black representations. As the reviews demonstrate, critics indeed attempted to thrust their interpretative context on the play, yet *Purlie Victorious* offers instead a meditation on black subjectivity that enables it to travel beyond the politics of respectability and civility as well as outside of uplift ideology's narrow confines. It refuses the arbitrarily imposed boundaries between black Christianity and black cultural nationalism and instead proposes that freedom does not reside only in holding Big Bethel's deed, collecting Cousin Bee's five-hundred-dollar inheritance, or eulogizing Cotchipee. While those events enable and support freedom, the play ultimately frames freedom as the ability to develop and sustain one's own self-concept through the embrace of the black southern nation within the nation and black cultural nationalist self-determination. In *Purlie Victorious*, freedom is ultimately about affirming black identities without what film critic Ed Guerrero, recasting James Baldwin, has called the burden of representation or "the burden of always being viewed as, and reduced to the voice and sign of the black community resident in the popular imagination" (189).

After Purlie eulogizes Cotchipee, he issues his final call to action—the call for self-affirmation, the acknowledgment of the nation within the nation, but most significantly the casting off of the burden of representation: "Be loyal to yourselves; your skin, your hair; your lips, your southern speech, your laughing kindness—are Negro kingdoms vast as any other! Accept in full the sweetness of your blackness—not wishing to be red, nor, white, nor yellow; nor any other race but this" (Davis, *Comedy* 81). Pointing to a specifically southern iteration of black identity, critic Darryl Dickson Carr argues that African-American satire "struggle[s] to define African American culture as something rich and diverse, but independent of any single definition of blackness, literature, or even American identity" (275), and Davis' play approximates that impulse. Through his exploration of southern iconography and stereotypical figures, Davis teases out a multiplicity of black southern identities drawn from what Davis called the truth of his own experiences. While the play counters cultural memory's oft repeated notion that cultural production simply supported the ostensibly more important work of direct action protests, *Purlie Victorious* illustrates the import of black representations that challenge the sometimes limited ways that black identity is framed in the Freedom Struggle era.

Reflecting on the play in 1989, actor Alan Alda, who played Charlie, recalled, "I think it was only after we had been playing for a few months that I began to realize what rich insight there was in this play. And it wasn't until much later that I began to think that maybe the play was probably 10 or 15 years ahead of its time" (Davis, *Commemorative* 95). Twenty-eight years after the play's debut, Alda suggested that he was just beginning to understand its significance. As we close in on another thirty years since Alda's realization about *Purlie Victorious*, perhaps we can follow his observations and revisit Ossie Davis' critically neglected and groundbreaking play. Perhaps we can find that, as Davis asserted, "*Purlie* is black laughter, and like all laughter, when it is humane, it is liberative" ("Purlie Told Me" 89).

Notes

1. Though iterations of both black cultural nationalism and black revolutionary nationalism appeared before this time, as historian James Smethurst points out, unlike 1960s era black nationalism, the development and expansion of a distinctly African-American culture was not central to those earlier iterations. Though many individuals and organizations differed in their expressions of black nationalism, generally black cultural nationalism offers an ideology that understands African Americans in the US as a nation within a nation with a distinct culture that necessitated liberation and self-determination. Smethurst asserts that it also includes a "notion of the development or recovery of a 'true' national culture that is linked to an already existing folk or popular culture" (17). While it adheres to black cultural nationalism's basic tenets, revolutionary nationalism differs in its "open engagement with Marxism" (16).

2. My designation of *Purlie Victorious* as a conversion narrative derives from historian William Van Deburg's discussion of the "negro-to-black conversion experience" informing black nationalism. Drawing on the work of psychologists and educators including Frantz Fanon, William Cross, and JoAnn Gardner, Van Deburg argues that such experiences "became an exercise in the recovery and transmission of psychologically empowering cultural forms" (60). Similarly, Davis' play frames its representations as

a recovery of a black southern culture and experience that challenges the notion of black southerners as disempowered as it charts its characters' transition into psychological agency. Consequently, I read *Purlie Victorious* as a conversion narrative as it follows the conversion experience's hallmarks within a dramatic text.

3. The mammy figure is a US archetypical representation of African-American women who worked as housekeepers or nannies in the homes of white families and often derives from the experience of chattel slavery in the United States. Similarly, the Uncle Tom is another archetypical representation of African-American men who worked in the homes of white families. One of the earliest appearances of both figures in U.S. popular culture is in Harriet Beecher Stowe's 1852 novel *Uncle Tom's Cabin*. The country ingénue is a variation on the ingénue, another archetypical representation of a young woman who is kind and lacks sophistication. The ingénue is usually involved in a romantic subplot in the narrative.

4. Minstrelsy was an immensely popular nineteenth century form of entertainment developed in the United States performed by white, usually male actors, in blackface to play the role of African-American people. These three-act performances ridiculed blacks by portraying them as dim-witted, lazy, and child-like as they staged dancing, music, comedy skits, and variety acts. Many of the stereotypical images of African Americans in the current historical moment derive from minstrelsy's legacy in the United States.

5. Philip Rose noted in *You Can't Do That on Broadway: "A Raisin in the Sun" and Other Theatrical Impossibilities* (2001) that Brustein's reaction to the play was not uncommon among white theatre-going liberals or, as he called them, "white progressive organizations and individuals" whom he said berated him for "putting on a show which not only made fun of Negroes but also portrayed an 'Uncle Tom' character" (168). Like both Alan Alda and Davis himself, Rose observed that *Purlie Victorious* "never received the recognition it deserved" because it was "ahead of its time both for the usual theatre audience and to a significant degree, for the black community" (172).

Works Cited

Ashe, Bertram. "Theorizing the Post-Soul Aesthetic: An Introduction." *African American Review* 41.4 (2007): 609-623.

Black, Susan M. Rev. of *Purlie Victorious*. New York: Cort Theatre. *Theatre Arts* Dec. 1961: 12.

Brustein, Robert. Rev. of *Purlie Victorious*. New York. Cort Theatre. *The New Republic* 6 Nov. 1961: 22.

Carr, Darryl Dickson. *African American Satire: The Sacredly Profane Novel.* Columbia: U of Missouri P, 2001.

Craig, Maxine Leeds. *Ain't I a Beauty Queen?: Black Women, Beauty, and the Politics of Race.* New York: Oxford UP, 2002.

Davis, Carol Bunch. *Prefiguring Blackness: Cultural Memory, Drama, and the African American Freedom Struggle of the 1960s.* Jackson: UP of Mississippi, 2015.

Davis, Ossie. *Life Lit by Some Large Vision: Selected Speeches and Writings.* Ed. Ruby Dee. New York: Atria, 2006.

_____. "Purlie Told Me." 1962. Davis, *Life Lit* 87-94.

_____. *Purlie Victorious: A Comedy in Three Acts.* New York: Samuel French, 1961.

_____. *Purlie Victorious: A Commemorative.* New York: Emmalyn Enterprises, 1993.

_____. "The Wonderful World of Law and Order." 1966. Davis, *Life Lit* 105-118.

Ford, Tanisha C. "SNCC Women, Denim, and the Politics of Dress." *The Journal of Southern History* 79.4 (2013) 635-658.

Gaines, Kevin K. "Racial Uplift Ideology in the Era of 'the Negro Problem.'" *Freedom's Story.* National Humanities Center, Apr. 2010. Web. 13 Dec. 2016.

Guerrero, Ed. *Framing Blackness: The African American Image in Film.* Philadelphia: Temple UP, 1993.

Norman, Brian & Piper Kendrix Williams, eds. *Representing Segregation: Toward an Aesthetics of Living Jim Crow and Other Forms of Racial Division.* Albany, NY: SUNY UP, 2010.

Rose, Philip. *You Can't Do That on Broadway: "A Raisin in the Sun" and Other Theatrical Improbabilities.* New York: Limelight, 2001.

Smethurst, James. *The Black Arts Movement: Literary Nationalism in the 1960s and 1970s.* Chapel Hill: U of North Carolina P, 2005.

"Uncle Tom Exhumed." Rev. of *Purlie Victorious* by Ossie Davis. New York. Cort Theater. *Time* 6 Oct. 1961: 88-89.

Van Deburg, William L. *A New Day in Babylon: The Black Power Movement and American Culture, 1965–1975.* Chicago: Chicago UP, 1992.

Haunting America: Racial Identity and Otherness in Civic Society

Mary K. Ryan

Upon spotting Rodney King speeding down the 210 freeway in Los Angeles, the California Highway Patrol engaged in a high-speed chase on March 3, 1991. King feared a traffic violation would cause his license to be revoked given that, at the time, he was on probation for a robbery offense. Eventually, King was caught by Los Angeles police officers. As the personal camera recording by local resident George Holliday captured, officers forced King out of his car and brutally beat him. As a result, Laurence Powell, Timothy Wind, Theodore Briseno, and Stacey Koon—the four LAPD officers involved—were indicted on charges of assault with a deadly weapon and excessive use of force by a police officer. After all four officers were acquitted of any wrongdoing in April 1992,[1] intense race riots swept across Los Angeles. More than fifty people were killed, more than two thousand were injured, and 9,500 were arrested for rioting, looting, and arson, resulting in approximately one billion dollars of property damage.

In response to these events, many journalists and news reporters covering the riots noted the dire economic climate plaguing the Los Angeles community, suggesting that the Rodney King beating reflected a tipping point for a community divided by income inequality, joblessness, racial profiling, homelessness, and unequal housing access. Mike Davis, for example, writes in a June 1992 article for the *Nation* that:

> [i]n two years of recession, unemployment ha[d] tripled in L.A.'s immigrant neighborhoods," resulting in "rapidly growing colonies of homeless *compañeros* on the desolate flanks of Crown Hill and in the concrete bed of the L.A. River, where people [were] forced to use sewage water for bathing and cooking. (743)

Moreover, because these issues were so widespread, affecting minorities of all ethnicities, Davis also addresses how racially and ethnically diverse the mobs and rioters were, including African Americans, Latino/as, and Caucasians—a multiracial outcry that underscored the decades of inequity ravaging the community. This ongoing tension between communities of color and local police helps to explain why police brutality against a black man would resonate so strongly with residents of the area; the community's shared experiences and socioeconomic struggles yielded a response that mirrored their common history.

For many in the 1990s, King thus became a household name. While his brutal beating and the investigations that followed were frequent news items, he also symbolized many of the problems between communities of color and authority figures, causing him to gain attention as a kind of crystallizing force for decades of racial pain in the United States. In a 2012 interview with Rory Carroll of the *Guardian*, King reflected on his experience: "I'm comfortable with my position in American history. It was like being raped, stripped of everything, being beaten near to death there on the concrete, on the asphalt. I just knew how it felt to be a slave. I felt like I was in another world" (par. 1). King also discussed his forgiveness of the officers who beat him: "No one wants to be mad in their own house. I didn't want to be angry my whole life. It takes so much energy out of you to be mean" (par. 12). While King's forgiveness may seem emotionally and spiritually mature, it begs a critical reflection. Citizens must consider why a victim of injustice is the one who must be kind and whose fragility is often in question. More to the point, King's comments enable us to ponder the affective struggle that inequity and abuse burdens people of color with at the hands of interpersonal racism and structural injustice.

In Los Angeles' case, people of color, especially African Americans, only became visible enough to produce public policy changes when they were harmed and outraged.[2] This phenomenon is not new; Martin Luther King Jr. observed in his 1967 "The Other America" that "a riot is the language of the unheard" and condemned the "contingent, intolerable conditions that exist in our society" (par. 7). One way to understand Rodney King's battery is to then consider it, on a theoretical level, as a trap of the ideological evil of racism, which frames society as tolerant and well-intentioned on the one hand yet ignores the systemic injustices and cruel realities of racism on the other. In their book *Racecraft: The Soul of Inequality in American Life* (2014), Barbara J. Fields and Karen Fields declare that "[t]olerance as an alternative to equality is so firmly rooted in good intentions that practitioners fail to recognize the evil. White persons are human beings until they choose not to be; black persons are not human beings until they earn the privilege, one at a time, by performing a meritorious act" (105). In this statement, a racial double standard emerges, urging readers to reconsider hollow understandings of harmony, which suggest that tolerance alone can foster community change. In fact, true equality cannot abound from the toxic roots of ideological racism, which often renders its victims invisible in American society.

Though the events surrounding Rodney King demonstrate the hyper-visibility of a single black person, American racial identity is overtly considered to be a function of visibility or invisibility. By investigating the layers underneath this outward, sanctioned process in three novels—Kiese Laymon's *Long Division* (2013), Ralph Ellison's *Invisible Man* (1952), and Toni Morrison's *Beloved* (1987)—we can explore how American racial identity is informed through the processes of haunting and memory. Furthermore, juxtaposing these works alongside real-world case studies, such as the Rodney King beating, riots, and trial in the early 1990s as well as the handling of Hurricane Katrina in 2005, aids in the elucidation of salient race critiques of cultural practices and policy or administrative bureaucracy in the late twentieth and early twenty-first centuries. Such incidents of horror, haunting, and history are, of course, vital considerations for why we still need a civil rights movement today yet, perhaps more significantly, also serve to justify why it is so hard to achieve systemic, lasting, and meaningful reforms. Therefore, assessing how we think about identity through these works can help our society better understand that civic engagement, democratic promise, and civil rights for a collective society are not rooted in false individualism but rather in a stronger civic community bound together through authentic lives.

Haunting Citizenship in Kiese Laymon's *Long Division*

American racism can manifest itself in many ways. Unlike the blatant hostility exhibited by police officers in the Rodney King case, the experience of African Americans during Hurricane Katrina functions as a counterexample, calling attention to the hyper-invisibility of black persons. The bureaucratic mismanagement of this natural disaster in August of 2005 showcased the racial tension in America by shining a spotlight on New Orleans. In the immediate aftermath of the hurricane, thirty thousand residents who were unable to evacuate, mostly African American and/or poor, found themselves stranded and overcrowded in the city's Superdome, while others were perched atop their flooded homes for several days awaiting rescue, food, clean water, and sanitary conditions (Sustar 12). Even today, there is no state or federal agency to track those missing post-Katrina, causing Americans to lack concrete statistical data about the severity of the hard-hitting natural and man-made disaster (Olsen par. 5). In "Discrimination's Effects on Katrina's Victims," Becca Hutchinson explains how the situation of the poorest New Orleans residents, who were overwhelmingly black, was no accident or surprise given the history of racism and racial segregation in America. Discriminatory housing practices, like redlining, have existed since the 1890s, contributing to the creation of subpar neighborhoods, white flight to the suburbs, and the isolation of African Americans to the point that they have become the most segregated ethnic group in the country (Hutchinson par. 9). Together, these structural conditions render African Americans into a statistical mass, grouping them into a dangerously powerless cluster that suffers from society's indifference to black lives.

Concerns surrounding Hurricane Katrina are a centerpiece of Kiese Laymon's 2013 debut novel *Long Division. Long Division*'s plot focuses, in part, on the notion of disappearance and social invisibility. The protagonists of the novel are two black teenagers from Mississippi, both named City Coldson, one of whom lives in

2013 and the other in 1985. Considering Katrina from the vantage point of 1985, City wonders what kind of storm could just make people disappear, implicitly referencing the 500 names that have never been released as victims as well as the hundreds of lives that have simply gone unaccounted for in the wake of Hurricane Katrina (Olsen par. 2). Here, City also invites the reader to pass judgment on the policies, cultures, and practices that demonstrate racialized inequity, such as educational disparity and neighborhood segregation. In doing so, he envisions Hurricane Katrina as a gateway into another major interest area of *Long Division*, that of citizenship.

This concept emerges in different ways throughout the book's evolution. Both Citys (full name Citoyen, meaning *citizen* in French) discover what rules apply and what opportunities are available for various ethnic or racial identities in American society during different periods in national history. For example, the novel considers which people would be considered free white persons under the Naturalization Act of 1790.[7] Broadly, the novel construes citizenship and racial visibility as constructions of power, turning identity into a performative, communal concept. In one sublime moment, for instance, near the end of the book's section called "Eyes Have It," 1985 City tells his friend and teenage crush Shalaya Crump that there "'ain't no reason to be scared. What can [white] people do to you, really?'" (Laymon 190). She replies, "'They can make you disappear,'" to which he reassures her, "'Yeah but then you're gone. I ain't afraid of disappearing. I bet disappearing doesn't even hurt, to tell you the truth'" (190). Just as Rodney King reported that he "felt like [he] was in another world" (qtd. in Carroll par. one) during his beating, City and Shalaya feel the need to imagine pain in an alternate time or place. This contemplation of what another world might look like reflects a friction of racial justice work.

While *Long Division*'s characters voice an intolerance of the status quo, they also indirectly offer a cautionary fear that the future may not be better. After all, Shalaya's fear, along with City's attempts to spin disappearance into something that is not painful and thus not something of which to be afraid, demonstrates the emotional duress internalized by African Americans after centuries of victimization, exploitation, colonialism, and capitalism. *Long Division*'s characters exhibit the emotional ramifications of our country's racist history and ideology, which "must be constantly created and verified in social life" (Fields & Fields 137). If "exercising rule means being able to shape the terrain" (140), then the novel bears witness to a kind of racial burnout through an existential quest of young African Americans who withstand fear, engage in optimism, and explore possibilities across time periods where they have never shaped the terrain.

While visibility can manifest itself in the literal presence of a person or through "seeing" an allegorical representation of a memory or ghost, conversely, society sometimes reveals times when invisibility is just as powerful or useful as visibility. *Long Division* employs time travel for an invisibility doubling as a kind of protective measure for its characters. Laymon employs time travel back to 1964, for example, to show the meeting of Shalaya, City, and a Jewish boy named Evan Altshuler, who is desperately trying to save his family from being harmed by the Ku Klux Klan during the Freedom Summer campaign. The remainder of this aspect of the novel yields insight into terror, neo-liberalism, religious freedom, and coming of age. In the present age, the characters encounter the destruction wrought by Hurricane Katrina and the Gulf oil spill, showing the reader that our country still has a lot of growing up to do.

Moreover, this novel cultivates ideas of identity and uses time travel to underscore that despite all of the positive events and progress of the twentieth and twenty-first centuries, many people, especially African Americans, remain imprinted by the damaging centuries of slavery and Jim Crow practices. City's 2013 classmates thus help the reader reflect on black self-identity in the "post"-Civil Rights Era. One girl, Baize Shephard, for example, is constantly daydreaming about introducing herself to the world and the companion image she will be presenting to others. She feels she must work even harder than her white counterparts to make a positive impression. Additionally, the novel begins as 2013 City competes in a grammar competition. The rivalry between City and classmate

Lavender Peeler, a self-proclaimed "exceptional African-American" (Laymon 33) who dreams of proving himself worthy of marrying Malia Obama, is also telling. For City and Lavender, the goal is not just to win the grammar competition but to be noticed by those in power. In Lavender's opinion, African Americans are generally thought to be more ignorant than white Americans, so when an African-American kid outshines a white one, especially in a white state like Mississippi, the African-American child is special. City's interest is less individualistic; he just wants to be a good example for his neighborhood. Both of these examples outline the need for recognition and approval within the African-American experience as well as pathways to achieve them. At the same time, neither of these examples is expressly political, which is a critical reminder of the ways in which racism permeates social life, orients identity, and constructs community interactions.

As we see, *Long Division* is interested in how modern life has been shaped, or haunted, by the nation's racist past. City of 1985 and Shalaya Crump, haunted by rumors concerning their grandfathers' deaths, time-travel back to 1964 to chase the ghosts of their grandfathers who died during the Civil Rights Movement. When they arrive in 1964, their own mortality becomes jeopardized as they are hunted by the Ku Klux Klan. Flashing forward to the status quo, 2013 City remains haunted by the passion of the civil rights generation, feeling an eternal push to keep running to make progress. Thoughts like this, along with the book's cover image of a rusted and broken chain, symbolize the ever-present pressure America's history with slavery brings to African-American lives. The idea of being valued and devalued based on skin color, along with a feeling of being perpetually aware of one's Otherness, runs throughout the novel. In each time period—1964, 1985, and 2013— the African-American characters encounter the threat of racial discrimination and violence. This precariousness contributes to the poignancy behind City's final conversation with his grandmother, who cautions him to "'do whatever it takes to protect you and yours. Especially in your dreams. Especially in your dreams, because you never know who else is watching'" (Laymon 265). This resonates with City who, earlier, during one of his time travels, was told that "'people can mash your heart in your chest while you're still alive. They can take people from you. That's something to be afraid of'" (190). No matter what the characters accomplish, whether it be academic excellence or time travel, their existence is never secure, suggesting our country still has strides to make before our work on civil rights and racial equity is complete.

Hope in Ralph Ellison's *Invisible Man*

While Laymon alludes to the election of Barack Obama and the murder of Trayvon Martin early in the novel, as they serve to represent the prime examples of twenty-first century African-American hope and hopelessness respectively, another novel, *Invisible Man* by Ralph Ellison, takes readers on a different journey of identity and awareness. *Invisible Man* is the story of a young, college-educated black man struggling to survive and succeed in a racially divided society that refuses to see him as a human being. Told in the form of a first-person narrative, *Invisible Man* traces the nameless narrator's physical and psychological journey from blind ignorance to enlightened awareness, transgressing the book's terminology of purpose, passion, and perception through a series of flashbacks in the forms of dreams and memories. Set in the United States during the pre-Civil Rights Era, when segregation laws barred black Americans from enjoying the same basic human rights as their white counterparts, the novel opens in the South (Greenwood, South Carolina), although the majority of the action takes place in the North (Harlem, New York). The book is a social and intellectual tour de force, incorporating the philosophies of black nationalism, Marxism, and Booker T. Washington as it examines identity and individuality.

The novel is framed by W. E. B. Du Bois' idea of double consciousness, an idea that taps into African-American literary heritage. Because of the invisible man's dual role as narrator and protagonist, the narrative is framed by the double consciousness of his grandfather. The grandfather's dying advice suggests two layers of action. He recommends pretending to uphold the racial ideology surrounding them while also proclaiming the need to undermine it. Specifically, he tells the invisible man, "'I want you to overcome 'em with yeses, undermine 'em with grins, agree 'em to death and destruction, let 'em swoller you till they vomit or bust wide open . . . Learn it to the young'uns'" (Ellison 29). Again, the reader sees that the authentic identity of African Americans is suppressed in a sociopolitical climate that does not allow black people to flourish, much less be genuine in their daily conduct as human beings. Such constrictions reshape the development of identity in two primary ways. Identity can be interpreted by white people—those who hold power and are external to the world of blacks—as either socially acceptable or unacceptable. In contrast, Ellison suggests that another option is possible, one in which black people doggedly preserve their authenticity and express only their own true thoughts and feelings, regardless of the implication for white people. Together, these dual approaches reflect an enduring monologue in the minds of black people battling to remain respectable and true to themselves as they navigate the cultivation of consistent public and private personas.

The invisible man's education and schema for interpreting the world are derived from the heritage of a grandfather and arguably, by extension, an entire generation that suggests African Americans cannot be respected authentically in public communities or the social world at large. *Invisible Man* is a gut-wrenching novel largely because of this troubling juxtaposition. Still, the invisible man believes in his American identity and his ability to make something of himself in American society. The tension to move beyond double consciousness is therefore palpable, yet the pathway is rigged with difficulties, including being tricked by white counterparts and given shock treatments, and the ensuing stresses this shoulders him with cause him emotional distress. *Invisible Man* reveals how one's personal haunting can function as a mask, which shows how being unable to infiltrate, much less survive in, the dominant white society can contribute to feelings of alienation. This isolation can in turn lead to hostility, yielding a more problematic result for all of society.

The genius of *Invisible Man* is the bridge built between internalized racism and collective hurt. The book shows how segregation drives wedges between communities, undermining the promise of communal decision-making—a major threat to cultivating effective democracy. Yet, perhaps most damaging of all, is the sustained re-creation of identity some African Americans take on in wearing the mask, which prevents authenticity and autonomy from guiding their lives. Racism as an ideological power can fool people, and, in turn, people can trick themselves into a false acceptance, generating a hollowness that erodes at their own quality of life while contributing nothing to the public either. This danger is revealed within the novel's conclusion that "being invisible and without substance, a disembodied voice, as it were, what else could I do? What else but try to tell you what was really happening when your eyes were looking through? Who knows but that, on the lower frequencies, I speak for you?" (Ellison 591). As we see, the African-American male experience of attempting to self-actualize but always reflecting the white man conveys a fruitless invisibility.

In *Ghostly Matters* (1997), visibility is hypothesized as "a complex system of permission and prohibition punctuated alternately by apparitions and hysterical blindness" (Gordon 17). Most importantly, this kind of visibility must be acknowledged because it helps us to reckon with racial injustice, but it also warrants our attention because of the implicit public death it threatens upon our social systems and civic virtues. *Invisible Man* is a powerful self-narration of a black man's soul in a bitter, overly calculated, and racial world, but it need not be all of our stories from this point forward. Ellison's hopefulness is apparent from the very beginning. He reveals in the prologue that the narrator is living in a basement hole within a whites-only building but that the light is bright and offers him the intellectual necessity of the truth. This invisibility of physically occupying the underground perspective is critically important to the saliency of Ellison's message. At the end of the novel, the narrator can resurface (after being lost in the Harlem riots that occurred earlier in the book) because overt actions have occurred. History, storytelling, and bringing invisibility to life matter. The invisible man, despite a barrage of obstacles from white society, remains hopeful of his ability for success. Flashing forward years later into mainstream society and the experiences of African Americans in the Rodney King beating or during Hurricane Katrina reveals the need for American society to remain vigilant to Ellison's voice. The past must haunt the present. The invisible must gnaw at and wrangle with the visible. These, as Ellison's book reveals, are the pathways to political change.

Identity in Toni Morrison's *Beloved*

Ultimately, *Invisible Man*'s conclusion of speaking for another evokes the idea of claim and autonomy later presented in Toni Morrison's Nobel Prize-winning 1987 novel *Beloved*. Set after the American Civil War, *Beloved* mirrors the story of an African-American slave, Margaret Garner, who escaped slavery in Kentucky in 1856 by fleeing to the free state of Ohio. In the book, Garner is portrayed as the protagonist Sethe who also escapes slavery by fleeing to Ohio. Just shy of a month of freedom, she encounters a group of white people who arrive to retrieve her, supported by the Fugitive Slave Act of 1850. In response to this duress, Sethe kills her two-year-old daughter, Beloved, instead of allowing her to be recaptured and raised in servitude. Years later, a woman presumed to be Beloved haunts Sethe's home at 124 Bluestone Road in Cincinnati. Morrison opens the book by revealing the ghostly haunting— "124 was spiteful. Full of a baby's venom" (3)—which persists throughout the novel.

Beloved, set in 1873, offers this salient look into the experiences of African-American people during slavery. The novel grapples with how individual identity is connected to autonomy and legitimacy and how these features contribute to reckoning with our country's racial ideology. Specifically, the existence of Beloved's two dreams— exploding and being swallowed—suggests that memory can help trigger or influence our actions, as Gordon explains: "When the living take the dead or the past back to a symbolic place, it is connected to the labor aimed at creating in the present a something that must be done" (175). The ghost of Beloved haunts the present, reflecting a displacement of memory that demands attention. Morrison's book can thus be seen as a call to action to examine the ways in which contemporary social ills may reflect unlearned or unacknowledged lessons. When Gordon asserts that "[t]o be haunted is to be tied to historical and social effects" (190), she, like Morrison, is urging us to find connections between our personal and political traumas. Particularly, Sethe's actions put forward the possibility of living in a way that one's surroundings suggest may not be viable as the only means to finally live an authentic life. This kind of cognitive dissonance reflects both the staunch optimism previously expressed in *Long Division* as well as the grappling with double consciousness that Ellison explores.

Despite being the namesake of the book, Beloved often represents an intangible presence, a person who almost functions as a thing, disorienting those around her. Here Morrison writes, "Everybody knew what she was called, but nobody anywhere knew her name. Disremembered and unaccounted for, she cannot be lost because no one is looking for her, and even if they were, how can they call her if they don't know her name? Although she has claim, she is not claimed" (323). Despite being "freed" by her mother, Beloved becomes a heavy weight on her mother's conscience, revealing that the reasons and impacts of our actions remain distinct from the actions themselves. As Gordon observes, "Twenty years after the Emancipation Proclamation, the characters in *Beloved* are struggling with the knowledge that 'freeing yourself was one thing; claiming ownership of that freed self was another'" (172).

More broadly, Morrison conveys the ways in which personal choices act as a sort of echo chamber for societal renderings, including racism, violence, and belonging. Many people, after all, repress horrific memories. In *Beloved*, the characters Sethe, Paul D., and Denver all repress memories of slavery in an attempt to forget the past. Yet, this separation leaves them barren, fragmenting their sense of self and leaving them lacking a sense of their original, authentic identities. As Gordon alludes to, part of claiming ownership of oneself is allowing for the integration of all aspects of oneself, even those wrapped up in painful or unspeakable moments. The plight of repression from slavery in *Beloved* therefore echoes the public/private split so dominant in *Invisible Man* as one's sense of identity often seems heavily entwined with external evaluations of one's worth.

As we see, characters in *Beloved* are living through the complexity of being able to physically eject themselves from a tumultuous place while struggling to move past, emotionally and spiritually, from a heartbreaking, complicated, and painful past. One tangible representation of this struggle in *Beloved* comes from analyzing the use of the English language throughout the book. While only two characters, Baby Suggs and Stamp Paid, officially rename themselves, all are attempting to come to grips with definitions and language forced upon them by slave owners and slavery as a system overall. In the process of self-exploration, language is a tool Morrison employs to make those who have always been defined by others into people who become free to define themselves. Importantly, Morrison does not leave this process to each character alone; she paints a community of shared aspirations and common histories, such as when the Georgia prison inmates sing together with Paul D. Just as with the other two aforementioned novels, truly transformative power emerges with collective discovery, not merely one person's self-awareness. Likewise, part of what makes the collective experience of public policy-oriented problems in the United States, like the Rodney King beatings and Hurricane Katrina, so potent in our society is that they become part of the public consciousness. While the direct experience transpires to far fewer people, those experiences trigger similar historical events in our collective memory; shape our racial understandings of power, trust, and community; and test our public appreciation for all human beings as members of a holistic political community.

Heeding the Haunt: Lessons for a Stronger US

In *Beloved*, *Invisible Man*, and *Long Division*, America's pervasive struggle with racism is explored across numerous time periods, offering a comprehensive look into the country's efforts to create policies and social or political reforms related to areas including criminal justice, education, housing, and employment. While the civil rights reforms of the 1960s are important steps in the country's efforts to cultivate equitable lives among citizens of all races, we can see, in a very small way from the Rodney King beating and riots as well as the handling of Hurricane Katrina, that racism is still a serious problem in America. After all, part of the reason for the thorniness of America's problems with racism is because it is larger than simply civic policy alone. For that reason, racism can be perceived as an ideology steeped in the political arena and thus a critical component in civil rights largely because it is able to "shape the terrain" of ideological practice (Fields & Fields 140).

Perhaps more significant to twenty-first-century civil rights efforts, though, is the Fieldses' closing call for collective action in *Racecraft*. Since racism lives on in social life, policy change is important but not sufficient alone to create lasting change. To reinforce this point, Fields and Fields invoke Harold Garfinkel's reflection that racism employs "seen but unnoticed features of social life," which "enter the memory" and "manifest as social order" (Fields & Fields 186). In this way, it becomes clear that racism is not simply a legal taboo to be amended or vetoed. It is a palpable inequality penetrating our society and threatening our democracy. While civil rights reform helps us to see that inequality is not a zero-sum issue, as the Fieldses put it, "Inequality never stands merely as fact: it requires moral reinforcement in collective beliefs" (277). The nation's moral codes and acceptance of racial ideology will, therefore, help to steer the necessary forthcoming progress in civil rights.

Just as the Fieldses suggest that "the law shows society in the act of inventing race" (130), twenty-first-century racial progress holds the promise of recreating our understanding of power. The need to infiltrate this power reflects a struggle, but in the present century, haunting offers American society an instructive guide. This struggle for power ought not to be about a particular racial or ethnic group gaining supremacy. Since, as the Fieldses note, "exercising rule means being able to shape the terrain" (140), democratic power must be shared across diverse identities to prevent the warping of the terrain for the interests of one identity alone. It is a collective struggle for all of us to break out of the racial ideology that has trapped this country since our foundational roots in slavery. Together, the novels thus make the case that all identity is haunted and all of our lives are performances of the political influences structuring the world in which we live. As such, civil rights in the twenty-first century requires a recognition of the political processes that have been sanctioned as legitimate, understanding which cultural and social practices are rooted in inequity, and identifying ways to break down policies that alienate and segregate people. Our nation's horrific racial past ought to haunt us, but it need not separate us into individualism or divide us by Otherness; it must compel us to unite and achieve the racial equality we all deserve.

Long Division, *Invisible Man*, and *Beloved* therefore offer critical insight into the myriad of psychological, material, and emotional ways that American racecraft operates as an ideological force on both collective and individual levels. In each book, there is a gap between personal and social expectations, public and private life, and objective versus subjective truths. Thus, in these ways, America can be viewed as "a haunted society, full of ghosts" (Gordon 98) from our collective past. Therefore, "the very way in which we discover things or learn about others or grapple with history is intimately tied to the very things themselves, to their variable modes of operation, and thus to how we would change them" (65). Depicting US society in this way, these three novels offer insight into how racism in America frightens, segregates, and undermines people while also revealing ways in which communities and people unite, empower each other, and flourish. However, it is a mistake for us to live in the haunting or be scared away by the ghosts in the country's social memory, so if the next wave of civil rights reforms comes, collective action will be necessary to spur strides for equality. Progress is not guaranteed without deliberative, conscious action to reconcile the ghosts of our past. It is up to us, along all racial lines, to ensure the historical bigotry highlighted in these novels as well as the inequity experienced in contemporary public life are mitigated and overcome in the future. Laymon, Ellison, and Morrison may deliver an idea of a haunted society, but the solutions rest with the American public itself.

Ta-Nehisi Coates' "Letter to My Son" voices this observation when he writes that his "great error was not that [he] had accepted someone else's dream but that [he] had accepted the fact of dreams, the need for escape, and the invention of racecraft" (par. 24). Instead of settling for living in the harmful racial dream of a false whiteness, our society should heed Coates's advice in his closing lines to his son: "I would not have you descend into your own dream. I would have you be a conscious citizen of this terrible and beautiful world" (par. 37). By owning up to and taking stock of all sides of our past as well as being present in the complexity of the status quo, we can better learn how to live in a world of constant transformation. America's ability to treat all races as equal requires us to move beyond an arbitrary rainbow catalogue of racial identity and into a new zone of wholeness, uniting memory with action and brokering new displays of power and belonging.

Notes

1. The United States Department of Justice filed federal civil rights charges against the officers; in August of 1992, two were found guilty while the others were again acquitted. As a result of a civil trial, King was eventually awarded 3.8 million dollars for the injuries he sustained.

2. This incident is explicitly connected to institutionalized racial intolerance, which spurred the investigation of an independent commission, informally known as the Christopher Commission. Accordingly, the incidents led to the resignation of LAPD Chief Daryl Gates, his replacement with black police chief Willie Williams, and other reforms related to citizen complaint systems and internal disciplinary measures.

Works Cited

Carroll, Rory. "Rodney King: I Had to Learn to Forgive." *The Guardian*. Guardian News and Media Limited, 1 May 2012. Web. 17 Dec. 2016.

Coates, Ta-Nehisi. "Letter to My Son," *The Atlantic*. The Atlantic Monthly Group, 4 July 2015. Web. 17 Dec. 2016.

Davis, Mike. "Urban America Sees Its Future: In L.A., Burning All Illusions." *The Nation* 1 June 1992: 743-746.

Ellison, Ralph. *Invisible Man*. New York: Random House, 1952.

Fields, Barbara J. & Karen E. Fields. *Racecraft: The Soul of Inequality in American Life*. Brooklyn: Verso, 2014.

Gordon, Avery. *Ghostly Matters: Haunting and the Sociological Imagination.* Minneapolis: U of Minnesota P, 1997.

Hutchinson, Becca. "Discrimination's Effects on Katrina's Victims." *University of Delaware Daily.* University of Delaware, 21 Sept. 2005. Web. 17 Dec. 2016.

King, Martin Luther, Jr. "The Other America." 1967. *Veterans of the Civil Rights Movement.* Tougaloo College/Bruce Hartford, n.d. 17 Dec. 2016.

Laymon, Kiese. *Long Division.* Chicago: Agate Publishing, 2013.

Morrison, Toni. *Beloved.* New York: Vintage International, 2004.

Olsen, Lise. "Five Years After Katrina, Storms Death Toll Remains a Mystery." *Houston Chronicle.* Hearst Newspapers, LLC, 30 Aug. 2010. Web. 17 Dec. 2016.

Sustar, Lee. "Hurricane Katrina Exposes Racism and Inequality." *Socialist Worker* 1 Sept. 2005.

CRITICAL
READINGS

Unpacking Notions of Citizenship through James Baldwin's *Another Country*

Hope W. Jackson

Hailing from Harlem, New York, noted novelist and playwright James Baldwin seems torn even at an early age between how his identity and citizenship conflate. Throughout his life as well as indicated through his writings, Baldwin struggles to reconcile both his as well as others' notions of identity and citizenship, not as separate but, for him, congruent. Provokingly titled, *Another Country*, his 1962 novel then enables him to interrogate identity but simultaneously trouble and juxtapose interpretations of American citizenship. The novel, after all, is intricate, highlighting complex issues under the context of America's metropolitan "melting pot," New York City. After World War I and World War II, the city was considered the mecca for postwar immigrants, as the Statue of Liberty—a gift to the United States from France during the nineteenth century—represents, "recognized as a universal symbol of freedom and democracy" ("The Statue of Liberty"). However, through the novel, Baldwin examines myopic behavioral patterns most associated with the bigotry of southern states but situated in the "Big Apple" with Lady Liberty in the background.

Within the title, he is challenging the actions of American citizens, who ideally represent the conglomerate or "melting pot" of individuals within the city. Merriam-Webster defines the word *another* as "different or distinct from the one first considered," so by using *another* in the title, Baldwin is suggesting that the United States is far from its superior claims as a *civilized* world power. In fact, America's democracy demonstrates hypocrisy for Baldwin because of its continued castigating judgments placed on others, i.e., non-white or non-normative individuals, regardless of whether they are US-born or not. In other words, America is, in actuality, no different than any other country.

This is evident even today as American citizenship and its rights seem to elude black folks. From the time of slavery to segregation to the present day, there are moments that remind members of the black community of their former non-person social status. Today, they remain vilified, demonized, and criminalized. If that were untrue, there would be no Tamir Rice, Eric Garner, Freddie Gray Jr., or feces-drawn swastikas at Mizzou. Yet, the irony continues resonating when Fox News journalist Bill O'Reilly declares #BlackLivesMatter a terrorist organization and not the revolutionary movement founded by young African Americans who decided that black lives do in fact matter ("How Black Lives Matter is Killing Americans").[1] Under this view, the United States is just "another country"—one that allows its own citizens to be maligned and mistreated based on race, gender, class, religious beliefs, as well as sexuality.

In particular, James Baldwin's identity as a black, homosexual man not only demonstrated his frustration with his own US citizenship, but his personal pain can be readily identified in *Another Country*, as he continues to speak out against the atrocities done to Americans by other Americans. Therefore, as dialogue of these issues ensues, a recognizable theme reoccurs: critical citizenship discourse. And, with twenty-first-century events in Ferguson, Baltimore, as well as Mizzou, the types of thought-provoking conversations undoubtedly developing in African-American literature and culture classes across the United States need to be brought to a larger audience, continuing the dialogue by troubling tenets of citizenship particularly through works such as James Baldwin's critical novel. Through his black male protagonist, Rufus, Baldwin necessarily challenges American citizenship. After all, before the deaths of Tamir Rice, Freddie Gray Jr., or Eric Garner, there was *Another Country's* Rufus Scott.

Another Country as Site of Memory: The Intersection of Memoir and Fiction

James Baldwin's narrative presence is evident and deliberate in his fictional novel, *Another Country*. While critics often assert how novels are fictional accounts, highlighting one's ability to convey an imaginary story, for black folks, especially James Baldwin, memoir and fiction are often inseparable. In "The Site of Memory," Toni Morrison writes that there are clear similarities between the two—

"places where those two crafts embrace and where that embrace is symbiotic" (65). As such, Baldwin's inclusion of personal experiences is deliberate. For instance, he chooses his hometown as the geographical landscape for *Another Country*, as New York City represents citizenship. Countless non-American citizens flock to New York City in an attempt to become citizens, inspired by Lady Liberty, which stands guard over the perimeter of this city as a representation of the amalgamation of America. Baldwin interrogates this locale as well as its perception by exposing the dichotomy of America and democracy in the city that represents all of the country's dreams of America. For Baldwin, the setting is therefore a key element in his work.

The setting, however, is not the only element that reflects the intersection of memoir and fiction in Baldwin's text. *Another Country*'s multilayered implications then resonate over sixty years after its publication precisely because it challenges its reader to navigate the taboo topics of homosexuality, bisexuality, infidelity, sexism, racism, as well as mental illness that Baldwin encountered during his life and that are still, to an extent, taboo subjects today. Baldwin thus implements a thought-provoking strategy to make people question their views of all of these issues. In addition, through his interrogation of these topics, he reveals complicated characters who must confront their fears and learn to cope with difference. The death of the protagonist, Rufus Scott, triggers this confrontation of self-reflection by most of the other characters in the novel. In turn, Baldwin challenges his readers to recognize the destruction of self-loathing and hate. Ultimately, he shows readers the importance of loving oneself as well as others despite internal and external heterogeneity—a key idea for the black community if its people are not only going to avoid being driven from their homes but also "make America what America must become" (Baldwin, *The Fire Next Time* 10).

He accomplishes this goal first by exploring the topic of mental illness, which even today remains a taboo subject. Early in the novel, Baldwin considers the complexity of mental illness through Rufus Scott as well as Scott's response to his own psychological anguish.

Unable to cope with the racist aggressions of his surroundings, Rufus lashes out and assaults his girlfriend, Leona, multiple times. In essence, Rufus' actions demonstrate W. E. B. Du Bois' theory of double consciousness. In *The Souls of Black Folk* (1903), Du Bois writes that this condition entails "always looking at one's self through the eyes of others, of measuring one's soul by the tape of a world that looks on in amused contempt and pity" (2). Rufus responds to the contempt others have for him through violence because he is unable to cope with what others think of him and his emotions, resulting in his "two-ness,- an American, [and] a Negro; two souls, two thoughts, two unreconciled strivings; two warring ideals in one dark body" (2). Unfortunately, Rufus lacks the "dogged strength" to "keep it from being torn apart" (2). Baldwin's inclusion of Rufus' torment therefore requires readers to confront both racism and its effects. In this instance, the effect of racism is Rufus' mental illness, though none of his friends take his violent behavior seriously until after his death. Only then do they begin to contemplate their participation and perhaps their own culpability in his death.

This perspective must be examined because of Baldwin's personal connection to it. By incorporating his own demons into his prose, he invites others into his pain. Doing so awakens some sympathy for the Rufus in his life but perhaps criticism for those who could have prevented his untimely death, Baldwin included. In his essay, "The New Lost Generation," he shares his last conversation with his best friend, Eugene, who, like Rufus, was in a relationship with a white woman. Also like Rufus, he was in a physical altercation with a group of white men after they see Eugene and his girlfriend together in the subway. Unfortunately, Baldwin and Eugene's last encounter was heated and left Eugene seemingly deflated and hopeless. Not long afterwards, he, like Rufus, "jumped from the George Washington Bridge" (Baldwin, "The New Lost Generation" 660)—an event that Baldwin conceivably reflects on in *Another Country*. It is easy, after all, to imagine that Baldwin may blame himself for the friend's suicide. If this event did not haunt him, it would have been omitted. By including his narrative voice in

Another Country, he boldly offers didactic prose to show the dangers of blind ignorance, especially when contextualized by racism.

Baldwin is therefore unapologetic with including other personal, taboo issues he has encountered, from racism to homophobia. He is challenging his readers to trouble the underbelly of American society, especially in a city that claims to include everyone. To accomplish that, Baldwin wants his audience to see, hear, feel, and taste through the experiences of his characters. Thus, he insists that all of his characters matter, especially Rufus, despite his transgressions. By adding a narrative element that shares his encounters with oppression and victimization, personal or witnessed, Baldwin has solidified the authenticity of his perspective. After all, several situations included in the novel are not fictional; by including his voice, he then invites the audience to participate in his citizenship dialogue, fulfilling Toni Morrison's demand that a novel should "provide the places and spaces so that the reader can participate. Because it is the affective and participatory relationship between the artist or the speaker and the audience that is of primary importance" ("Rootedness" 59).

The ability of the reader to engage in *Another Country*'s citizenship dialogue is also a core reason for the novel's continued appeal today. Like the character of Rufus, many black men who have been killed by white police officers have been further victimized in death. For instance, Eric Garner's previous arrest record was released, while Michael Brown was accused of stealing cigars, thus supposedly contributing to his own death. Yet, Baldwin offers that black lives matter, regardless of whether they are criminals or not. Moreover, he asserts that their character assassinations reveal more about the living than about the dead, especially the continuing racist sentiments of this American society. In the novel, Rufus Scott is not allowed to rest in peace because his experiences will not be laid to rest; several white characters in the book harp on his unforgivable transgressions, while the other characters relay the continued bigotry that contributed to his death. This is important because the dominant narrative of "he deserved what he got" continues all while emphasizing the prevailing racist sentiments. As such, these experiences of double consciousness must be (re)told by others who recognize that Rufus' suffering, like the suffering easily imagined for Garner and Scott, demonstrate the social injustices still prevalent today. Accordingly, his story will not be silenced through death but continues to resonate loudly by those who recognize the price of citizenship for some who are deemed unworthy of it.

The American Problem: Rufus' Perceptions of North versus South in *Another Country*

The novel takes place in New York City during the 1950s, a seemingly more progressive locale than the South. After all, the perception of the South during this time is as the lynching capital of the United States. In fact, it is in the Deep South of the 1950s that Emmett Till, a Chicago native, was murdered while visiting Mississippi during his summer vacation because he allegedly made an inappropriate gesture towards Carolyn Bryant, a white woman. Blacks are, therefore, fleeing such oppressive living conditions by escaping from the segregated South to a supposedly more tolerant North. This historic period, defined as the Great Migration, saw millions of blacks migrate to various northern cities like New York, looking to escape the despotic sharecropping system and to find safer living conditions as well as better job opportunities for their families. Baldwin's first citizenship dichotomy can be found in Rufus' North versus South perceptions.

It is important to recognize that not only was Rufus gainfully employed as a jazz musician, but he had white friends, a white girlfriend, decent living conditions, as well as an active, diverse social life—a seemingly perfect life would likely be impossible in the South. After all, the reputation of southern racism is not subtle but direct and, at times, confrontational. During the historical setting of this novel, southern black boys and men were been lynched for charges of violence against white women. Ida B. Wells-Barnett suggests that "any mesalliance existing between a white woman and colored man is a sufficient foundation for the *charge* of rape" (679, emphasis added). Lynchings of black folks, especially black men, were common practice all across the United States, prompting the National Association for the Advancement of Colored People (NAACP) to campaign to bring public awareness to these atrocities.[2]

This is the historical context for Rufus Scott. And his white girlfriend, Leona, is a constant reminder of a society that perceives him as inferior, thus positioning him as a second-class citizen. Yet, Rufus himself is perplexed and does not understand why he strikes Leona on multiple occasions. This deliberate inclusion of a violent, black northerner is intentional; while racism seems to be a southern problem, Baldwin suggests that it is, in fact, an American problem. Baldwin writes, "To be a Negro in this country and to be relatively conscious is to be in a rage almost all the time" (qtd. in *The Price of the Ticket*).

A frustrated Rufus reaffirms this, saying, "'You got to fight with the landlord because the landlord's *white*! You got to fight with the elevator boy because the mother fucker's *white*'" (Baldwin, *Another Country* 62). Rufus' words highlight an important issue. Rufus seems to suppress his anger in public, but when he is home, his anger is unleashed. Baldwin only describes Rufus' acting on that anger in violence when he should be in a "safe space" where he is able to let his guard down. Yet, this private space does not seem to exist, more importantly, in the greatest city in the world because he resides with his white girlfriend, who does not recognize Rufus' painfully lived experience as a black man. In fact, she inadvertently calls him "boy" without understanding it as a microaggression, though she quickly apologizes to Rufus by saying, "'I didn't mean nothing by it, honey,'" while taking his arm (31). Such small instances were once avoidable at home, but with Leona's cohabitation, they are inescapable. Even in a northern landscape, he cannot escape the subtle, innate bigotry that continues today. As such, she and her whiteness become a constant reminder of the racism he endures on a daily basis. As a result, Rufus lives in a constant state of rage yet does not know why. Unsurprisingly, his anger manifests itself in violence towards Leona and continues escalating until she finally leaves him.

Despite the illusion of Rufus' ideal lifestyle for a black man, the psychological effects of living in this northern city and enduring daily racist macro- and microaggressions were as equally damaging as living in a southern city. Baldwin's intent is not to say that life in the North is not as threatening as life in the South; rather, he purposefully dispels this myth. In a racist United States, Baldwin reveals that Rufus was unsafe no matter his location. As a result, the effects of social and environmental stressors contributed to Rufus' psychological breakdown—a common fate for blacks nationwide. In "Racism and Mental Health: The African American Experience," David R. Williams and Ruth Williams-Morris write that racism "can lead to physiological and psychological reactions that bring about adverse changes in mental health status" (243). While this undeniable revelation becomes immediately evident in Rufus' decision to commit suicide, James Baldwin's nonfiction writings further support this sentiment. In his essay, "A Talk to Teachers," delivered a year after *Another Country*'s publication, he writes:

> [A]ny Negro who is born in this country . . . runs the risk of becoming schizophrenic. On the one hand he is born in the shadow of the stars and stripes and he is assured it represents a nation which has never lost a war. [The Negro] pledges allegiance to that flag which guarantees "liberty and justice for all." He is part of a country in which anyone can become President, and so forth. But on the other hand he is also assured by his country and his countrymen that he has never contributed anything to civilization—that his past is nothing more than a record of humiliations gladly endured. He is assured by the republic that he, his father, his mother, and his ancestors were happy, shiftless, watermelon-eating darkies . . . [and] that the value he has as a black man is proven by one thing only—his devotion to white people. (679)

For Rufus, this is certainly a lived reality. At the height of his psychosis, he even attempts to explain his frustration to his white best friend, Vivaldo. He says, "'How I hate them—all those white sons of bitches out there. They're trying to kill me, you think I don't know? They got the world on a string, man, the miserable white cock suckers, and they tying that string around my neck, they killing *me*'" (Baldwin, *Another Country* 62). This scene in the novel is key because here Baldwin attempts to reveal with a white man a black man's frustrations being treated as inferior. After all, Rufus' friends were mainly white, including his girlfriend, yet even they cannot make him feel equal to them. Rufus shares these sentiments with Vivaldo, saying, "'[W]ouldn't it be nice to . . . go someplace . . . where a man could be treated like a man'" (62). Rufus made the mistake of believing that by his attempts to assimilate into the white society, he would be accepted by them. After all, he had white friends, lived in the Village (a predominately white area of New York City), and had a white girlfriend. Yet, he still was not white. He mistakenly thought all of these actions would "lift [him] into a higher social sphere" (Wright 1404). Sadly, he was still called a nigger and attacked while socializing with these same so-called friends. His association with them did not prevent his oppression. In fact, his devotion to them likely fueled his psychotic episode and led to his eventual suicide.

Another Country's Citizenship Dichotomy: Stigmas of Race

At the time of Rufus' suicide, his whereabouts remain unknown to his family and friends. He simply goes "missing." Baldwin thus uses this opportunity to further discussions regarding this dichotomy of race, as Rufus' sister, Ida, searches for him. She visits the home of his white friends during her quest and explains that she has been to the police to no avail: "'They said it happens all the time—colored men running off from their families. They said they'd try to find him. But they don't care. They don't care what happens—to a black man!'" (Baldwin, *Another Country* 89). One white male character, Richard, quickly responds, "'Oh, well now,'" his face red, "'is that fair? I mean, hell, I'm sure they'll look for him just like they look for any other *citizen* of this city'" (89, emphasis added).

Nonetheless, Ida seeks help from them in her continued search for Rufus, and Vivaldo offers to assist her. She indicates that she wants to visit the Village but "ha[s] the feeling they [will] think [she is] being hysterical" (Baldwin, *Another Country* 89). This is another dichotomy that Baldwin highlights about race and gender perceptions. Here, Ida seems emotional over Rufus' missing status.

She is hesitant to visit her brother's last-known hangout because she believes they, i.e., men, will think she is hysterical, i.e., paranoid. However, Vivaldo quickly comes to her rescue by soothing her anxiety in his offer to help her look. He states, "'I'll come with you. They won't think *I'm* hysterical'" (89). Vivaldo's words exude the whiteness of the patriarchal savior. Even Richard grins at Vivaldo's response. The implication is clear: a black woman cannot be taken seriously, but a white man can. In other words, they will believe Vivaldo because he is a white he and not a black she.

While Vivaldo seems more helpful in this search, throughout the novel, Richard vilifies Rufus. Even though he has been missing for six weeks, Richard dismisses any need for concern. Similarly, while Ida's growing hysteria seems justified, Richard eschews her anxiety, stating, "'I really don't see the point of all this. Rufus is probably just sleeping it off somewhere'" (Baldwin, *Another Country* 89). Afterwards, Ida and Vivaldo leave in search of Rufus, but even after Rufus' suicide is revealed, Baldwin demonstrates that even in death, Rufus remains judged by Richard. He states, "'I don't love Rufus, not the way you did, the way all of you did. I couldn't help feeling, anyway, that one of the reasons all of you made such a kind of—*fuss*—over him was partly just because he was colored. Which is a hell of a reason to love anybody. . . . And, I couldn't forgive him for what he did to Leona'" (93). His words indicate a symbolic lynching of Rufus, despite the fact that Rufus is already dead. Even in death, he nor his actions can be forgiven. Richard engages in this exhumation if you will, for although Rufus is dead, it is not enough. Richard must dig him up again. Why? From Richard's perspective, Rufus committed the ultimate crime; he hit a white woman and was never charged or punished for this crime, rendering him the quintessential brute Negro.[3] Therefore, since Richard cannot lynch him literally for his actions, he annihilates his memory through a figurative murdering of his character.

Such sentiments easily explain why today's black lives continue to be in peril. Noted anti-racist scholar, Tim Wise refers to the deaths of Trayvon Martin; Eric Garner; Michael Brown; and other young, African-American victims as "extrajudicial killings." In one of his politicians are arguing over erecting walls around the US/Mexican border as well as deporting Muslim individuals because of their supposedly questionable political alliances, Baldwin understood the necessity for two elements regarding perceptions of others: love and reflection. He recognized that without both equity amongst all people could never be acknowledged. In *The Price of the Ticket*, Baldwin therefore stated, "No label, no slogan, no skin color, no religion is more important than a human being." In *Another Country*, Vivaldo finally recognizes this after Ida professes her love for him. In this scene, Vivaldo stares into a cup of coffee. "noting that black coffee was not black, but deep brown" (Baldwin, *Another Country* 361). In fact, he realizes that "[n]ot many things in the world were really black, not even the night, not even the mines. And the light was not white, either" (361). It is during this conversation that for the first time, Vivaldo is unconsumed with categories. During his "coffee reflection," Vivaldo realizes that race does not define who we are. No matter our exterior appearance, we are all emotional individuals capable of love. Such poignant words should remind us that regardless of race, gender, religion, or sexuality, all Americans are entitled to all the benefits of full citizenship.

Notes

1. James Baldwin always proclaimed the value of black lives through his literature. In a letter written to his nephew in the introduction to *The Fire Next Time*, Baldwin writes, "Well, the black man has functioned in the white man's world as a fixed star, as an immovable pillar, and as he moves out of his place, heaven and earth are shaken to their foundations" (9). He continues, "You don't be afraid. I said it was intended that you should perish, in the ghetto, perish by never being allowed to go beyond and behind the white man's definition," though he also recognizes that many in the African-American community have challenged that prescribed fate by becoming exactly what white men have said they could never become (9). Through these words, Baldwin reminds his nephew that "this is your home, my friend, do not be driven from it; great men have done great things here and will again, and we can make America what America must become" (10).

2. In 1919, the NAACP published a report entitled, *Thirty Years of Lynching in the United States, 1889–1918*. This research documented the lynching of more than 2,500 blacks. During the mid-1930s, a haunting site hung outside the corporate headquarters for the NAACP in Harlem, New York.

blog posts, he indicates that black men, like Trayvon Martin, had "no right to be treated like a citizen, indeed like a human being. No rights to due process, to peaceably assemble on a public street, to free speech . . ., to be free from cruel and unusual punishment (such as extra-judicial execution . . .). No rights at all" (Wise). More importantly, he adds, "'Regardless of their guilt or innocence, these black folks were denied their right to a trial to determine their guilt or innocence" (PCC Videos). What these events reveal is that there is a history of convicting African Americans for their own deaths in the United States. After all, it is more important that Freddie Gray Jr.'s autopsy results indicated that he had traces of cocaine in his system. Similarly, some argued that twelve-year-old Tamir Rice had no business playing with a toy gun. Like Rufus, these young black individuals were charged, tried, and convicted based on perceptions of guilt and without due process. And, one of the most basic citizenship rights Americans are entitled to is due process under the law, included in both the Fifth and Fourteenth Amendments of the US Constitution.

Ironically, Vivaldo reveals that he is capable of violence, too, though he is untarnished by the stigma associated with his race. In a cab ride with Richard's wife Cass, Vivaldo reveals his participation in the gang rape of a homosexual man. Baldwin writes:

> "One time," he said, "we got into a car and drove over to the Village and we picked up this queer, a young guy, and we drove him back to Brooklyn. . . . We drove into this garage, there was seven of us, and we made him go down on all of us and then we beat the piss out of him and took all of his money and took his clothes and left him lying on that cement floor, and, you know, it was winter. . . . Sometimes I still wonder if they found him in time, or if he died, or what." (Baldwin, *Another Country* 97)

The narrator seems to be the conscience that Vivaldo lacks, and it is possible that Baldwin himself represents this omniscient narrator. As such, Baldwin remarks with disgust at Vivaldo's indifference to his participation in such a violent, horrific sexual assault and robbery. The narrator, Baldwin, supports this, indicating, "[Vivaldo] regarded it with a fascinated, even romantic horror, and he was looking for a way to deny it" (*Another Country* 98). And while Vivaldo never denied it, he is also never held accountable for it. He is not castigated for his participation in this man's assault or perhaps even his death. More importantly, Vivaldo is not demonized or criminalized even though he is admittedly culpable as well as a participant in this violent attack. Cass responds to his admission with silence. And this silence suggests muted acceptance of his participation in an act of rape, which seems much more appalling than the accusations made towards Rufus.

James Baldwin and the Civil Rights Struggle

Ultimately, Baldwin infers that some of Rufus' experiences as a black man with an ambiguous sexuality is likely autobiographical. While Baldwin was openly gay, he was in constant conflict with and reflected on his role as a black man in America. For example, in *The Fire Next Time*, James Baldwin shares an experience of discrimination at Chicago's O'Hare airport where he and his companions are refused bar service. After they provide evidence that they are legally eligible to consume alcohol, their drinks are brought to them. When a white man standing nearby questions them, Baldwin indicates that "he hadn't wanted to talk to us earlier and we didn't want to talk to him now" (*The Fire Next Time* 56). One of Baldwin's companions adds that the dispute in the bar should have also been this white man's fight, too, but the young man replied, "'I lost my conscience a long time ago,'" and he departed (56). Though Baldwin appears better able to internalize the hatred imposed on him by his fellow countrymen during segregation, he, like Rufus, does eventually "take his exit."

While Rufus commits suicide in the novel, Baldwin leaves the United States. In fact, in 1947, while writing *The Fire Next Time*, he leaves for France. He shares in *The Price of the Ticket* that he becomes disillusioned with America because he realizes that his citizenship rights will continually be denied him. All the while, he continues to write and publishes his first novel, *Go Tell It on the Mountain* (1953). Fortunately, Baldwin, an avid reader, becomes

moved by the atrocities he sees being done to his black co[...] during the Civil Rights Movement, and his conscience pr[...] towards engaged involvement in the civil unrest of black[...] September of 1957, he flies to the American South and [...] gather information that contributed to his next book, publ[...] 1961, *Nobody Knows My Name* (Pierpont). In addition, he b[...] publically speak out for social justice issues and continued [...] until his death.

That deeper concern for the rights of blacks makes Ba[...] writings quite relevant to today's headlines of extra[...] lynchings, student protests, as well as the Black Lives [...] Movement. While Rufus' death in the novel seems abrupt, it [...] him undeniable and unforgettable. His death is not a simple o[...] remains complex, like the issues of racism and citizenship [...] today. In the same way, James Baldwin's literature and the cr[...] it engenders leaves a lasting impression, like Rufus' death. The[...] abrupt yet unapologetic. National Book Award-winning poet [...] Finney acknowledged this when she recently participated in a [...] discussion entitled, "The Legacy of James Baldwin," at the [...] Presidential Library in Boston, Massachusetts, on June 11, 2[...] She paraphrased Baldwin, indicating that he would likely say:

America refuses to look at itself as a complicated place. There are[...] things that Americans consider virtuous: simplicity and sinceri[...] And, I was thinking about that because we're living in this ti[...] where Baldwin is so current; he's so present. . . . Every time I h[...] somebody *sincerely* say, "Well I held that young black girl down[...] the grass because I *sincerely* thought I was keeping the neighborho[...] safe. . . . I *sincerely* thought that black man who was—who I w[...] arresting—was reaching for my Taser," and so if it were not for th[...] camera, we would believe in the *sincerity* of that person we ha[...] hired to protect us. (JFK Library)

Finney concludes, "Baldwin is with us, if we would but listen" (JFK[...] Library), though the clues are not difficult to decipher. In the end,[...] his works reveal a consistent advocacy for the citizenship rights[...] of oppressed people—from black folks to the poor. While today's[...]

The iconic flag blew in the wind and read, "A Man was Lynched Yesterday." This symbol was an important visible reminder of blacks' fear while living in a racist society, especially in the South, which "account[s] for 9/10 of the lynchings" during the turn of the twentieth century (Myrdal qtd. in Gibson par. 3). Another astonishing statistic indicates that "in the South, an estimated two or three blacks were lynched each week in the late 19th and early 20th centuries" (*The American Experience: Emmett Till*).

3.   See Sterling Brown's explanation of "Brute Negro" in "Negro Characters as Seen by White Authors" (191-192).

Works Cited

"Another." Def. 1. *Merriam-Webster Online*. Merriam Webster, Incorporated, 2016. Web. 18 Dec. 2016.

The American Experience: Emmett Till. Writ. Marcia A. Smith. Dir. Stanley Nelson. PBS. New York, 11 Aug. 2016.

Baldwin, James. *Another Country*. New York: Dell, 1962.

_____. "A Talk to Teachers." *James Baldwin: Collected Essays*. New York: The Library of America, 1998. 678-686.

_____. *The Fire Next Time*. New York: Vintage, 1993.

Brown, Sterling A. "Negro Character as Seen by White Authors." *The Journal of Negro Education* 2.2 (1933): 179-203.

Denard, Carolyn C., ed. *What Moves at the Margin*. Jackson: UP of Mississippi, 2008.

Du Bois, W.E.B. *Souls of Black Folks*. New York: Dover, 1994.

Gates, Henry Louis, Jr. & Nellie McKay, eds. *The Norton Anthology of African American Literature*. 2nd ed. New York: Norton, 2004.

Gibson, Robert A. "Lynchings." *The Negro Holocaust: Lynching and the Race Riots in the United States, 1880–1950*. 4 Feb. 1979. Yale-New Haven Teachers Institute, 2016. Web. 18 Dec. 2016.

JFK Library. "The Legacy of James Baldwin." *YouTube*. YouTube. 11 June 2015. Online video clip.

O'Reilly, Bill. "How Black Lives Matter is Killing Americans." *FoxNews*. Fox News Network, LLC, 26 May 2016. Web. 18 Dec. 2016.

Morrison, Toni. "Rootedness: The Ancestor as Foundation." Denard 56-64.

_____. "The Site of Memory." Denard 65-80.

The Price of the Ticket. Dir. Karen Thornsen. California Newsreel, 1990.

PCCvideos. "Ferguson and Beyond: Racism, White Denial, and Criminal Justice." *YouTube*. YouTube, 10 Feb. 2015. Online video clip.

Pierpont, Claudia Roth. "Another Country: James Baldwin's Flight from America." *New Yorker*. Condé Nast, 9 Feb. 2009. Web. 18 Dec. 2016.

"The Statue of Liberty." *National Park Service*. National Park Service/US Dept. of the Interior, n.d. Web. 18 Dec. 2016.

Wells-Barnett, Ida B. "*The Red Record*." Gates Jr. & McKay 676-682.

Williams, David R. & Ruth Williams-Morris. "Racism and Mental Health: The African American Experience." *Ethnicity & Health* 5.3/4 (2000): 243-268.

Wise, Tim. "Trayvon Martin, White America and the Return of Dred Scott." *TimWise.org*. Time Wise/WordPress27, 27 Mar. 2012. Web. 18 Dec. 2016.

Wright, Richard. "Blueprint for Negro Writing." Gates Jr. & McKay 1403-1410.

"On Revolution and Equilibrium": Barbara Deming's Secular Nonviolence

Sheila Murphy

From eighteenth-century pacifist Quaker sects to abolitionists, anarchists, labor union advocates, and anti-war demonstrators, nonviolence has a long and varied history in the United States.[1] As a strategy, though, nonviolent direct action is most closely associated in American history with Martin Luther King Jr. and the Civil Rights Movement. Additionally, the rise of other social movements in the 1960s, '70s, and '80s—including the Women's Rights Movement, environmental justice movements, and the spread of emerging democracies—reinforced the concept of political and cultural change through peaceful strategic protest. In *Political Protest and Cultural Revolution: Nonviolent Direct Action in the 1970s and 1980s* (1991), Barbara Epstein points out that "[t]he main accomplishment of the direct action movement is that it has taken the first step toward articulating a politics of cultural revolution that unites these currents with the philosophy of nonviolence" (22). While these movements often demonstrated important commonalities in their goals of promoting significant cultural changes through the strategy of nonviolent direct action, those commonalities often took a parallel, rather than overlapping, path.

For example, while King and others labored tirelessly for the freedoms which the Civil Rights and Voting Rights Acts would eventually bring, equality for women remained frustratingly elusive. The oppression of women in American culture—including civil rights organizations—was a ubiquitous and overt feature of society at the time. As Gwendolyn Zoharah Simmons explains in her essay on her experiences with the movement, "Sexism was definitely a problem throughout all civil rights organizations. Dr. King, not surprisingly—like most if not all of the men in the movement who were products of the Black Church and American culture—was sexist" (194). Despite this, the commonalities between the women's movement and the Civil Rights Movement were then, as now, undeniable. It is no surprise, then, that a feminist peace politics arose in the ensuing years as women claimed agency in the politics of the personal and as American involvement in foreign conflicts lost public support in dramatic and historic ways.

While feminist peace politics that explored the intersection of feminism and nonviolence enjoyed a surge in popularity in the 1980s and 1990s, the twenty-first century has not enjoyed the kind of sustained scholarly interest in the topic that marked the immediately preceding decades. Of the two areas of interest, certainly feminism has remained a focus of inquiry, shifting and expanding research and discussion as it moved from second- to third-wave feminism as well as the inclusion of womanist perspectives, accompanied by significant changes in the lives of women and the roles they play in current society. Nonviolence, though, has not enjoyed the same continuous exploration and scrutiny. Although it remains the topic of occasional works (largely focused on international protest movements), nonviolence would seem to be primarily regarded as a relic of the recent past, tied inextricably to the Civil Rights Movement but stuck fast, as it were, in the amber of history.[2] We may peer at it through sepia tones now and then and polish it up for our schoolchildren every February, but in general, we are happy to leave it alone, displayed on a shelf, attractive, shiny, and harmless.[3]

Continuing to do so, however, would be a mistake. The challenges for equality and justice in the twenty-first century—including racial equality, women's equality, LGBTQ rights, economic justice, environmental justice, heath care and education access, and international conflicts—all demand that we revisit our history of nonviolent direct action. The rising generation deserves more from us than advancements in violent force. We must, then, explore and develop those methods and strategies for creating societal change that will build up, rather than tear down, the global community. Writer Adam Sanchez makes this very point in his recent article for the Zinn Education Project, which is geared primarily toward elementary and secondary educators. In his piece, "What Happened to the Civil Rights Movement After 1965? Don't Ask Your Textbook," Sanchez calls out our education system for presenting the Civil Rights Movement as if it ended with the passage of civil rights legislation:

> Not only does this narrative tell students that politicians and judges are more important than activists and organizers, it reinforces the myth that structural racism is a relic of the past and the United States is on an unstoppable path of progress. As Black Lives Matter activists once again take up the fight against racial inequity and police brutality, excavating the long, grassroots history for students is crucial if we hope to use the past to inform our struggles today.

Using the past, though, has proven to be somewhat problematic for those engaged in today's struggles. Despite its important, history-changing successes, the grassroots history of the Civil Rights Movement is burdened with its own mistakes and anachronistic methods, such as the sexism previously noted, and its heavy reliance on individual leaders who could make or break those successes. Jelani Cobb, in his recent article on the development of the Black Lives Movement for *The New Yorker*, points out that "Black Lives Matter has been described as 'not your grandfather's civil-rights movement,' to distinguish its tactics and its philosophy from those of nineteen-sixties-style activism. Like the Occupy movement, it eschews hierarchy and centralized leadership." Indeed, at a time when we find ourselves under siege, both metaphorically and literally, from violent forces intent on doing people harm, the very concept of nonviolence may seem quaint or naïve. When there is no longer any such thing as a noncombatant and when theaters, bars, churches, schools, and street corners may be turned into the next battleground, it may even seem dangerous to suggest that the idea of nonviolent direct action deserves our attention. There are, however, significant lessons from the past that we would do well to explore and heed.

A long overlooked but important contributor to this grassroots history of nonviolence is feminist activist and author Barbara Deming. As Ira Chernus points out in his book, *American Nonviolence: The History of an Idea* (2004), Deming may be one of the least known theorists of nonviolence in US history, yet she is one of the most significant, for "[s]he is the most influential thinker who developed a systematic argument for nonviolence with no religious basis" (182). Deming's theory of explicitly secular nonviolence represents a clear and significant departure from Dr. King's exhortations to a divinely-inspired, beloved community. It also offers multiple insights for protest movements in twenty-first century America, whose citizenry has grown both markedly more diverse and considerably more secular than it was forty or fifty years ago.

Deming's Theory of Nonviolence

While Deming began writing poetry in the 1940s, her political writing came to prominence through publication in *The Nation* and *Liberation* in the 1960s, with such pieces as "The Peacemakers" (*The Nation*, 1960) and "Southern Peace Walk: One Issue or Two?" (*Liberation*, 1962).[4] As early as 1960, Deming became involved in the Civil Rights Movement, working with the Committee for Nonviolent Action and The Peacemakers and later corresponding with King at the Southern Christian Leadership Conference. As a result of her participation in civil rights protests in Alabama and Georgia, she was jailed multiple times—experiences she details in her 1966 book *Prison Notes*. Deming's experiences led her to not only support nonviolent direct action as a specific, targeted technique in the struggle for civil rights, it also provided a concrete manifestation of a theory of peace politics rooted in the feminist concept of equality and respect for all persons.

Deming's essay "On Revolution and Equilibrium" provides the clearest explanation of her views on nonviolent direct action as an alternative to violent force.[5] Published in February, 1968, the essay appeared a few years after the Civil Rights and Voting Rights Act had been passed, at a time when many activists had grown impatient with the lack of progress toward equality and disillusioned with the promises of King's Christian vision of a beloved community. While King insisted that "Christ furnished the spirit and motivation" ("Pilgrimage to Nonviolence" 38) for the Civil Rights Movement, Deming's conception of nonviolence considers this reliance on a religious basis for nonviolent action to be too meek, too trusting.

She writes, "I argue with the contention that nonviolent action can only be prayerful action" (Deming 174). Rather than "remain naïve" (174), she claims nonviolence not only could but must become much more radical in order to effect the kind of societal change toward which the movement aimed: "The pressure that nonviolent moves could put upon those who are opposing change, the power that could be exerted in this way, has yet to be tested," she proclaims (174).

Throughout the essay, Deming presents her arguments from a distinctly personal perspective, which underscores the decidedly feminist approach she urges for her readers. In the same way that King's "Letter from Birmingham Jail" was written in direct response to the criticisms others brought against the nonviolence campaigns he led, Deming's essay responds to specific criticisms of nonviolence brought by other influential writers who urged violent force as the only means of exercising genuine power. Responding to arguments by such writers as Frantz Fanon, Carl Oglesby, Andrew Kopkind, and Stokely Carmichael, Deming presents their claims and then reflects, evaluates, and challenges those claims as she explains her deeply held belief in the superiority of nonviolence for effecting positive and lasting social change. For instance, early in the essay, Deming refers to Frantz Fanon's *The Wretched of the Earth* (1961), recounting a vignette from Fanon's text in which he describes a former terrorist who finds it difficult to contemplate the idea that those whom he had killed might have been like the friends he has now made. Thinking of his enemies like that, he explained, caused him to feel "'what might be called an attack of vertigo.' Then he asks a poignant question: 'But can we escape becoming dizzy?'" (qtd. in Deming, 169). This is Deming's key question for herself and those to whom she writes. She challenges her readers to determine for themselves what it is that would make them dizzy. Her exhortation to nonviolence rests on this key idea: that we must all choose, as individuals, actions that do not disrupt our own balance— our "equilibrium": actions that will offer no conflict between what we believe and how we act in the world.

While King's many writings emphasized the larger community, the role of Christian love in refusing to physically harm one's adversary, and the importance of viewing all people as members of the metaphorical and universal body of Christ, Deming makes no such assertions. Instead, Deming keeps the focus of her discussion at the individual and personal level. Their varying purposes make the need for this difference clear. King's purpose was to promote—on as wide a scale as possible—building a "beloved community" ("Stride Toward Freedom" 487). He is concerned with and addresses the greater community of Christian followers who find their commonality in their faith and who together comprise a loving community seeking to expand that love and embrace their oppressors, transforming them from adversaries to allies. Deming, too, seeks to transform her adversaries into allies, but she approaches that goal from a much more focused, individualized perspective. Rather than concern herself with the larger community, Deming's feminist perspective approaches the issue from the standpoint of individuals as individuals, since her concern is the very specific effect on the personal, conscious lives we all must inhabit. "The living question" she poses "is: What are the best means for changing our lives—for really changing them?" (Deming 169).

"God Terms" in Deming's Theory

As a method of inquiry, Kenneth Burke's cluster analysis provides a useful means of assessing the primary perspective from which writers draw their assertions. As Burke explains in *Attitudes Toward History* (1937), "significance" can be determined "by noting what subjects cluster about other subjects" (232). In cluster analysis, the "god terms"—or ultimate terms towards which the speaker or writer strives—are identified. Close analysis of "On Revolution and Equilibrium" shows three ultimate terms—*change*, *lives*, and *control*—around which Deming frames her concept of nonviolence. Along with identifying these ultimate terms, identifying associated terms—the cycle or "cluster" of terms—allows examination of the relationships among those terms. As William Rueckert clarifies in *Kenneth Burke and the Drama of Human Relations* (1982), "The object of a cluster analysis is to find out what goes with what and why" (84). Because Deming is writing in response to specific arguments made by others, the god terms she employs are somewhat constrained by the assertions those others are making. However, she is quite selective with the passages she chooses to highlight from the works of these other writers, which only reinforces, rather than detracts from, their role as god terms in her overall position. A closer look at the god terms in play here makes this clear.[6] In her very first paragraph, she notes that Frantz Fanon claims his desire in setting out his revolutionary ideas in *The Wretched of the Earth* is to "set a foot a new man" (qtd. in Deming 168). Proclaiming her solidarity with this goal, Deming writes, "I stand with all who say of present conditions that they do not allow men to be fully human and *so they must be changed* [emphasis added]" (168).

Change is the first god term presented in this piece, and it is the primary motivation around which she builds her argument. Given that she is specifically writing to other activists with similar political leanings, this is not at all surprising. The goal of their activism is to elicit change—change in the societal structures that oppress them, change in the minds and actions of their opponents, and change in specific laws and policies that work against their full freedom. The cluster of terms associated with change makes this focus of motivation even more explicit. Deming positions the word *change* with the words *action* and *struggle* repeatedly throughout the piece. Not only are these terms implicit in any call for change, their role in this symbolic motivation toward perfection is made explicit in her challenge of Fanon's endorsement of violence. She writes,

> But I ask all those who are readers of Fanon to make an experiment: Every time you find the word 'violence' in his pages, substitute it for the phrase 'radical and uncompromising *action*.' I contend that with the exception of a very few passages this substitution can be made, and that the *action* he calls for could just as well be nonviolent *action*. (Deming 170, emphasis added)

Burke notes, though, that the cluster of terms is incomplete unless one also considers their linguistic opposites. He writes, "The essential distinction between the verbal and the non-verbal is in the fact that language adds the peculiar possibility of the negative"

("A Dramatistic View" 252). The demand for change would be meaningless if our minds could only conceive of a constant status quo. The exhortations to action therefore only gain meaning when held up against the pitiful inaction that is causing the unrest to begin with. Quoting Fanon to emphasize her point about substituting nonviolence for violence, Deming includes these words: "Without that struggle, without the knowledge of the practice of action, there's nothing but a fancy dress parade" (170). That pitiful inaction, the "fancy dress parade," loses its power and meaning—is demystified— in the face of the action for which the activists call. For Deming, though, that "practice of action" must be nonviolent. "Violence," Deming reminds us, "makes men dizzy; it disturbs the vision, makes them see only their own immediate losses and fear of losses" (181). Nonviolent action allows people to maintain an equilibrium of spirit, which permits the possibility of genuinely changing lives.

The second god term pervasive throughout the essay is the term *lives*. While Deming directly connects the concept of change to the word *lives* early on—as in "What are the best means for changing our lives . . . ?" (169)—the word is prominent throughout the essay, along with related clustered terms. These include *selves, humanity, people, men, women,* and *one*. These terms present the striving toward the perfection of the self—specifically, individual selves, about whom Deming writes as independent, autonomous, self-determined, and acting according to specific individual needs. To emphasize both the primacy of individuality but also our shared humanity, she often utilizes the first-person plurals, *we* and *our*. Her query to her readers does not ask them to consider what it is that might make society dizzy, or a community dizzy, or even a small group of activists dizzy. Her concern is at a personal level. She speaks of her own personal equilibrium and the equilibrium of others on an individual level. Acknowledging the concomitant negative of this god term, the word *other* appears frequently throughout the text as do *victims* and *enemy* as well as the contrasting of *rebels* and *nice guys*. Again, though, her focus is on enemies as individual persons, as humans who deserve the same consideration one would want for oneself. While loving one's enemies may be beyond the practical abilities of a person who suffers from systematic violence or oppression, focusing on individuals as individuals can strengthen one's ability to at least refrain from enacting physical harm: "What *is* possible is to act toward another human being on the assumption that all men's lives are of value, that there is something about any man to be loved, whether one can *feel* love for him or not" (Deming 175-176).

The third god term to serve as a focus of motivation in Deming's writing is *control*. However, in speaking of control, Deming is careful to continue her explicit distinction between societal control and personal control. In rejecting the need for violent force, she insists: "It is my stubborn faith that if, as revolutionaries, we will wage battle without violence, we can remain very much more in control—of our own selves, of the responses to us which our adversaries make, of the battle as it proceeds, and of the future we hope will issue from it" (Deming 169). Control on a larger scale, then, must be grounded in and is only ever made possible by the deliberate control of the self in response to violence and oppression. In making such a claim, Deming emphasizes "control" in the sense of personal will rather than in any sense of subjection or dominion. Mastery is over one's own urge to lash out, to respond to violence in kind, or to destroy one's adversary as a means of gaining advantage. "Vengeance," she points out, "is not the point; change is" (179). Related terms that cluster around this idea of control, further clarifying its significance, include such words as *power, pressure, force, leverage,* and *balance*. With all of these terms, Deming underscores, again and again, the idea that while nonviolence refuses to inflict physical injury on human persons, it remains an effective and moral method for waging conflict, or, as she puts it, "[N]onviolent battle is still battle" (180).

When taken together, these three god terms—*change, lives,* and *control*—demonstrate the rhetorical framework within which her theory of nonviolence operates and reveal a dialectical relationship that supports the delicate equilibrium of which she writes. It is the interplay among these terms and their associated clusters of terms that anchors the concept of nonviolence firmly in a feminist concept of personhood. As Nancy Hirschman explains in *Rethinking Obligation: A Feminist Method for Political Theory*

(1992), "Feminist recognition involves not a subject and object, a self and other, but two subjects, two selves, with the object and the other absorbed into the dynamic of the relationship between subjects and selves" (250).[7] By focusing on human beings as individual human beings, the activist gives nonviolent direct action its power. Deming recognizes and illuminates the power within this dynamic interplay between two selves when she explains the superiority of nonviolence:

> We can put *more* pressure on the antagonist for whom we show human concern. It is precisely solicitude for his person *in combination with* a stubborn interference with his actions that can give us a very special degree of control . . . We put upon him two pressures—the pressure of our defiance of him and the pressure of our respect for his life— and it happens that in combination these two pressures are uniquely effective. (177-178)

For Deming, the strength of nonviolence lies not in the idea that one is acting in a loving or Christian manner toward one's opponent. Instead, it is the interplay of one's respect for the opponent as another subject—another self—together with the defiance of oppressive actions that make nonviolence a more constructive method of waging conflict. This interplay also supports the promise of more positive and long-lasting results.

This is not to say that Deming does not recognize the violence being imposed by that "other self" through unjust systems or even by direct physical violence taken against the oppressed. She points out that casualties in battle are accepted as a given so that losses in nonviolent battle should not be equated with *defeat*. She writes:

> It is an intriguing psychological fact that when ghetto uprisings provoked the government into bringing out troops and tanks—and killing many black people, most of them onlookers—observers like Kopkind decided that the action had been remarkably effective, citing as proof precisely the violence of the government's response. But when James Meredith was shot, just for example, any number of observers editorialized: "See, nonviolence doesn't work." (Deming 179-180)

Clearly, nonviolent methods constitute waging battle every bit as much as troops and tanks. For Deming, what it does not do—what a focus on the interplay among change, lives, and control will not allow—is a vengeful exacting of punishment from other selves, who may be just as much at the mercy of an oppressive system as those who rebel against that system.

Reflections, Deflections, and Equilibrium

A cluster analysis and evaluation of the god terms involved in any symbolic action must include what Burke refers to as "terministic screens."[8] Under this concept, any terminology, however carefully selected, must by definition be incomplete. Burke explains that "[m]en seek for vocabularies that will be faithful *reflections* of reality. To this end, they must develop vocabularies that are *selections* of reality. And any selection of reality must, in certain circumstances, function as a deflection of reality" (Burke, "A Grammar of Motives" 59). These terministic screens reveal the deflections of reality that necessarily occur by the emphasis placed on god terms. That is, if the god terms reflect a particular view of reality, they also deflect other views, keeping them hidden so that the motives of that view of reality are difficult to ascertain. The purpose, then, of a cluster analysis is to reveal those motives, to pull back the curtain, as it were, on the screens created by the privileging of one view over another. According to Burke, it is only by examining and revealing these hidden mysteries, these implied and privileged symbolic motives, that we can hope to transform our realities.

Deming recognizes this problem with language as incomplete when she laments in her essay that part of the difficulty with nonviolent action is, in fact, a question of finding the proper terms. She writes, "If people doubt that there is power in nonviolence, I am afraid it is due in part to the fact that those of us who believe in it have yet to find for ourselves an adequate vocabulary" (Deming 175). Appeals to truth and love, she notes, fall short, since power is often only associated with violence. Her essay attempts to shift that focus: to present power as a product of nonviolent control, to present change as a possibility without resorting to violence, and to privilege individual lives over systems, institutions, and larger societal groups.

It must be admitted, though, that Deming's own terms and clusters of terms also deflect some important realities. Deming clearly insists on the importance of personal connections and individual commitment: her conversational tone as she discusses her own reflection on nonviolence and her use of first-person pronouns to introduce herself help establish a personal rapport with her reader. Her descriptions of personal encounters and appeals to conscience illustrate the individual nature of this grappling with the problem of violence. These stylistic techniques point to the personal and interpersonal dialectic she wishes to emphasize. The larger issues, though, of systemic violence and intractable policies that keep the status quo well supported do not get addressed with any serious consideration.[9] It is true, as Deming asserts, that "[w]e can put more pressure on the antagonist for whom we show human concern" (177). However, that does little to get to the root of the issue that caused one's "antagonist" to be an antagonist in the first place. And as Zara Chandler points out in her essay "Antiracism, Antisexism, and Peace," "There cannot be any serious consideration of ending the evils of racism, sexism, and war without speaking of the termination of their root causes in the world systems of injustice" (30).

Deming also points out that in waging the nonviolent struggle, "Words are not enough here . . . [W]hat is needed is this—to *cling* to the truth as one sees it. And one has to cling with one's entire weight" (176). While she follows this exhortation with examples of personal actions—such as boycotting a particular store or refusing to pay a particular tax—she does not actually acknowledge or address the complicated difficulties in actually following through with such a commitment, of genuinely clinging "with one's entire weight" (176) to this truth. Similarly, while she notes that the writers on whom she reflects attempt to address these very issues, Deming herself remains focused on the personal and individual. She is almost apologetic when she actually does mention that real disruption, genuinely radical action, can have unintended consequences that take the struggle beyond the personal by inducing second- and third-order effects. For example, while insisting that "[i]t is quite possible to frustrate another's actions without doing him injury," she also includes a footnote with that comment: "It is possible but not always simple. When we stage an act of massive obstruction in a city . . . there is always the risk that we will prevent some emergency call from being answered—prevent a doctor's car from getting through, perhaps. One has obviously to anticipate such situations and be ready to improvise answers to the human problems raised" (177). A curt nod, however, to the problem of creating major problems with infrastructure that could very well endanger some unknown person's life hardly seems compatible with the overriding concern for an antagonist as an individual.

Further, Deming notes in several instances in her essay that harm, punishment, and revenge are not the goals; rather, change is the goal. She barely considers that for many people who have suffered tremendous loss under an unjust societal system, revenge may, in fact, be one of their goals. While she attempts to remain rational and logical in her explications of the power of nonviolence, this rationality may be irrelevant to people who are so driven by negative, irrational emotion that the goal of change does not cancel out the desire for punishment. Deming recognizes this difficulty when she observes that for those who wish to see more opponents than allies hurt, "a complete mental readjustment is required of them . . . [V]ictory has nothing to do with their being able to give more punishment than they take" (179). However, simply stating that fact does little to address the deeply ingrained and culturally reinforced emotions it represents. While Deming's insistence that "to refuse one's cooperation is to exert force" (176) may be theoretically correct, it is also a sad reality that sometimes the point of exerting force really is to injure.

Despite these drawbacks in Deming's vision, the value of her work as both a representative text on nonviolence as well as a feminist text lies in her insistence on the primacy of perceiving and dealing with others as individual human beings. Always acknowledging, always respecting one's antagonist as a human being whose life is always deserving of respect presents both the promise of a more just and inclusive society as well as a tremendous challenge as to how one might actually accomplish such a feat. Recognizing that challenge, Deming places violent force, punishment, and revenge in the category of phenomena that throw our lives out of balance. Because one cannot engage in violent force without also violating the basic moral concept that we are all humans, each deserving of the same protections from harm, to engage in causing such harm makes us, in the words of the recovering terrorist, "dizzy."

Deming goes to great lengths to contemplate and attempt to resolve this condition of psychological vertigo. For Deming, overcoming that dizziness requires balancing the primacy of self with the primacy of the Other. As long as we continue to consider our opponents "Other," though, our dizziness remains. Debates about which lives matter—black? blue? LGBTQ? immigrant? the comforting but demonstrably untrue assertion of "all"? —rely on a societal view that denies the very idea that both self and Other can have equal primacy. The solution, Deming insists, is to use the interplay of nonviolent pressure and concern for the human whom we would oppose. "The most effective action," she writes, "*both* resorts to power *and* engages conscience" (Deming 175). This "both/and" approach offers concrete action accompanied by moral balance. Unlike King, for whom power was based in the certainty and superiority of Christian love, Deming claims the power of revolution lies in that moral balance, "this life-saving balance—this equilibrium between self-assertion and respect for others" (188). As our culture has become more expansive, more diverse, and more integrated into the larger world, turning to Deming is vital, as the struggle to find equilibrium—that life-saving balance—still faces us today.

Notes

1. In their extensive work, *Nonviolence in America: A Documentary History* (1995), editors Staughton and Alice Lynd provide a comprehensive chronicle of this history. They note that while nonviolence is often assumed to have its beginnings in the writings of Thoreau and Tolstoy, it has, in fact, a long history in the United States dating back to the seventeenth century. But, as Lynd and Lynd observe, "With the Montgomery bus boycott of 1955–56

and still more with the student sit-ins of 1960, nonviolence became a more significant social force than at any earlier period in the history of the United States" (xxxi).

2.   Lynd and Lynd note that "[i]n the United States . . . after a period (late 1960s, early 1970s) in which many activists scorned nonviolence as `bourgeois' and sought to imitate Third World guerillas, there followed years of apparent apathy and ideological retreat" (xxxvi). They further observe that while later activists engaged in civil disobedience against the war, for example, many "did not consider themselves pacifists, but concluded that any war waged by the United States under current and foreseeable conditions would be an unjust war" (xxxvii). See David S. Meyer, "Civil Disobedience and Protest Cycles," for a discussion of the cyclical nature of protest movements and the shifts in power and participation as activists win public attention and concessions, while simultaneously losing support for more dramatic actions.

3.   While many recent protest actions, such as the Occupy Wall Street Movement and the Black Lives Matter Movement have used peaceful protest to advance their respective causes, nonviolence as the foundational core for a deeply rooted and sustained cultural movement has not received much focus in the United States since the successes of the Civil Rights Movement of the 60s.

4.   Deming's other numerous contributions in *The Nation* include "The Ordeal of SANE" (1961), "International Peace Brigade" (1962), and "In the Birmingham Jail" (1963). Another well-known piece published in the left-wing magazine, *Liberation*, was "Letter to WISP" (1963).

5.   First published in *Liberation*, "On Revolution and Equilibrium" was reprinted in 1971 in Deming's book, *Revolution and Equilibrium*.

6.   The cluster analysis on which this essay draws was originally done as part of a chapter on feminist nonviolence in my 1996 dissertation, *The Rhetoric of Nonviolent Conflict Resolution: Towards a Philosophy of Peace as a Social Construct*.

7.   This feminist view of self and Others offers an interesting perspective on the difficulty of the "Black-White Binary" in critical race theory. In their excellent introduction to that field, Richard Delgado and Jean Stefancic explain that "[t]he black-white—or any other—binary paradigm of race . . . simplifies analysis dangerously" (78). This dichotomous framing of interpersonal relations is precisely what enables and encourages violence against an objectified Other. Similarly, Delgado and Stefancic go on to explain that the black-white binary, unlike the feminist conception of self, "weakens solidarity, reduces opportunities for coalition, deprives a group of the benefits of the others' experiences, makes it excessively dependent on the approval of the white establishment, and sets it up for ultimate disappointment" (79).

8. By "terministic screens," Burke is referring to those terminologies under which we choose to operate. Even at the most basic level of definition, choosing a terminology for any symbolic action, whether that choice is deliberate or spontaneous, will "direct our attention to quite different kinds of observation" (Burke, *Language as Symbolic Action* 44). This effectively serves to screen, by way of terminology, one's perspective on any subject.

9. See Sheila Murphy's *The Rhetoric of Nonviolent Conflict Resolution* (1996), 210-213.

Works Cited

Burke, Kenneth. "A Dramatistic View of the Origins of Language." *Quarterly Journal of Speech* 38 (1952): 251-263.

_____. *Attitudes Toward History, Third Edition*. 1937. Berkeley: U of California P, 1984.

_____. *A Grammar of Motives*. 1945. Berkeley: U of California P, 1969.

_____. *Language as Symbolic Action: Essays on Life, Literature, and Method*. Berkeley: U of California P, 1966.

Chandler, Zara. "Antiracism, Antisexism, and Peace." *Rocking the Ship of State: Toward a Feminist Peace Politics*. Ed. Adrienne Harris & Ynestra King. Boulder, CO: Westview P, 1989. 25-34.

Chernus, Ira. *American Nonviolence: The History of an Idea*. Maryknoll, NY: Orbis, 2004.

Cobb, Jelani. "The Matter of Black Lives Matter." *The New Yorker.* Condé Nast, 14 Mar. 2016. Web. 18 Dec. 2016.

Delgado, Richard & Jean Stefancic. *Critical Race Theory.* New York: New York UP, 2012.

Deming, Barbara. "On Revolution and Equilibrium." *We Are All Part of One Another.* Ed. Jane Meyerding. Philadelphia: New Society Publishers, 1984. 168-188.

Epstein, Barbara. *Political Protest and Cultural Revolution: Nonviolent Direct Action in the 1970s and 1980s*. Oakland, CA: U of California P, 1991.

Hirschman, Nancy J. *Rethinking Obligation: A Feminist Method for Political Theory*. Ithaca, NY: Cornell UP, 1992.

King, Martin Luther, Jr. "Pilgrimage to Nonviolence." Washington 35-40.

_____. "Stride Toward Freedom." Washington 417-490.

Lynd, Staughton & Alice Lynd, eds. *Nonviolence in America: A Documentary History.* Maryknoll, NY: Orbis, 1995.

Rueckert, William. *Kenneth Burke and the Drama of Human Relations, Second Edition*. Oakland, CA: U of California P, 1982.

Sanchez, Adam. "What Happened to the Civil Rights Movement After 1965? Don't Ask Your Textbook." *Teaching A People's History: Zinn Education Project.* Zinn Education Project, 14 June 2016. Web. 18 Dec. 2016.

Simmons, Gwendolyn Zoharah. "Martin Luther King, Jr. Revisited: A Black Power Feminist Pays Homage to the King." *Journal of Feminist Studies in Religion* 24.2 (2008): 189-213.

Washington, James M., ed. *A Testament of Hope: The Essential Writings and Speeches of Martin Luther King, Jr.* New York: HarperCollins, 1991.

"[B]ut yesterday morning came the worst news": Margaret Walker Alexander's *Prophets for a New Day*_____

Seretha D. Williams

On June 12, 1963, Medgar Evers was murdered in the driveway of his home at 2332 Guynes Street in Jackson, Mississippi. Evers, who had been instrumental in investigating the murder of Emmett Till and in desegregating the University of Mississippi, was shot in the back by Byron De La Beckwith. De La Beckwith was arrested, but he was not convicted of the crime until 1994. Such was the climate of the United States; racists responded to nonviolent activism with violence, and local governments failed to uphold justice, resulting in personal and communal losses that shook the country. In particular, Evers was the neighbor of Margaret Walker[1] who was the first to purchase a home in 1955 in this neighborhood developed specifically for the black middle class.[2] Evers and his wife Myrlie moved in in 1957, and thus Walker knew the Evers family well. In her journal entry for June 13, Walker captures her sentiments about this time, writing:

> The demonstrations for Negro Rights were in full swing in Jackson and I got much material for poetry and an article—but yesterday morning came the worst news. Medgar Evers—our neighbor and NAACP Field Secretary had been shot and fatally wounded as he stepped out of his car midnight Tuesday. By 2 am Wednesday, he was dead—shot in the back leaving a young widow and three small children. The worst tragedy of the whole movement for equality—the deaths at Oxford and the deaths of Smith in Brookhaven, and now Medgar Evers—tragic, and overwhelming in its horror.[3]

Although she initially processes Evers' death as a trend, a part of a broader reality for civil rights workers, her grief intensifies over time, and she returns to the subject of Evers' death at various points in her life. On July 10, 1963, for instance, Walker writes, "Guynes Street also much in my thoughts. I can see the neighborhood and neighbors shocked over Evers death and standing around in groups—every house with a light on and folks unable to go back to bed and sleep."

Walker does not literally see this scene or the murder of Evers, as she was enrolled in a doctoral program at the University of Iowa when Evers was assassinated. But she, too, suffers from the trauma of violence, his death becoming an impetus for the civil rights poems she began to compose in her journals throughout the year 1963. Many of those drafts in fact became poems included in Walker's 1970 collection *Prophets for a New Day*, in which she re-imagines civil rights figures as biblical prophets, documents a racial memory of struggle, and articulates the psychological and physical traumas caused by racial violence. In the collection, Walker captures the verve of the Civil Rights Era and invokes the memory of iconic figures such as Martin Luther King Jr. and Malcolm X. Yet, *Prophets for a New Day* transcends eulogy, functioning as a guide for moving forward; Walker shows us the worst news—the horrors of American hatred—but encourages us to look toward the new day.

"The Struggle Staggers Us": Walker's Early Work as a Poet Activist

Walker, a member of the 1930s South Side Writers Group[4] in Chicago and an integral voice of the Chicago Black Renaissance,[5] understood the potential of art as social protest. Although she never joined the Socialist or Communist parties, Walker travelled in literary circles with writers like Richard Wright who were aligned with such groups, and she studied socialist and communist texts, including Hewlett Johnson's *The Soviet Power: The Socialist Sixth of the World* (1939) ("Journal 19" 26). Her journal entries thus reveal an abiding concern with the economic, political, and social rights of black Americans. Further influenced by her mentor Langston Hughes, whose literary productivity was characterized by its leftist leanings, Margaret Walker wrote realist poetry and prose that examined the lives of the folk and seldom romanticized the American South. For example, her first collection, *For My People* (1942), included poems such as "Southern Song," "Sorrow Home," and "Delta" that juxtapose the beauty of the South's topography with the vileness of its embedded racism and hatred. *Prophets for a New Day* retains some of the lush description of the previous collection, but gone are what R. Baxter Miller interprets in *For My People* as scenes of the "restorative potential of nature" (85).

Continuing to explore the social justice issues prevalent in US history, *Jubilee*, Walker's 1966 neoslave folk novel, recounts the horrors of slavery and the terrorism newly emancipated blacks experienced postbellum. Like *Prophets*, *Jubilee* documents African-American history and serves as a work of social protest, and so its publication in the midst of what Walker calls the Negro Revolution is poignant. *Jubilee* is a mandate that calls for America to examine its racist and violent character one hundred years after the end of the Civil War. In it, Walker provides a lens through which to view the conflicts of the 1950s and 60s and implicitly asks us to consider how far America has come. Joyce Pettis suggests that the publication of *Jubilee* and *Prophets* "may be seen as the beginning of the second phase of Walker's career, for these publications located her amidst a younger generation of writers" (46). This is certainly correct, though Walker was invested, from the beginning of her literary career, in "the earlier tradition of protest, realism, and rebellion out of which *Prophets for a New Day* came" (46).

Walker's Social Justice Pedagogy

By her own account, Walker, as a woman in academia, endured numerous affronts by administrators who attempted to undermine her career and silence her voice. In the essay "Black Women in Academia," Walker writes, "As for myself, my teaching career has been fraught with conflict, insults, humiliations, and disappointments. In every case where I have attempted to make a creative contribution and succeeded, I have immediately been replaced by a man" ("Black Women in Academia" 29). Occupying a tenuous position on the faculty of Jackson State College (now Jackson State University), Walker did not feel secure enough to engage directly in the politics of the day.

While her journals indicate a willingness to speak out and act, Walker recognized that the potential repercussions could be costly to her and her family. According to Jelani Favors and Julius Eric

Thompson, Walker, nevertheless, intentionally radicalized students in her courses, teaching "three or four courses per academic semester. In this regard, she was truly a cultural worker, since she came into contact with so many students over the years" (Thompson, *Black Life in Mississippi* 99). In a 1965 seminar on Herman Melville, for example, Walker included Melville's "Benito Cereno," a fictionalized account of a revolt aboard a Spanish ship, and paired it with contemporary critical texts such as Sterling Brown's *The Negro in American Fiction* (1969) ("Journal 75" 9-10). After all, as she writes in her journal,

> Personally I detect the note of tendency in American literature which attached mystery to the Negro—unfathomable depths, darkness, and in extremity evil—not pretending to understand Negroes because as James Baldwin says whites in America do not have the courage to look at themselves because they would not like what they would see. (Walker, "Journal 75" 27)

In many of her courses, she, therefore, incorporated her *Jubilee* research on the antebellum South and the period of Reconstruction into her lectures and connected the "bloody revolution" of the Civil War to the Civil Rights Movement ("How I Wrote *Jubilee*" 63) in an attempt to engage her students with the African-American struggle throughout history.

Jackson State students actively participated with civil rights groups such as the NAACP and in Freedom Ride activities. Some of these students were enrolled in Walker's classes. Although she was not in the streets marching, as an educator at a historically black college, Walker prepared the youth who would demonstrate by arming them intellectually with the history of black struggle. Although Walker does not actively publish during the 1960s, as we see, she does employ a pedagogy of social justice in her classes that reflects the timbre of the Civil Rights Movement.

Despite her success and influence as professor, Walker believed that her calling was as a writer. She writes, "As for my role as a writer, I believe and still contend I have something important to say as a Voice of the Southern Negro" ("Journal 69" 13). Rightfully,

Walker is concerned that the national conversation concerning civil rights and black culture does not adequately include the voices or perspectives of black southerners. She observes in another entry that:

> "all the Negroes listed as important are Northern Negroes with very few exceptions yet the Revolution is stemming from the South and the Southern Negro. . . . It is true the articulate Negroes has *[sic]* always been Northern like Thurgood Marshall and Adam Clayton Powell, and Roy Wilkins, and James Baldwin—a little more flamboyant than the conservative Southern Negroes but not any more militant!" (Walker, "Journal 69" 31)

Moreover, few, if any, women leaders and writers were called upon to offer their perspectives on the current social and political climate. Not until the late 1960s and the 1970s do we see the growth of black-owned publishing companies and, consequently, a surge in the publication of books written by black authors, in particular by black southern authors. James L. Conyers notes, "More collections of poetry, in book form, were produced by Mississippi's black poets during the 1970s than in any other previous decade" (219). Walker's *Prophets for a New Day* is one of three collections published by a black Mississippi author in 1970.

Walker as a "Voice of the Southern Negro"

In the months following Evers' death, Walker writes numerous entries in her journal regarding the hostile and increasingly dangerous climate of the South. On July 6, 1963, for instance, she writes, "I should like very much to write material for [the NAACP Commandoes] to use in this last ditch campaign in the all out war against segregation. Six more difficult months of 1963 lie ahead and the tide is not yet completely turned in our favor. Hostile reaction can very easily eclipse everything" (Walker, "Journal 69" 7). The next day, her birthday, she writes, "This country may well turn on the crisis of [the Negro Revolt and proposed Washington March] toward a new ideology and how dangerous can that be? . . . We seem on the brink of a very serious crisis in race relations and liberal issues in this country" ("Journal 69" 12). Recognizing the importance of literature in the social protest movement, by August 1963, Walker begins to compose poems in her journal that address the crises of the revolution, as Walker refers to the Civil Rights Movement.

The majority of the poems in *Prophets* were composed during this time, though the collection is not published until 1970. The timeliness of the poems is apparent, however, as understanding that the collection was written in the throes of the struggle alters how we engage with the text. Ultimately, *Prophets* is not merely a reflective text; Walker is not looking back at an era. She is writing in the moment, and the moment is replete with violence. She says:

> I was thinking at dinner about two revolutions, the Negro Revolution and the Black Revolution. In the late fifties and early sixties we had a half-dozen civil rights leaders. Men who have vision, who had purpose, who were able to use effective tactics and who got out in the street and accomplished something. It doesn't seem like much because it was primarily public accommodation and transportation and voting rights. And then integration of jobs through economic boycotts and marches . . . But the Black Revolution did something else for black people. . . . And this was a revolution of the minds—to change the minds of black people about themselves . . . The Black Revolution was tremendous because it offered to give back to black people manhood and womanhood (Giovanni & Walker 118).

Although Walker chronologically belongs to an era predating the Black Revolution, her poetry is consonant with the zeitgeist of the Black Arts Movement, an ideology that parallels and overlaps the Civil Rights Era. Walker's earlier poems such as "For My People," "We Have Been Believers," "Delta," and "People of Unrest" with their jeremiad and rebellious undertones lay a foundation for the poetry of the Black Arts Movement, which can best be summarized as confrontational and politically conscious in scope. Reinforcing this view, Richard Barksdale describes *Prophets* as "the premier poetic statement of the death-riddled decade of the 1960s" (114). It "reflect[s] the full range of the Black protest during the time" (114).

Moreover, the slim volume, only thirty-two pages in length, was published by Dudley Randall's Detroit-based Broadside Press—a black-owned press established in 1965. Broadside Press promoted the works of black writers who needed a venue for articulating a burgeoning black identity and became a vital organization in the Civil Rights Movement. Walker was already an established writer published by Yale University Press and in *Poetry* magazine, so her decision to support Broadside Press should be seen as another example of her activism and radicalism. Aligning her career with Broadside was risky. As Julius Thompson notes, "During the Black Arts movement, Dudley Randall and Broadside Press were targets of government surveillance because of the cultural, social, and political implications of the literary work published by the company" (*Dudley Randall* 131).

Walker's poem "Ballad of the Free" was one of the press' earliest broadsides, and her poem about Malcolm X inspired Randall and his coeditor, Margaret Burroughs, to publish an anthology dedicated to him.[6] Randall, in an August 4, 1969 letter, thanks Walker for giving Broadside the right to publish her poetry collection. Dudley Randall's letter to Walker concerning the form and content for her submitted manuscript is telling. Concerned with the focus and size of the publication, he writes, "I have read it again and think we should emphasize the civil rights aspect of the book. That will give the book unity, and also cut it to a size where I can manage it financially. I think it could be published in 1970, early." Randall surmises that the audience and purpose of Walker's collection will be different from her first collection, *For My People*. The poetic aesthetics of *For My People* guided the organization and theme of the book more than its political message did. In contrast, the message of *Prophets* would be of primary concern, a hallmark of the Black Arts Movement. Furthermore, he writes, "I've been thinking of a title. First I thought of Cities and Men, the Prophets and Men (very Lewis Mumfordish) then I think this is it! Black Prophets. It would go with your section 'Prophets of a New Day,' and it contains the magic word, 'black.'" Ultimately, Walker and Randall would settle on *Prophets for a New Day* as the title, with the eponymous poem of the collection establishing the book's identity.

Detroit-based Shirley Woodson (now Shirley Woodson Reid) designed the collage for the cover of *Prophets*. The original Broadside Press cover featured multiple images of Martin Luther King Jr. and Malcolm X and a single image of W. E. B. Du Bois from whose face King appears to emerge and to replicate. Du Bois, then, is a precursor to the prophecy of Malcolm X and King. The images of Malcolm X are from different stages of his career, while the multiple Kings are replicas of a single image. Superimposed over the images is the title, composed in letters clipped from newspapers or magazines. The title and Walker's name are lowercase. The word *prophets* is centered on Malcolm X's head. The sheer size and number of Malcolm X images suggests his primacy or importance in the collection. However, only one poem in the collection is dedicated to him. Yet, Malcolm X figures prominently in the design because, Woodson said, she "felt he was a prophet. His philosophy was based on a demand for full citizenship," though "[a]ll three were radical." The cover of the collection thus syncretizes Walker's social protest poetry written over the course of twenty years and the discourse of the Black Revolution. All the while, Woodson and Randall package Walker's collection to appeal to a new audience.

In the same letter, Randall praises Walker's elegy "For Andy Goodman—Michael Schwerner—and James Chaney," writing it is "different from the usual thing being written today about rats and roaches, with its beautiful natural images." The poem eulogizes three murdered civil rights workers—Goodman and Schwerner who were Freedom Summer volunteers and Chaney, a local activist. Walker opens the poem with synecdoche. The slain activists are "[t]hree faces . . . / mirrored in the muddy stream of living" (ll. 1-2). The three faces become "[t]hree leaves / Floating in the melted snow" and then "Three lives / turning on the axis of our time" (ll. 11-12, 24-25). The repetition of the mystical number three, the seasonal imagery, and the language of resurrection imbues the poem with an air of prophecy, which Randall suggests can unify the collection.

He also suggests including her Malcolm X poem. Randall writes, "Surely he would be accepted as a prophet. Can you think of a prophet who paralels [sic] him?" Walker's "For Malcolm X" does not directly align the slain leader with a prophet as she does with other civil rights figures in the collection; however, the poem recasts Malcolm X as a central figure—not a marginal voice—in civil rights. He is a martyr and bears the stigmata of martyrdom. In the poem, Walker eulogizes Malcolm X dead in his coffin, insisting, "Our blood and water pour from your flowing wounds" (l. 11). She celebrates his "sand-papering words" (l. 10) that force black Americans to see America and their situation through a different lens. Finally, as she does with other slain leaders in the collection, Walker proposes the spirit of black struggle transcends the flesh of a single black leader. She asks, "When and Where will another come to take your holy place? / Old man mumbling in his dotage, or crying child, unborn?" (ll. 13-14). Malcolm X, more than Martin Luther King Jr., becomes the face and inspiration of the Black Power Movement[7] whose followers were impatient with the slow pace of social change through legal avenues. Moreover, the murders of Malcolm X, King, and others called into question the viability of a nonviolent ideology as a path to true revolution. Walker's poem speaks to that angst. Thus, Melba Joyce Boyd notes, "With uncanny skill, Walker's powerful civil rights poems, such as 'For Andy Goodman—Michael Schwerner—and James Chaney' . . . exalted the historic moment in the freedom struggle and provided aesthetic direction for aspiring poets" (170).

Although scholars such as Boyd praise *Prophets* for capturing the essence of the era, little has been written about the collection's patriarchal framing of civil rights. The prophets are all men, but certainly Walker was aware of the contributions of Fannie Lou Hamer and other women activists. The lack of women's voices and experiences in *Prophets* skews readers' understanding of black women's activist roles and leadership. However, women are not wholly absent or silent in the text. The collection opens with the poem "Street Demonstration," in which Walker introduces the reader to the everyday activities of the revolution through the perspective of an eight-year-old child in 1963. In it, Walker makes visible the invisible work and contributions of women and young people who sacrificed safety and suffered abuse for the cause of justice, as they are heard and located squarely on the frontlines of the revolution. For example, the speaker implores Lucille to hurry up because the plan is to be arrested. As we see, the children are not alone. They are "hoping to be arrested" (l.1), a strategy of the Children's Crusade in Birmingham. A child, the speaker is unexpectedly wise and mature, suggesting black children are not afforded the luxury of innocence. The speaker recognizes, "And some of us will die" (l. 7) —a reminder that not even children are immune or protected from the violence.

The poems "Now" and "Sit-ins" build on the defiant tone of the first two poems, "Street Demonstration" and "Girl Held Without Bail," establishing footing for the more explicit condemnations of racism in the remainder of the collection. In particular, "Now" speaks to the immediacy of the struggle. The speaker recounts the indignities and suffering caused by intolerance and Jim Crow segregation, citing the all-too-common humiliation of having to enter through backdoors, to use segregated washrooms, to remain silent when whites called adult women out of their names, and to the violence embodied and enacted by the Ku Klux Klan. In "Sit-ins," Walker undertakes the Greensboro, North Carolina, sit-ins of 1960. The poem is a praise poem celebrating the heroism of one of the earliest groups to use civil disobedience[8] to challenge segregated lunch counters. These youths are the trailblazers, the visionaries, and the action-takers of the movement. They are "[t]he first to blaze a flaming path for justice / And awaken consciences / Of these stony ones" (ll. 8-10). The Greensboro sit-ins were not the first civil rights sit-ins, but they were the most visible in the media.[9] The speaker invokes Jesus calling him "Bold Young Galilean," and the Greensboro Four are likened to his disciples. "Sit-ins" and "Now," like "Street Demonstration" and "Girl Held Without Bail," attest to the potential dangers of political agitation. Walker suggests that the selfless deeds of these named and unnamed actors are epic, on par with the acts of Old Testament biblical figures who spoke out and stood up for justice.

Astutely, R. Baxter Miller describes Walker's prophetic poems about figures such as Martin Luther King, Jr., Benjamin Mays, Roy Wilkins, John Lewis, James Farmer, and Medgar Evers as "typological poems" (88). Typology, the Christian theological doctrine that proposes events and people of the New Testament are prefigured or symbolized by events and people in the Old Testament, is an integral characteristic of black theology and collective consciousness. James Cone argues that "almost all blacks in America—past and present—have identified Egypt with America, Pharaoh and the Egyptians with white slaveholders and subsequent racists, and blacks with the Israelite slaves" (63). Walker's use of figural tradition in *Prophets* then connects the oppression and violence of the 1960s to the horrors of American slavery through an extended metaphor of human struggle against evil.

Moreover, she argues that the lives of the prophets of the Old Testament are models for the exemplars of the Civil Rights Movement. For Walker, Benjamin Mays is a "type" of Jeremiah, Roy Wilkins is a type of Isaiah, John Lewis is a type of Joel, James Farmer is a type of Hosea, Medgar Evers is a type of Micah, and Martin Luther King Jr. is a type of Amos. The biblical prophets warned of sin and its consequence, foretold of the fall of kingdoms, conveyed messages of salvation and restoration, and spoke truth in the face of ridicule and punishment. In the poem, "Prophets for a New Day," Walker proposes these new prophets pick up the mantle of earlier prophets. She writes, "So the Word of the Lord stirs again / These passionate people toward deliverance" (ll. 9-10). The battle of the African-American Civil Rights Movement is thus prefigured in the epic battles between good and evil in the Old Testament. The people and places change, but the battle is the same. The embattled sites of Egypt, Samaria, Jerusalem, and Judah therefore become Jackson, Mississippi; Oxford, Mississippi; Birmingham, Alabama; and Washington, DC in Walker's poetic configuration, enabling her to explore the historical struggles blacks faced in each site.

"Jackson, Mississippi," for example, does not directly address the murder of Medgar Evers, nor does it reference the Friday, May 15, 1970 Lynch Street police assaults on students at Jackson State. Nevertheless, the violent deaths of Evers and of Phillip Lafayette Gibbs and James Earl Green, who were killed by police during the Lynch Street assault, form the backdrop for Walker's poem. Similarly, the poem "Birmingham" does not name specific events, but the city was one of the primary sites of contention and violence. The September 1963 bombing of the Sixteenth Street Baptist Church, which resulted in the deaths of four black girls, was but one of many horrific acts committed by staunch segregationists. In the poem, Walker again indicts the South for its "bitter hate" (l. 32). Likewise, in "Oxford is a Legend," Walker confronts the ensuing violence precipitated by the forced integration of the University of Mississippi. James Meredith's enrollment in Ole Miss sparked massive riots that necessitated the deployment of US Marshalls and the National Guard. However, these acts of violence are not the first in Oxford. It is the site of the Civil War as well as the site of the "war" of integration. Walker juxtaposes imagery of both, placing "rebel yell" (the battle cry of Confederate soldiers), "rebel flag" (the flag of the Confederacy), and "scholars yelling 'nigger'" next to each other in stanza one (l. 5). Twice she tells us that Oxford burned over race.

However, her purpose in "At the Lincoln Monument in Washington August 28, 1963" is slightly different. Instead of connecting traumas to a site, she writes about resistance to oppression. She likens the March on Washington for Jobs and Freedom to the exodus of the Israelites out of Egypt. Martin Luther King Jr. is depicted as a type of Moses, a leader who takes his people to the Promise Land but will not make it there himself. The South is described as a biblical Egypt, a site of oppression, but the marchers "overflow out of Egypt / The Red Sea cannot stop them" (ll. 25-26). It is important to note that although "*Prophets*" is replete with anecdotes of violence, its ultimate message is one of hope. As Eugenia Collier observes, *Prophets* records the generation of the sixties' contribution to the history of bloody struggle against

oppression and the soul-deep conviction that we—that all people—
are meant by nature to be free" (107).

"We Live Again": Walker's New Day and a Poetics of Hope

The year 1963, when Walker began to compose the majority of
the poems collected in *Prophets for a New Day*, was pivotal in the
Civil Rights Movement. The Children's Crusade in Birmingham,
during which police turned dogs and high-pressure water hoses
against youth, the murder of Medgar Evers, and the bombing of
the Sixteenth Street Baptist Church all occurred in 1963. Walker's
poems reflect the violence exacted against black bodies and call
attention to the human toll of nonviolent protest. In this same year,
Martin Luther King Jr. delivered his "I Have a Dream" speech at
the March on Washington for Jobs and Freedom, and Malcolm X
criticized the march and the nonviolent strategy of the Civil Rights
Movement. In "Message to the Grassroots," his last speech as a
minister of the Nation of Islam, Malcolm X asks, "How can you
justify being nonviolent in Mississippi and Alabama when your
churches are being bombed and your little girls are being murdered
. . . ?" Walker, too, asks this question, but because she is rooted
in the humanist tradition of black letters, her response differs from
Malcolm X's and the poets of the Black Revolution. Her message is
one of hope: "Change will come and there is hope for a better world.
But that world must be founded on a new humanism instead of the
old racism" ("The Humanistic Tradition" 130).

Optimism is an integral characteristic of African-American
culture and spiritual practices, and Walker, even in the midst of
despair, returns to this theme in her work. *Prophets* thus closes with
the poem "Elegy" and ends with the lines:

We live again
In children's faces, and the sturdy vine
Of daily influences: the prime
Of teacher, neighbor, student, and friend
All merging on the elusive wind. (l. 33-37).[10]

For Walker, the struggles of the Civil Rights Movement were epic in proportion and inextricably linked to biblical battles of good versus evil. However, Walker does not focus on the divine elements of prophesy; instead, she focuses on human actions against hate and illuminates the potential goodness of humanity. For this reason, Walker suggests in "Elegy" and throughout the collection that the spirit of freedom is persistent and transcends the mutable or mortal self. Until freedom reigns, new prophets will emerge to speak out and stand up against injustice.

In the end, as *Prophets for a New Day* reveals, Margaret Walker Alexander was a writers' writer. Poets, novelists, and literary critics alike cite Walker's influence on their work and literary careers. Born in 1915 in Alabama, Walker developed a career that spanned six decades. She was close friends with literary luminaries, a contributor to the literary scene of the Chicago Black Renaissance, faculty at multiple colleges, literary conference organizer, and founder of the Institute for the Study of the History, Life, and Culture of Black People (now the Margaret Walker Center). Perhaps because she was a woman, a southern woman, and an academic writing during eras before the emergence of women's studies programs and second-wave feminism, Walker's voice has been muffled by black male leaders and writers. Through her poetry, her lectures, and her creation of the Institute for the Study of the History, Life, and Culture of Black People, however, Margaret Walker Alexander attests to the importance of protest and the preservation of those acts of defiance, all the while mentoring the next generation of poets and activist as well as the writers of the Black Arts Movement within whom she saw the promise of the Civil Rights Movement.

Notes

1. Dr. Walker Alexander published under the name Margaret Walker, so Walker will be used throughout the essay.

2. In 1981, the city of Jackson renamed Guynes Street Margaret Walker Alexander Drive. The neighborhood where Walker and Evers resided was designated as the Medgar Evers Historic District. The neighborhood was the "first modern subdivision designed for middle-class blacks after World War II in Mississippi" ("National Register").

3. Lamar Smith was shot and killed in front of the Brookhaven Courthouse on August 13, 1955, as he helped African Americans who wanted to vote fill out absentee ballots.

4. In 1936, Richard Wright organized a group of black writers residing in Chicago. Group members included Margaret Walker, Arna Bontemps, Frank Marshall Davis, and others. See *The Black Chicago Renaissance* (2015) edited by Darlene Hine Clark and John McCluskey Jr.

5. Beginning in the 1930s and extending to the late 1950s, the Black Chicago Renaissance was a period of high cultural productivity in literature, music, and visual arts. Gwendolyn Brooks and Lorraine Hansberry are authors associated with this period. See *The Black Chicago Renaissance* (2015), edited by Darlene Hine Clark and John McCluskey Jr.

6. According to Melba Joyce Boyd's research and Margaret Walker's personal papers, Dudley Randall and painter Margaret Burroughs heard Walker practice reading "For Malcolm X" at the 1966 Writers Conference at Fisk and made plans to compile an anthology of Malcolm X poetry. The anthology, *For Malcolm: Poems on the Life and Death of Malcolm X*, was published in 1967. The 1966 Fisk Conference was a milestone for the Black Arts Movement, bringing together major black writers and fostering ideological and aesthetic debates that would shape the future of black poetry. Randall published the poets from the conference in the first set of broadsides. Margaret Walker's "Ballad of the Free" was fourth in the series.

7. The phrase "Black Power" is first associated in 1966 with Willie Ricks and Stokely Carmichael, activists within the Student Nonviolent Coordinating Committee. Carmichael, frustrated by the slow pace of change using the model of nonviolence, broke ranks with Martin Luther King Jr. and the leadership of the Civil Rights Movement. Advocates of Black Power called for a realignment of social, political, and economic resources. Peniel Joseph's scholarship on Black Power expands the scope of Black Power activism from the 1950s to the 1980s. See Joseph's *The Black Power Movement: Rethinking the Civil Rights-Black Power Era* (2013).

8. Civil disobedience is a peaceful form of political action through which individuals or groups refuse to comply with laws or practices they deem unjust. Mahatma Gandhi and his followers used this form of nonviolent resistance in their struggle for Indian independence.

9. The Greensboro Four—Joseph McNeil, Franklin McCain, Ezell Blair Jr., and David Richmond—were students at North Carolina Agricultural and Technical State University. They sat down at the lunch counter in a Woolworth in February 1960, and by that spring, the sit-in movement spread to other cities and lunch counters.

10. Walker dedicates "Elegy" to Manford Kuhn, a leading scholar of symbolic interactionism at University of Iowa who died in 1963. Kuhn's "Iowa

School" methodology emphasized quantitative methodology, a stance that stood in contrast to the humanist approaches of the Chicago School.

Works Cited

Barksdale, Richard K. "Margaret Walker: Folk Orature and Historical Prophecy." *Black American Poets Between Worlds, 1940–1960.* Ed. R. Baxter Miller. Knoxville: U of Tennessee P, 1986. 104-117.

Boyd, Melba Joyce. *Wrestling with the Muse: Dudley Randall and the Broadside Press.* New York: Columbia UP, 2003.

Collier, Eugenia. "Fields Watered with Blood: Myth and Ritual in the Poetry of Margaret Walker." Graham, *Fields* 98-109.

Cone, James. *For My People: Black Theology and the Black Church.* Maryknoll, NY: Orbis Books, 1984.

Conyers, James L. *Africana Studies: A Disciplinary Quest for Both Theory and Method.* Jefferson, NC: McFarland, 1997.

Favors, Jelani. "The Greatest Art is the Greatest Propaganda: The Fascinating and Tragic Life of Margaret Walker Alexander." *The Review of Black Political Economy* 43.2 (June 2016): 111-127.

Graham, Maryemma, ed. *Fields Watered with Blood: Critical Essays on Margaret Walker.* Athens, GA: U of Georgia P, 2001.

_____. "'I Want to Write, I Want to Write the Songs of My People': The Emergence of Margaret Walker." Graham, *Fields* 11-27.

Margaret Walker Alexander Personal Papers. Margaret Walker Center's Digital Archives Project, Jackson State University, Jackson, MS.

Miller, R. Baxter. "The 'Etched Flame' of Margaret Walker: Literary and Biblical Re-Creation in Southern History." Graham, *Fields* 81-97.

"National Register of Historic Places Registration Form." *Medgar Evers Historic District.* National Park Service, n.d. Web. 19 Dec. 2016.

Pettis, Joyce. "Margaret Walker: Black Woman Writer of the South." Graham, *Fields* 44-54.

Randall, Dudley. Letter to Margaret Walker. 4 August 1969. Margaret Walker Alexander Personal Papers.

Thompson, Julius Eric. *Black Life in Mississippi: Essays on Political, Social, and Cultural Studies in a Deep South State.* Lanham, MD: UP of America, 2001.

_____. *Dudley Randall, Broadside Press, and the Black Arts Movement in Detroit, 1960–1995.* Jefferson, NC: McFarland, 1999.

Walker, Margaret. "Black Women in Academia." Walker, *How I Wrote "Jubilee"* 26-32.

_____. "How I Wrote *Jubilee.*" Walker, *How I Wrote "Jubilee"* 50-65.

_____. *How I Wrote "Jubilee."* New York: The Feminist P, 1990.

_____. Journal 19. Margaret Walker Alexander Personal Papers.

_____. Journal 69. Margaret Walker Alexander Personal Papers.

_____. Journal 75. Margaret Walker Alexander Personal Papers.

_____. *Prophets for a New Day.* Detroit: Broadside P. 1970.

_____. "The Humanistic Tradition of Afro-American Literature." Walker, *How I Wrote "Jubilee"* 121-133.

_____. *This is My Century: New and Collected Poems.* Athens, GA: U of Georgia P, 1989.

Woodson, Shirley. Personal Interview. 12 June 2016.

X, Malcolm. "Message to the Grassroots." *YouTube.* YouTube, 22 Feb. 2012. Online video clip. 19 Dec. 2016.

The Mothers' Tragedy: Loss of a Child in the Works of Gwendolyn Brooks, Dudley Randall, and Michael Harper

Eric J. Sterling

Accounts of civil rights struggles tell of the unfortunate and brutal demise of the fallen victims but too often overlook the pain and suffering of the family members who live on, grieve, and call for equality and justice. Gwendolyn Brooks considers it important to stress the suffering and pain of survivors, such as grieving mothers, so that people can understand why African Americans must continually fight for justice. From her perspective,

> "NOW the address must be to blacks; that shrieking into the steady and organized deafness of the white ear was frivolous—perilously innocent; was 'no count.' There were things to be said to black brothers and sisters and these things—annunciatory, curative, inspiriting—were to be said forthwith, without frill, and without fear of white presence" (Brooks, *Capsule* 4).

Brooks' two Emmett Till poems, like Dudley Randall's ballad about the Birmingham bombing and Michael Harper's verse regarding the Algiers Motel police brutality case in Detroit, clearly articulate the pain experienced by the maternal survivors of victims of brutal, racially-inspired murders. This essay analyzes the suffering of victims' grieving mothers during the Jim Crow era and the Civil Rights Movement as told through the ballad genre—a genre that unfortunately has received far less attention than the novels, plays, music, and other facets of the Black Arts Movement in regard to lynching and racism. The aforementioned poems focus on racially motivated murders that deal with prejudiced men who kill young African Americans while also desecrating their bodies, leaving their mothers to witness and bury the dismembered bodies of their children as they painfully mourn.

A Black Mother's Heart Breaks While a Racist Woman is Indifferent: A Juxtaposition

Pulitzer Prize-winning poet Gwendolyn Brooks believed that racial bigotry should be confronted and examined bluntly in literature, with poets eschewing flowery language that might distract readers by obfuscating the prejudice with which African Americans were besieged:

> In the early days of the revolution, she explains, the aesthetic program of the Black Arts poets discouraged "decoration," "dalliance," and "idle embroidery" as techniques of "avoidance, avoidance of the gut issue, the blood fact. Literary rhythms altered! Sometimes the literature seemed to issue from pens dipped in blood, stabbed in, writhing blood" (Ford 372)

Both sides of the poet appear in her works, with Brooks offering a subdued and subtle approach in "A Bronzeville Mother Loiters in Mississippi. Meanwhile, A Mississippi Mother Burns Bacon" (1960) but making her anger and frustration regarding bigotry apparent in her companion piece, "The Last Quatrain of the Ballad of Emmett Till" (1960).

In both of these works, Gwendolyn Brooks focuses on the aftermath of the horrific murder of the Chicago teenager who was brutally tortured and killed on August 28, 1955, for allegedly wolf-whistling at Carolyn Bryant, a white female grocery store owner in Money, Mississippi. Devoting most of the former poem to Bryant's ambivalent thoughts regarding her false accusation against and racist behavior toward Till, Brooks juxtaposes Bryant's indifference to the murder with the heartbreak Till's mother experiences. While Mamie Till mourns the death of her son, Bryant's primary concern seems to be that she has burned some bacon. She throws out the ruined bacon because it, unlike Mamie Till's son, is replaceable, and although the bacon is burnt, it is recognizable and can be identified, unlike the body of Emmett Till. The killers, after all, were acquitted partly because their brutality was so devastating that examiners could not positively identify the body as Till during the trial and were not even sure that the corpse was of an African American.

The life of the white woman in this poem seems carefree compared to that of Emmett Till's mother, whose life has been torn apart by this act of racism. Yet, Bryant is certainly not unaffected. She despises "that snappy-eyed mother, / That sassy, Northern, brown-black—" (Brooks, "A Bronzeville Mother" ll. 82-83) and steels herself to the suffering of Till's mother over the senseless death of her teenage son. At the same time, Bryant's husband Roy and his half-brother J.W. Milam (the men who killed Emmett) believed that they should not be punished for the murder because they lived in the South, where many white men felt that they needed to protect white women from miscegenation, and because Jim Crow laws superseded the suffering of black mothers. These cultural values are apparent, as Brooks writes:

> Nothing could stop Mississippi. . . .
> They could send their petitions, and scar
> Their newspapers with bleeding headlines. Their governors
> Could appeal to Washington. (ll. 88, 92-94)

The indifference of the vast majority of Mississippians (and the white Mississippi media) to the lynching of Till indicates a great deal about virulently racist attitudes regarding segregation and miscegenation in the state. When confessing to the murder after his acquittal, J.W. Milam mentioned in a magazine interview that he and Roy Bryant possessed the moral authority to slay Till: "As long as I live and can do anything about it, niggers are gonna stay in their place. Niggers ain't gonna vote where I live. . . . They ain't gonna go to school with my kids. And when a nigger gets close to mentioning sex with a white woman, he's tired o' livin'" (qtd. in Huie). Many Mississippians shared Milam's prejudiced views, and some even served on the jury during the trial. Thus, Brooks' ballads are not merely about the horrific and unprovoked murder of one fourteen-year-old teenager but also about the institutional racism that pervaded the Deep South. This point is abundantly clear in the poem when an all-white jury acquits the two men who even confess in court that they kidnapped Till on the night he disappeared. The jury acquits the men unanimously after merely sixty-seven minutes, part of which was spent getting and drinking Coca Cola (l. 133), manifesting the indifference of the Jim Crow Mississippi Delta society to the killing of unarmed African Americans.

Gwendolyn Brooks' narrator in "A Bronzeville Mother Loiters in Mississippi. . . " immediately introduces the ballad form. A ballad is a narrative story told in verse. The story's focus in a ballad is quite narrow so that the poet may concentrate on a significant event and compelling emotional intensity. That is why Brooks focuses not on Till's life and death but only on the short trial, only on the aftermath of the lynching. Instead of covering Till's life before he visited Mississippi or his tragic death, Brook's upends the genre and reader expectations by linking the murder to its root cause: racist white southerners' indifference to the value of African-American life.

In the poem, the narrator calls attention to the ballad tradition while subverting it, just as the nameless ingénue supposedly representing Carolyn Bryant subverts the damsel-in-distress tradition because she is not endangered at all. The narrator claims that the lady's precarious situation "had been like a / Ballad" (Brooks, "A Bronzeville Mother" ll. 1-2). The simile indicates that although there is the appearance of a threat, it merely seems so. In the poem, Carolyn Bryant exaggerates, or even invents, the threat posed by Till to be noticed by her husband when, historically, Bryant pretended to be a threatened white female victim, helpless against a lecherous black man. Like most ballads, the plot is melodramatic, with good versus evil supposedly dichotomized. The "milk-white maid. . . / Of the ballad" (ll. 6-7) is being "Pursued / By the Dark Villain" (ll. 7-8). The simplistic bigotry of the Deep South is epitomized by the white-versus-black color imagery, with white representing purity and innocence and black representing lechery and corruption of innocence. Legend had it that Carolyn Bryant was a gorgeous beauty queen, who was so beautiful that men stared at her often; thus, she is worthy of being the subject of a ballad, and it is unsurprising that males such as Till would desire her. The notoriety regarding her beauty helped Roy Bryant accept without question and act upon his wife's false accusation against Till. Thus, the innocent fourteen-year-old becomes the ballad's Dark Villain.

But can the teenager truly be the Dark Villain when such monsters are invariably cruel and do not have loving mothers who mourn their loss? Till was merely a teenager and not the threat that she and society made black men to be, which should have been obvious when Till fled in fear. As Brooks writes, this mother's son "should have been older" (l. 19), and "his menace possessed undisputed breadth, undisputed height, / And a harsh kind of vice . . . / With the bones of many eaten knights and princesses" (ll. 21-22, 24). Instead, in this anti-ballad:

> the Dark Villain was a blackish child
> Of fourteen, with eyes still too young to be dirty
> And a mouth too young to have lost every reminder
> Of its infant softness. (ll. 26-29)

Instead of raping women, the punished ballad villain is actually more innocent than the woman who falsely accuses him and is still bound to his mother, as a soft infant should be. The ballad tradition is therefore subverted because the "Dark Villain" who allegedly attacks the "milk-white maid" is actually not evil or even a threat at all. Furthermore, the Fine Prince rescues the woman from an attack that never occurs, rendering his actions not protective or heroic but racist and cowardly. Through this depiction, Brooks' anti-ballad stresses the woman's attempt to be valued by her spouse by falsely claiming to be a vulnerable victim, a ruse that perpetuates the history of torture and murder of black men in the United States.[1]

At the same time, a ballad is a plot-driven poem that often tells a heroic tale of courage, yet in this work even the female protagonist questions her own version of the events that led to the torture and lynching of Till. Brooks' poem, in particular, is not only a ballad but also an anti-ballad partly about a woman who, ironically, is too ignorant to comprehend what a ballad is, let alone how her racist conduct and false accusation destroyed the life of an innocent black teenager. Bryant's account has the danger ("the beat inevitable" and "blood"—l. 2) and "wildness" that is often contained in the "four-line stanzas of the ballads she had never quite / Understood—the ballads they had set her to, in school" (ll. 3-5). Bryant's ignorance is crucial because she is too foolish (or apathetic) to understand the personal and social ramifications of her actions—how her racist behavior not only cost Emmett Till his life but also left his mother perpetually in mourning.

From there, the narrator notes that the Mississippi mother "made the babies sit in their places at the table" (l. 52) and that "[i]t was necessary / To be more beautiful than ever. / The beautiful wife" (ll. 54-56). As these lines reveal, the woman feels the need to look beautiful continually because her story depends upon it; furthermore, the husband has risked his freedom by murdering the teenager, so she wants to look beautiful so that her husband will consider her worth his sacrifice. In the process, she orders her children to sit still, which she can do because her kids are still alive, unlike Emmett Till. Here, the Mississippi mother demonstrates no love for her children and takes them for granted, while the Bronzeville woman loves her child, although he is now dead. Instead, there are "[d]ecapitated exclamation points in that Other Woman's eyes" (l. 130). The grieving mother's eyes, just like the face and body of her beloved son, have been destroyed as the loss experienced is shared. The narrator further demonstrates this when she refers to Mamie Till as "the other woman." None of the historical characters in Brooks' poem are named because, although Emmett Till's death was tragic, it was not an anomaly. Many black teenagers were murdered in the Deep South by racist white men, so the dead African Americans and their grieving mothers exist as a paradigm, an entry in a long list of examples. Providing names would individualize a murder that was one of a long pattern and paramount concern.

Readers can also discern the perspective of the mourning mother in Brooks' companion piece, "The Last Quatrain of the Ballad of Emmett Till." The mother:

sits in a red room,
drinking black coffee.
She kisses her killed boy.
And she is sorry.
Chaos in windy grays
through a red prairie. (ll. 3-8)

As with all the ballads in this essay, the mother grieves over the loss of her child, who has died senselessly and far too young in an unprovoked attack. Brooks' poem is thus short and truncated, just like Emmett Till's life and his time with his mother. When the teenager boarded the train to Mississippi, he forgot to kiss his mother good-bye. Mamie asked him to descend the stairs and kiss him. She lamented to him prophetically, "'How do I know I'll ever see you again?'" (20). Sadly, she never did.

In the poem, the mother "kisses her killed boy" (l. 5) as he lies unrecognizable from his injuries, adding greatly to the poignancy of their relationship, which is now over at least on earth. Readers can juxtapose Mamie Till kissing Emmett with Carolyn Bryant disciplining her children and Roy Bryant hitting his son: "the Fine Prince . . . slapped / The small and smiling criminal" (ll. 93-94). If Roy Bryant slaps the son he loves, readers can only imagine what he, a bigoted man, has done to Mamie Till's son, whom he accuses of flirting with his allegedly pure wife. The father who slaps his son is called a Fine Prince, while the young boy is called a criminal—another indictment by Brooks demonstrating how innocence and ballads are subverted, just as in the Mississippi courtroom, good and evil were turned upside down.

The emphasis on colors in the ballad is also significant, as it indicates Brooks' correlation between skin color and violence. The two references to red suggest the bloody end of Till's life, with witnesses reporting a large amount of blood in the back of Roy Bryant's truck.[3] A person who overheard the attack mentioned that in his last words, Emmett Till cried out not to his cousins or the sheriff for help but to his loving mother: "Mama, Lord have mercy. Lord have mercy" (Whitfield 40). Knowing of his suffering, Mamie Till wanted the world to know that her son was brutally murdered, so she blocked Mississippi officials from quietly burying her son there (and attempting to bury the physical evidence and infamy along with the body) and insisted upon an open-casket funeral, with thousands of people serving as eyewitnesses to the racist killing. Brooks' poems thus serve as another record of these tragic events.

A Mother's Concern for Her Daughter's Safety and the Klan's Disdain for Black Lives: A Juxtaposition

Dudley Randall's poignant work "Ballad of Birmingham" (1963) tells the story of the tragic and horrific bombing of the Sixteenth Street Baptist Church on the morning of Sunday, September 15, 1963, in Birmingham, Alabama. This shocking atrocity brought Birmingham immediately to the forefront of the Civil Rights Movement with the violence in this segregated city exemplifying the bitter racial hatred that pervaded the Deep South. In fact, as a result of the church bombing, it became apparent that racial violence in Birmingham surpassed that of any other city in the nation. The bombing, after all, was just one event in the long history of racial violence that blacks faced in the city.

For instance, two years earlier, Birmingham witnessed such violence as Klan members assaulted Freedom Riders in an attempt to intimidate black protestors and discourage their fight for equal rights. Birmingham Commissioner of Public Safety Theophilus Eugene "Bull" Connor, who controlled both the police force and the fire department, allowed racist agitators to brutally attack the Freedom Riders for fifteen minutes without police intervention when they rode into the city on Sunday, May 14, 1961—Mother's Day. The Trailways bus of the Freedom Riders was stopped and attacked, and when the riders left the bus, they were viciously beaten. When asked why he did not stop the violence committed against them, Connor mendaciously blamed Mother's Day: "No policemen were in sight as the buses arrived, Connor claimed, because they were visiting their mothers" (Dierenfield 66).

The bombing, like the open display of Till's body and the battered faces of the Freedom Riders, transformed into an unforgettable and shocking symbol of unrestrained racial hatred, particularly as the civil rights discourse turned to nonviolent protests for desegregation, equal job opportunities, and voting rights. At the same time, the four African-American children who perished also became a symbol of this ongoing strife: Addie Mae Collins, age fourteen; Denise McNair, age eleven; Carole Rosamond Robertson, age fourteen; and Cynthia Wesley, age fourteen.[2] The heinous murder of four innocent black children was so horrific that it manifested even to some segregationists (but certainly not all) that the hatred and violence toward African Americans had escalated too far, allowing them to finally empathize with the victims and their families. After all, many prejudiced white southerners had children of their own and pondered how they would respond if their children were murdered in a house of worship as they prayed.

Ultimately, the visual images of the dead children and the bombed church portrayed in newspapers and on television throughout the world transformed public opinion irrecoverably in favor of blacks striving for equality, rendering the murder of the children a significant turning point in the Civil Rights Movement. It is no coincidence that President Lyndon B. Johnson signed the Civil Rights Act of 1964 only nine months after the bombing—the same attack that was designed to intimidate people and, ironically, to prevent the passage of such an act because it included the desegregation of schools and other public places and the establishment of full voting rights for minorities. Although four young children died in the attack and the media preoccupied itself with the deaths, in "Ballad of Birmingham," Randall chose instead to focus on the heart-wrenching tragedy of a mother.

In Randall's ballad, words such as *baby* and *dear* manifest the close bond between mother and daughter—a bond that is irreversibly and shockingly compromised as a result of the bombing. The mother in this work is very protective of her child, which is logical given the violent time and the precarious situations that African Americans endured in Birmingham in the 1960s with black people being shot, assaulted, threatened, and even bombed for no reason other than their skin color. Although it was the twenty-first bombing in Birmingham since 1955, earning the city the ignominious nickname of "Bombingham," because of the recent plan to implement the desegregation of Alabama's public schools, it was the fourth bombing in Birmingham that month and the third in the past ten days, contributing to the mother's fears.

In Randall's ballad, the mother's loss of her daughter is disturbing not only because the girl is so young, dutiful, and innocent but also because the murder and destruction of the church is seemingly pointless, forever robbing the mother of her child and the child of her future. Instead of witnessing the death of the girl, however, readers and listeners dwell on how her demise affects her mother, who never expected to bury her child. In the historical account of the Sixteenth Street Baptist Church bombing, when the dead bodies of the girls were being removed from the church, "one youth broke away and tried to touch one of the blanket-covered forms. . . . 'This is my sister,' he cried. 'My God, she's dead.' Police took the hysterical boy away" ("Six Dead"). This heart-wrenching account became well known, so Dudley Randall most probably was familiar with it. The poet changes the role of the mourner from a brother to a mother, perhaps to create more sympathy because of the close mother-daughter bond.

Randall then skillfully distinguishes the volatile protests and bloody freedom marches, on the one hand, from the nonviolent, peaceful worship in God's church on the other, "suggest[ing] a division between those willing to risk violent injury by challenging Jim Crow through direct action and those unwilling to take such risks" (Sullivan 33). Being a devoted mother, she wants to protect her daughter from the violence at the protests and the brutality of racist police officers at the marches. Consequently, the mother rejects her daughter's request to march:

"No, baby, no, you may not go,
For the dogs are fierce and wild,
And clubs and hoses, guns, and jail
Aren't good for a little child." (ll. 5-8)

The refusal in the first line emphasizes the mother's fear of police and Klan attacks at Freedom Marches and other protests as well as her need to protect her daughter from harm. She knows about Bull Connor's use of fire hoses and police dogs to attack African-American protestors and thus wants to insulate her innocent daughter from such brutality and racial hatred.

The caring mother attempts to protect her daughter by sending her to church instead because she naively believes that even committed racists have some semblance of decency and thus would never attack innocent children in a Christian house of worship. Even rabid Klansmen attended church regularly and considered themselves Christians. The mother's naiveté demonstrates how shocking and abhorrent the thought of bombing a house of worship and killing children would have been to those who witnessed, and suffered because of, the tragedy.[4] It is noteworthy, then, that when the stained glass windows of the church were blown out by the bomb, only one remained—the glass window portraying Jesus leading a group of children. The face of Christ Himself was blown out, symbolizing that the bombing served a blow not only to the black community but also to their faith; mothers such as the one in Randall's ballad wondered why their children were not being protected and how racists could act in a manner that even transcended the commonplace cruelty that they had come to know so well.

A Mother Bitterly Reacts to Police Brutality that Resulted in Her Son's Murder

Michael Harper's "A Mother Speaks: The Algiers Motel Incident, Detroit," like "A Bronzeville Mother Loiters in Mississippi . . .," focuses on the unprovoked and racially-motivated murder of a young black male by bigoted white Americans and the heart-wrenching reaction of the victim's mother. Harper based his poem on John Hersey's account of the murder, but the poem narrows his focus exclusively to the mother's reaction to her son's death. In Harper's poem, the mother sees the disfigured body of her deceased teenage son, Aubrey Pollard, who was at the Algiers Motel when a police raid occurred. The incident evoked civil rights concerns since the police acted violently, beating and shooting blacks without cause. Pollard, in particular, was beaten for not relinquishing a gun, though he was unarmed and had no weapon to give. According to Hersey's account, when Pollard could not produce a weapon, the enraged police officer, Ronald August, brutalized the defenseless Pollard and then shot and murdered him.

The grieving mother in Harper's poem (Rebecca Pollard) looks on as the undertaker, like August, demonstrates no respect for the body, pushing "his body / back into place with plastic and gum / but it would not hold water" (ll. 4-6). The undertaker simply wants to get rid of the body and exhibits no concern for how it will look at the funeral or what he has to do in order to get the body parts back in place. The undertaker's responsibility is to reconstruct the deceased teenager's body to make it presentable for viewing, yet the man instead leaves the body in worse condition than when he began work. The body is dismembered, just like the corpse of other lynching victims. That the corpse is missing an eye, like the undertaker cutting away the body's arm, "affirms racist social structures by demonstrating white license to destroy black personhood while silencing witnesses' critiques of violence and the ideology that it buttresses" (Kieran 247). The undertaker thus treats Aubrey Pollard just as cruelly in death as the murderous policeman and other racists did while Pollard was living.

Harper's ballad then reveals the horror of Pollard's mother as she is forced away from her son's corpse:

> I was led away without seeing
> this plastic face they'd built
> that was not my son's.
> They tied the eye torn out
> by shotgun into place
> and his shattered arm cut away
> with his buttocks that remained. (ll. 8-14)

David Kieran astutely likens the language on Pollard's injuries to lynching and power, writing, "'Back into place' takes on multiple meanings, recalling both lynching's historically disciplinary function and Harper's consistent evocation of a culture in which white authorities desire to obliterate 'transgressive' African Americans"

(246). Apparently, the white police officer did not consider Pollard to be sufficiently submissive to him, so he beat up and shot the black teenager to the point that his body would have been unrecognizable to his own mother. Furthermore, Kieran writes, "Harper emphasizes not only the mutilated body's function as spectacle but also the degree to which Rebecca Pollard's account of her son's injuries parallels Mamie Till-Mobley's account of seeing Emmet *[sic]* Till's body" (246). The brutality Aubrey experiences must have been horrific because her son's body is unrecognizable, like that of Till: it is no longer human but now plastic, and the mother asserts that the face is "not my son's" any longer, not after the cruelty of the police and the harshness of the undertaker.

In *The Torture of Mothers* (1968), his book on how police brutality and racism psychologically hurts the mothers of African-American victims, civil rights activist Truman Nelson claims, "There is a special, an excruciating torture which comes out of love. It comes mainly out of uncertainty and fear . . . out of wanting to protect, in this case, and not being able to find the object of the compulsion to protect. One can have a rage to shelter, to enclose" (25). When Mrs. Pollard realizes that her son is dead, a victim of racism and police brutality, she experiences this "excruciating torture" (25). The mother feels tortured for losing her son, just as her son was tortured (and dismembered) by a police officer whose job was to protect, not destroy.

This is only compounded by the fact that, like Till, Pollard seems to have comported himself passively and deferentially during his precarious situation but to no avail. Mrs. Pollard told author John Hersey that her son "wasn't even looting, wasn't even after curfew hours, he was just in his own place what he was renting. . . . I want to know why [Ronald August] killed him like that." Furthermore, Pollard told Hersey that not only did Aubrey refrain from fighting back, he did not defend himself and even apologized for the damage caused to the police officer's gun when he smacked it on Pollard's head: "Oh I'm so sorry, officer / I broke your gun" (ll. 17-18). Harper adds the word *officer* to Pollard's last words, emphasizing the victim's submissive behavior and the unprovoked nature of the brutality. These last lines suggest that Pollard's subservience and pleas were insufficient to calm the bigoted hatred of the Detroit police officer, so the mother's "son's gone by white hands" (l. 15). Pollard's apology manifests his innocence and the extremity of the police brutality. Harper's poem should, therefore, remind readers of the ballads by Randall and Brooks in the destruction of the bodies, the senseless violence, and the racial hatred that motivated the murders.

Conclusion

As evidenced by the aforementioned poems, three brutal murders—in which bodies became spectacles—call attention to racially-motivated violence against innocent African Americans. Mamie Till, for instance, wanted the nation to see the horrific brutalization of her son, so she demanded that Emmett's body not be buried in Mississippi (one must ponder what gave Mississippi officials the thought that they could bury the teenager without his mother's permission) and be sent to Chicago for an open-casket funeral. She wanted the world to see how horribly disfigured her son was from the lynching and drowning. As a result, more than fifty thousand people visited the Chicago funeral parlor to see the corpse, and with the horrific photograph published in newspapers across the country, millions of Americans saw the shame of brutal bigotry. A photograph of Emmett and his mother smiling together was also published in newspapers, humanizing him, showing them as a family, and manifesting what the mother had lost irrecoverably because of the murder of her son.

As with the aforementioned cases, the grieving mother plays a significant role in shaping public awareness and calls for justice. The "excruciating torture" (25) that Nelson discusses is prevalent in all these cases, for the mothers of these unfortunate victims wish they could have protected their children from racial violence. They feel a sense of helplessness for not protecting their loved ones and despair for realizing that they will never see their children again. Yet, it is difficult to protect children from every event on every day when violence can be provoked merely by a wolf whistle, a visit to a church, or a mistaken report of a gun. And the pain that the mothers feel over the senseless violence and loss is compounded by the indifference to their suffering and the sight of the dismembered physical bodies in the aftermath of the deaths. These three cases helped change public opinion about what we now call hate crimes and inspired the Civil Rights Movement, enabling current murders, such as the killings of Trayvon Martin and Michael Brown, to garner much public scrutiny. Therefore, the works of Gwendolyn Brooks, Dudley Randall, and Michael Harper remain important texts, keeping their tales and their mothers' sorrows ingrained in the American cultural imagination as a testimony of racial prejudice and lost lives.

Notes

1. Though the lady is supposedly innocent (as in, "milk-white maid"), according to Scott Shepherd—a friend of Carolyn Bryant's family—it was well-known that Bryant flirted often with men, even with the black male customers in her store, who, unlike Till, were experienced enough to know not to flirt back if they wanted to remain alive. Mamie Till warned her son that life was harder for African Americans in the Deep South than in Chicago and that he had to be careful: "'Even though you think you're perfectly within your right, for goodness sake take low. If necessary, get on your knees and beg apologies. Don't cross anybody down there because Mississippi is not like Chicago . . . . No matter how much it seems you have the right, just forget your rights while you're in Mississippi" (qtd. in Hudson-Weems 235). But Emmett, in an effort to impress his friends by flirting with Carolyn Bryant, failed to heed his mother's sagacious warning. He had not yet learned what Richard Wright terms, "the ethics of living Jim Crow" (1).

2. Their names need to be mentioned because far too often they are simply labeled the four victims of the bombing, as if they are a statistic, not individuals. They were wonderful children and individuals with hopes, dreams, and talents.

3. Emmett's body was mutilated; he was shot in the head and tossed into the Tallahatchie River, weighed down with a gin fan so that his body was bloated.

4. As James Sullivan notes in *On the Walls and in the Streets: American Poetry Broadsides from the 1960s*, "the child's body and the mother's naïve faith in the limits of hatred and violence have been destroyed, as the ballad leaves the mother transfixed among the 'bits of glass and brick,' where she can find only her little girl's shoe but not the girl herself" (32). The Sixteenth

Street Baptist Church bombing was therefore a significant event in African-American history, for it revealed how deep-seated racial violence was in the United States.

Works Cited

Alexander, Elizabeth, ed. *The Essential Gwendolyn Brooks.* New York: The Library of America, 2005.

Anderson, Devery S. *Emmett Till: The Murder that Shocked the World and Propelled the Civil Rights Movement.* Jackson: UP of Mississippi, 2015.

Brooks. Gwendolyn. "A Bronzeville Mother Loiters in Mississippi. Meanwhile, a Mississippi Mother Burns Bacon." Alexander 61-67.

_____. *A Capsule Course in Black Poetry Writing.* Detroit: Broadside P, 1975.

_____. "The Last Quatrain of the Ballad of Emmett Till." Alexander 68.

Dierenfield, Bruce J. *The Civil Rights Movement.* New York: Pearson Longman, 2008.

Ford, Karen Jackson. "The Last Quatrain: Gwendolyn Brooks and the End of Ballads." *Twentieth-Century Literature* 56.3 (Fall 2010): 371-395.

Harper, Michael. "A Mother Speaks: The Algiers Motel Incident, Detroit." *The Algiers Motel Incident.* By John Hersey. New York: Alfred A. Knopf, 1968. 328-335.

Hersey, John. *The Algiers Motel Incident.* New York: Alfred A. Knopf, 1968.

Hudson-Weems, Clenora. *Emmett Till: The Sacrificial Lamb of the Civil Rights Movement.* 4th ed. Bloomington, IN: AuthorHouse, 2006.

Huie, William Bradford. "The Shocking Story of Approved Killing in Mississippi." *Killers' Confession in Look (January 1956).* University of Missouri-Kansas City School of Law.

Kieran, David. "Lynching, Embodiment, and Post-1960 African American Poetry." *Demands of the Dead: Executions, Storytelling, and Activism in the United States.* Ed. Katy Ryan. Iowa City: U of Iowa P, 2012: 239-254.

Nelson, Truman. *The Torture of Mothers.* Boston: Beacon P, 1968.

Randall, Dudley. "Ballad of Birmingham." *Words of Protest, Words of Freedom: Poetry of the American Civil Rights Movement and Era.* Ed. Jeffrey Lamar Coleman. Durham, NC: Duke UP, 2012: 65-66.

Shepherd, Scott. "Carolyn Bryant: The Untold Story." *Youtube.* Youtube, 19 Jul. 2014. Online video clip.

"Six Dead after Church Bombing." *Washington Post.* The Washington Post, 16 Sept. 1963. Web. 19 Dec. 2016.

Sullivan, James D. *On the Walls and in the Streets: American Poetry Broadsides from the 1960s.* Urbana, IL: U of Illinois P, 1997.

Thompson, Julius E. *Dudley Randall, Broadside Press, and the Black Arts Movement in Detroit, 1960–1995*. Jefferson, NC: McFarland, 1999.

Whitfield, Stephen. *A Death in the Delta: The Story of Emmett Till*. Baltimore, MD: Johns Hopkins UP, 1991.

Wright, Richard. "The Ethics of Living Jim Crow: An Autobiographical Sketch." *Uncle Tom's Children*. New York: HarperPerennial, 2008. 1-15.

Alice Walker and Claudia Rankine: Reclaiming the Ocularity of the Self _____

Margaret Cox

Alice Walker once stated, "Activism is my rent for living on the planet," and her literary works are reflective of such payments. Her 1976 novel *Meridian*, set in the 1960s during the Civil Rights Era, not only explores a woman's courage to become an activist, but it also examines the turmoil that women face under constant criticism for the choices that they make. Decades later, Claudia Rankine, through *Citizen: An American Lyric* (2014), shifts the scrutiny and places it upon the societal eye, which has become all too powerful to the extent that people change their behavior so that the comfort level of the hegemonic society will not be disrupted. As a result, the personal comfort of the individual in his or her own skin is no longer paramount. This is a constant problem in such an image-based society—a common theme that Walker and Rankine interrogate in their works of literature with respect to reclaiming the ocularity of the self—a concept that refers to how individuals constantly reconfigure their "lens" in acceptance of societal ocular dominance. Under this system, the privileging of society's eye over the individual's skews the acuity and validity of his or her self-image. Both Alice Walker and Claudia Rankine therefore succeed as writers who find a place for variations in voice within African-American prose narratives and poetics while challenging that societal ocular dominance that proves so detrimental to black men and women.

Literary Predecessors: Countering the Marginalization of Black Women Writers

It was a long journey, however, to reach the point that Walker and Rankine have achieved—a journey that included literary periods such as the Harlem Renaissance and the Black Arts Movement in which black women were important yet under-recognized and underappreciated figures. In his article titled, "The Sexual Mountain and Black Women Writers," Calvin Hernton raises this issue about the marginalization of the literary voice of black women writers that prevailed since the inception of Afro-American writing and how black women writers have historically received back-burner status. Hernton notes that despite the presence of black women writers such as Nella Larsen, Dorothy West, and Jessie Redmon Fauset, "it has been almost impossible to read the critical works and general history of the New Negro/Harlem Renaissance of the 1920s and get any impression other than that the 'New Negroes' were entirely of the male sex" (140). Hernton makes a valid point since even the aforementioned black women writers remained largely unmentioned in academic course curriculums across America.

It is noticeable that despite the challenges that black male writers faced in not being part of the mainstream, predominantly white literary scene, they did not face as much adversity as their female counterparts. There seemed to be a double standard with respect to the reception of works by black men and black women, as evident in the response to Richard Wright's *Native Son* and Ann Petry's *The Street*.[1] As Hernton asserts, "*Native Son* (1940), devoted to the plight of America's black male youth, was and is hailed as a masterpiece" (140). *Native Son* focuses on the struggles of African-American males who stand no chance of surviving a system that is put in place to oppress them. Similarly, Hernton notes, "Ann Petry's 1946 novel *The Street* [was] devoted to the tragedy of a young black female who is crippled, exploited, and driven to murder by the oppressive misogynous systems of the white and black man" (140). Yet, how much attention was given to the female protagonist in the context of the African-American literary canon? It is notable that *Native Son* is not only in print, but it is widely taught in secondary and postsecondary educational settings. In contrast, *The Street*, for a period of time, was out of print and is somewhat unheard of in educational institutions even today. What sort of message does this send? Both works were about black youths in America and the effects of race and socioeconomic issues upon their lives. Does this suggest that the experiences of black males supersede those of black females?

Although Ann Petry's work is not widely known, there were ultimately literary success stories of women whose works were published during the Harlem Renaissance. Zora Neale Hurston is such an anomaly. However, she, too, came under harsh scrutiny. Though addressed with mixed reviews, *Their Eyes Were Watching God* (1937) received negative reviews that attacked Hurston's validity as a writer. Could it have been because she chose not to write based on the standard of writing set by her black male counterparts, such as Richard Wright, who was among her most serious critics? Could it have been because she chose to write in her own voice, based on experience and anthropological observation? Instead of offering negative criticism, perhaps Wright should have promoted a sense of solidarity between his writing and that of Hurston, his black female contemporary. Perhaps the Harlem Renaissance would have been even more successful if the women's voices were not diminished to insignificance. Hurston, after all, suffered from her temporary disappearance from the literary scene until scholars Larry Neal and Alice Walker engaged in the recovery of her work, returning a degree of prominence decades after her death.

What does this say about the mindset behind American literary criticism? About the mindset behind black literary criticism? Do black women writers need to gain validity in a posthumous manner? Or, does the status or lack of status of black women writers need to undergo a revolution? And who should be called upon to "lead the charge"? Historically, notable black women writers, such as Nikki Giovanni, Sonia Sanchez, and Maya Angelou stepped to the forefront to remedy the situation. Emerging in 1965, the Black Arts Movement came about as an attempt to reestablish the presence of the black literary voice collectively through poetic and dramatic enactments that enforced elements of activism and solidarity parallel to the Black Power Movement—a social and political movement that gave credence to the voice of blacks in America. However, as in any movement whose goals are social and political justice, some voices remain muted among the booming voices of its leaders. Like the Black Power Movement, the Black Arts Movement was overtly masculine and justified as such because the black man has historically been marginalized in America, from the period of slavery, in which his masculinity was puppeted under the chattel system, through the period of Reconstruction, in which he faced the challenge of rebuilding his identity without clear reference points and resources.

In a movement like the Black Arts Movement, he is educated in the institutional sense as well as in the experiential sense, possessing a powerful literary voice to resound upon the masses of those inside and outside of the struggle. He will be heard, and his literary voice will be his megaphone. Larry Neal suggests that "history weighs down on all of this literature. Every black writer in America has had to react to this history, either to make peace with it, or to make war with it. It cannot be ignored" (15). Through this statement, Neal effectively articulates the need for activism within the Black Arts Movement. Without an activist stance towards the discontents generated in the history, the black writer's words would be written in vain. It is also commendable that Neal's statement draws reference to black writers of both sexes. Despite the gender impartiality of his statement, however, this practice was not common throughout the Black Arts Movement and some of the literary work that it produced, including Neal's. While the literary voices of these black men were heard, there were women in the background and sometimes by their sides who echoed the rhetoric of the men and also had rhetoric of their own, though too often these sentiments remained unheard. As Cheryl Clarke asserts in her essay, "Queen Sistuh: Black Women Poets and the Circle of Blackness," within the Black Arts Movement, "[The Black] 'Woman' is elided with 'Black'. No space for black women's multiple identities is given between race and gender in the best of all possible Black (male) worlds. And there is no space for black women to be identified as nonconcentric to or separate from black men" (49).

Clarke's argument criticizes the assertions made by Don L. Lee in his poem that addresses the "blackwoman" as "an in and out rightsideup action-image of her man" (54). Such an assertion indicates that a black woman should imitate her man's actions and thoughts as opposed to engendering her own. There appears to be a trend in relation to this viewpoint. For instance, in "Poppa Stoppa Speaks from His Grave," Larry Neal has the narrator of the poem request that his woman pass on or, to an extent, give life to his story so that he will not be forgotten. This is a legitimate request, but in the act of passing on Poppa Stoppa's story, the woman runs the risk of forgoing the telling of her own. Furthermore, in this poem, Neal also sandwiches the woman between Poppa Stoppa and another man, as though her existence is irrelevant without one. It is doubtful that Neal's intentions were to marginalize the black woman, but ingrained in the psyche of man is the tendency to engage a woman in the sharing of responsibility without asking whether she already shoulders the weight of her own, thus regarding her primary purpose as being to support men.

During an interview in which she was part of a collective of black female literary/activist voices on the *Phil Donahue* show, Alice Walker along with Maya Angelou, Angela Davis, Ntozake Shange, and Michele Wallace agreed that the black female voice has historically been silenced. It is notable that during the show, Walker and the other black women panelists who assert their own voices were counteracted by the dynamics of the talk show. The panelists offered their criticisms, as did Donahue and some of the audience members. However, out of a somewhat racially balanced and gender-balanced audience, representatives from each race and each gender voiced their opinions, except for the black women in the audience. The camera captured their nods of agreement to statements made by the panelists, yet they were not offered the opportunity to step up to the microphone that Donahue made available to audience members. This appears to have been an intentional silencing of the voice of the black woman. It was as if to say that it was sufficient enough that the five authors/activists were able to express themselves, never mind that there were black women in the audience with similar concerns.

This episode of the *Donahue* show should, therefore, serve as validation of what author/activists, such as Angelou, Davis, Walker, Wallace, and Shange have been depicting all along in their works of poetry, drama, fiction, and sociopolitical commentary—all works that capture the theme of inequalities and the marginalization of black women while taking on issues that society sometimes tries to avoid discussing. This is why Walker and Rankine remain important literary figures today. They carry on the struggle of their literary predecessors while reclaiming the ocularity of the self so vital in countering the marginalization and silencing of black women.

Questioning Submissiveness: Walker's Meridian as a Model of Civil Rights Activism

In *Meridian*, Alice Walker demonstrates how an African-American woman, Meridian Hill, and her white counterpart, Lynne Rabinowitz, remain steadfast in determining their roles in a well-intentioned liberation movement that, at times, marginalizes and imperils them. For Meridian, becoming involved in civil rights activities means making sacrifices in regards to her family. Recently divorced and thrust into single motherhood without a viable support system from family and friends, she chooses obtaining a higher education over raising her child. Although giving up one's child after months of bonding with him seems brutal in the eyes of those who are close to her, particularly her own mother, Meridian cannot count on anyone to help her raise her child while she sets out to improve herself. It is therefore not a cold choice but a hard one. She has "nightmares of the child, Rundi, calling to her, crying, suffering unbearable deprivations because she was not there, yet she knew it was the opposite: Because she was not there he needn't worry, ever, about being deprived" (Walker 89-90). Although she knew in her heart that she had made the right decision, "she felt condemned, consigned to penitence for life" (90).

After making this difficult decision, Meridian begins to cultivate her activism at Saxon College, an institute rooted in precepts of provincialism that attempts to contain and hinder the development of progressive ideological thinking in its students.[2] Formerly a plantation, it maintains the practices of keeping its black female residents in their place of subservience. Though not physically whipping them into compliance, the college manipulates them into adhering to the status quo. However, strong-willed and freethinking students like Meridian and some of her colleagues reject conformity. Walker writes, "Meridian and the other students felt they had two enemies: Saxon, which wanted them to become something—ladies—that was already obsolete, and the larger, more deadly enemy, white racist society" (95). The surrounding Atlanta community provides them with constant reminders that the finishing school-oriented academic environment could not shield them from racially motivated civil liberty violations, as "[o]ne of Meridian's classmates, a gentle drama student from Ohio, had been dragged out of a picket line by four thugs and forced, on the main street in Atlanta, to drink a pint of ammonia" (95). While picket line protests pose no physical threat to persons or entities that are protested against, it calls attention to the need to shift the weight in the distribution of social equity—a call often met with violent opposition. Instead of the assailants receiving punishment for committing the brutal act, the socially conscious student is traumatized and receives no advocacy and support from Saxon College, ultimately prompting her to withdraw.

From that encounter, Meridian, more a student of life than academics compared to the other women at Saxon, becomes even more seasoned with regards to the atrocities that African Americans face in an intensively racialized society. She bears witness to what "caused the majority of her waking moments to seem fragmented, surreal. She saw small black children, with short, flashing black legs, being chased by grown white men brandishing ax handles" (Walker 95). It was not only the young who were attacked, for "[s]he saw old women dragged out of sorts and beaten on the sidewalk, their humility of a lifetime doing them no good" (95). While obtaining a postsecondary education holds significant value, after Meridian witnesses these events, the lives of blacks matter more to her. Therefore, she joins the movement and participates fearlessly: "While other students dreaded confrontation with police, she welcomed it, and was capable of an inner gaiety, a sense of freedom, as she saw the clubs slashing down on her from above" (97). For Meridian, Saxon College, built on a plantation that in the recent past forced enslaved Africans into labor against their will, presently attempts to keep young black women enmeshed in docility.

Her experiences thus cause her to question why she should practice or exhibit submissiveness when faced with acts of aggression from legal agents of authority as well as certain self-sanctioned citizens who take it upon themselves to victimize black people.

Walker's depiction of the 1960s Civil Rights Movement serves as a gateway to a better understanding of modern protests, such as to the Black Lives Matter Movement, and helps to expose the current state of racial issues in the United States. The leadership roles of women in the Black Lives Matter Movement is more noticeable than they were in various segments of the Civil Rights Movement, such as the Student Nonviolent Coordinating Committee and the Black Panthers. Founded by Alicia Garza, Patrisse Cullors, and Opal Tometi in 2013, "Black Lives Matter is a chapter-based national organization working for the validity of Black life" ("About"). As part of a growing movement, they have addressed the increasingly frequent incidents of violence against African Americans, their efforts made available through the spread of technology and social media. Bystanders record acts of violence committed against African Americans and broadcast them within minutes or even livestream them via social media. In some instances, police dashboard or body cameras capture these occurrences. In the month of July 2016, for instance, at least three cases involved police shooting African-American men. Minnesota cafeteria supervisor, Philando Castile, riding in the passenger side of a car was fatally shot. This took place less than twenty-four hours after Baton Rouge police fatally shot Alton Sterling, whom they confronted while he sold CDs outside of a convenience store. Approximately two weeks later, behavioral therapist Charles Kinsey, who attempted to bring an autistic patient under his care back to the care facility, faced similar peril but survived being shot in the foot.

It seems that in all three instances, African American men are assigned an image that defines them as a threat. Allison L. Skinner and Ingrid J. Haas, researchers from the University of Washington and the University of Nebraska-Lincoln, conducted a four-tiered study that addresses the issue of how racial biases impact policing in interactions with African-American men. The sampled populations consisted of students and adult community members, with the majority being white. Central to their study were "high-profile police altercations with Black men, including those resulting in the deaths of Michael Brown and Eric Garner in 2014" (Skinner & Haas 1). They concluded that, "[a]s threat associated with police officers increases, participants are increasingly supportive of restrictive and reformed policing policies. Yet, as threat associated with Black men increases participants are increasingly resistant to restrictive and reformed policing policies" (13). Skinner and Haas's findings also indicated that "publicizing racially charged police encounters may actually promote *resistance* to policing policy reform among those who perceive Black men as threatening" (15).

Unfortunately, this notion of "black equals threat" is not applicable to black men alone. Racially biased hegemonic institutes within society apply this image to black women as well. Police dashboard camera footage showed an Austin police officer body slamming a petite black schoolteacher, Breaion King. The arrest took place in June 2015. When King questioned the officer, as she sat hand-cuffed in the back seat of the squad car, as to why she was being treated this way, his response was that "[n]inety-nine percent of the time . . . it is the black community that is being violent. . . . That's why a lot of white people are afraid. And I don't blame them" (qtd. in Miller). This conversation was recorded by a camera inside the police vehicle. In a public address regarding this assault, Austin Police Chief Art Acevedo indicated that he found this to be problematic: "For those that think life is perfect for people of color, I want you to listen to that conversation and tell me we don't have social issues in this nation. . . . Issues of bias. Issues of racism. Issues of people being looked at different because of their color" (qtd. in Miller).

Similarly, a police dashboard camera recorded Sandra Bland's arrest, also in Texas. The officer stopped her because she failed to signal before changing lanes. The interaction escalated after Bland refused to extinguish the cigarette that she smoked while seated in her vehicle. Her lack of compliance on this irrelevant matter and her "back talk" toward an authority figure added to the officer's apparent reason for arresting her. Days later, Sandra Bland died while in police custody. Her death, according to an autopsy report, was the result of suicide due to asphyxiation. Further investigation is pending, however, as a guard at the facility admitted to falsifying the log entry that allegedly indicated that he checked in on Bland an hour before she died.

Incidents such as these beg the question of whether black women pose a perceived threat of violence or is it that they exercise their right to speak up when confronted in a situation in which authority figures disregard their humanity? According to Malcolm X, "The most disrespected woman in America, is the black woman. The most unprotected person in America is the black woman. The most neglected person in America is the black woman." Police officers' treatment of Sandra Bland, Breaion King, and other black women reflect this sentiment, not far removed from what Meridian experiences in Walker's work. Together, they reveal that the United States is a nation whose gender inequity is deeply rooted in chauvinism.

This chauvinism, however, has not applied to black women to the extent that it has been applied to white women. Consider the social dynamics within the institution of slavery. As Angela Davis notes in *Women, Race & Class* (1981), "Required by the masters' demands to be as 'masculine' in performance of their work as their men, Black women must have been profoundly affected by their experiences during slavery" (11). She points out that a number of women "were broken and destroyed, yet the majority survived and, in the process, acquired qualities considered taboo by the nineteenth-century ideology of womanhood" (11). Of course, the standard of womanhood is modeled in whiteness. By these standards, white women were viewed as fragile, in need of assistance, and more aesthetically desirable, whereas black women were seen as the opposite.

In *Meridian*, Alice Walker examines this dichotomy by providing comparative narratives of Meridian and Lynne with Truman at the center. Truman, a black man of mixed ancestry, expresses interest in both women, who contribute to the movement in their own individual way. Although Truman has feelings of desire and love for Meridian, he chooses Lynne and ultimately marries her. Yet, over the years, he reaches out to and interacts with Meridian on a more emotional level. Then why does he choose Lynne in the first place? Does this decision stem from the idea that black women are seen as less feminine and more aggressive? Furthermore, does the fact that Meridian takes on a role of leadership within the movement pose a threat to his masculinity? Walker presents Meridian as blend of the New Negro and the New Woman. She is confident about her racial identity as well as that of her gender role. She does not buy into the expectations imposed by society when it comes to either category, and it seems to be too much for Truman to handle.

Lynne, on the other hand, takes on a supportive role, remaining on the sideline and in silence, often to her social, physical, and emotional detriment. Walker demonstrates how, at times, Truman's and Lynne's marriage fosters sentiments of white guilt: "By being white, Lynne was guilty of whiteness. [Truman] could not reduce the logic any further, in that direction. Then again was it possible to be guilty of color?" (Walker 140). In such passages, Walker brings up the touchy subject of white privilege and the guilt associated with that privilege—an interesting subject given that a major goal of the movement is to move toward an America with equitable rights for all citizens regardless of race or ethnicity, an America where racial prejudice and discrimination no longer exists. However, this post-racial utopian society is far from the horizon in the 1960s. Although the term *post-racial* has been constantly utilized since the actualization of a black president, equality still eludes society. Are white people, such as Lynne—who is not only part of a movement but is married to a black man active in the movement—culpable for the racial discrimination that other whites and institutions controlled by whites practice? As Walker writes, "Of course, black people for years, were 'guilty' of being black. Slavery was punishment for their 'crime'" (140). Some would argue that Lynne, having benefitted from the color of her skin, is guilty. It is arguable, however, that the fact that she is in the struggle with her black husband exempts her from that guilt. She gives up a lot, after all. Narrow-minded whites view her as consorting with the enemy against her own kind. They believe that she degrades herself by being with black people, much less married to a black man. To an extent, she sacrifices her whiteness. All of these issues are central to *Meridian* and Walker's efforts to depict the racial landscape of the United States.

A New Awareness: Rankine's *Citizen* and Moments of Privilege and Non-Privilege

Over the last few years, race, privilege, and awareness have become increasingly critical issues in American society, especially when it comes to societal perception versus self-perception. Actor Jesse Williams, who is biracial, is lauded for the "Stay Woke" speech that he delivered upon his acceptance of a Black Entertainment Television (BET) award. In this speech, Williams discussed the value of the black lives lost due to institutional racism. He stressed how blacks are treated differently than whites when confronted by the police, stating, "What we've been doing is looking at the data and we know that police somehow manage to de-escalate, disarm, and not kill white people every day." He commemorated Tamir Rice, one of the youngest victims who lost his life at the hands of police who said that they mistook the young man's toy gun for a real gun. Williams declares, "I don't want to hear any more about how far we've come when paid public servants can pull a drive-by on a twelve-year-old playing alone in a park in broad daylight, killing him on television and then going home to make a sandwich." Many African Americans respect Williams for being enlightened. Thus, the privilege that he experiences for being half-white is not extensively scrutinized. He also owns up to the fact that he has benefited from being light-complected and having blue eyes but has used this to gain access and ultimately open doors to gain information to which darker-complected black people do not have access.

Like Williams, Jamaican author Claudia Rankine captures various moments of access and inaccess, privilege and non-privilege, in *Citizen: An American Lyric*, a finalist for the National Book Award. Along with the everyday incidents in which societal ocular dominance skews the acuity and validity of the African-American self, she illustrates hegemonic society's attempts to marginalize African Americans who have obtained celebrity status. Grand slam champion Serena Williams has been the constant target of such an imposition. In *Citizen*, Rankine asks, "What does a victorious or defeated black woman's body in a historically white space look like?" (25). She points out that both "Serena and her big sister Venus Williams brought to mind Zora Neale Hurston's [notion that] 'I feel most colored when I am thrown against a sharp white background'" (25). Whether it is a referee who penalizes her committing a fault or a foul during a match when the playback video and the sports commentators observed otherwise or an American fan in the stadium seat rooting for her opponent from another country, Serena Williams is vulnerable under the judgmental societal eye. It scrutinizes her. It mocks her. It upsets her. And when she exhibits dissatisfaction in response to the scrutiny and mockery, she is further criticized for living up to the stereotype of the angry black woman.

Undoubtedly, Williams expresses her disagreement with the referee's call in a combative way. However, there is a double standard. At the height of his career, John McEnroe exhibited similar behavior for the same reasons. As a white man, he was afforded such privilege. But as a woman, and especially as a black woman, Williams is viewed as a threat, much in the same way as Sandra Bland, Breaion King, and arguably the average African-American female citizen. As Rankine posits, "To understand is to see Serena as hemmed in as any other black body thrown against our American background" (32). This is compounded by her physicality and athlete's strength. Williams's physical appearance is often the focus of media scrutiny, especially on social media. Her muscular body, developed from intensive training that has led to her being the best female tennis player, evokes a perceived image of masculinity. In actuality, it is not the muscles that threaten white hegemony; rather, it that African-American women such as Serena Williams have achieved high status in spite of the racial inequity that exists in American society, all while refusing to reconfigure their lens. Williams, after all, does not allow the harsh criticisms to silence her as she continues to persevere, inspiring black women and black girls to achieve beyond the limits placed before them.

Such experiences, however, are not restricted to celebrities in the African-American community. For the everyday black American citizen, male or female, there are daily incidents that skew the validity of the self. In *Citizen*, for example, Rankine highlights perceptions of reverse discrimination due to a white parent's child allegedly losing an opportunity for admission to a college or university because a black student received a scholarship under affirmative action. A parent who feels slighted has no reservations about discussing this matter with his/her black friend. Furthermore, that parent expects his/her black friend to be understanding of the predicament. Later in the work, Rankine describes a black man who babysits for a friend in a neighborhood that is predominantly white. He goes outside to use his cellphone, though his pacing makes him appear suspicious to the neighbor who previously met him but does not recognize him. This incident reflects a trend of occurrences, big and small, that are to the detriment of black people's ocularity of the self, for the police are called, and he is encouraged to go into the backyard if he needs to use the phone again—a request that renders him invisible. It seems that no matter how a black person views him/herself, segments of the white hegemonic society constantly reconfigure the black individual's lens to the extent that the acuity and validity of the self is skewed. As Rankine writes, "Yes, of course, you say. Yes, of course" (15).

In some instances, natural disasters, such as Hurricane Katrina, and the slow push to render aid also have a way of revealing societal perceptions about African Americans. Claudia Rankine examines this in *Citizen: An American Lyric* when she utilizes various quotations from the CNN program, *The Situation Room*. Without utilizing much poetic license, Rankine exposes the viewpoints across a spectrum of commentary collected from the news program and developed with the help of John Lucas. For instance, Rankine writes, "Faith, not fear, she said. She heard that once and was trying to stamp the phrase out of her mind. At the time she couldn't speak it aloud. He couldn't tolerate it. He was angry. Where were they?

Where was anyone? This is a goddam emergency, he said" (83). Not only is this plea for help indicative of the urgency of the situation, but it also suggests, according to the person crying out, that there is a sense of a lack of urgency when rescuing African Americans from the disaster. She continues, "Then someone else said it was the classic binary between, the rich and the poor, between the haves and the have-nots, between the whites and the blacks, in the difficulty of all that" (83). This statement confirms the cognizance of inequity that pushed this event into the national conversation on race, even though Hurricane Katrina affected all lives.

Added to this is the apparent disdain for blackness that some individuals possess towards African Americans, even when they are in need of help. Here, Rankine addresses the following statement among many others: "You simply get chills every time you see these poor individuals, so many of these people almost all of them that we see, are so poor, someone else said, and they are so black" (85). In this instance, blackness is associated with poverty and is also seen as a detriment. Through these random statements, made by those who offered their commentary, Rankine exposes the mindsets that serve as a means to continue to skew the validity of the African-American self. Holly Bass makes a valid point in her *New York Times* review of *Citizen*, when she says, "The challenge of making racism relevant, or even evident, to those who do not bear the brunt of its ill effects is tricky. Rankine brilliantly pushes poetry's forms to disarm readers and circumvent our carefully constructed defense mechanisms against the hint of possibly being racist ourselves" (BR9). In such passages, Rankine's lyrical activism is subtle and bold at the same time as it engages readers across cultures so that they can take the opportunity to own up to their biases, publicly or privately.

Looking Ahead: Walker, Rankine, and the Legacy of African-American Literature

As *Meridian* by Alice Walker and *Citizen: An American Lyric* by Claudia Rankine reveal, works of literature have historically been effective sites of reflecting on the various cultural, socioeconomic, political, gendered issues that complicate the lives of people across the United States and throughout the world. Through such works, writers have critically engaged audiences in order to explore and empower communities. The Harlem Renaissance and the Black Arts Movement, in particular, accomplished that with their respective representative writers—an effort that continues today with activist authors such as Alice Walker and Claudia Rankine leading the way. Whether artistic or political, they have the ability to help reshape the ocularity of the self, calling attention to the fact that society's perception ought not to supersede that of the individual. As literature continues to address these issues—in the Black Lives Matter Movement and beyond—Walker and Rankine provide a clear sense of direction for looking ahead: the ocularity of the self must be reclaimed by black men and black women alike to counter the history of cultural oppression and silence that far too often renders them invisible in the American tale.

Notes

1. According to Hernton, "Despite the legacy of this double standard—lack of equal reward for equal work—black women, like black men, continued to write throughout the Depression years on into the 1960s" (140).

2. Meridian's experience at Saxon parallels that of Helga Crane, the protagonist of Harlem Renaissance writer Nella Larsen's novel *Quicksand*. Helga also faces the dilemma between performing "good Negro" behavior and attempting to affect progress.

Works Cited

"About the Black Lives Matter Network." *Black Lives Matter*. #BlackLivesMatter Organization, 2016. Web. 20 Dec. 2016.

Clark, Cheryl. "Queen Sistuh: Black Women Poets and the Circle of Blackness." *After Mecca: Women Poets and the Black Arts Movement*. New Brunswick, NJ: Rutgers UP, 2004. 47-93.

Bass, Holly. Rev. of *Citizen: An American Lyric* by Claudia Rankine. *New York Times*, 24 Dec. 2014: BR9.

Davis, Angela. *Women, Race & Class*. New York: Vintage, 1983.

Hernton, Calvin. "The Sexual Mountain and Black Women Writers." *The Black Scholar* 16.4 (1985): 2-11.

Lee, Don L. "blackwoman." *A Broadside Treasury*. Ed. Gwendolyn Brooks. Detroit. Broadside, 1971.

Miller, Michael E. "Video: Austin police body-slam black teacher, tell her blacks have 'violent tendencies.'" *Washington Post. Nash Holdings LLC,* 22 July 2016. Web. 20 Dec. 2016.

Neal, Larry. "And Shine Swam On: An Afterword." *African American Literary Theory: A Reader.* Ed. Winston Napier. New York: New York UP, 2000. 69-80.

Rankine, Claudia. *Citizen: An American Lyric.* Minneapolis, MN: Graywolf, 2014.

Skinner, Allison L. & Ingrid J. Haas. "Perceived Threat Associated with Police Officers and Black Men Predicts Support for Policing Policy Reform." *Frontiers in Psychology* (2016): 1-18.

Walker, Alice. *Meridian.* 1976. Orlando: Harcourt, 2003.

"Jesse Williams' Fiery BET Awards Speech." *YouTube.* Youtube, 27 June 2016. Online video clip.

X, Malcolm. "Who Taught You to Hate Yourself?" Funeral Service of Ronald Stokes, Los Angeles, 5 May 1962.

"Crooning [the] Lullabies [of] Ghosts": Reclamation and Voices of Witness as Sociopolitical Protest in the Short Fiction of Alice Walker

Christopher Allen Varlack

[The notion that women across history and across the world were once expected to ask for permission to speak] is heartbreaking. Not just for black women who have struggled so *equally* against the forces of oppression, but for all those who believe subservience of any kind is death to the spirit. But we are lucky in our precedents, for I know that Sojourner Truth, Harriet Tubman—or a young Fannie Lou Hamer or Winson Hudson—would simply ignore the assumption that "permission to speak" *could be given them,* and would fight on for freedom of all people, tossing White Only signs and Men Only signs on the same trash heap.

(Alice Walker, "Staying Home in Mississippi," italics original)

In her 1987 article, "'The Darkened Eye Restored': Notes Toward a Literary History of Black Women," Mary Helen Washington challenges headfirst the widespread marginalization of African-American women writers—those same "intellectuals and activists, who in the 1890s had taken on such issues as the moral integrity of black women, lynching, and the education of black youth" but who were largely considered, at the time, "social decorations" (444). For Washington, this marginalization not only denies the vital role that black women writers have played (and will continue to play) in the ongoing fight for equal rights but also "underscores an attitude toward black women that has helped to maintain and perpetuate a male-dominated literary and critical tradition" (445). Historically, the literary and cultural works produced by black women authors across the United States have been ignored or too often forgotten until years after their author's deaths—a fact that speaks to a more widespread marginalization of black women at large, often placed in the background of the struggle for civil rights. As Washington aptly questions, "Why is the fugitive slave, the fiery orator, the political activist, the abolitionist always represented as a black *man*? How does the heroic voice and heroic image of the black woman get suppressed in a culture that depended on her heroism for its survival?" (444).

This is one of the fundamental issues that Pulitzer Prize-winning author Alice Walker addresses in her novels and short fiction works, cataloguing the untold stories of black men and women once silent or silenced. For instance, in her seminal essay, "In Search of Our Mothers' Gardens," Walker notes that the same heroic women who guided the black community through centuries of discrimination and cultural oppression still "dreamed dreams that no one knew—not even themselves, in any coherent fashion—and saw visions no one could understand" (421). Far from silent, despite living in a society that discouraged not only their education but also the free exercise of their voices in public space, these women were at the frontier of a burgeoning artistic and cultural tradition: black women breaking their forced silence in seemingly unconventional ways as simplistic as tending a garden, writing a poem, or making a patchwork quilt. These same women, according to Walker, had "wandered or sat about the countryside crooning lullabies to ghosts, and drawing the mother of Christ in charcoal on courthouse walls" (421), just a small inkling of the individualized talents that black women across the United States learned as vital forms of self-expression aimed at preserving their stories and combatting their cultural erasure.

Throughout her short fiction and autobiographical works, Alice Walker has thus engaged in a lifelong quest to find her mother's and grandmother's neglected "gardens," tracing the rich histories of artistic and creative expression pursued by black women in a discriminatory society virtually unwilling to ever truly "acknowledge them, except as 'the mule[s] of the world'" ("In Search" 421). Her works attempt to bear forth that necessary obligation central within African-American literature—an obligation to share the stories once untold, to speak for those rendered voiceless, and to search for the voice buried deep inside—just a faint whisper of that late-night croon, that bedtime lullaby to ancient and familial ghosts. Her stories, actively seeking to reclaim the tales of black men and women that would otherwise be stifled within them, are therefore a valuable form of social and political protest, asserting the value of black lives and, in particular, the value of black women as orators, activists, and the keepers of tales. By examining her fiction works and their concerted efforts to challenge the suppression of black women, we reach a better understanding of how these very women engaged the fight for civil rights, not always by laying their bodies before the national conscience (779), as Dr. Martin Luther King Jr. demanded in his "Letter from Birmingham Jail," but by keeping alive a tale of the African-American struggle that so many across centuries tried to erase. In other words, through an intensive study of Walker's fiction, we can see the ways in which black women "fight on for freedom of all people" (Walker, "Staying" 880) all while refusing to ask permission to speak.

"Ke[eping] Alive . . . The Notion of Song": The Aesthetic Project and Cultural Foundation of Alice Walker's Short Fiction

Published in 1983 in a collection of the same name, "In Search of Our Mothers' Gardens" attempts to trace the millions of gardens that we have left untended over time and the rich heritage that exists there, somewhere in the fertile soil buried beneath the weeds. In this essay, Walker establishes a foundation for the larger aesthetic endeavors of her fiction works, beginning through approaching "the lives of women who might have been Poets, Novelists, Essayists, and Short-Story Writers (over a period of centuries), who died with their real gifts stifled within them" ("In Search" 422). From the slave mother who birthed a field of slave children to the objectified women of the post-Reconstruction South to the multitudes of Mammies who were not actually so cheerful inside, these women are the women whom Walker essentially recreates, sharing their stories and reclaiming their voices in order to unearth that spirituality "so intense, so deep" but restricted by a series of detrimental socio-political concerns (420). As Walker notes, racism and sexism in the United States kept such women "unaware of the richness they held" (420). African-American people, after all, were ultimately forbidden to read, or write, or even dream without consequence, stripped of dignity or stripped of life for that one stray dream—that one bright glimmer of song.

While much of black history has been marred by cultural imperialism and the attempt to erase that knowledge of who we are and from where we came, Walker's works attempt to move beyond the stagnation she sees, beginning the arduous task of breaking that equally detrimental silence by taking back a piece of history that is too often forgotten and by delving into the lives and the voices of black people who otherwise might have "perished in the wilderness" ("In Search" 423). To that end, however, Walker asserts that "all the young women—our mothers and grandmothers, *ourselves*—have not perished in the wilderness. And if we ask ourselves why, and search for and find the answer, we will know beyond all efforts to erase it from our minds, just exactly who, and of what, we Black American women are" (423). In "In Search of Our Mothers' Gardens," Walker begins this process through exploring the lives of individuals, including Lucy Terry and Phillis Wheatley, noted among the few black women to publicize their artistic gifts and to use their voices at a time when blacks were expected to remain subservient and silent. For Walker, what they revealed is that "[i]t is not so much what you sang, as that you kept alive, in so many of our ancestors, the notion of song" that otherwise would have been erased by the lash or the whip (425). Her stories then tell the struggles of black men and black women who toiled to keep alive the notion of song and the story of the African-American experience as a reminder not only of the oppression blacks faced but also of the ways in which blacks have forever shaped the mosaic of American life.

Through stories such as "To Hell with Dying," Walker salvages and redeems the lives of black figures past, all the while infusing the spirituality and civil rights struggle so essential to the African-American people—a direct challenge to the overwhelming and flawed perspective of black women's writing as overly sentimental and apolitical. In this text, Walker accomplishes this goal through her literary "reincarnation" of the character Mr. Sweet, a fisherman and a guitar player by trade. Silenced in an era of discrimination and prejudice, Mr. Sweet represents a larger sector of the disenfranchised black community, wanting "to be a doctor or lawyer or sailor, only to find that black men fare better if they are not. The South was a place where a black man could be killed for trying to improve his lot" ("To Hell" 130). Through telling his all-too-common story, Walker then ensures that his experiences and his history do not die in the wilderness. Her work is therefore inherently an act of preservation and sociopolitical protest, reflecting the "everyday practices to reform and resist the [very] structures of oppression" (Marable & Mullings xvii) that limited access to opportunity for people like Mr. Sweet while also working "to renew their community through imagining and enacting its continuity" (xvii-xviii).

In the story, readers are introduced to Mr. Sweet, "a diabetic and an alcoholic and a guitar player [who] lived down the road from us on a neglected cotton farm" (Walker, "To Hell" 129). Such description emphasizes the ramifications of unfulfilled dreams, as Mr. Sweet is denied not only an opportunity at upward socioeconomic mobility but also a true sense of life, liberty, and the pursuit of happiness fundamental to achieving the American Dream. For much of the story, then, Mr. Sweet is dying in his "very poor shack," tears flowing along the deep crevices and whiskers of his face (133). "To Hell with Dying," told from the perspective of an adoring young girl, thus memorializes, even eulogizes, the character of Mr. Sweet after death, calling attention to the memorable (and at times tragic) experiences of his life as a vital part of the African-American and American tales. From the melancholy and sadness that poured from his bluish eyes to the late afternoons caressing his head in an attempt to bring him back to life, these moments Walker finds worth saving, not merely as a portrait of an old man unforgotten but also as a clear picture of the South as it is and as it should always be remembered.

Like her nonfiction, these stories, too, often emerge from real-life situations and peer into the past—in this case, the 1940s and 1950s—of the black men and black women who were influential in shaping our notions of song. Mr. Sweet is just one such example, pulled from the middle of Georgia and Walker's memories of her childhood past as a reminder of the people and places that inherently inform who we are. In her 1989 nonfiction collection *Living by the*

Word, Walker refers to Mr. Sweet as "a fixture, a rare and honored presence in our family, and we were taught to respect him—no matter that he drank, loved to gamble, and shoot off his gun" ("The Old Artist" 38). Here Walker is concerned with the notable fixtures within the African-American community—individuals like Mr. Sweet, who embody a sense of time and place for which we are ultimately nostalgic. At the same time, Walker also acknowledges that "he was an artist. He went deep into his own pain and brought out words and music that made us happy, made us feel empathy for anyone in trouble, made us think" (38). In telling his tale, she and the adoring young girl who tends his needs therefore strive to keep his music alive as he kept them alive, using his music as the first sweet note of an African-American tale that refused to be erased.

In essence, the story thus embodies Walker's aesthetic notion of honoring and cherishing old men—those within the African-American community whose struggles and stories are most enlightening. Mr. Sweet, after all, was loved by the narrator and their surrounding neighbors, remembered for his frequent dances around the yard and for the cold steel tang of his old guitar. The reverential tone through which his life is described thus parallels the overarching respect that Walker holds for the great writers of the African-American past. "We must revere their wisdom," Walker notes in her "Unglamorous Duties" essay (135). We must "appreciate their insight, love the humanity of their words" (135). Though these statements directly mention the James Weldon Johnsons and Langston Hugheses of the world, Walker's larger aesthetic project indicates a more universal reverence—a deep spiritual connection with her ancestors. Therefore, by sharing the tale of old Mr. Sweet, Walker is accomplishing that vital aesthetic and cultural goal, "nurtur[ing] and renew[ing]" her African-American community by "creating and maintaining" the notion of song just as the political and social leaders often credited in the annals of history worked to erect "institutions to provide goods, services, and cultural and educational sustenance" (Marable & Mullings xviii).

Throughout her short story collection, *In Love & Trouble* (1973), Walker thus weaves between the personal and the detached,

---

in essence drawing interconnecting lines between herself and those who came before, in each work juxtaposing those artists, those influential figures within the black community, with a witness of a different generation. In her short story, "The Flowers," for instance, Walker briefly describes the experiences of Myop, a ten-year-old girl captivated by song and "the harvesting of the corn and cotton, peanuts and squash, . . . each day a golden surprise that caused excited little tremors to run up her jaws" (119). Innocent, "nothing existed for her but her song, the stick clutched in her dark brown hand, and the tat-de-ta-ta-ta of accompaniment" as she practiced her beat on the fence posts alongside the pigpen (119). Still, in exploring the woods behind "her family's sharecropper cabin," Myop, like the narrator in "To Hell with Dying," is most significant here as a witness to American history—as that connection between the present and the past so vital to much of Walker's work (119).

Like her other works, "The Flowers," too, is primarily an investigation into the African-American past—an effort to reclaim and re-discover the untold stories of black men and black women unable to speak for themselves as a result of concerted efforts at cultural silencing and erasure. In this text, Myop serves as witness to a tall black man, with "large white teeth, all of them cracked or broken, long fingers, and very big bones," lynched from a nearby tree like the hundreds, if not thousands, of black people lynched and forgotten in the weeds (Walker, "The Flowers" 120). Through juxtaposing the image of an innocent Myop as she searches the woods for flowers with this image of a decaying black corpse, Walker calls attention to those silent and sometimes horrific moments when we stumble upon our history that some intentionally forget—the millions of gardens and the millions of graves hidden across the American landscape. While "the summer was over," signifying the loss of innocence or the damaging psychological effects of this discovery on the character of Myop (120), "The Flowers" is predominantly a story about the laying of flowers at the foot of unmarked graves, about the importance of remembering and refusing to forget the tradition of violence against black bodies that unfortunately continues even today.

In this particular scene of this arguably under-read and under-appreciated story, "*to save* someone, in Walker's eyes, includes the obligation to liberate her/him from an oppressive cycle of violence" (Smith 438), to rescue young black girls like Myop from the violence of lynchings and the realization of hatred pervasive in the American South just as much as she rescues this dead and forgotten man from perishing unnoticed any longer. Though fiction, the story naturally accomplishes that all-important goal of both creating and recreating with the sole purpose of offering a type of redemption—self-discovery or a chance to speak—for those millions of black men and women who Walker believes had something important to say that was stifled inside them. From "the rotted remains of a noose, a bit of shredding plowline, now blending benignly into the soil" to the "wild pink rose" barely noticed nearby, this scene (and the man that it strives to remember) serves as a reminder of a not-so-distant past and as an indication that we will continue growing like roses from the garden and from the grave, despite the cycle of violence that may befall us (Walker, "The Flowers" 120).

Contrary to Alice Hall Petry's assertion in "Alice Walker: The Achievement of the Short Fiction," this story is not therefore an exploration into the shattering of Myop's childhood and "her attitudes toward her self and her world," at least not as much as it delves into "the blunt social reality of lynching" as a marker of who we are or from where we came (13). Instead, "The Flowers" is far more redemptive in accordance with Walker's aesthetic endeavors, seeking to salvage by reclaiming a history so heavily marred by violence and oppression in the past. This understanding, however, is only reached through examining Walker's works in conversation, using the artistic and cultural focus outlined in her nonfiction works as a veritable looking glass through which we can interpret her artistic endeavors. Alice Walker, after all, embodies the spirit of the black revolutionary artist she examines in her nonfiction essays. And from *The Color Purple* to her story of this murdered black man, she adopts a revolutionary approach, concerned with the empowerment (even after death) of disempowered figures already beaten down in this world while honoring the lasting impact they have had on emerging generations—a fact made clear as the fictional Myop chooses to lay down her gathered flowers: an homage to the unknown black man no longer disregarded beneath her feet.

Interrogating the "Social Matrix of Black Consciousness": Redemption and Group Empowerment in Walker's Short Fiction

For artists like Alice Walker, engaged in this arduous process of resurrecting an untold African-American past, "To acknowledge our ancestors means / we are aware that we did not make / ourselves" ("Fundamental Difference" ll.1-3). Consistent with her artistic and cultural goals, it is therefore important to resurrect that all-important bridge between the present and the ancestral past, using her fiction as a reminder to readers that "it / is an easy thing to forget: that we / are not the first to suffer, rebel" (ll. 5-7). In that sense, throughout her short fiction, Walker embraces the notion of writing as "a cultivated awareness of the reciprocal saving potential of art, . . . keeping alive the connection between ancestral spirits and their living descendants" (Smith 438). Through the processes of writing, creating, and recreating, Walker can foreground the continued importance of the ancestral spirits to the collective African-American identity and, at the same time, demonstrate the spirit of reverence and remembrance she finds so integral to the zeitgeist of the day. Through this artistic approach, Walker is engaging "the social matrix of black consciousness" (Marable & Mullings xviii) while "providing the wisdom of the past both to ensure the continuity of the folk ethos and to serve as a blueprint for personal and communal survival for those who require artistic models" (Smith 438).

In her fiction, Walker is more concerned with the common and the everyday, peering into the lives of the average black man and the average black woman whose stories too often perish and drift away. In her short story, "Everyday Use," for example, Walker shares the experiences of a family of black women, each at different stages in embracing their beauty and their cultural roots and each an illustration of a larger community of everyday African-American women. Here Walker begins with the recreation of the suffering yet silent black woman. In this case, readers are introduced to the character of Maggie, physically and emotionally scarred, "stand[ing] hopelessly in corners, homely and ashamed of the burn scars down her arms and legs, eying her sister with a mixture of envy and awe" ("Everyday Use" 47). For much of the story, she is like "a lame animal, perhaps a dog run over by some careless person rich enough to own a car," always "chin on chest, eyes on ground, feet in shuffle, ever since the fire that burned the other house to the ground" (47). Telling her story is just one way of breaking that silence expected of women, of highlighting the experiences of the millions of Maggies, "chin on chest," somehow too scarred to look beyond the world at their feet.

In the end, as demonstrated in this work, Walker chooses to foreground the redemption of characters like "Maggie, the supposedly uneducated sister, who has been nowhere beyond the supposedly uneducated black South"—the type of woman likely to be forgotten in the weeds (Christian 760). Maggie, after all, "loves and understands her family and can appreciate its history. She knows how to quilt and would put the precious quilts to 'everyday use,' which is precisely what, Walker suggests, one needs to do with one's heritage" instead of leaving it as an ornament of one's past to fade on living room walls (760). Maggie, too, is an artist, like many of Walker's other redeemed characters, keeping alive that notion of song, in this case, through her quilting, which was passed down from generation to generation—that all-important link between the present and one's ancestry. So in telling Maggie's story, Walker thus asserts her importance to a larger African-American tale, signifying how the black woman artist is fully empowered, far from the feeble and silent figure that some believe her to be. Maggie, like the millions of mothers-turned-artists, does not need the quilts to be redeemed; she carries within her the tradition of quilting—that notion of song so vital to the African-American identity—and with that she will always be able to maintain her grandmother and great-grandmother's legacies even in a society that devalues that ancestral past. More importantly, however, she reminds us to put that notion of song to everyday use as part of the ongoing fight for civil rights and the countermovement to cultural oppression that continues today.

That same feeling of connectedness and ancestral understanding is also prevalent in short stories like "Roselily," in which Walker strives to acknowledge the internal (and external) burdens that continuously affect the lives of the black women all around her. Here Walker familiarizes readers with the character of Roselily—a single mother of three illegitimate children, who finds herself tired of working, tired of fighting, and tired of being alone. Essentially torn between two difficult possibilities, for Roselily, building a life in Chicago inherently represents an opportunity at obtaining "respect, a chance to build. Her children at last from underneath the detrimental wheel. A chance to be on top" (Walker, "Roselily" 4). At the same time, she associates her impending marriage with "ropes, chains, handcuffs, his religion. His place of worship. Where she will be required to sit apart with covered head," forced instead to sacrifice yet another part of herself (4). The result is an existence plagued by silence, screaming internally beneath the echo of wedding vows she might not mean and feelings of overwhelming apprehension. For Roselily, she buries any notion of song behind that silence—too burdened, too conflicted at a crossroads so many African-American women also face in a society where their disenfranchisement is two-fold—where being black and female affords one a second-class status as best.

In this regard, Roselily is a direct parallel to the mothers and grandmothers who Walker examines in "In Search of Our Mothers' Gardens"—a rich heritage of women, "not Saints, but Artists; driven to a numb and bleeding madness by the springs of creativity in them from which there was no release" (422). Similar to the study Walker offers in nonfiction texts, "Roselily" is concerned with the psychosocial factors that leave Roselily unhinged with no release, standing on the front porch of her house in Mississippi, in the midst of a wedding to a man she does not love. If Walker's central concern in searching for our mothers' gardens is to ultimately discover that "respect for the possibilities—and the will to grasp them" ("In Search" 422), her goal in this story is also to trace the desire "to live for once" ("Roselily" 8), to breathe even when the women who so desperately uphold that desire do not "know quite what that means"

(8). Both projects converge at this crucial point, for this tale is not merely Roselily's tale; it is the richly textured tapestry of human experience, sewn together thread by thread with the encounters of African-American women torn asunder by two conflicting paths, two warring ideals. Roselily, after all, is disenchanted with an American Dream that seems to exclude her, torn between economic ruin and a loveless marriage because of the limited economic opportunities for black women too often forced into the meager existence of black domestic work.

Unlike many of Walker's other stories, "Roselily" seems to lack the appearance of overt redemption. Roselily, in the end, is not the empowered black woman, like Celie in *The Color Purple*, creating her own path and forging her own destiny. Roselily, instead, appears suspended in time, consumed with her own intricate thoughts, described as "ignorant, wrong, backward" (Walker, "Roselily" 9). And while in this text "opposition is not necessarily insurmountable: struggles and crises can lead to growth" (Petry 13-14), Roselily is not saved, not rescued like Mr. Sweet or Maggie are saved; she is still trapped in a life without true love. Redemption, then, must engage an alternative definition, what Sam Whitsitt, in his analysis of "Everyday Use," identifies as epiphany—a sudden self-realization and discovery. Roselily is redeemed only by giving voice to thoughts once silently buried, by having her story told even when she does not fully understand it herself.

For Walker, these stories exist in mutual conversation. As she acknowledges in her essay "The Black Writer in the Southern Experience," "What the black Southern writer inherits as a natural right is a sense of community"—a sense of involvement in something larger beyond the self, as evident in the tales of Maggie, Myop, and Mr. Sweet (17). By and large, this approach is predominant within Walker's aesthetic project, connecting individual experience (of real-life figures, like Zora, or fictionalized characters, like Roselily) with the community of men and women whose intersecting stories weave that first fresh stitch, a new corner of the American fabric. On the other hand, "we inherit a great responsibility as well, for we must give voice to centuries not only of silent bitterness and hate but also neighborly kindness and sustaining love" (Walker, "Black Writer" 21). As revealed in stories like "Roselily," Walker also explores the centuries of suffering and internal dilemma just as common within the black community, hoping to provide a voice to the multitudes of Roselilys struggling and searching for themselves. Only through this comparative and cross-genre approach, however, does the full picture of Walker's aesthetic endeavor become clear; she is concerned with cataloguing experiences of the African-American South, searching for her mothers' and grandmothers' gardens in order to spark conversation amongst the emerging generations of black men and black women now listening all across the United States.

The "Duties of the Black Revolutionary Artist": Reclamation as Sociopolitical Protest in African-American Literature

In "The Unglamorous But Worthwhile Duties of the Black Revolutionary Artist, or of the Black Writer Who Simply Works and Writes," presented to the Black Student's Association at Sarah Lawrence College in 1970, Walker tests the thesis she later expands throughout "In Search of Our Mothers' Gardens," contending that "the work of the black artist is also to create and to preserve what was created before him," even against the forces that consistently seek to silence and to erase (135). Here Walker asserts the importance of historical and cultural preservation as central to the work of both resistance and renewal at the heart of African-American literature, claiming that the black artist is inherently "the voice of the people," speaking through the carefully crafted words of a short story or the intricate stitching of her latest patchwork quilt ("Unglamorous" 137). In the process, she is able to rediscover the voice of those once rendered voiceless, all while honoring the artists who came before her and keeping their stories alive, even the stories they kept silent to the grave. From Walker's perspective, after all, *we are a people. A people do not throw their geniuses away.* And if they are thrown away, it is our duty *as artists and as witnesses for the future* to collect them again for the sake of our children, and if necessary, bone by bone" ("Zora" 92).

For Walker, on the one hand, this process occurs primarily through her investigations into the lives of Toomer, Hurston, and more, as revealed in essays such as "The Divided Life of Jean Toomer" or "Looking for Zora." Within these nonfiction texts, Walker delves into the real-life experiences of artists whose roles were critical to the development of the African-American literary tradition—figures such as Hurston, who "followed her own road, believed in her own gods, pursued her own dreams, and refused to separate herself from 'common' people" ("Zora" 91). These figures, after all, have had an undeniably resounding impact on literature produced by black authors, providing a clear model for the poetry, stories, and plays that not only climbed the racial mountain but that deconstructed (or at least attempted to deconstruct) the color line so prominent in the twentieth-century United States. On the other hand, this process is also evident in her fiction works, as Walker recognizes those whose names may never have been recorded in history but whose backs were broken under the weight of the nation they were building, whose song still echoes in the spirituals or work songs carried across voices until they finally reached someone gifted with a skill for the pen.

In her 1992 critical article, "Alice Walker's Redemptive Art," Felipe Smith builds upon this notion, arguing that Walker's works "indicate her belief in the actual, not figurative, saving power of art— the ability of the artist to liberate people from their tragic histories" (449). For the black revolutionary artist, this notion is particularly important. Creating and recreating in a field that has traditionally enabled black artists to express the beauty of the black community as well as unburden themselves of those tragic histories, Walker's art is redemptive in its ability to save the artist herself and the people depicted in her work. Smith contends, however, that "the process involves much more than acknowledging Zora Neale Hurston, to cite one example, as a literary 'foremother'; it suggests instead a determined effort 'literally' to reincarnate and redeem her as text-within-text" (439), particularly through her employment of what Trudier Harris identifies as "black folk materials" (8). As Walker's works "reflect a keen insight into the folk mind" and the notion that "folk culture is an inseparable part of the black folk at any level of existence" (Harris 8), she not only reincarnates her literary and artistic influences—Hurston, Toomer, Chesnutt, and more—as a way of drawing deep connections between texts and between times but also works tirelessly to preserve the stories that otherwise might perish in the wilderness.

In the end, each collection of works that Walker toiled to create is therefore just one more leg in her search to find her mother's garden, in her lifelong journey to trace that moment when women of color, much like herself, overcome that burden that builds so deep inside and find their beauty—that distant dancer so close, so dear— and the world gleaming brightly in once blind eyes. By tracing the histories of African-American women and men whose stories otherwise might never be told, Walker demonstrates the renewed importance of storytelling in the African-American artistic tradition. Like the vigils once held for the victims of the Seventeenth Street Baptist Church Bombing or the 2015 memorial services held for those killed at the Emanuel African Methodist Episcopal Church by Dylann Roof, these works also serve a clear civil rights function too often under-recognized—a reminder so that we do not "forget that we have our own light—it may be small, it may be flickering, but it's actually there. And so what we need to do, I think, is to be still enough to let that light shine, and illuminate our inner landscape and our dreams—especially our dreams" (Walker, "A Conversation" 286). Only then can the lasting gift of our mothers and their gardens be truly realized: when we take time to find that voice inside, when we take the time to acknowledge (in fiction, in poetry, in any form of creative expression) those who dared to dream, when we take a moment to croon the "lullabies [of ancestral] ghosts" (Walker, "In Search" 421).

Works Cited

Christian, Barbara T. "'Everyday Use' and the Black Power Movement." *An Introduction to Fiction*. Eds. X. J. Kennedy and Dana Gioia. 9th ed. New York: Pearson/Longman, 2005. 760-762.

Harris, Trudier. "Folklore in the Fiction of Alice Walker: A Preparation of Historical and Literary Traditions." *Black American Literature Forum* 11.1 (1977): 3-8.

King, Martin Luther, Jr. "Letter from Birmingham Jail." 1963. Carson 777-794.

Marable, Manning & Leith Mullings, eds. *Let Nobody Turn Us Around: Voices of Resistance, Reform, and Renewal.* Lanham, MD: Rowman & Littlefield, 2003.

Petry, Alice Hall. "Alice Walker: The Achievement of the Short Fiction." *Modern Language Studies* 19.1 (Winter 1989): 12-27.

Carson, Clayborne et al., eds. *Reporting Civil Rights.* 2 vols. New York: Library of America, 2003.

Smith, Felipe. "Alice Walker's Redemptive Art." *African American Review* 26.3 (1992): 437-451.

Walker, Alice. "The Black Writer and the Southern Experience." *In Search of Our Mothers' Gardens* 15-21.

_____. "A Conversation with Marianna Schnall from feminist.com." *The World Has Changed: Conversations with Alice Walker.* Ed. Rudolph P. Byrd. New York: The New P, 2010. 285-302.

_____. "Everyday Use." *In Love & Trouble* 47-59.

_____. "The Flowers." *In Love & Trouble* 119-120.

_____. "Fundamental Difference." *Revolutionary Petunias and Other Poems.* San Diego: Harvest, 1973. 1.

_____. *In Love & Trouble.* San Diego: Harcourt Brace Jovanovich, 1973.

_____. *In Search of Our Mothers' Gardens.* New York: Mariner, 2003.

_____. "In Search of Our Mothers' Gardens." *50 Essays.* Ed. Samuel Cohen. 3rd ed. Boston: Bedford, 2011. 420-429.

_____. "Roselily." *In Love & Trouble* 3-9.

_____. "Staying Home in Mississippi." 1973. *Reporting Civil Rights* 871-881.

_____. "The Old Artist: Notes on Mr. Sweet." *Living by the Word: Selected Writings, 1973-1987.* New York: Mariner, 1989. 37-40.

_____. "To Hell with Dying." *In Love & Trouble* 129-138.

_____. "The Unglamorous But Worthwhile Duties of the Black Revolutionary Artist, or the Black Writer Who Simply Works and Writes." *In Search of Our Mothers' Gardens* 130-137.

_____. "Zora Neale Hurston: A Cautionary Tale and a Partisan View." *In Search of Our Mothers' Gardens* 83-92.

Washington, Mary Helen. "'The Darkened Eye Restored': Notes Toward a Literary History of Black Women." 1987. *Within the Circle: An Anthology of African American Literary Criticism from the Harlem Renaissance to the Present*. Ed. Angelyn Mitchell. Durham, NC: Duke UP, 1994.

Whitsitt, Sam. "In Spite of It All: A Reading of Alice Walker's 'Everyday Use.'" *African American Review* 34.3 (200): 443-459.

The City and The Country: Queer Utopian Spaces in John Rechy's *City of Night* and Patricia Highsmith's *The Price of Salt*

Derrick King

In August of 2016, the US Department of Agriculture and the National Center for Lesbian Rights co-sponsored the Fifteenth National LGBT Rural Summit in Des Moines, Iowa. Like the previous stops in the series, the event provided a space for the LGBT+ population living in the nearby rural areas to meet and share their experiences. This particular stop also drew the ire of the right-wing media. Rush Limbaugh, for instance, portrayed the summit as a conspiratorial attack on conservative rural America that would "convince lesbians to become farmers," which was particularly shocking to him because he "never in [his] life knew that lesbians wanted to become farmers" (Percelay). Limbaugh, and no doubt many of his listeners, could not imagine queerness associated with the rural Midwest. Ironically, rural Iowa is a central location in Patricia Highsmith's 1952 Cold War lesbian classic *The Price of Salt*: Therese and Carol kiss for the first time in Waterloo, Iowa—something they could not do in New York City. In *Carol*, Todd Haynes' 2015 film adaptation of the novel, Waterloo is also retained as the site of the couple's first sexual encounter. In these works, lesbian desire is not only possible in Iowa but is actually enabled by the privacy of the rural country.

It is true, however, that the queer imaginary has largely focused on the city as a site for liberation, leading theorists like Jack Halberstam and Scott Herring to critique what they term queer "metronormativity," an ideology that forecloses upon anti-urban queer projects by making a non-urban queer identity unimaginable (Halberstam 36-8; Herring 14-16). Indeed, from its beginnings in the early 1950s, the LGBT+ Civil Rights Movement has largely been associated with major coastal cities like New York and San Francisco. The Mattachine Society, an early homophile organization that explicitly cited gay civil rights violations when publicizing a 1952 court case against police entrapment (Faderman 64), was formed in Los Angeles and moved to San Francisco in the mid-1950s. The Daughters of Bilitis, the first lesbian civil rights organization in the United States, likewise began in San Francisco. In contrast to the era's political movements, however, the queer literature of the 1950s and 1960s includes a healthy mixture of both queer city novels—including John Rechy's *City of Night* (1963) and Ann Bannon's Beebo Brinker series—as well as novels in which queer sexuality is located in rural areas, such as *The Price of Salt*, Jane Rule's *Desert Hearts* (1964), and Carl Corley's gay pulp novels set in the US South.

Focusing specifically on *City of Night* and *The Price of Salt*, we can better understand how the tension between the rural country and the urban city structures queer literature during the early stages of the gay and lesbian civil rights movement, extending roughly from the founding of the Mattachine Society in 1950 until the Stonewall uprising in 1969.1 Elements of both novels echo key aims of this burgeoning movement. *City of Night* portrays large cities as queer spaces in which a variety of sexual practices can flourish while *The Price of Salt* imagines the transformative power of queer love. Not only do they advance these goals while maintaining a focus on both urban and rural spaces missing from historical accounts that only focus on cities like San Francisco and New York, but it is actually through this juxtaposition of rural and urban spaces that *City of Night* and *The Price of Salt* can gesture towards what José Muñoz calls "queer futurity," an impossible-to-imagine queer "then and there" that transcends the limits of the here and now (97). Extending beyond the political realities of the early moments of the gay and lesbian civil rights struggle, these novels enable us to conceptualize both the city and the country as queer, potentially utopian spaces.

Historicizing the City and the Country in Cold War Queer Literature

This spatial opposition between the city and the country has a particular relevance for mid-twentieth-century queer literature. As John D'Emilio's pioneering essay "Capitalism and Gay Identity" (1983) demonstrates, the migration from rural to urban spaces required by capitalist industry was central to the development of the LGBT+ civil rights movement in the United States:

> In divesting the household of its economic independence and fostering the separation of sexuality from procreation, capitalism has created the conditions that allow some men and women to organize a personal life around their erotic/emotional attraction to their own sex. It has made possible the formation of urban communities of lesbians and gay men and, more recently, of a politics based on sexual identity. ("Capitalism" 7)

In D'Emilio's account, the process of capitalist industrialization inadvertently created the foundations for a collective gay identity. For example, D'Emilio discusses how urban spaces like gay and lesbian bars, cruising spots, bathhouses, social clubs, and YMCAs create the possibility of "a group life" for lesbians and gay men ("Capitalism" 8-9). It was precisely these sorts of collectivities that allowed for the formation of political organizations like the Mattachine Society and the Daughters of Bilitis, the latter of which even originated as a social club providing a space for lesbians to meet outside of bars (Faderman 76).

As Halberstam argues, however, historical narratives that focus exclusively on rural-to-urban migration risk naturalizing queer metronormativity, thereby limiting the kinds of identities that are legible as "queer." Not only does queer metronormativity silence the experiences of queers living in rural areas, but it misses how these rural spaces might allow for innovative forms of queer expression or politics. Instead, metronormativity represents the queer as inherently urban by equating the process of moving to the city with the process of "coming out of the closet": "the metronormative narrative maps a story of migration onto the coming-out story . . . since each narrative bears the same structure, it is easy to equate the physical journey from small town to big city with the psychological journey from closet case to out and proud" (Halberstam 36-37). So while queer urban enclaves do indeed create the conditions of possibility for a collective queer identity, we should not reify these spaces as the only ones in which a queer identity is imaginable.

Halberstam's juxtaposition of "coming out" narratives and metronormativity is particularly useful in the Cold War context. In an essay on "the closet" and the Cold War, Michael Bibler rejects "coming out of the closet" as a universal paradigm for queer self-definition, arguing that it is not particularly well suited to pre-Stonewall gay and lesbian cultures. While "coming out" would become key to the development of LGBT+ civil rights after Stonewall, many queers responded to the vicious harassment of the early Cold War period "not by embracing or lamenting the secrecy of the closet, but by asking for the right of the privacy of the closet" (Bibler 123). Furthermore, in a brief reading of *The Price of Salt*, Bibler suggests that a theorization of privacy is more relevant to the novel than the concept of the closet: "what these women want is not to be invisible but to be left alone" (133). As we will see later, *The Price of Salt* also reconfigures this opposition as a geographic one: the rural Midwest provides the women privacy to act on their sexual desire, while the city is associated with the Cold War surveillance state.

Indeed, the Cold War surveillance state provides a significant reason for queer people in the early 1950s to value privacy over the ability to gather in spaces that would reveal their sexuality. As D'Emilio notes, while urban enclaves allowed for a collective gay identity, they also exposed gays to the outside world: "should society find a reason to persecute its homosexual members' activity, the changing structure of gay life guaranteed that it would locate them" (*Sexual Politics* 40). Such a reason would be found in the McCarthy era, during which gays were labeled "national security risks" because of their alleged susceptibility to blackmail by communist agents (41-43).[2] Then, after the 1950 Senate investigations into homosexuals in the government, the era's security apparatus began to target sexual minorities: the FBI began compiling data on gay bars (46-47) and local police forces began vicious crackdowns on bars and cruising areas (49). The same urban spaces which allowed for the creation of a gay subjectivity also created the conditions for increased police surveillance and harassment. So while the city is a site of freedom from the familial and social pressures of rural life, rural spaces might in turn allow queers to escape the surveillance state of the city and live "under the radar."

A counter-metronormative theory of pre-Stonewall queer literature therefore needs to take both possibilities into account. While *City of Night* represents the city as a space in which queer relationships can flourish, *The Price of Salt* demonstrates how the country provides a degree of privacy for Carol and Therese. By representing queer sexuality in both the city and country, these texts enact a powerful critique of the Cold War era's attempt to silence queer identities and sexual practices. This is not to say that we should collapse the distinction between urban and rural spaces, however, or simply try to compare the different modalities of oppression that queers face in each. Rather, as Raymond Williams argues, they key is to move beyond a contrast between the city and the country and "go on to see their interrelationships and through these the real shape of our underlying crisis (297).[3] By attending to both the utopian possibilities and the limits of the city and country, we can reach beyond the limits of metronormativity to see a wider range of ways in which queer authors can draw attention to the homophobic oppression of the Cold War era and imagine forms of resistance.

This queer utopian hermeneutic reads the city and country opposition as a way in which we can imagine a better world, but the content of such a utopia cannot be given direct expression in either text. Rather, this utopian horizon should be imagined in the crisscrossing of city and country occurring in both novels. It is travel, rather than the stasis of either location, that defines the city/country opposition. In *City of Night*, the narrator travels to different cities throughout the course of the novel, each time finding a temporary utopia in the groups of hustlers and gay men he encounters. These "cities" are contrasted with an imagined "country" described by the narrator and the men he meets throughout the text. In contrast, *The Price of Salt* begins with the imprisonment of the city and imagines utopia through Therese and Carol's escape to the Midwest. Once again travel is central to the novel's narrative: they drive across the Midwest, trying to elude a detective sent to spy on them. While *City of Night* remains caught in an endless loop of travel between the

---

different cites of the novel, *The Price of Salt* points toward a queer utopian potentiality exceeding what was imaginable during the pre-Stonewall stage of the gay and lesbian Civil Rights Movement.

Queer Collectivities in *City of Night*[4]

City of Night is a semi-autobiographical tale of an unnamed young man who flees his home in El Paso, Texas, and begins a trek across the country, integrating himself into underground communities of queers and male hustlers in New York, Los Angeles, and New Orleans. The novel's episodic narrative structure emphasizes fleeting moments of connection with other young hustlers he meets in these cities. The novel is not exactly a travelogue, however: while locations like Times Square are described in detail, they are all subsumed under what the narrator calls "The City of Night," his designation for the "city" as an abstract concept (1) "The City of Night" functions in the novel as a figuration for a certain organization of social space: a site of sexual freedom existing below the radar of straight life. The same cast of characters and situations repeat themselves throughout the novel, making the specific makeup of a given city seem irrelevant. After traveling to Los Angeles from New York, the narrator notes the similarities between the two cities, stating, "Instantly I recognize the vagrant youngmen [*sic*] dotting those places: the motorcyclists without bikes, the cowboys without horses, AWOL servicemen or on leave . . . and I know that moments after arriving here, I have found an extension, in the warm if smoggy sun, of the world I had just left" (88). While the novel is about geographic movement, it is only the movement from city to city that is important.

Indeed, this is a novel of cities in which the country remains phantasmatic—it is literally skipped over when the narrator recounts his travels from city to city but still structures the unconscious of the text. It is almost as if the rural country can only be imagined in the movies. For instance, when talking to another hustler who envies the narrator's Texas home, the narrator:

> [smiles] now at the thought of his Texas and the Texas I had known: the city, not the plains of which he had dreamily conceived in

Georgia, longing for Cowboy Country. The cactusstrewn [*sic*] desert . . . not the cactus which for me had grown in a feeble cluster outside that window, in the vacant lot . . . the Texas I knew . . . Memories of the wind . . . like dirt . . . the tumbleweeds . . . my dead dog . . . That wind blowing not freely across the plains that threateningly sweeping the paved streets into that injured house . . . El Paso . . . Texas . . . for me, not the great-stretching, wide-plained land of the movies—but the crushing city where I had been raised in stifling love and hatred. (135, ellipses in original)

The recontextualization of Texas in this passage is particularly notable given the presence of the hustlers dressed as cowboys in the passage quoted above. The country, especially as imagined in western film, continues to exert a pull on the imaginary of these characters even when their lives are completely urban. In a reading of the classic hustler film *Midnight Cowboy* (1969), Kevin Floyd notes a similar "deterritorialization of the cowboy; a shuttling of this distinctly American image of both masculinity and nationalism out of the frontier and into the big city" (156). The gay urban cowboy transforms a heterosexual figure into a queer one—a process Floyd refers to as the "working of masculinity's weakness" (155)—which is a politically useful way of deconstructing an important icon of heteronormative masculinity. However, by recoding a rural signifier into an urban one, *The City of Night* also erases the possibility that this transformation could happen in the rural country, once again privileging the city as the only location for queer politics.

Without direct access to the country, "The City of Night" is imagined as completely insular: a utopian enclave indifferent to its actual geographic location. The hustlers in spaces like Times Square have a complex relationship to the outside world: "I saw the army of youngmen [*sic*] [. . .] pretending to be reading the headlines flashing across the Tower—but oblivious, really, of the world those headlines represent (but an integral part of it); concerned only with the frantic needs of Inside—*Now!!*" (29, emphasis in original). Through this separation from the straight world, the novel can imagine a queer collectivity: later the narrator describes "homosexuals ritualistically protectively assembled in one close area—like flotsam on the beach—as if symbolically defying the world that shut them out" (212). These queer enclaves allow for new forms of sociality and community extending beyond the social structures of the outside world. While the novel does not conceptualize these communities as political, they are precisely the kinds of locations that D'Emilio argues were central to the formation of a collective queer identity and, because they brought together large groups of queers who shared similar experiences of oppression, the LGBT+ Civil Rights Movement. These queer enclaves are also utopian examples of what Lauren Berlant and Michael Warner call queer culture building, or projects that "support forms of affective, erotic, and personal living that are public in the sense of accessible, available to memory, and sustained through collective activity" (203). Their mere existence is, as Rechy's narrator puts it, an act of defiance to the heteronormative world (212).

Indeed, these enclave spaces give the narrator a glimpse of a queer utopia. Participating in these communities allows him to experience a radically different way of being in the world:

> For me then there followed a period of untrammeled anarchy as a felt my life stretching toward some kind of symbolic night, as the number of people I went with multiplied daily. With those many people—only in those moments when I was desired . . . I felt an electric happiness, as if the relentless flow of life had stopped, poised on the very pinpoint of youth; and for those moments, youth was suspended unmoving. (120)

Through this representation of queer sexuality, the novel provides a glimpse of what life could be like without homophobic oppression. For José Muñoz, such moments are "an anticipatory illumination of a queer world, a sign of actually existing queer reality, a kernel of political possibility within a stultifying heterosexual present" (49). Rechy's narrator is "performing utopia" through his participation in these erotic encounters. While these moments are temporary, they unlock a vision of a better world. As "anticipatory illumination[s] of a queer world" (Muñoz 49), these momentary glimpses of utopia can sustain concrete political programs like the struggle for LGBT+ civil rights.

However, while the city allows for these utopian moments of connection, the novel does not imagine how they might develop into a collective queer politics. The novel instead focuses on the emotional emptiness of the city, represented through a series of failed romantic relationships that stand in allegorically for his inability to imagine queer futurity. In part, it is the temporariness of his sexual encounters: "I had an acute sense of the incompleteness intrinsic in sharing another's life. You touch those other lives, barely—however intimately it may be sexually . . . their lives will continue, you'll merely step out" (82). There are several points in the novel during which the narrator seems to fall in love with another man—with other hustlers in New York, a man he picks up in California, and finally a man named Jeremy in New Orleans—but is unable to imagine a future with any of them. Early in the novel, he and another hustler named Pete see "a French movie about lesbians in a girl's school"—presumably *Olivia* (Jacqueline Audry, 1951)—but while Pete can understand "guys making it with each other for money," he has difficulty imagining "two chicks could dig each other that tough" (47). Pete stays with the narrator that night, and the two fall asleep holding hands, after which they "were never together for long anymore" and soon actively avoid each other (49). Like the rural country, queer love is something that can only be realized in the movies.

The connection between queer love and the country is made explicit later in the novel, when the narrator contemplates a relationship with Jeremy while staying in New Orleans. Here, he explicitly opposes their potential relationship against his life as a hustler in the cities across America: "Cities joined together by emotional emptiness, blending with dark-city into a vastly stretching plain, into the city of night of the soul [. . .] Jeremy . . . the undiscovered country which may not even exist and which I was too frightened even to attempt to discover" (372). Here Jeremy—an "undiscovered country"—is the other term in the opposition between city and country. Once again, the novel creates an opposition between love and "the city." In a conversation with Jeremy, the narrator says that "he never loved any *one*" (347, emphasis in original). Jeremy tells him, "I think you could love me" (366). "Yes, maybe you're right," the narrator thinks to himself, "maybe I could love you. But I won't. The grinding streets awaited me" (368). The novel ends soon after with the narrator's return to his home in El Paso, and since the novel also begins in El Paso, its narrative structure forms a closed circular loop that refuses the promise of queer futurity.

Love and the Country in *The Price of Salt*[5]

A similar opposition between the city and the country also operates in *The Price of Salt*, although here "love" and the country are the primary terms opposed to the emptiness of the city.[6] In this novel, the city signifies heteronormative entrapment, beginning with the department store in which Therese is working part time during the holidays. In the first pages of the novel, Therese describes the store as "a single huge machine [. . .] They should have a church, too, she thought, and a hospital for the birth of babies. The store was organized so much like a prison, it frightened her now and then to realize she was part of it" (12). The machine-like store is then associated not only with the conventional confinement of a prison, but also the ideological entrapment that Lee Edelman calls "reproductive futurism," which "impose[s] an ideological limit on political discourse as such, preserving in the process that absolute privilege of heteronormativity" by framing the future exclusively through the image of the "Child" (2). Therese realizes these locations suggest a normative life narrative in which she would work at the department store, get married in a church, and give birth in a hospital.

At the beginning of the novel, she seems to be destined for precisely such a future: she is a struggling set designer whose boyfriend Richard is pressuring her into marriage. For Therese, this vision of the future is indeed a kind of prison:

> [She] knew it was the hopelessness that terrified her and nothing else [. . . .] The hopelessness of herself, of ever being the person she wanted to be and of doing the things that person would do . . . it was the terror of this hopelessness that made her want to shed the dress

and flee before it was too late, before the chains fell around her and locked. (23)

The repetition of the prison imagery in this passage is important because it juxtaposes space—the space of the department store but also that of the city itself—with an inability to imagine a positive—or queer—futurity. By defining the future solely in terms of heterosexual reproduction, reproductive futurity forecloses alternative visions of what it means to be an adult. This is why visions of utopia are so crucial for queer literature: they articulate alternate models of futurity that do not equate adulthood with heterosexual coupling and children. For Therese, the city—as figured by the department store—disallows any such alternatives.

Into this urban entrapment comes Carol, an older woman who meets Therese's gaze one day at the department store. Carol is associated with the country: her home is located outside of town in an isolated area, ensuring the women privacy when she invites Therese to visit. This association is further secured when Carol invites Therese on a road trip "out west" so that Carol can get away from the pressures of her contested divorce with Harge, who is trying to use Carol's sexuality in order to gain custody of their daughter.

It is the country that unlocks the possibility of queer sexuality for Carol and Therese, evidenced in part as Highsmith utilizes nature imagery to describe the progression of the couple's relationship, deepening further the association of the country with the possibility of a queer utopia. After they spend a Sunday afternoon together at Carol's country house, Therese "flung herself on her bed and drew a line with a pencil on a piece of paper. And another line, carefully, and another. A world was born around her, like a bright forest with a million shimmering leaves" (74). This imagined world provides Therese with an alternative to the feelings of restriction that the novel associates with the city. Similar imagery is used when they act on their feelings for each other: after they kiss for the first time in Waterloo and cuddle together in bed, Therese thinks "happiness was like a green vine spreading through her, stretching fine tendrils, bearing flowers through her flesh. She had a vision of a pale white flower, shimmering as if seen in darkness, or through water" (189). In this passage, Highsmith's language combines eroticism with visions of unruly wildlife, situating their romantic and sexual desire far away from the machine of the city.

It is through their journey west that Highsmith is able to gesture toward a queer utopia that would provide an alternative to reproductive futurism. Muñoz argues that "to see queerness as horizon is to perceive it as a modality of ecstatic time in which the temporal stranglehold that I describe as straight time is interrupted or stepped out of" (32). Therese finds precisely such an alternative temporal mode when the couple stops for a night in the Colorado Mountains:

> Once they came upon a little town they liked and spent the night there, without pajamas or toothbrushes, without past or future, and the night became another of those islands in time, suspended somewhere in the heart or in the memory, intact and absolute. Or perhaps it was nothing but happiness, Therese thought, a complete happiness that must be rare enough, so rare that very few people ever knew it. But if it was merely happiness, then it had gone beyond the ordinary bounds and become something else, become a kind of excessive pressure. (214)

Sexual pleasure here is divorced from the chronology of "straight time"—the past and future—and invokes a modality of happiness that seems to exceed language itself. Crucially, this temporal utopian leap is grounded within a certain organization of space. It is the freedom to be apart from the eyes of heteronormative culture that unlocks the vison of utopia in this passage. The phrase "islands of time" captures precisely this temporal and spatial relationship.

This utopia is short-lived, however, as a private detective sent by Carol's ex-husband repeatedly catches up to them. Shortly after their night in the mountains, they spot the detective and discover the Dictaphone he has been using to record them for Harge to use in the divorce proceedings (218). When they confront the detective, he explicitly tells Carol to go back to New York, which she eventually does. The detective is thus associated with the city: he uses advanced technology that contrasts with the nature imagery dominating these passages, he is from New York himself, and it is his presence that forces Carol and eventually Therese to return there. As Victoria Hesford argues, "The detective sent on their trail becomes a symbol and enactor of surveillance—an extension of the City of spectacle they have just left" (134). Finally, the detective marks the return of homophobic oppression:

> [Therese] remembered the detective's face and the barely legible expression that she realized now was malice. It was malice she had seen in his smile, even as he said he was on no side, and she could feel in him a desire that was actually personal to separate them, because he knew they were together. She had seen just now what she had only sensed before, that the whole world was ready to become their enemy. (230)

Here, the contradiction between the city and the country comes to the forefront of the text, as the intrusion of the city into their rural moments of utopia brings with it all of the forces potentially aligned against the couple. While their time in the West provided a utopian escape from this oppression, the detective's return serves as a reminder of how precarious such a sense of security is for queer individuals.

Unlike *City of Night*, which remains caught in an endless loop of travel, *The Price of Salt* imagines a more positive solution to the city/country contradiction. Therese comes back to the city transformed: she remembers how a certain street once filled her with "a sense of oppression" but now "filled her with tense excitement, made her want to plunge headlong into it, down the sidewalk with all the signs and theater marquees and rushing, bumping people" (273). Her experience with Carol in the Midwest has changed her experience of the city. It is also from within this transformed subjectivity that she can reimagine her relationship with Carol:

> It was Carol she loved and would always love. Oh, in a different way now, because she was a different person and it was like meeting Carol all over again, but it was still Carol and no one else. It would be

Carol, in a thousand cities, a thousand houses, in foreign lands where they would go together, in heaven and in hell. (287)

Her love for Carol breaks free of geography, allowing Therese to imagine a utopia that is not limited to the country. Their love is no longer imagined as an escape from the city, but as a transformation of the world.

While such a political transformation cannot be directly imagined in the text, the novel's justifiably famous ending points toward this utopian horizon. The couple's reunion suggests a suspension of time: their gazes meet in a restaurant where Therese has rushed to join Carol and the novel ends with the sentence, "Therese walked toward her" (287). Therese walks toward her, but the novel never describes their meeting. This is where they step out of straight time; the novel gestures toward a queer utopia it cannot put into words. On the one hand, this suspension suggests the limits of the historical moment: it is impossible for Highsmith to imagine them reaching each other while still in the public space of the city. However, this suspension of time is also a provocation, a reminder that utopias have to be brought about through organized political struggle. Only the ongoing struggle for queer liberation can fulfill the promise of the novel's happy ending. The novel's vision of queer love is an animating force for queer politics because it is "an insistence on potentiality or the concrete possibility for another world" (Muñoz 1).

Civil Rights Literature and LGBT+ Politics: A Direction Moving Forward

While these novels do not directly give expression to the political possibilities of the burgeoning gay and lesbian civil rights organizations like the Mattachine Society and the Daughters of Bilitis, their insistence on the right to occupy public places or to be with the person one loves without the threat of harassment or physical violence mirrors key political goals of these groups. Read together, these novels insist on the visibility of both queer sexuality and queer love in the face of the Cold War era's institutionalized homophobia. These novels are also both fundamentally about the claiming of space: the space to explore the possibility of erotic encounters but also the space to be left alone. While the goals and tactics of the LGBT+ movement would grow immensely following the radical utopian possibility unlocked by the Stonewall rebellion, this focus on space remains a key element of queer politics. It is also worth returning to pre-Stonewall-era literature, which reminds us that this queer utopian imagination is not reducible to either city or country but can be understood as a potentiality embedded in the tension between these different spaces. This potentiality is nothing less than queer futurity itself, which it is still our task to bring about.

Notes

1. See Lillian Faderman's history *The Gay Revolution* (2015), pages 53-168, for an account of the early gay and lesbian civil rights movement and the differences between this era and what she calls the post-Stonewall "new gay politics." Following Faderman, I will also use terminology consistent with historical usage: when describing the pre-Stonewall civil rights struggle, I will use "gay and lesbian." When describing the movement as a whole (from 1950 to the present), I will use "LGBT+." In instances when I am not directly referring to the civil rights struggle, I have used "queer," by which I simply mean not (hetero)normative. While "LGBT+" names positive identity categories that are crucial for civil rights discourse, "queer" is more expansive in that it is not an identity category but an open signifier that, as José Muñoz argues, "exists as an ideality that can be distilled from the past and used to imagine a future" (1).

2. See Robert Corber's *Homosexuality in Cold War America* (1997) and David K Johnson's *Lavender Scare* (2004).

3. For a related framework informing my conceptualization of the city/country opposition, see Fredric Jameson's "The Politics of Utopia," in which he theorizes the relationship between the city and the country in science fiction. Jameson proposes that we should imagine each term "negatively," as a critique of the other (50). The goal is an ideological "neutralization," or a utopian neither/nor position that can open a space to imagine the radically new (50). For a discussion of the value of "neutralization" for queer theory, see my essay "Narrative, Temporality, and Neutralization in Sarah Orne Jewett's Queer Utopias" in *South Atlantic Review* (2016), in which I argue that neutralization is a way to break free of the heteronormative modes of temporality structuring the nineteenth-century realist novel.

4. Unless otherwise noted, all quotations in this section are from John Rechy's *City of Night*.

5. Unless otherwise noted, all quotations in this section are from Patricia Highsmith's *The Price of Salt*.

6. The importance of space in *The Price of Salt* has been explored in criticism of the novel, particularly in Victoria J. Hesford's essay, "A Love Flung Out of Space." Where my account differs is the importance of the city and country: Hesford argues that Waterloo and the other rural areas the couple visits are "merely an extension, or a displaced manifestation, of a space offered the lovers in the City" (129). In contrast, I read these spaces in opposition.

Works Cited

Berlant, Lauren, and Michael Warner. "Sex in Public." *Publics and Counterpublics*. By Michael Warner. New York: Zone, 2002. 187-208.

Bibler, Michael B. "The Cold War Closet." *The Cambridge Companion to American Gay and Lesbian Literature*. Ed. Scott Herring. New York: Cambridge UP, 2015. 122-138.

Corber, Robert J. *Homosexuality in Cold War America: Resistance and the Crisis of Masculinity*. Durham: Duke UP, 1997.

D'Emilio, John. "Capitalism and Gay Identity." *Making Trouble: Essays on Gay History, Politics, and the University*. New York: Routledge, 1992. 3-16.

_____. *Sexual Politics, Sexual Communities: The Making of a Homosexual Minority in the United States, 1940–1970*. Chicago: U of Chicago P, 1983.

Edelman, Lee. *No Future: Queer Theory and the Death Drive*. Durham: Duke UP, 2004.

Faderman, Lillian. *The Gay Liberation: The Story of a Struggle*. New York: Simon and Schuster, 2015.

Floyd, Kevin. *The Reification of Desire: Toward a Queer Marxism*. Minneapolis: U of Minnesota P, 2009.

Halberstam, Jack. *In a Queer Time and Place: Transgender Bodies, Subcultural Lives*. New York: New York UP, 2005.

Herring, Scott. *Another Country: Queer Anti-Urbanism*. New York: New York UP, 2010.

Hesford, Victoria J. "'A Love Flung Out of Space': Lesbians in the City in Patricia Highsmith's *The Price of Salt*. Paradoxa 18 (Summer 2003): 117-135.

Highsmith, Patricia. *The Price of Salt*. New York: Norton, 2004.

Jameson, Fredric. "The Politics of Utopia." *New Left Review* 25.1 (Winter 2004): 35–54.

Johnson, David K. *The Lavender Scare: The Cold War Persecution of Gays and Lesbians in the Federal Government*. Chicago: U of Chicago P, 2004.

King, Derrick. "Narrative, Temporality, and Neutralization in Sarah Orne Jewett's Queer Utopias." *South Atlantic Review* 81.4 (Winter 2016). 12-27.

Percelay, Rachel. "Right Wing Media: 'Lesbian and Transgender Hillbillies Are the Latest Threat to Conservatism." *Media Matters for America*. Media Matters for America, 19 Aug. 2016. 30 Jan. 2017.

Muñoz, José. *Cruising Utopia: The Then and There of Queer Futurity*. New York: New York UP, 2009.

Rechy, John. *City of Night*. New York: Grove P, 1963.

Williams, Raymond. *The Country and the City*. New York: Oxford UP, 1975.

"B(l)ack up on the Shelf: The Erasure of Black Queerness in Martin Luther King Jr.'s *Why We Can't Wait*"_____

Robert LaRue

Reflecting on the African-American Civil Rights Movement and the 1963 March on Washington for Jobs and Freedom, historian John D'Emilio asks, "Why have we forgotten Bayard Rustin?" (12). "How," D'Emilio continues, "could [Rustin] have figured so prominently at the time and yet be so peripheral to historical memory today?" (12). Furthermore, D'Emilio questions, "What do we suppress when we forget him?" (12). On the one hand, D'Emilio's queries demand answers because, by many accounts, Rustin helped define social protest as we currently conceive of it. In addition to his leadership during the 1963 March on Washington for Jobs and Freedom and providing black protestors access to important political figures, such as Lyndon B. Johnson, Rustin served as a close friend and advisor to Martin Luther King Jr. As his advisor, Rustin helped King see the value in and power of nonviolent protesting. Rustin was also instrumental in helping King expand his ideas so that they came to include economic and social revolution for all underprivileged peoples. Therefore, attending to Rustin's absence provides a better understanding of the values resting at the heart of the Civil Rights Movement.

On the other hand, D'Emilio's queries speak to a much deeper problem, a problem of which Rustin is only the most apparent example. Questioning the absence—or what this essay terms "the erasure"—of Rustin points to a more pervasive tendency: the tendency to assume black leadership, or dare it be said, black power, as solely heterosexual. This is part of a trend throughout history in which the black community has been stereotyped as a monolithic unit. During America's foundational period, for example, the pervading idea was that blacks were little more than property, and after the emancipation of the slaves, the prevailing stereotype was that blacks were lazy and unproductive. It was against such stereotypes that black individuals such as Phillis Wheatley, Frederick Douglass, Harriet Jacobs,

Booker T. Washington, and William Edward Burghardt Du Bois fought.[1] Contemporaneously, monolithic notions of blackness can be found in the assumption that black men are "thugs" or potential criminals or that black women are welfare queens. And like their predecessors, individuals such as William Julius Wilson, Karyn R. Lacy, and Eugene Robinson have all worked to show the diversity of the black community.[2] Nonetheless, while attempts have been made to diversify the representations of blackness, comparatively few of these attempts have sought to call attention to sexual difference, especially as it pertains to the Civil Rights Movement.[3] Therefore, in addition to contributing to a better understanding of the guiding values of the Civil Rights Movement, Rustin's experience proves instructive for those currently continuing the battle for civil rights.

The Legacy of a Movement: Why King, and Why *Why We Can't Wait*?

This essay directly responds to D'Emilio's concern for the marginalizing of Rustin, by arguing that Rustin has been pushed to the periphery, in part, because of a transition of black (American) bodies from one form of materiality (corporeal—that is, bodily materiality) to another form of materiality (capital-ism—that is, exchangeable goods). One crucial way in which this transition manifests is through the production of texts aimed at re-presenting blacks as productive—and (re)producing—American citizens. To be clear, this is not to suggest that King's textual production was a new concept. As Henry Louis Gates Jr. argues, for centuries, "[t]he production of literature was taken to be the central arena in which persons of African descent could, or could not, establish and redefine their status within the human community," though "black people . . . had to represent themselves as 'speaking subjects' before they could even begin to destroy their status as objects, as commodities, within Western culture" (*The Signifying Monkey* 129). Or, put in different terms, given that black individuals have been using the production of texts as a means for redefining notions of blackness ever since Wheatley's time,[4] it is not King's writing of a text per se that is of importance here.[5] What is of importance is that King's textual production and the marginalizing of Rustin that accompanied it are strategically employed as an additional tool for the construction of a new image of blackness precisely at the point when black social demands were receiving the most public attention.

By examining the discourse surrounding the March on Washington for Jobs and Freedom, as presented within Martin Luther King Jr.'s text, *Why We Can't Wait* (1964), this essay takes seriously Robert Reid-Pharr's suggestion that "'blackness' is as much a fetish object for Black Americans as it is for whites" (*Once* 129). To this end, the essay works to demonstrate how the production of a consumable text and the desire to re-present a marketable black body intermingle, leading to the marginalization of queer figures, like Rustin. King and the Civil Rights Movement, rather than the Black Power Movement, are given focus precisely because such a focus prevents the assertion that homophobia is the product of a militant black mindset commonly associated with black nationalism.[6] As Henry Louis Gates Jr. points out, homophobia "is an almost obsessive motif that runs through the major authors of the Black Aesthetic and the Black Power movements," where "national identity became sexualized in the 1960s, in such a way as to engender a curious subterranean connection between homophobia and nationalism" ("Black Man's Burden" 234). A focus on King, then, allows for an accounting of the larger and more pervasive structures at play in what is often attributed as "black homophobia." Importantly, not only does King's text offer a firsthand description of an important year in black history, a year in which blacks found themselves able to slide into the larger fabric of American society in ways they had previously been denied, but it also offers an examination of more than King's speeches, which are, more often than not—with the exception of his "Letter from Birmingham Jail" (1963)—the object of study.[7]

The presence of King's textual productions signals his efforts to communicate blackness on a number of different fronts. King's addresses to the black community were most often expressed as oral speeches delivered in person as he traveled from city to city, from town to town, meeting with congregations, activists, and individuals in those places.[8] *Why We Can't Wait*, however, aims to recount his travels and motivations for an audience that could not be present for his face-to-face addresses. More than anything, the narrative structure of the text works to provide an insider's look into the daily lives of blacks for white readers—for those readers who had no day-to-day southern Negro experiences—a point made clear by his inclusion of his "Letter from Birmingham Jail" in this text and by his many explanations of situations of which blacks would be well-aware. Redirecting attention to King and his relation to issues of homosexuality as presented in his text-based persona then allows a more complex understanding of the demands for posturing[9] (that is, the presentation of certain attitudes) required by needs to "represent"—or re-present—blackness for a larger American context—posturing that is often associated only with the more militant black nationalists, such as Eldridge Cleaver, Ishmael Reed, Amiri Baraka, and Nathan and Julia Hare.[10] In short, the emphasis on King, and the example of Bayard Rustin, arises from a desire to contest common narratives of an inherently homophobic black community and to facilitate a more nuanced understanding of public responses to queerness made by black individuals. More than simple acts of homophobia, or reflections of some intrinsic brutality, these responses, including King's *Why We Can't Wait*, often are and have been, at least in part, responses to the demands of the dominant American society.[11]

Defining Queer: Black Queers, Queer Blacks

Because it occupies a crucial place in the following argument, it is important to note the multiple meanings of the term *queer(ness)* being put forth in this argument. The first meaning, queer(ness) as something strange or not ordinary, needs little elaboration. The second, however, does. This second meaning of *queer(ness)*, implying homosexuality, as it is being applied to this discussion of 1963, is somewhat anachronistic. On the one hand, the term *queer* as it is being used here did not come into fashion until the 1980s when the spread of AIDS inspired gays and lesbians to vocally, and sometimes physically, protest social silences on the deaths suffered by the community. Similar to contemporary black usage of the term *nigga*, *queer* became an appropriation of a once negative term and was used as a means of unabashedly claiming one's sexual difference. Under such politics, movements such as ACT UP (AIDS Coalition to Unleash Power) and Queer Nation sought to contest what they saw as a mandate for heterosexuality. As Michael Warner has defined it, to be queer means to always be fighting about the ways in which:

> stigmatization is connected with gender, the family, notions of individual freedom, the state, public speech, consumption and desire, nature and culture, maturation, reproductive politics, racial and national fantasy, class identity, truth and trust, censorship, intimate life and social display, terror and violence, health care, and deep cultural norms about the bearing of the body. (xiii)

Somewhat ironically, however, *queer* has risked becoming an umbrella term, sheltering everyone from homosexuals to heterosexuals who refuse the tradition of marriage. As queer theorist Annamarie Jagose notes, "As queer is unaligned with any specific identity category, it has the potential to be annexed profitably to any number of discussions" (2). This is to say, *queer* maintains a fluidity that allows it to crop up in the least suspecting of places. It is this fluidity, and slight irony, onto which this essay latches in order to build its case. It is crucial to recognize that at the very heart of attempts to re-write blackness—whether they be Wheatley's, Douglass', Washington's, Du Bois', Wilson's, or Lacy's—exists a desire to disassociate blackness from notions of queerness. Or, to put this differently, in those attempts to show that blacks are or can be just like everyone else creeps an anxiety about the perceived queerness of being different. Rather than avoid the association, this essay seeks it out. However, this anxiety is not pursued so as to call forth what might be called King's homophobia; it is pursued so as to examine what also sits behind it. In this way, this essay takes seriously its own warning against presenting a monolithic answer. Following Hortense J. Spillers' suggestion that America "needs [blackness], and if [it] were not here, [it] would have to be invented" (65), this essay works to demonstrate that King's anxiety, as presented via his text, points more towards a desire to respond to that which American society demands of him than it does to his own sentiments and fears.[12]

Why We Can't Wait: Writing Strategically

Published in July of 1964, eight months before Daniel Patrick Moynihan published his highly controversial report, *The Negro Family: The Case for National Action* (1965), and established the black family as queerly matriarchal and, therefore, dysfunctional, King's *Why We Can't Wait* sought to fill in the "part[s] of history which ha[ve] been censored by the white writers and purchasers of board-of-education books" (King ix). In its move to recover a censored history, however, the text also demonstrates an investment in writing out the queerness of black images, as King never explains the ways in which queer blacks, just like their heterosexual counterparts, have also "done more than their share" of labor (ix) or on the picketing lines, as demonstrated by Rustin. This omission is all the more glaring considering King's decision to narrate the events culminating in the 1963 March on Washington for Jobs and Freedom, an event in which Rustin's labor should be most visible, since he served as the march's principle organizer. Nowhere is this omission more apparent than in the following passage:

> It took daring and boldness to embrace the idea. The Negro community was firmly united in demanding a redress of grievances, but it was divided on tactics. It had demonstrated its ability to organize skillfully in single communities, but there was no precedent for a conviction of national scope and gargantuan size. Complicating the situation were innumerable prophets of doom who feared that the slightest incidence of violence would alienate Congress and destroy all hope of legislation. Even Without disturbances, they were afraid that inadequate support by Negroes would reveal weaknesses that were better concealed (King 112).

It is clear that King is interested in recounting the events for those unfamiliar with the scope, power, and significance of the Negro

Revolution of 1963. Opening with the novel yet polarizing idea to conduct a single massive march, King then explains the success of what many thought would be a failure, yet he curiously leaps from beginning to end in spite of his recognition that the mere idea of such a task was enough to strike fear into the hearts of many within—and outside of—the Negro movement. As with the pages that precede this quotation, nowhere is there a mention of Rustin, "the man who, more than anyone, made the March on Washington happen" (D'Emilio 12) or the leadership roles he undertook in earlier civil rights protests.[13] King's omission of Rustin should, then, be taken not as a simple matter of "omitting" but as an active writing out of a key figure in the march's organizing and success.

It might be suggested that Rustin's absence from the text results from King's desire to avoid praising an individual in lieu of the movement itself, which could be supported by the tendency of King's rhetoric to emphasize the community rather than the individual. After all, King's stated purpose is to shed light on not only the choice and power of "nonviolent direct action" (King 12) but also on the Negro "group [that] seized the streets, the squares, the sacrosanct business thoroughfares and the marbled halls of government to protest and proclaim the unendurability of their oppression" (2). However, a re-examination of the quoted passage suggests this is not entirely accurate. In his description, King singles out A. Philip Randolph, the "dean of Negro leaders" (112), as the progenitor of the march. Yet, it is not enough for King to refer to Randolph as a "great" leader, which he no doubt was, or to submit that in proposing the march, Randolph was speaking for the spirit of the people. Instead, King elevates Randolph to the highest level of veneration and, in the process, makes him more than the community, making him a trans-communal voice. According to King, it is in response to the events of the summer of 1963 that Randolph proposes his "answer"; the community, when it reenters the picture, simply has to respond to that answer. Moreover, the veneration of Randolph succeeds numerous other individuals (Rev. Fred Shuttlesworth, Ralph Abernathy, and Harry Belafonte, to name a few) whose hard work and valiant efforts contributed to the success of the Negro Revolution, culminating in the march, and whom King names throughout his text. Therefore, while it can be said that King preferred raising the community over its individuals, this response oversimplifies the erasure of Rustin.

The question then remains: if Randolph and others are venerated, why was Rustin, quite literally, erased from these pages? One might offer King's role as a Southern Baptist preacher or his increasing "commit[ment] to economic radicalism" (Jones 34). Yet, as Michael G. Long suggests, rather than reading King's emphasis on personal strength over religious conviction as a misstep for the Baptist leader, one should recognize that in selecting his emphasis, King "identified himself with liberal pastoral counselors of his time and separated himself from ministerial colleagues and fellow Christians who used [the Bible and Christian theology] to condemn" (55). Interestingly, in his description of the moments leading up to the march, of the effects of the march, and of the treatment of the march, not once does he reference the Bible. Instead, everything mentioned he discusses according to the earthly efforts of the Negro. As King notes, it is *the Negro's* organization and *his* determination to stand "in majestic dignity as witnesses to their single-minded determination to achieve democracy in *their* time [emphasis added]" (King 113) that led to the new respect brought about by the march.

The very structure of *Why We Can't Wait* suggests that the text is not only, if at all, for black Americans, as he narrates experiences with which blacks would be knowledgeable (e.g., the bombing of the church in Birmingham or the impossibility of sitting at a lunch counter in the South). Such narration stands in stark contrast to the face-to-face speeches, meetings, and advice columns King used to converse with the black community (Long 39-53). In fact, as Long notes, while speaking directly to a black audience, King personally responded to a young boy who wrote his advice column seeking help with his homosexuality (39-53). So, it is beyond safe to say that King is neither oblivious nor unsympathetic to the presence of queers within the black community. This text, then, seems invested in further presenting blacks as respectable and determined citizens not for blacks themselves but for a white readership who, at worst, were on the fence about the place of blacks in society and those who, at best, might consider themselves "moderates" on the issue. To this end, black queerness becomes a dangerous quality, threatening this project and must therefore be erased. By erasing the presence of Rustin, King is able to bring his notion of blackness one step closer to being in line with mainstream society's heterosexual narrative.[14]

An economic mandate for the erasure of queer presences can be found in King's desire to create "a new and wholesome healing" (King 142). This mandate touches on both meanings of the term as used in this essay. On the one hand, King's concept of the "wholesome" points to the residue of the heteronormative marketing practices that surround both black representation and textual production. The appeal to a "wholesome" healing harkens back to King's (re) positioning the black community as a "wholesome" family unit, as he does in his discussion of his time in the Birmingham jail (62). On the other hand, King's concept of "wholesome" displays the privation daily experienced by the Negro. King, and the Negro community, intends to make clear that "equality meant dignity and dignity demanded a job that was secure and a pay check that lasted throughout the week" (10). Not only does "wholesome" suggest the proper way things should be, but it also suggests the necessity for the economic means with which to secure the family, which stands at the heart of American society. In making this connection, King connects the Negro cause with the underlying capitalist spirit of America as a way to sell the Negro cause as viable and productive for America. The Negro, when one looks beyond the smoke, the gas, and the pickets, is presented as simply wanting to be a part of the American family.

King's positioning of the family as an intricate part of the capitalist system is in direct line with the capitalist logic of reproduction as proposed by Karl Marx in volume one of *Das Kapital* (1867). According to Marx, capitalism can only sustain itself if and when it sustains its labor force through a process of continual reproduction (69). This is to say, in order for capitalism to continue, workers must continue having children who will then grow up to become workers in the capitalist system. And while the cycle permits a number of individuals to replace the owners of capital (that is, to become bosses), this founding principle of this exchange remains the same. Under the capitalist system, bodies become part of "the production of commodities, their circulation, and the more developed form of their circulation called commerce" (59). What is important to point out here is that, as they participate in the production of consumable goods, laboring bodies work to naturalize heterosexuality as the foundation of the capitalist system by leaving uncontested the ways in which non-reproducing bodies (i.e., sexually queer bodies) also contribute to the labor process. In a similar way, in publishing his argument for a white readership without drawing attention to the labors of queer individuals such as Rustin, King becomes complicit in the construction of a presumably heterosexual and dequeered, black laboring body.

Critical of Marx's heterosexual foundation, Andrew Parker posits Marx's inability or unwillingness to think of other forms and uses of sex as the result of his own anxiety about his relationship with his friend, and often coauthor, Friedrich Engels. This is to say, "Marx may have realized, in effect, that it takes one to know one" (Parker 29). It, then, becomes possible to see how the circulation of texts made it possible to silence queer black voices/presences. In a similar way, King found his relationship with Rustin questioned by Representative Adam Clayton Powell Jr., who threatened to have Rustin presented to the press as his gay lover (Long 75). In response to this threat, King chose to have Rustin publically "step down as [his] assistant," relegating Rustin's involvement to "behind the scenes" support (76). The equivalent of this request comes in King's omission of Rustin from the body of his text, *Why We Can't Wait*. Rather than reflecting a sense of homophobia, King's response to have Rustin step down, and his decision to not include Rustin in his discussion of the 1963 march, reflects his anxiety over the media's power to topple the image of the black community he was working to construct. As Rustin explained after the incident, "King 'was terrified of the press'" (qtd. in Long 75).

King's strategic erasure of queerness becomes apparent on two levels: on one level, King's reliance on economic equality as a way to wedge the black man into society not only worked to counter the notion of the lazy, disinterested black man but also to reaffirm the black man's commitment to the process of procreation that grounded social values. On another level, King's concept of "wholesome[ness]" becomes less about Rustin's actual sexuality and more about how it would be perceived by the rest of the world and how that perception might impact the image King worked to present. He performs this task by emphasizing the domesticity of blackness, such as his wife and home, and then, at other times, remaining silent on—that is, erasing evidence of—matters of sex and sexuality. Queerness, as either difference or homosexuality, was not a possible point of power or resistance. Given the moment in which he is writing, King is without the expanded notion of queerness that it is permitted today. He is, therefore, not in a position to wield the political force of queerness sought by Warner and other proponents of queerness today. Consequently, erasure became the only available means he saw for shoring up the notion of an acceptable black body.

"When My Brother Fell": The Importance of Re-Membering Black Queerness

To conclude, in "Brother to Brother," Joseph Beam insists that "we take care of our own kind when the night grows cold and silent" and that "these days the nights are cold-blooded and the silence echoes with complicity" (191). By proposing that Martin Luther King Jr.'s 1964 text is a product grounded in a specific system of exchange and use, this essay has attempted to bring some warmth to our nights. This essay has sought to dissociate the black male from notions of an inherent homophobia by arguing that, in part, this homophobia is the product of the language of the text, which mandates a validation and reproduction of the heteronormative framework grounding not only the market of textual production but also the dominant American society in which those texts are disseminated. In order to aid "the average Negro . . . [in] his struggle to escape his circumstances" of "want and deprivation" (King 9), King must engage America in terms that the times understand: economics. This much is evident, as the title of the 1963 march shows us: the March on Washington for Jobs and Freedom.

But none of this is to suggest that the complicities of texts such as King's are off the hook. Rather, while invested in dissociating the black male from the assumption of an inherent homophobia, this essay has been equally invested in reminding readers of the consequences of forgetting that "*the master's tools will never dismantle the master's house*" (Lorde 112), so long as those tools retain their original anxieties. As Charles Nero points out, overwhelmingly, the production of black texts has promoted heterosexuality as the de facto state of blackness, thus erasing gay and lesbian experiences (229). We must yearn, as Robert Reid-Pharr contends, "for a vision of the good, for a public dialogue and a civic life that celebrates multiplicity, that prizes ambiguity, that recognizes the play of identity and difference that makes possible community as well as change" (*Black Gay* 175). However, in order to make this vision a reality, we must first recognize what legacies we are carrying on.

Therefore, while this essay began by questioning what we risk when we forget Rustin, a reversal of such a question is in order: what do we gain when we remember him? More specifically, what do we gain when we remember that blackness and queerness have never been so far removed? Perhaps in remembering (or rememorying, to use Toni Morrison's powerful construction)[15] to ask what we gain by remembering Rustin, we might be able to actualize Cathy Cohen's hope for politics, one that embraces queerness, rather than eliding it (131).

Notes

1. For more information on Phillis Wheatley, Douglass, Jacobs, Washington, and Du Bois, see Henry Louis Gates Jr., *The Trials of Phillis Wheatley: America's First Black Poet and Her Encounters with the Founding Fathers* (2003); Frederick Douglass, *Narrative of the Life of Frederick Douglass, An American Slave* (1845); Harriet Jacobs, *Incidents in the Life of a Slave Girl* (1861); Booker T. Washington, *Up from Slavery* (1900); and W. E. B. Du Bois, *The Souls of Black Folk* (1903).

2. See William Julius Wilson, *More than Just Race: Being Black and Poor in the Inner City* (2009); Karyn R. Lacy, *Blue-Chip Black: Race, Class, and Status in the New Black Middle Class* (2007); Eugene Robinson, *Disintegration: The Splintering of Black America* (2010).

3. Though they do not focus on sexuality in the Civil Rights Era, for more scholars and authors who have traced the connection of black bodies to sexualizing histories in an attempt to account for the connections of racism to the body see: Frantz Fanon, *Black Skin, White Masks* (1952); Toni Morrison, *Beloved* (1987); Hortense J. Spillers, "Mama's Baby, Papa's Maybe: An American Grammar Book"; Isaac Julien and Kobena Mercer, "True Confessions: A Discourse on Images of Black Male Sexuality"; Siobhan B. Somerville, *Queering the Color Line: Race and the Invention of Homosexuality in American Culture* (2000); and Robert Reid-Pharr, *Once You Go Black: Choice, Desire, and the Black American Intellectual* (2007) and *Black Gay Man: Essays* (2001).

4. Part of the work of Wheatley's poetry was to attest to the capacity of blacks to produce culture and art on par with American and European minds.

5. For a more detailed discussion of the use of writing as a form of black protest, see Henry Louis Gates Jr., *The Signifying Monkey: A Theory of Afro-American Literary Criticism* (1988) and *Tradition and the Black Atlantic: Critical Theory in the African Diaspora* (2010); Alain Locke, *The New Negro: An Interpretation* (1925); Richard Wright, "Blueprint for Negro Writing" (1937); and James Baldwin, *Notes of a Native Son*, especially the essay "Everybody's Protest Novel" (1955).

6. Though manifested in various forms, some of which condoned the use of violence, the Black Power Movement sought both to instill a sense of racial pride in African Americans and to redress the many social inequalities daily experienced by blacks. In general, the movement believed it was impractical to wait for white society to change and therefore preferred more direct forms of action. Among other goals, the Black Power Movement sought sovereignty for black lives, full employment for black people, and adequate and appropriate housing.

7. For a cogent defense of the selection of King's writing over his oral speeches, see Wesley T. Mott, "The Rhetoric of Martin Luther King, Jr.: Letter from Birmingham Jail."

8. King also interacted with his black audience in a column he wrote for *Ebony* magazine between September 1957 and December 1958, entitled "Advice for Living."

9. For a detailed analysis of black attitudes and behavior, see Elijah Anderson, *Code of the Street: Decency, Violence, and the Moral Life of the Inner City* (1999). In this text, Anderson argues the importance of recognizing that black culture is guided by a need to negotiate power differences. Part of this negotiating is learning the proper "code" for survival.

10. Stating this does not mean to accuse all black nationalists or all members of the Black Power Movement of being homophobic or anti-homosexual. In fact, Black Panther Party cofounder, Huey P. Newton, suggests that "when

we have revolutionary conferences, rallies, and demonstrations, there should be full participation of the gay liberation movement and the women's liberation movement. . . . We should be willing to discuss the insecurities that many people have about homosexuality" (158). Newton goes so far as to caution "using those terms that might turn our friends off. The terms 'faggot' and 'punk' should be deleted from our vocabulary, and especially we should not attach names normally designated for homosexuals to men who are enemies of the people, such as Nixon or Mitchell. *Homosexuals are not enemies of the people*" (159).

11. No attempt is made to apologize for these behaviors, nor is it suggested that there is no homophobia in the black community. To reiterate, this essay is less concerned with origins per se. It is concerned with assumptions. It aims to complicate how black responses to queerness are understood.

12. For a detailed analysis of Spillers' work, see Alexander G. Weheliye, *Habeas Viscus: Racializing Assemblages, Biopolitics, and Black Feminist Theories of the Human.*

13. For more details on the specifics of Rustin's efforts, see Nancy D. Kates and Bennett Singer, *Brother Outsider: The Life of Bayard Rustin* (2003), and William P. Jones, "The Unknown Origins of the March on Washington: Civil Rights Politics and the Black Working Class" (especially p. 38).

14. It is important to note that it is not until the Stonewall riots of 1969, and then the queer movements of the 1980s, that mainstream society becomes forced to move towards incorporating queerness (i.e., homosexuality) into its narrative.

15. For a definition of "Rememory," see Morrison's *Beloved*, (especially p. 36-37).

Works Cited

Beam, Joseph. "Brother to Brother: Words from the Heart." *In the Life: A Gay Black Anthology.* Ed. Joseph Beam. Boston: Alyson, 1986. 180-91.

Cohen, Cathy. "Death and Rebirth of a Movement: Queering Critical Ethnic Studies." *Social Justice* 37.4 (2011): 126-132.

D'Emilio, John. "Remembering Bayard Rustin." *OAH Magazine of History* 20.2 (Mar. 2006): 12-14.

Gates, Henry Louis, Jr. "The Black Man's Burden." *Fear of a Queer Planet: Queer Politics and Social Theory.* Ed. Michael Warner. Minneapolis: U of Minnesota P, 1993. 230-38.

_____. *The Signifying Monkey: A Theory of Afro-American Literary Criticism.* New York: Oxford UP, 1988.

hooks, bell. *We Real Cool: Black Men and Masculinity*. New York: Routledge, 2004.

Jagose, Annamarie. *Queer Theory: An Introduction*. New York: New York UP, 1997.

Jones, William P. "The Unknown Origins of the March on Washington: Civil Rights Politics and the Black Working Class." *Labor: Studies in Working-Class History of the Americas* 7.3 (2010): 33-52.

Julien, Isaac & Kobena Mercer. "True Confessions: A Discourse on Images of Black Male Sexuality." *Brother to Brother: New Writing by Black Gay Men*. Ed. Essex Hemphill. Boston: Alyson. 167-173.

King, Martin Luther, Jr. *Why We Can't Wait*. New York: Signet Classic, 2000.

Long, Michael G. *Martin Luther King Jr., Homosexuality, and the Early Gay Rights Movement: Keeping the Dream Straight?* New York: Palgrave Macmillan, 2012.

Lorde, Audre. *Sister Outsider: Essays and Speeches*. New York: Ten Speed, 1984.

Marx, Karl. *Das Kapital—Capital, Vol. 1: Critique of Political Economy*. Trans. Samuel Moore & Edward Aveling. Chicago: Aristeus, 2012.

Morrison, Toni. *Beloved*. New York: Plume, 1987.

Mott, Wesley T. "The Rhetoric of Martin Luther King Jr.: Letter from Birmingham Jail." *Phylon* 36.4 (4th Qtr., 1975): 411-21.

Moynihan, Daniel Patrick. United States. Department of Labor. Office of Policy Planning and Research. *The Negro Family: The Case for National Action*. Washington: GPO, 1965.

Nero, Charles I. "Toward a Black Gay Aesthetic: Signifying in Contemporary Black Gay Literature." *Brother to Brother: New Writing by Black Gay Men*. Ed. Essex Hemphill. Boston: Alyson. 229-52.

Newton, Huey P. "The Women's Liberation and Gay Liberation Movements; August 15, 1970." *The Huey P. Newton Reader*. Ed. David Hilliard & Donald Weise. New York: Seven Stories, 2002. 157-59.

Parker, Andrew. "Unthinking Sex: Marx, Engels, and the Scene of Writing." *Fear of a Queer Planet: Queer Politics and Social Theory*. Ed. Michael Warner. Minneapolis: U of Minnesota P, 1993. 19-41.

Reid-Pharr, Robert. *Black Gay Man: Essays*. New York: New York UP, 2001.

_____. *Once You Go Black: Choice, Desire, and the Black American Intellectual*. New York: New York UP, 2007.

Spillers, Hortense J. "Mama's Baby, Papa's Maybe: An American Grammar Book." *Diacritics*, 17.2 (Summer 1987): 64-81.

Warner, Michael. "Introduction." *Fear of a Queer Planet: Queer Politics and Social Theory.* Ed. Michael Warner. Minneapolis: U of Minnesota P, 1993. vii-xxxi.

Writing Civil Rights after James Byrd, after Matthew Shepard

Tasia Milton

Historically, classifying a bias-motivated crime as a "hate crime" has allowed the community to cast the incident as an aberration and the act as well as its perpetrators as anachronistic with the progressive present. Such an understanding releases the community from the responsibility of dismantling the systemic forces (e.g., racism, homophobia, sexism, and xenophobia) that produced such crimes.[1] For instance, the cities of Jasper and Laramie both claimed racialized and anti-gay violence were not values of their towns after the murders of James Byrd and Matthew Shepard in 1998. In Laramie, as Shepard lay in a hospital in Colorado, 450 anti-hate protestors marched in the University of Wyoming's homecoming parade, carrying signs with slogans including, "Hate Is Not a Small Town Value—No to Violence and Evil" and "No Hate Crimes in Wyoming." In Jasper, news outlets praised the townspeople's choice:

> Instead of living in simmering bitterness, instead of erupting in racial conflict, blacks and whites have joined in prayer vigils, rallies and sometimes just one-on-one discussions over chicken-fried steak, all intended to bind up the wounds caused by that crime and to show the outside world that what happened here hurt and outraged all the town's people, not just its blacks. (Bragg A8)

In both cases, the crimes committed by individuals cut how the towns perceived themselves and were perceived by others from the ideal image of a town free of violence and inclusive of all community members, thus requiring attempts at representational suture.

The conception of hate crimes as acts committed by strangers and people living on the fringes of the community, however, ignores the varieties of anti-LGBT violence that are intertwined with the pursuit of the fulfillment of sexual desire or platonic connection. Frequently in reports of hate crimes, an acquaintance or even a friend lures the victim. For example, Byrd and Shawn Berry knew each other because they shared a parole officer. Aaron McKinney and Russell Henderson masqueraded as gay to lure Shepard away from a campus hangout. In the case of the first crime prosecuted under the 2009 Matthew Shepard and James Byrd, Jr., Hate Crimes Prevention Act (HCPA), Kevin Pennington was lured by two women who he thought were his friends, after which he was attacked by cousins Anthony and David Jenkins as the two women watched and cheered. As poet Saeed Jones explains, the victims' desires for connection, natural of course, at times create the opportunity for violence:

> We take risks and we put other people in risky situations, whether it's physical or emotional. There's this very natural practice of the first kiss, of sneaking out of the house and going into the woods, of skinny dipping. And then, [for some men], when you're not a child anymore, and when you have a performance of masculinity to uphold—that's where the risk becomes violent, often. It's a reaction against fear. (qtd. in Halperin, "What It Means to Be 'Wanted'")

Implicit in this statement is the idea that identity is formed through our interactions with other people and through culture. Particularly, expressions of sexuality are a crucial aspect of identity, especially in the transition from adolescence to adulthood. In this case, cultural demands to maintain standards of masculinity deform the natural process of sexual exploration and boundary testing—issues that Jones seeks to tackle in his 2014 collection, *Prelude to Bruise*.

Background: Byrd, Shepard, and the Debate Over Hate Crime Legislation

Two events shape how we conceive of hate crimes in the present—the murders of James Byrd Jr. and Matthew Shepard. On the evening of June 7, Shawn Berry, Lawrence Russell Brewer, and John King offered Byrd a ride home in the East Texas town of Jasper. Instead of taking Byrd home, the three men took him into the woods, beat him, and dragged him, still conscious, behind their pickup truck for two miles. The descriptions of Byrd's body in newspaper accounts match the crime, brutal and unsparing:

> Byrd's body was found on the morning of June 7, torn apart as if some wild animal had set upon it. His torso was at the side of a country road. His head and an arm were just over a mile away, ripped from his body as it hit a concrete drainage culvert. Police marked a piece of flesh here, his dentures there, his keys somewhere else—75 red circles denoting body parts and belongings along a two-mile stretch of asphalt. Fingerprints were the only key to Byrd's identity. (Chua-Eoan & Hylton 34)

For many, Byrd's murder felt like a repetition-with-a-difference in the long line of violence perpetrated against black bodies since Reconstruction. This description of Byrd's body torn to pieces is reminiscent of descriptions of lynching in which a mob would take "souvenirs" from the remains of the deceased to commemorate the event. In fact, journalists as well as cultural critics and producers frequently compared Byrd's murder to the murder of Emmett Till nearly fifty years before. According to the media outlets narrativizing the crime, Byrd's murder was a natural outgrowth of a town "more Deep South than Lone Star—and still carries some of the baggage of the Old Confederacy" (Van Boven & Gesalman 33). What surprised the nation was that an all-white and majority-white juries convicted Byrd's murderers. The court sentenced Berry to life in prison and Brewer and King to death. Texas state senators would later use the convictions of the three men as evidence that legislation against hate crimes was unnecessary, arguing that present laws and punishments were enough.

Four months later in Laramie, Wyoming, Aaron McKinney and Russell Henderson robbed and tortured Matthew Shepard and left him to endure below freezing temperatures tied to a fence in a rural area. McKinney's romantic partner told police the men were motivated to commit the crime in part because of Shepard's sexual orientation; Shepard supposedly had embarrassed McKinney by making a sexual advance toward him. Like with the murder of James Byrd, the brutality of the crime inspired public outcry and unprecedented media coverage. The public was mesmerized by a "horrendous image—like the body of a waiflike young man strung up on a fence, his face so bloody from pistol-whipping that his flesh shows only through the streaks of his tears" (Goldstein 64). As a result, Shepard—a blonde, five-foot, two-inch, 105-pound college freshman with the face of the boy next door—became the face of a shift in the gay rights movement. Rather than use open resistance, subversion, and cleaving to queer subcultures, organizations such as the Human Rights Campaign (HRC) turned to humanizing images that show the LGBTQ community living in accord with mainstream, heterosexual values.[2] That the public attributed innocence to Shepard and identified with his upper-middle-class background was in line with this agenda. Ultimately, juries convicted McKinney and Henderson of Shepard's murder and sentenced them to life in prison.

Although the deaths of both men sparked debate about the continued necessity of hate crime legislation and whether the definition of protected classes should be expanded to include sexual orientation, Congress did not take action at the federal level until eleven years later with the 2009 Matthew Shepard and James Byrd, Jr., Hate Crimes Prevention Act, which forever weds the two men in the American imaginary based on their shared identity as victims of hate crimes. The HCPA provides support for "state, local, and tribal jurisdictions to . . . investigate and prosecute hate crimes" ("Hate Crimes Prevention Act"). The law also makes it a federal crime to attempt to or to cause bodily injury with a dangerous weapon because of a person's "actual or perceived race, color, religion, natural origin" and expands the protected classes to include "gender, sexual orientation, gender identity, or disability" if the crime can be broadly conceived of as affecting "interstate or foreign commerce" ("Hate Crimes Prevention Act"). Such laws prosecuting hate crimes not only aim to declare bias-driven crimes as especially heinous and worthy of enhanced punishments. Advocates for hate crime legislation stress that acknowledging that perpetrators of such crimes commit them in order to terrorize an already vulnerable population is necessary to begin healing the community and to assert the intrinsic value of the targeted group. Ironically, for targeted individuals and groups to receive this affirmation, they must be victims of a crime and redress can only occur retroactively.

Prelude to Bruise within the Tradition of Anti-Lynching Writing

In the absence of full acceptance from their wider communities, LGBTQ people form communities and spaces where they can define themselves, freely express a wide range of emotions, relate their experience, and articulate the identities they self-fashion. By providing an aesthetic space to represent the intimacy of hate crimes, poetry enables readers to understand hate crimes as normative, an outgrowth of a society that routinely punishes non-heterosexual expressions of sexual identity. In so doing, turning to poetry allows authors to voice the often unspeakable violence committed by a family member, violence committed by a lover, or violence committed by an acquaintance often ignored when society conceptualizes hate crimes as acts committed by strangers. Jones' *Prelude to Bruise* takes on such a project.

Jones, born in the mid-1980s, writes in a moment of optimism shadowed by the potential of terror. The passage of the HCPA in 2009—which holds the possibility for redressing race, gender, religious, and sexual identity-based violence—and the Supreme Court's 2015 marriage equality ruling with the *Obergefell v. Hodges* case both point to a future of acceptance. However, gay, lesbian, transgender, and gender nonconforming people of color continue to face discrimination and violence on the basis of either identity at rates higher than their peer groups.[3] In a short essay, "A Poet's Boyhood at the Burning Crossroads," Jones describes learning a crucial lesson watching news reports of Byrd's and Shepard's murders as a thirteen-year-old: *"Being black can get you killed. Being gay can get you killed. Being a black gay boy is practically a death wish."*

The mythic figure Boy in *Prelude to Bruise* was birthed in part by the murders of Byrd and Shepard as well as the longstanding violence against the LGBTQ community. The collection is tied together by Boy's journey to manhood, a process shaped by his vulnerable position as young, queer, and black living in the

---

South. While Boy must contend with a homophobic father and his grief produced by the loss of his mother, *Prelude to Bruise*'s poems are also marked by what Anna Journey describes as "an anguished or taboo eroticism" as Boy negotiates his relationships with men. Poems invoking boys of Greek and biblical myth (Icarus, Ganymede, and Isaac) and describing the beautiful but menacing Southern landscape intermingle with Boy's journey. The father-son and lover-beloved dyads the collection invokes reveal the limits of subjectivity; neither the father nor the lover can possess Boy as the object of their hopes and desires. The violence present within the volume can be understood as efforts to bridge this gap between two subjectivities, to police both Boy's behavior and their own. In Boy's struggle to define himself, he must cut through the futures his father and his lovers project upon him.

In describing Boy's journey to manhood, Jones' use of the bruise as a motif offers a means of understanding older millennials' relationship to the past, from slavery through Jim Crow, as well as their current moment.[4] An ephemeral marker of memory, the bruise as it appears in millennial poetry differs from a tradition of representing maimed and fatally wounded black male bodies. A bruise is evidence of being touched roughly but not necessarily without consent. While marking moments of trauma, the bruise is not a scar; it will fade away. For Jones, the bruise motif thus offers a means of representing fraught interactions between white and black people that are not defined strictly in terms of oppressor/oppressed or inflictor of violence/subject of trauma—interactions the law and narratives of historical events cannot convey without falling into binary oppositions.

He achieves this project by emphasizing the "prelude," the moment of potential and anticipation before trauma. In "Prelude to Bruise," in representing a white man's erotically charged sadistic demands to an anonymous black male subject, Jones delays the realization of desire and makes ambiguous whose desire is expressed. The prelude is also a space for interior meditation. For example, Jones represents Byrd's final thoughts before he is murdered in "Jasper, 1998." This representation of a moment of quiet provides an opportunity to explore "the black interior," what Elizabeth Alexander describes as "black life and creativity behind the public face of stereotype and limited imagination" (x). In moving away from the gruesome representations of Byrd's decapitation and dismemberment towards representing Byrd's fear at the moment, Jones reveals that resistance in the moment and post-event, often unduly expected from black people, is not always possible.

At the same time, Jones inherits a tradition of anti-lynching writing across multiple genres in African-American literature and departs from this tradition in his willingness to depict instead the interiority of victims of such crimes. For example, in depictions of lynching in works such as James Weldon Johnson's *Autobiography of an Ex-Colored Man* (1912) and James Baldwin's short story "Going to Meet the Man," writers explore the interiority of white and black characters complicit in the crime as observers. In "A Bronzeville Mother Loiters in Mississippi. Meanwhile, A Mississippi Mother Burns Bacon," Gwendolyn Brooks explores the interiority of one of the wives of Emmett Till's murderers, Carolyn Bryant, who is complicit in the crime in her role as catalyst. Lucille Clifton's "jasper texas 1998" comes closest to Jones' representational strategy in that she chooses as speaker Byrd's decapitated head. Clifton's first stanza depicts the horror of Byrd's dismemberment; one concrete image—"the arm as it pulled away/pointed toward me, the hand opened once/and was gone"—lingers with the reader (ll. 3-5). In the next two stanzas, the poem's speaker refuses to respond to calls for reconciliation between Jasper's black and white citizens in response to such tragedy. The outrage the community offers is too little, too late. The speaker rejects the logic that being vulnerable to such violence dehumanizes its victim. Rather, Byrd's humanity is affirmed by his relationship with his family and his capacity to bleed.

Key differences separate Jones' poem from Clifton's, specifically his focus on the crime as it happened rather than its aftermath. The title of Jones' "Jasper, 1998," like Clifton's, locates the reader in time and place. "Go back," repeated in the first lines of the first and second sections doubles as a command to the reader to remember Jasper and the fateful moment in which Byrd accepts a ride from Berry, Brewer, and King. Although both poems are written in memory of Byrd, the reader is left to infer that he is the speaker of the poem through the perspective described. Rather than emphasize Byrd's decapitation and dismemberment, Jones' first stanza focuses on the body parts necessary for speech. Byrd promises to speak even with a "throat still/crowded with dirt/and loose teeth" (Jones ll 1-3). This zooming in functions in the service of subverting conceptions of black resistance that insist speaking out or protesting is the ultimate demonstration of strength. That Byrd by the end of the poem is able to articulate what happens to him is little solace in the face of his murderers' depravity. The direction to "go back" is an injunction for the reader to go along for the ride, to enter Byrd's mind, and to move away from the body and even the voice towards the black interior.

The second section transports the reader to the truck's cab. Tension mounts throughout as Byrd realizes that the men have no intention of taking him home and as he struggles to question the men's actions. In contrast to Byrd's promise to speak in the first stanza, in the truck's cab, he is quiet, contributing to the tension of the scene. Kevin Quashie explains that "[s]ilence often denotes something that is suppressed or repressed, and is an interiority that is about withholding, absence, and stillness" (22). In this representation of interiority, Byrd is a person whose most minute actions are defined by a system of racial dominance. "Smile, ride, quiet" (Jones l. 18; 25) repeats as Byrd follows the imperative created under a white supremacist society for black men to portray docility, to not question the men's choices, though following this implicit rule does not save him.

In the final section, the chain dragging him behind the truck, Byrd's body, and the road's pavement unite in song, disrupting the uneasy quiet of the previous section. The section begins with the repetition of the line, "Chain gang, work song, back road, my body" (Jones l. 46; 48). With these lines, Jones introduces another form of violence directed toward black bodies—the forced labor of the chain gang. In so doing, he blurs the line between past and present. The work song is equal parts compliance with white supremacy—as chain gangs used the work song to keep rhythm and, as a result, increase productivity—and resistance to being transformed into a tool of the state. The men transform Byrd into a tool for their entertainment or to enact fantasies of total domination, as indicated by the lines, "These men play me dirty" (l. 50), and "they take my teeth/ for piano keys" (ll. 59-60). However, the last lines, "Hear me, Jasper./Hear me for miles" (ll.67-68), recover some agency for Byrd with the switch to the imperative voice and with the poem's fulfillment of Byrd's promise to speak given in the first stanza.

The Bruise Motif

Byrd's existence as a man and cultural figure limits a full exploration of the erotic within violence. The brutality of Byrd's murder inhibits any attempt to read meaningful connection between Byrd and his murderers. In proving an individual's humanity, prose writers and poets often emphasize interiority in response to the circulating representations that emphasize the entertaining, the abused, or the laboring body. For Jones, in "Prelude to Bruise," the skin becomes a means of escaping this conundrum produced by this split between interiority and the body. As Didier Anzieu and Naomi Segal have argued, the skin as an organ marks the relationship and boundary between the body, the psychic self, and the social self. It receives both pain and pleasure through touch as well as signifies race, offering a means of understanding social relationships as a key to identity formation (Segal 44-45; Anzieu 36-39). In bringing the skin into focus, "Prelude to Bruise" productively straddles the line between presenting the desires of the individual and working towards a larger redemptive project within African-American literature, that of recovering histories of domination. In addition to adding to the canon of representations of black men suffering abuse at the hands of white men, the sexual resonances present within the scene also recover the often elided history of same-sex coerced and consensual sexual encounters.[5]

In "Prelude to Bruise," humanity and therefore interiority are assumed, allowing Jones to explore even fantasies that cannot be mobilized in service of the political. In the title poem, "the burly man" addresses an unnamed black man, presumably the boy who unites the entire collection, directing him to spit-shine his boots under the threat of violence. Jones' choice of a bootblack, in addition to representing the menial jobs that white supremacy and segregation relegated to black men, also resonates in the context of the leather BDSM community.[6] The poem trades in scopic and sonic pleasures even in the absence of the bootblack's voice and a full description of his body through the speaker's fetishization of the bootblack's skin, his explicit statements of what he will do to the bootblack, and use of the imperative voice. The poem's sexual elements are also apparent in the tempering of the burly man's threats of violence with praise ("Good boy" repeats twice) and his promise, "I'm gonna break your back in" (Jones l. 12), a phrase frequently used as slang for anal penetration. Images of boot-licking and spit-shining leather boots hold iconic status within this community. It is worth stating, however, that not all bootblacks are submissive. Bootblacking is a skill that a bootblack can enjoy performing for its own sake. Nevertheless, in this representation, the bootblack appears submissive, as indicated by his acquiescence to the burly man's commands.

For readers who reject the erotic potential within the poem, the focus on the bootblack's skin—represented by the lines, "Your back, blue-black" (Jones l. 4; 22), which repeats later in the poem, and "Black boy, blue-black boy" (l. 24)—emphasizes his alienation and status as racial Other. But reading reciprocity and inclusion into the encounter offers a means of conceptualizing their relationship as one that affirms the black subject's humanity. The two interpretations of the poem open it to align with the "two different ways of knowing blackness and interacting with the other" (10) that Michelle Stephens identifies in *Skin Acts: Race, Psychoanalysis, and the Black Male Performer* (2014). Racialized abuse and interracial sexual acts, like performance, enable one to experience himself as "epidermal skin," operating within the restrictions of the history-laden symbolic order and "sensational flesh" (10).

When exploring the tension between sexual desire and violence, the burly man's pleasure is much more apparent than the bootblack's. Maintaining the fantasy white supremacist masculine identification offers requires explicit or de-facto segregation (in order to protect one's purity) or staging encounters that will assert one's dominance. In addition to these performances of race, in the cultural imagination, white men either perceive the black man as guilty and worthy of punishment or fetishize him. This scene enables the burly man to enact these fantasies. In order to submit to this secondary process, the burly man must renounce identification with the feminine, queerness, and blackness and the pleasures these other identifications can offer. Separately and together, these identifications have been theorized to allow for a *jouissance* not available through a phallocentric order. However, for subjects like the burly man, these pleasures become possible through taking on the sadistic point of view. As Kaja Silverman puts it, "The fascination of the sadistic point of view is merely that it provides the best vantage point from which to watch the masochistic story unfold" (5). In the process of touching another, an individual touches himself. But the bootblack is not only an object of the burly man's gaze; he is also a recipient of his touch. The bootblack's flesh presses back.

That "Prelude to Bruise" precedes "Jasper, 1998" by one poem may make it troubling to conceive of the bootblack receiving any kind of psychic fulfillment in this encounter. To do so would seem to argue for the victims' complicity in their abuse and murder. However, imagining the bootblack and burly man's encounter as containing an element of reciprocity is actually a rejection of masculinist white supremacist ideology, which is supported by fantasies of total domination and the privileging of the white man's pleasure. The poem can be read as demonstrating that sometimes sexual desire does not follow the politics that our identity seems to demand; as Leo Bersani explains, "The logic of homosexual desire includes the potential for a loving identification with the gay man's enemies" (208). Gay men can believe in the same standards of masculinity used to judge them as inadequate and perceive of themselves as inadequate. The same logic can be applied to race, since being a racial minority does not prevent one from holding white supremacist beliefs.

The poem's BDSM resonances expand the affective possibilities for encounters that physically and psychically bruise for the bootblack and the reader through re-naming and the use of "you" as a possessive adjective, a direct address, and as a direct object. The possibility of the bootblack's pleasure enters the poem in the fifth and sixth stanzas when the burly man addresses the bootblack, asking:

> See this burnished
> brown leather belt?
> You see it, boy?
> Are you broke, or broken? (Jones ll. 8-11)

Later the burly man threatens, "[O]r I'll bend you over my lap–*rap rap*" (l. 15). The making of a "boy" is a sociogenic and intersubjective process. As an epithet, "boy," which whites frequently used regardless of a black man's actual age in order to assert their superiority, has the power to interpolate, to position the so-named as an object of power. The appellation "Boy" as a direct address, mentioned in the first line, changes for the rest of the poem to "you." That Boy is unnamed produces an emptiness within the pronoun that allows readers to insert themselves. The poem also engages the reader's sonic sense through the use of onomatopoeic "*rap rap*" (l.15) and the rhythm achieved through alliteration of "black boy, blue-black boy" (l. 24). If the reader is able to identify with "boy" as well as feel erotically stimulated, he or she has internalized "boy" and its social logic. The historical weight it carries and that its use openly articulates power relations give "boy" its erotic power—a point Darieck Scott argues about "nigger" in black-authored BDSM representations (255). Jones' representation of this scene of domination makes visible the process of interpellation. This visibility, Scott argues, makes such scenes "amenable to various uses and transformations" (255). Reading the poem as also representing the bootblack's masochistic perspective allows the reader to choose to identify with the much-maligned passive role in the male/female, active/passive divisions that structure gender relations. This authorial choice makes possible empathetic identification with both the burly man and the bootblack.

In *Prelude to a Bruise*, Jones insists on registering the trauma caused by racism and homophobia at a societal level. At the same time, however, Jones' poetry also depicts circumstances in which black queer bodies desire—and actively participate in—their own erotic subjugation. In so doing, Jones exposes a major limit within hate crimes legislation and the cultural values these laws reflect: that to gain inclusion in the wider community, the queer person of color can only speak as a subject of trauma. This is not to say hate crimes legislation does not perform important community work. Acts such as the HCPA are necessary for asserting the citizenship of vulnerable populations as well as affirming that violence is unacceptable. However, the law is constrained by the biases of the population it serves. For imagining a future in which individuals can bring their whole selves and still be extended kinship, we must turn to the arts.

Notes

1. Clara S. Lewis argues this point at length in *Tough on Hate?: The Cultural Politics of Hate Crimes* (2014).

2. The Human Rights Campaign, founded in 1980, advocates for the equal rights of lesbian, gay, bisexual, transgender, and queer people through political lobbying and public education campaigns.

3. Hate crime statistics are notoriously difficult to track in part because of the reluctance of local police departments to declare an incident of violence a hate crime and because victims, afraid of coming out or mistreatment from the police, choose not to report attacks. The National Coalition of Anti-Violence Programs, which tracks hate crimes in twenty-two states, reports the following statistics in the report on "Lesbian, Gay, Bisexual, Transgender, Queer, and HIV-Affected Hate Violence in 2015": 62 percent of victims of homicides were black and latin/a, 67 percent were transgender and gender non-conforming, and 54 percent were transgender women of color (Waters, Jindasurat, & Wolfe).

4. Nathan Heller helpfully provides an explanation of what differentiates older millennials from their parents and a younger cohort within the same generation in "The Big Uneasy: What's Roiling the Liberal-Arts Campus?" Formative events for older millennials, born during the 1980s, include: the terrorist attacks of September 11th, the wars in Afghanistan and Iraq, the increased militarizing of local police departments and surveillance domestically, and the world-wide Great Recession beginning in 2007. In response to the uncertain future these events produced, older millennials

developed conservative lifestyle ideals, an entrepreneurial spirt, and an approach to activism that emphasizes gradual progress and compromise.

5.   In representing such a scene, Jones performs a cultural work that fulfills what Sigmund Freud terms "the repetition compulsion" (13), the effort to repeat a traumatic event in an effort to master it. Literary scholars and authors have only begun to probe the possibility of men suffering sexual abuse at the hands of men. For example, in "'The Strangest Freaks of Despotism': Queer Sexuality in Antebellum African American Slave Narratives," Aliyyah I. Abdur-Rahman turns to Luke's interpolated narrative in Harriet Jacobs' *Incidents in the Life of a Slave Girl* (1861) as an incident of same-sex sexual abuse and supports this reading by pointing to similarities in the veiled language used to describe heterosexual rape in the narrative, descriptions of the floggings Luke received, and the detail that Luke's master only permitted him to wear a shirt. In fiction, this secret history is represented in a white man's caress of the penis and testicles of a man about to be lynched in Baldwin's "Going to Meet the Man" and the sexual abuse Paul D experiences and witnesses on the chain gang in Toni Morrison's *Beloved* (1987).

6.   Jones attended the International Mr. Leather Competition, which holds a bootblack competition in which judges score the participant on skills, interview, personality, stage presence, and ballot collecting in May 2016. While biography cannot be confused with artistic production, this information provides some context for noting the BDSM resonances within the poem.

Works Cited

Alexander, Elizabeth. *The Black Interior*. Minneapolis, MN: Graywolf, 2004.

Anzieu, Didier. *The Skin Ego*. Trans. Chris Turner. New Haven, CT: Yale UP, 1989.

Bersani, Leo. "Is the Rectum a Grave?" *October* 43 (Winter 1987): 197-22.

Bragg, Rick. "For Jasper, Just What It Didn't Want: Klan and Black Militants Head for a Little Town Trying to Heal." *The New York Times*. 27 Jun. 1998: A8.

Chua-Eoan, Howard & Hilary Hylton. "Beneath the Surface." *Time* 151.24 (1998): 34.

Clifton, Lucille. *Blessing the Boats: New and Selected Poems, 1988–2000*. Rochester: BOA Editions, 2000.

Fanon, Franz. *Black Skin, White Masks*. Trans. Richard Philcox. 1952. New York: Grove P, 2008.

Freud, Sigmund. *Beyond the Pleasure Principle*. Trans. C. J. M. Hubback. London: International Psycho-Analytical P, 1912.

Goldstein, Richard. "The Hate That Makes Men Straight." *Village Voice*. 22 Dec. 1998: 64. *Factiva*. Web. 14 Dec. 2016.

Halperin, Moze. "What It Means to Be 'Wanted': Saeed Jones on His Book 'Prelude to Bruise.'" Books. *Flavorwire.com*. Flavorpill Media, 29 Sept. 2014. Web. 14 Dec. 2016.

Jones, Saeed. "A Poet's Boyhood at the Burning Crossroads." *Opinionator*. *New York Times* 19 Jan. 2015.

_____. *Prelude to Bruise*. Minneapolis: Coffee House, 2014.

Journey, Anna. "The Queer Baroque: On Saeed Jones's Prelude to Bruise." *Kenyon Review*. The Kenyon Review, Fall 2014. Web. 14 Dec. 2016.

"Murdered for Who He Was." Editorial. *The New York Times* 13 Oct. 1998: A18. *Factiva*. *Factiva*. Web. 14 Dec. 2016.

Quashie, Kevin. *The Sovereignty of Quiet: Beyond Resistance in Black Culture*. New Brunswick, NJ: Rutgers UP, 2012.

Scott, Darieck. *Extravagant Abjection: Blackness, Power, and Sexuality in the African American Literary Imagination*. New York: New York UP, 2010.

Segal, Naomi. *Consensuality: Didier Anzieu, Gender and the Sense of Touch*. Amsterdam: Rodopi, 2009.

Silverman, Kaja. "Masochism and Subjectivity." *Framework* 12 (Spring 1980): 2-9.

Stephens, Michelle Ann. *Skin Acts: Race, Psychoanalysis, and the Black Male Performer*. Durham, NC: Duke UP, 2014.

Van Boven, Sarah & Anne Bell Gesalman. "A Fatal Ride in the Night." *Newsweek* 131.25 (1998): 33.

Waters, Emily, Chai Jindasurat, & Cecilia Wolfe. "Lesbian, Gay, Bisexual, Transgender, Queer, and HIV-Affected Hate Violence in 2015." Rep. New York: New York City Gay and Lesbian Anti-Violence Project, 2016.

"The Process of Becoming Nobody": Reflections on E. Franklin Frazier's *Black Bourgeoisie: The Rise of a New Middle Class*

Leonard A. Steverson

In 1957, at the dawning of the US Civil Rights Movement, leading African-American sociologist E. Franklin Frazier published a scathing report on the rising black middle class in America. His thesis was that the black bourgeoisie did little to aid lower-class African Americans in their efforts at upward social mobility in the post-World War II era[1] and that this group of business, religious, and political leaders contributed to a racial inferiority complex for African Americans as a whole. Predictably, the work was met with condemnation by these leaders, but it also attracted a large reading audience of scholars and non-scholars alike. The groundbreaking book, *Black Bourgeoisie: The Rise of a New Middle Class* (1957), presented a pessimistic view of racial struggles of upward mobility that is still being considered at a time when the first African-American president has been elected to office.

Decades before the publication of the work, W. E. B. Du Bois, one of the nation's most prominent sociologists, issued a clarion call for the top black leaders of the day—the so-called "talented tenth"—to address the issue of the upward social mobility of African Americans and to work toward increasing their prominence on the national and global stage.[2] Years after the publication of *Black Bourgeoisie*, civil rights legislation that improved African-American access to career opportunities as well as adequate and affordable housing was promulgated to promote social mobility for blacks, and it did so in significant ways. The Civil Rights Act of 1964, the first major federal legislation since Reconstruction, sought to eliminate some of these inequities, notably in the areas of job and educational discrimination and access to public services. This legislation was soon followed by the Voting Rights Act of 1965, which sought to ban barriers to minority voting (such as literacy testing) and allowed federal intervention in voter registration activity when voting irregularities were discovered. While there is still a gap between socioeconomic conditions for black and white Americans, significant changes have been made and more African Americans will continue to experience movement into middle and upper-class status. Through a sociological lens, we explore the reactions to Frazier's controversial work in order to better understand its historical significance as well as its continued implications today.

"Gladiator in Every Sense of the Term"

To begin, it is important to have an understanding of the man behind this important work and the influences that inevitably shaped *Black Bourgeoisie.* Specifically, Edward Franklin Frazier was born in Baltimore, Maryland, in 1894 to a bank messenger and a housewife who had five children. His upbringing was certainly not of the black bourgeoisie he would later investigate. He attended area public schools and later matriculated at Howard University, where he obtained his bachelor's degree with honors. He taught at schools in various states and claimed his two major teaching influences were a high school teacher who instilled in him a love of learning and the famed sociologist and activist W. E. B. Du Bois (Cromwell 31-32).

After receiving his master's degree from Clark University in 1920 and completing additional graduate work at the New York School of Social Work and the University of Copenhagen, he continued to teach at a number of schools. Frazier decided to pursue his PhD at the University of Chicago, an institution well known for its development of a micro-level sociological theoretical known as symbolic interactionism and the research methodology known as ethnology (or field research), in which researchers study social life in its natural environment. An early example of this approach can be found in his doctoral dissertation at Chicago, entitled *The Negro Family in Chicago.*

There were many key figures in the so-called Chicago School of Sociology, including Robert K. Park, who became a major influence on Frazier. Park had suggested a notion that finds its way into Frazier's analysis of the black bourgeoisie; in his examination of migrating people, Park introduced the concept of the "marginal man," a hybrid of two types—a newcomer to an area who possesses characteristics of the native area. Park mentions the conflict that arises from the existence of the "divided self" that exists between "the old self and the new" (892). Since the transplanted individual is separated from native customs, this social type lacks the support needed to endure change. This bifurcation of self can be found, albeit at different levels of analysis, in Du Bois' conceptualization of "double consciousness" and in Frazier's analysis of the black bourgeoisie.

After his time at the University of Chicago, Frazier became involved in many sociological organizations and was elected president of the American Sociological Association in 1948. He was a true scholar of race relations and published ten books on the subject, which particularly focused on African-American families. As a young scholar, he drew his ideas primarily from Du Bois and Booker T. Washington as well as the ideas espoused in the popular African-American publication, *The Messenger*.

Frazier was not only a scholar but, as was the case with Du Bois, had a strong proclivity for activism. Hylan A. Lewis describes him as a "gladiator in every sense of the term" (28) who prompted his students and leaders in the black community to work diligently for the betterment of the black experience. Not one to run from controversy, Frazier supported Du Bois at a point when many black intellectuals rejected him, taught Marxism to students during the McCarthy communist witch hunts, and brought to his classes at Howard University the radical sociologist C. Wright Mills, who, although Caucasian, was not welcome as a speaker at many white colleges and universities.

During Franklin's career, he published numerous scholarly articles and also contributed to Gunnar Myrdal's highly influential 1944 study on race relations, *An American Dilemma: The Negro Problem and Modern Democracy*. His specific interest in the emerging black middle class, however, can be traced to his youth, as he became a keen observer of this group, though his family never made it to that level (Platt 72). Ultimately, Frazier's scholarly writing on the black bourgeoisie can be traced to the 1920s in his master's

---

thesis, in a number of articles and essays, and in a 1928 article called "La Bourgeoisie Noir" in *Modern Quarterly*. In 1929, for instance, Frazier penned an essay called "Durham: Capital of the New Middle Class" in which he wrote with some degree of hope for economic in-roads for a group in Durham, North Carolina. The essay, although adopting a very positive and hopeful tone, had seeds of discontent with the development of the black middle class that would surface later in *Black Bourgeoisie*.

The Polemic that Started the Controversy

The work was first published in France (as *Bourgeoisie Noir*) in 1955 and in America in 1957. In it, E. Franklin Frazier makes clear the purpose of his groundbreaking and controversial sociological examination about the rising African-American middle class. *Black Bourgeoisie: The Rise of a New Middle Class* offers readers a thorough analysis of the "real or objectively existing economic and social status of this group"[4] and the "standards of behavior and values of the isolated social world of this segment of the Negro population which has come into existence as a consequence of racial discrimination and racial segregation" (Frazier 23). The work, therefore, is organized around these two concerns. In the first part of the book, Frazier describes the consequences of African-American movement into the higher classes, the movement into an area in which they are held in abeyance between their own heritage and an unaccepting white world that refuses to allow this group the full benefits of upward mobility.

The second part of the work focuses on the consequences of identity formation in the development of the black middle class—a world of "make-believe" and myths that were perpetrated by black-owned newspapers that African Americans are meeting their own needs (based on the dominant ideology of the white upper class) and rising in social and economic status as their white counterparts. The newspapers that helped perpetuate the myth included the *Guardian*, the *Defender*, and the *New York Age*—the newspaper that supported the ideas of Booker T. Washington, the person who "institutionalized" the myth (Frazier 155). Frazier also mentioned magazines that assisted in perpetuating the myth—*Ebony, Jet, Hue,* and *Tan*— alongside publications in the vein of *Life* magazine that depicted romanticized images of African Americans (178-179).

This myth then created confusion and frustration; the black bourgeoisie are stuck in a level of consciousness between the inability to attain the same material and social benefits as the white bourgeoisie and, at the same time, unable to draw from their traditional values to mitigate this conflict. This particular quandary was similarly described earlier by sociologist and civil rights activist W. E. B. Du Bois in his concept of double consciousness. In his seminal work, *The Souls of Black Folk,* Du Bois described double consciousness as "a peculiar situation . . . this sense of always looking at one's self through the eyes of others" (45). The consequence, he believed, was that "[o]ne ever feels his two-ness—an American, a Negro; two souls, two thoughts, two unreconciled strivings; two warring ideals in one dark body, whose dogged strength alone keeps it from being torn asunder" (45). In contrast, Frazier relocates Du Bois' idea of double consciousness from a social and psychological condition experienced by all African Americans to that common experience of just the emerging black middle class.

With the skills of a historian, Frazier then explains the roots of the black bourgeoisie from the time the first slave ships brought large numbers of Africans to the American shores until large numbers of freed slaves were able to make their way into business enterprises—business ventures primarily for African Americans. After emancipation (and prior to it for those who were already free), African Americans ventured into the business world and opened stores, shops, and even some larger business ventures, supported by the Freedman's Bank, which was created to assist these entrepreneurs in their endeavors. A number of independent black-owned banks were formed to assist business undertakings, including, among others, African-American newspapers, restaurants, funeral homes, clothiers, and pharmacies (Frazier 29-42).

Frazier also addresses the economic and financial situation, educational system, and political power of black leaders of the post-Civil War era. Those African Americans who were rising in socioeconomic status had to choose between two avenues—distancing themselves from the lower classes or attempting to achieve solidarity with them (Evans 213). This created a unique situation that influenced the black bourgeoisie for generations to come. Attempting to mimic the white middle and upper classes, the black bourgeoisie, many believed, made those in the lower classes feel inferior, resulting in their perception of the black bourgeoisie as "sellouts" and "Uncle Toms." Losing that base of support, the black bourgeoisie had to place their hope in the white bourgeoisie to consider them as equals and to share the opportunities of a rapidly growing capitalism. This, according to Frazier, was a futile undertaking. He believe that, under this approach, both groups would continue to languish in their own inferiority complex—what some would say is still a quandary for upwardly mobile African Americans today.

In addition to the insights on the socio-historical situation of the black bourgeoisie, Frazier uses some social psychological concepts that resonate with this analysis. For instance, he refers to the "inferiority complex" that this group possesses, describing a diminished self-esteem that comes from constantly seeking status and acceptance that will never be attained from white society, the result being a collective self-hatred. Frazier's repeated use of the term "make believe" throughout the work is also an intriguing one. The status that is obtained by the African-American middle class is one of "status without substance" (Frazier 195). The status of "society" (which has its genesis in the life of the house servants during slavery) refers to the social life of the community and a means of escape for the black middle class. The result, however, is emptiness, as the lifestyle that emerges from this pursuit is basically meaningless. Finally, the metaphor of "the process of becoming nobody" (26)—perhaps the book's major theme and the author's main concern for the black bourgeoisie—is a powerful one and identifies a cautionary tale for those who continue to immerse themselves in the unachievable quest for status by relying on excessive consumerism and conspicuous consumption. This frivolity and materialism, Frazier argues, is causing the black middle class to lack real substance.

A "Most Controversial but Least Understood Work": Reactions to *Black Bourgeoisie*

Because of these ideas, there was much discussion over *Black Bourgeoisie*, considered by James E. Teele to be Frazier's "most controversial but least understood work" (1). According to Teele, after its release, *Black Bourgeoisie* was generally rejected by many reviewers. These were not actually rejections as most of the reviews at the time accepted these four key points as true: the mythology of the successes of the black business owners, the promotion of the materialistic nature of the black middle class by African-American news media, the existence of a pervasive inferiority complex among this group, and the experiences and concerns of the African Americans in the classes beneath them socially. However, the points of contention also follow a similar path: the public and embarrassing nature of Frazier's rebuke of African Americans who have achieved success, the embellishment and exaggeration of his claims, the basing of his claims on an insufficient sample, and his refusal to objectively and critically evaluate some of the claims of his sources (9). Scholarly book reviews that were proffered shortly after its publication provide some additional insight into these critiques.

One review was published a year after the original French version was released. After describing Frazier's general thesis about the predicament of the black bourgeoisie, with emphasis on the resulting inferiority complex, Barbara Hockey Kaplan explains that while Frazier has some supporting documentation for his claims (historical texts, meetings reports, personal statements, and the press), she states readers must simply believe the author's comments about the numbers of middle-class African Americans who suffer the deleterious psychological effects created by the quandary of the black bourgeoisie. She also criticizes the work for failing to adequately define this group and questions if it refers to everyone above the lower class. Kaplan also states that while Frazier focused on the newly well-to-do, he neglected to address those who had already gained some degree of financial success. Her comment that the work is "more polemic than scientific" (Kaplan 335) is, therefore, an obvious one. She concludes by asserting that the most salient characteristics of this group—notably, its obsessive concern with social status and material goods—could simply be an indication of cultural integration with whites. And this, she notes, should be of interest to the advancing middle-class status for blacks in French Africa.

In his review of the English version of the work, Wilson Record is clear in describing the scholarly reviews as being mixed and potentially more insightful than the work itself. Noting its provocative and controversial but also insightful nature, Record sees the value that results from seriously contemplating Frazier's ideas. On one hand, he notes that the work won the coveted MacIver Award handed out by the American Sociological Society for its outstanding sociological research. On the other hand, it was pilloried by an official of the NAACP as being superficial and unlikely to receive the same level of esteem by other African Americans as it did by the white academic community; in fact, Record suggests Frazier would be seen by the emerging black middle class as a sell-out. There is, Record suggests, a middle ground between these positions—one that he seems to espouse. From his view, Frazier addresses a series of observations that are important; however, Record also acknowledges that these observations lack the quantitative support that would provide a better examination, have questions in the selection and interpretation of data, and fail to note the similar conditions of rising middle-class existence within other groups. In addition, he claims that the work tends to view the black bourgeoisie as a homogenous group of egoistic individuals, missing the fact that many people in this group are politically active in altruistic pursuits to better their neighborhoods and their lives generally. Another key point in this review is that while the emerging black middle class seems preoccupied with socioeconomic status, this characteristic should be seen for what it is—a reflection of the standards of white success with goals that all black citizens can attain.

Other reviews see less merit in Frazier's work. F. D. Freeman, for example, after giving a general description of Frazier's thesis, provides a very unflattering critique of the work. He sees the description of the black bourgeoisie—as being opportunistic, self-centered, confused, materialistic, hollow ("nobody" as described by Frazier), and living in a world of "make believe"—as being too simplistic and unqualified for a scientific analysis. Frazier is described by Freeman as obviously "indignant" and writing "out of character" (181). Similarly, John E. Coogan describes *Black Bourgeoisie* as "this stripping of the white-collar Negro's soul" (171) and wonders about Frazier's lack of concern and pity for African Americans ("his own"). Coming from a Christian perspective, Coogan is concerned with the nothingness that comes from obsessions with gambling, alcohol, and sexuality that Frazier claims are characteristics of the black middle class.[3] Furthermore, social work scholar Louis Towley, in a dual review of Frazier's works (*Black Bourgeoisie* and *Race and Culture Contacts*), notes the dark tone of the book and expresses a concern over Frazier's treatment of African-American social workers of the period. He questions the claim that social work programs were financed by white philanthropists, allowing little independence of thought and decision-making, as he does the idea that the black bourgeoisie was simply a homogenous group of selfish individuals unconcerned with the affairs of African-American communities.

In addition, journalist Jesse H. Walker takes issue with what he considers a depressing indictment of the black middle class. Referring to Frazier's previous awards and accolades, Walker surmises that he would receive no awards from the group he characterized as overly materialistic, ritualistic, and status-seeking (qtd. in Telle 8). Similarly, a columnist of the era lambasts the work for being merely leftist propaganda and stated the book would be better received by white racists and white supremacist groups. G. Franklin Edwards, from the vantage point of reviewing the work almost two decades later, critiques the work for its failure to emphasize or acknowledge that the black bourgeoisie of the period did indeed have elements of stability and functionality.

Despite these critiques, as Robert M. Ratcliff suggests, *Black Bourgeoisie* is an important work that deserves renewed consideration. He implores readers to delve more deeply into Frazier's words to discover what he considers truths—that the idea of the successful African-American business is a myth, that black educators deemed themselves of higher status than those they were entrusted to educate, and that when blacks entered higher socioeconomic status, their lives became incomplete (cited in Teele 8-9)—in effect, nothing. In other words, Frazier's comments created a needed discussion on the topics he raised—a discussion all the more important in the twenty-first century.

The Gladiator Responds to His Critics

In response to the mixed criticism his work received, Frazier, in the preface to the 1962 edition of *Black Bourgeoisie*, offers a rejoinder to some of the charges leveled against him and the work. He notes that when the book was released in France, it expected little attention and when it was published in the United States, the controversy it ignited shocked him. However, he states that the reaction from African Americans was understandable as they "were able to see themselves for the first time" (Frazier 7). After that initial "shock of self-revelation" (7), anger set in as the black middle class felt as if he had betrayed them through his provocative (but, in his view, correct) analysis. He notes there were even suggestions of violence against him by one African-American newspaper and that one scheduled invitation by a college sorority was cancelled due to the high levels of animosity by some members. In fact, one member complained that he had "set the Negro race back fifty years" (qtd. in Franklin 7). On the other hand, he also notes that the work was appreciated by a number of black leaders, some of whom reported on his courage to publish such a work.

Frazier also calls attention, as a comparative analysis, to the difference between the reactions of white people inside and outside the United States. White Americans generally reacted negatively as opposed to whites in Europe and Latin America, who questioned Americans' negative responses. Frazier believes that many white Americans were concerned that *Black Bourgeoisie* challenged the hopeful theme that African Americans had been emancipated from the evils of slavery and now, through the acquisition of civil rights, were on their way to economic freedom. In other words, although slavery was now over, racism has diminished, and assimilation is rapidly occurring in capitalistic America, *Black Bourgeoisie* contested these notions and exposed how African Americans were still outsiders, floundering on the lower rungs in white society. He states that the myth of rising black entrepreneurs gaining entrance into the elite circles was also exposed, something that many whites did not want the outside world to see.

In addition, Frazier explores the question of whether the work should have been updated five years after the original American version. He believed at the time that blacks still experienced similar socioeconomic conditions as in the original and were still living in a make-believe world fueled by social status and conspicuous consumption. Frazier notes, however, a difference between the original and the 1962 version—that of the appearance of middle-class blacks who were involved in the civil rights protests. These are not the black bourgeoisie as originally described but also not the masses of lower-class black citizens. They were seen by Frazier as an amalgam of the genteel and folk traditions.

In the 1962 preface, Frazier also addressed two major criticisms of the book: the claims that his source materials were inadequate and that there was nothing peculiar about this group of middle-class citizens (as opposed to other groups). To the former, Frazier refutes the criticism and explains that his reliance on case materials, letters, comments, personal observations, media reports, and student responses was methodologically appropriate (he compared his method of data collection to that of an anthropologist). The latter critique he addressed by mentioning that this was specifically a study of African-American, middle-class individuals and not a comparative study with the white middle class, Jewish middle class, or others. But most importantly, he also answers the criticism that the book was too cruel to the black middle class with a statement found in Coogan's review: "A sad truth is better than a merry lie" (11).

Implications and the Current Situation

Some changes have certainly taken place in America since *Black Bourgeoisie* was released, but that does not negate the sad truths that

Frazier revealed. The decade following the publication of the work introduced federal reforms that improved African-American access to better employment, political power, housing, and accommodations that were restricted earlier (Evans 40). Also, due to greater economic advantage and federal oversight, many middle-class blacks live in integrated communities, many more than when Frazier's work was published. Furthermore, as noted by Paul Attenwell et al., the "talented tenth" envisioned by W. E. B. Du Bois—that is, the well-educated black professionals who would lead the masses from their lower status—is a moniker that no longer applies to the large numbers of middle-class African Americans, especially since the Civil Rights Era, as many blacks have surpassed whites in their attainment of upward social mobility (6). Still, scholars note that while Du Bois would likely be pleased with the status increase of blacks in America, he would probably be perplexed that it has taken so long to achieve and upset that the gap is still so great between upwardly mobile minority and nonminority citizens. It is assumed the same could be said about Frazier.

In his widely acclaimed work *Race Matters* (1994), Cornell West asks why the nation has not produced black leaders in the mold of Frazier, Du Bois, and others (56). He, in classic Frazier fashion, defines what he sees as the newly emerging African-American middle class since the 1960s, in effect updating *Black Bourgeoisie*, which he mentions specifically. In a view similar to Frazier's analysis, West states that the economic upturn (in spite of the political upheaval) of the 1960s created the situation in which goods and services were for the first time available to the throngs of middle-class Americans, including the black middle class. The achievement of a more materialistic lifestyle has created a situation in which "black communities are in shambles, black families are in decline, and black men and women are in conflict (and sometimes combat)" (56). Also echoing Frazier and *Black Bourgeoisie*, he states that "the new class divisions produced by black inclusion (and exclusion) from the economic boom and the consumerism of hedonism promoted by mass culture have resulted in new kinds of personal turmoil and existential meaninglessness in black America"

(56). The movement into the "existential meaninglessness" is certainly a nod to the "process of becoming nobody," as Frazier describes in *Black Bourgeoisie*.

Current analyses into the group Frazier examined might contain different insights than offered by West and Frazier's earlier critiques. Many African Americans have moved beyond the categorization of middle class and into the upper classes. Questions currently arise as to how, due to social changes involving interraciality. It is often stated, for instance, that Barack Obama is our nation's first black president, though he is, by current terminology, "biracial." Would he still fit in the categorization of black bourgeoisie? Since Frazier's work, the idea of the social construction of race forces us to see such issues in terms that are less binary. And if scholars of race are truly to investigate aspects of social life and to address current problems, such as the animus that exists today between the police and African-American communities, then understanding the intersection between race and class examined in Frazier's seminal work is crucial in providing such an analysis. Such scholars must depend on these important works in the literature to guide their investigations, as continuing to neglect the insights of works such as *Black Bourgeoisie* would result in a less than complete exploration of race relations, economic advancement, and upward social mobility in the United States.

Notes

1. At mid-twentieth century, African Americans continued to experience racial discrimination in access to adequate education, employment, housing, and political representation. Extreme acts of violence against African Americans, including lynching, continued into the 1950s.

2. Du Bois was a key figure among intellectuals who strove for racial equality in the twentieth century and beyond. The first African American to receive a PhD from Harvard University, Du Bois was not only a scholar who introduced such ideas into the landscape of sociology and black studies as the color line, the veil, and double consciousness, but he was also an editor of a leading black publication and a civil rights activist, who helped created what would become the National Association for the Advancement of Colored People (NAACP). During his career, he conceived of the idea of the "talented tenth" as a group of the top ten percent of African-American

academics and community leaders who would lead black people in the struggle for racial equality.

3. Coogan sees in Frazier's work a proclamation (albeit accidental) that this void can only be adequately filled by religion and that Catholics should unite to ensure that the Church will be accommodating and available for filling this need. Therefore, the work is seen as a sad commentary but one that should be addressed. Coogan suggests a means to that end. It should also be noted that, according to Anthony Platt, Frazier held no favor with organized religion, so if his ideas filled a spiritual void, it was (as noted by Coogan) probably unintentional ("Between Scorn" 72).

Works Cited

Attenwell, Paul, David Lavin, Thurston Domina, & Tania Levey. "The Black Middle Class: Progress, Prospects, and Puzzles." *Journal of African American Studies* 8.1-2 (2004): 6-19.

Coogan, John E. Rev. of *Black Bourgeoisie: The Rise of a New Middle Class* by E. Franklin Frazier. *The American Catholic Review* 18.2 (1957): 171-172.

Cromwell, Adelaide M. "Frazier's Background and an Overview." Teele 30-43.

Du Bois, W. E. B. *The Souls of Black Folk*. New York: Signet, 1995.

Edwards, G. Franklin. "E. Franklin Frazier." *Black Sociologists: Historical and Contemporary Perspectives*. Chicago: U of Chicago P, 1974.

Evans, Arthur, Jr. "Black Middle Classes: The Outlook of a New Generation." *International Journal of Politics, Culture, and Society* 6.2. (1992): 211-228.

_____. "The New American Middle Classes: Their Social Structure and Status Ambivalence." *International Journal of Politics, Culture, and Society* 7.2 (1992): 209-228.

Frazier, E. Franklin. *Black Bourgeoisie: The Rise of a New Middle Class*. New York: Free, 1957.

_____. *Black Bourgeoisie: The Rise of a New Middle Class*. New York: Free, 1962.

Freeman, F. D. Rev. of *Black Bourgeoisie: The Rise of a New Middle Class* by E. Franklin Frazier. *Social Forces* 37. 2 (1958): 181.

Kaplan, Barbara Hockey. Rev. of *Black Bourgeoisie: The Rise of a New Middle Class* by E. Franklin Frazier. *American Journal of Sociology* 63.3 (1956): 335.

Lewis, Hylan. "Howard University and Frazier." Teele 21-29.

Park, Robert K. "Human Migration and the Marginal Man." *American Journal of Sociology* 33.6. (1928): 881-893.

Platt, Anthony. *E. Franklin Frazier Reconsidered.* New Brunswick, NJ: Rutgers, 1991.

_____. "Between Scorn and Longing: Frazier's Black Bourgeoisie." Telle 71-84.

Record, Wilson. Rev. of *Black Bourgeoisie: The Rise of a New Middle Class* by E. Franklin Frazier. *Social Problems* 5.1 (1957): 44-46.

Teele, James E, ed. *E. Franklin Frazier and Black Bourgeoisie.* Columbia: U of Missouri P, 2002.

Towley, Louis. "Book Review: Black Bourgeoisie." *Social Work* 58.3 (1958): 83-84.

West, Cornell. *Race Matters.* New York: Vintage, 1994.

Toward a More Inclusive America: Jesse Jackson's 1984 and 1988 Democratic National Convention Addresses ____

Enrico Beltramini

In 1984 and 1988, Jesse Jackson ran for president on a platform that gave voice to the disenfranchised and focused on issues such as wealth inequality and racial injustice. Jackson earned prime-time convention speaking slots, and his convention speeches remain among the most significant speeches of recent political history. Successive roars of applause swelled over the audience at the convention centers, while the television audience of tens of millions of viewers followed Jackson's gospel-cadenced, impassioned oration. In both speeches, Jackson relied heavily on a delicate balance between passion and analysis, conviction and compromise, to deliver an image of peace and justice to the audiences' minds. Still, despite historians' vast research on the Civil Rights Movement, scant attention has been paid to contemporary civil rights leaders' political speeches, especially post-1968. The significance of this study is punctuated by the idea that Jackson used a civil-rights-centered rhetorical approach to capture diverse audiences while bringing to the national spotlight issues that are still relevant today. After all, his campaigns ignited for national politics a resurrection of the civil rights imagination that Barack Obama would ultimately adopt in his successful campaign for president of the United States in 2008.

The Emergence of the Rainbow Coalition: Jackson's 1984 San Francisco Address[1]

At the 1984 Democratic National Convention in San Francisco, Jackson made a forceful case for the extension of the Democratic tent to the poor and warned against the threat of Reaganism. Opening night featured a keynote address that belonged to first-term New York Governor Mario Cuomo. Cuomo reimagined America as a divided nation—"the lucky and the left out, . . . the royalty and the rabble"—and argued that the Democratic Party would be better off to defend the middle class, "the people not rich enough to be worry free but not poor enough to be on welfare"—"those who work for a living because they have to" ("Tale of Two Cities"). It was a most memorable keynote address and raised the bar for all speakers to follow, particularly Jesse Jackson, who took the stage the following evening, July 18, with his wife and five children. By then, he represented only 3.3 million votes, or 18 percent of the Democratic vote.[2] During the primaries, he had won almost 400 delegates, or 12 percent, finishing behind Walter Mondale (the nominee) and Gary Hart. More television viewers watched his address than any other part of the convention, reaching 33 million by its end. CBS News Anchor Dan Rather even remarked that more Americans saw Jackson's speech than the broadcast of Martin Luther King Jr.'s "I Have a Dream" speech at the 1963 March on Washington.

His address began with a prayer, "our faith in a mighty God," and then continued to define his constituency, which in the primaries stretched beyond his urban base of blacks to distressed farmers, coal miners, and both white- and blue-collar workers. He declared, "My constituency is the desperate, the damned, the disinherited, the disrespected and the despised. They've voted in record numbers. They have invested faith, hope and trust that they have in us. The Democratic Party must send them a signal that we care," he claimed, implying that the Democratic leadership was far too focused on the middle class. The first part of Jackson's speech, however, was not simply a description of his constituency; rather, it was a gateway that admitted the audience to a world all its own—a biblical world.

In this world, Jackson believed that politics was for the good: "to feed the hungry; to clothe the naked" (Matthew 25:36). He also believed that the disenfranchised have acted as a congregation and "have invested . . . faith, hope, and trust" (1 Corinthians 13:13) in the Democratic Party. In this world, "there is [a] call of conscience, redemption, expansion, healing, and unity" (Hebrews 9:14; Romans 8:29-30) that leadership must heed. Not only that, but "leadership can part the waters and lead our nation in the direction of the Promised Land" (Exodus 14:1-31). In this world, "there is a proper season for everything" (Ecclesiastes 3:1); there is a time to sow and a time to reap. There exists a time to compete and a time to cooperate. The scripture is clearly an important source for Jackson's political imagination, which he demonstrated by relying heavily on biblical stories and references to create enduring images in the minds of the audience, all while maintaining a gospel-cadenced, impassioned oration that galvanized his listeners.

Then Jackson called on his delegates to ratify support for him, while he pledged to support Mondale's candidacy, seeking to heal the divisions created by a stormy election campaign that highlighted deep internal differences. In this context, he also addressed the damage created by his reference to Jews as "Hymie" and to New York as "Hymietown."[3]—Although Jackson apologized for his unfortunate remark, he also proposed a definition of leadership that would inspire an entire generation of black politicians, stating, "This campaign has taught me much; that leaders must be tough enough to fight, tender enough to cry, human enough to make mistakes, humble enough to admit them, strong enough to absorb the pain, and resilient enough to bounce back and keep on moving."

While Cuomo articulated the image of the two cities, or two Americas,[4] Jackson instead advanced a vision of the American nation as a rainbow:

> Our flag is red, white and blue, but our nation is a rainbow—red, yellow, brown, black and white—and we're all precious in God's sight. America is not like a blanket—one piece of unbroken cloth, the same color, the same texture, the same size. America is more like a quilt: many patches, many pieces, many colors, many sizes, all woven and held together by a common thread. The white, the Hispanic, the black, the Arab, the Jew, the woman, the native American, the small farmer, the businessperson, the environmentalist, the peace activist, the young, the old, the lesbian, the gay, and the disabled make up the American quilt.

As we see, Jackson offered his audiences the promise of a multicultural society in which the faithful could share the same vision of inclusion, even if they do not share the same God. Jackson's vision of the United States as a rainbow is inclusive of all minorities and also of non-Christian religions as long as they are theistic in their faith (Christians, Jews, and Muslims), indicating his belief that we are all precious in God's sight. That was a familiar sentiment in Cuomo's speech, but Jackson took it even further into black church-talk, arguing that the ultimate inclusive American value is not mere tolerance but actual love.

Eventually, Jackson's vision of the United States as a rainbow initiated the Rainbow Coalition, which represents a significant expansion of the old, black, church-based coalition of the Civil Rights Movement. Here Jackson argues that "[t]wenty years later, we cannot be satisfied by just restoring the old coalition. Old wine skins must make room for new wine. We must heal and expand." As a result, he sought to include Arab Americans, Hispanic Americans, farm workers, Native Americans, Asian Americans, young Americans, disabled veterans, and small farmers excluded from the Democratic coalition of the past. Still, he recognized the Civil Rights Movement story that led to his place at the podium. His speech celebrated Fannie Lou Hamer and heroes of the movement like Medgar Evers, Martin Luther King Jr., Michael "Mickey" Schwerner, Andrew Goodman, James Chaney, and Viola Liuzzo, but he also included Malcolm X and the Kennedys in his list of martyrs, unlocking the civil rights pantheon of heroes to black radicals and white liberals.

Jackson's civil rights message of love and togetherness, however, did not stop him from challenging Reaganism and Reaganomics. As he said, "Reaganism is a spirit, and Reaganomics represents the real economic facts of life." However, Jackson focused criticism on Reaganomics, addressing both the supply-side economics and the military Keynesianism of the Reagan administration.[5] Jackson declared that if not "big corporations and rich individuals who received the bulk of a three-year, multibillion tax cut" or one of "the 37,000 military contractors who have benefited from Reagan's more than doubling of the military budget in peacetime," one must endure a life more miserable than ever. He continued, "There are now 34 million people in poverty, 15 percent of our nation." From his view, economic recovery was merely a dream for the poor.

The point is, Jackson said, that "rising tides don't lift all boats," which is a remark with specific meaning for US politics. President Kennedy used the original sentence, that is, "a rising tide lifts all boats," to promote the idea that improvements in the general economy would benefit all participants in that economy. Although the metaphor appeared in several of Kennedy's speeches, the phrase entered the history of US politics when President Kennedy used it in a 1963 speech to combat criticism that a tax cut he proposed to Congress was unnecessary to sustain strong economic growth. President Reagan's economic guru Arthur Laffer adopted the Kennedy quotation to preach the gospel of supply-side economics, specifically a cut that targeted the marginal tax rates for profitable corporations and wealthier individuals. However, he did not explain the difference between the two tax cuts. As a matter of fact, President Kennedy's tax cut was an example of Keynesian stimulus to boost the demand side of the economy; in contrast, President Reagan's tax cut was an example of supply-side economics to encourage investment and expand output. Make the average wage earners richer, Kennedy argued, and they will spend more. Make the rich richer, Reagan argued, and the wealth would trickle down to everyone. The illusion Jackson mocked in his Atlanta address was the idea of general economic prosperity proposed by Laffer's supply-side economics.

As a result of his criticism, Jackson's speech leaves no aspect of Reaganomics untouched. He denounced Reagan's increase of defense spending during peacetime, the cutting of government programs for the poor, and a budget cut that included nine permanent Social Security benefit cuts. Reagan racked up a double-digit unemployment (for the first time since the Great Depression), thanks to fiscal and monetary policies that drove the rate of increase in inflation down. Jackson criticized a permanent high real interest rate and argued that a "cumulative budget deficit for [Reagan's] four years is more than the sum total of deficits from George Washington to Jimmy Carter combined." In 1980, candidate Reagan had promised a balanced budget, but instead, lower income taxes and greater military spending caused a record 200-billion-dollar budget deficit. Jackson linked the budget deficit with its twin, the foreign trade deficit, as both are the product of high real interest rates.

After posing his critique of an economic policy that only further disenfranchised minorities and the poor, Jackson returned to the religious framework of his political vision in the final part of his address. Near the end, Jackson made a plea for a Democratic coalition based on values—justice and peace—in which minorities and groups with specific interests come together without losing their identities. In San Francisco, Jackson campaigned in poetry, to borrow Cuomo's famous aphorism, as political poetry was his style (Cuomo, "We campaign in poetry"). To reclaim the voice of the poor, he talked about principle not policies, all the while establishing his campaign theme and setting the marker for his 1988 campaign: "As I develop and serve, be patient: God is not finished with me yet."

Toward a Common Ground: Jackson's 1988 Atlanta Address[6]

At the 1988 Democratic National Convention in Atlanta, Jackson continued to build upon the ideas of his 1984 address, delivering an optimistic message of hope and togetherness. Again, Jackson took the stage on July 19, the second evening of the convention. At the start of his address to the delegates in Atlanta, he represented nearly 7 million votes, or 29 percent. During the primaries, he had won over 1,200 delegates (or 30 percent)—second to Michael Dukakis (the nominee)—and a dozen primaries or caucuses. He bested Hart as well as Senator Joe Biden, Senator Al Gore, Senator Paul Simon, and Congressman Richard Gephardt.[7]

His theme was how every generation of Democrats has worked together to build "common ground," to make America a more inclusive, more just nation. For instance, he recapped the African-American journey: from slavery to emancipation, from Jim Crow to the Civil Rights Movement, from Fannie Lou Hamer and Aaron Henry—the head of the Mississippi Freedom Democratic Party—to the present convention. He recalled Martin Luther King Jr. and the four little girls who died in a bombing at a church in Birmingham, Alabama. He also recalled the assassinations of Jimmie Lee Jackson,

Michael Schwerner, Andrew Goodman, James Chaney, and Viola Liuzzo as a reminder of a not-so-distant past.

But most importantly, Jackson's speech recognized the trajectory of the city of Atlanta, from the cradle of the Old South to a modern intersection of the New South. For Jackson, that transformation underscored the running theme of his address while also enabling him to summarize his own personal story with the statement, "From racial battlegrounds by law, to economic common ground"—the theme at the heart of this Atlanta address. Common ground, as exemplified in Atlanta, resembles Jerusalem, the birthplace for Judaism, Christianity, and Islam. Under the pursuit of this newfound unity, he touted common ground between the left wing and right wing of the party, between boundless liberalism and static conservatism, between lions and lambs (Isaiah 11:6-9).[8]

Why was the notion of a common ground then so important to Jackson and his vision for the United States? After all, Jackson did not indicate interest in victory. He did, though, mention survival and self-preservation as essential for the nation moving forward:

> The only time that we win is when we come together. In 1960, John Kennedy, the late John Kennedy, beat Richard Nixon by only 112,000 votes—less than one vote per precinct. He won by the margin of our hope. He brought us together. He reached out. . . . [But w]hen do we not come together, we never win. In 1968, the division and despair in July led to our defeat in November. In 1980, rancor in the spring and the summer led to Reagan in the fall. When we divide, we cannot win. We must find common ground as the basis for survival and development and change and growth.

Thus, Jackson's civil rights message of justice and togetherness was offered as a template for the entire party: Democrats win when they come together, and they survive and develop (and continue to exist) when they win.

He also introduced the audience to his theory of profit margin, which took on many versions across Jackson's lifetime. Probably the first evidence of Jackson's propensity to look at the profit margin of a business as a liability to exploit goes as far back as his initial involvement in civil rights demonstrations. After transferring to North Carolina A&T University in Greensboro, North Carolina, Jackson became involved in the Civil Rights Movement, joining the Greensboro chapter of the Council on Racial Equality (CORE). In 1963, Jackson helped to organize several sit-ins, desegregating local restaurants and theaters in Greensboro. During these civil rights demonstrations, he apparently developed the initial framework of the "theory of profit margin." His friends remember long conversations about strategy and Jackson making the point that one does not have to "spoil all the milk" to make a winning point to shopkeepers who refused to serve blacks. Instead, Jackson argued, "All you gotta do is spoil the part called 'profit.'"[9]

By the 1970s, Jackson had articulated the so-called "Kingdom Theory" and formalized his original intuition.[10] He wrote that "blacks and non-whites, we control, potentially, the margin of profit on most of the consumer items and nearly all of the basic consumer items in the nation" (qtd. in Reynolds 429). In other words, in industries where the margin of profitability is small, even if black customers are only a fraction of the total, they can still determine the success or failure of the business; they control the ultimate results. In Atlanta, Jackson proposes a political version of this original theory: in it, he states that where the margin of victory is small, even if the votes of the Rainbow Coalition are only a fraction of the total, they can still determine the success or failure of the election. In the context of the Kingdom Theory, the common ground becomes, in Jackson's words, a direct invitation to Michael Dukakis for "a commitment to a shared national campaign strategy and involvement at every level."

As we see, the motif of common ground became the expedient for Jackson to unpack his Rainbow Coalition: from blue-collar workers, farmers, teachers, and students to women, Hispanics, and the sick, particularly those without health insurance. Jackson decried "those who view social good coming from private interest, who view public life as a means to increase private wealth." He argued that Republicans were "prepared to sacrifice the common good of the many to satisfy the private interests and the wealth of a few." In contrast to his view of "a government that's a tool of our democracy in service to the public," he critiqued a vision of government as "an instrument of the aristocracy in search of private wealth."

Ultimately, Jackson held that if Reaganism promised aristocracy, Reaganomics promised reversed Robin Hoodism. Jackson told his audience that Reaganomics is "based on the belief that the rich had . . . too little money and the poor had too much." His critique of Reaganomics here takes a different path than the one from four years earlier. Back then, his criticism focused on the inefficiency of President Reagan's economic paradigm: supply-side economics and military Keynesianism. In Atlanta, Jackson seemed more concerned with the inherent inequalities of the paradigm, saying, "Seven years later, the richest 1 percent of our society pays 20 percent less in taxes. The poorest 10 percent pay 20 percent more." Jackson thus became most passionate when criticizing the Reagan administration for not using federal funds to build decent housing, educate children, wipe out slums, and put America back to work. He asked why, if the federal government willingly bailed out Continental Bank and Chrysler, it did not in turn bail out the family farmer. The pendulum must swing in the direction of protectionism, he argued, in order to protect jobs and small businesses at home.

Jackson's speech recasts the image of the poor against the notion of their perceived laziness and perpetual welfare. Rather, Jackson argued, the poor do not have a chance; they are in pain, and they cannot find jobs. When they work, they work hard and cannot get a union contract, and they cannot get insurance when they are sick: "Someone must defend them . . . [T]hey cannot speak for themselves." At the same time, his words attacked the idea that minorities universally indulge in drugs, calling for "a real war on drugs . . . at the level of supply and demand." For instance, he mentioned a conversation with black people at Watts: "We can go and buy the drugs by the boxes at the port. If we can buy the drugs at the port, don't you believe the Federal government can stop it if they want to?" Jackson's point was that the crack cocaine epidemic that exploded in the black neighborhoods in the 1980s was partially due to the federal government ignoring drug trafficking, and thus action was needed to truly give the poor a chance.

The final part of Jackson's address stands as a fine piece of rhetoric, starting with a statement from "The Call of the Open Sea," a poem of Daisy Rinehart, and ending with a portrait of himself as a young man, experiencing the struggle and the same sense of exclusion and vulnerability of the people that he represented at the convention: "I know abandonment, and people being mean to you, and saying you're nothing and nobody and can never be anything." He understood when people feel invisible, irrelevant, or like an embarrassment to the media and to the rest of society, stating, "Every one of these funny labels they put on you, those of you who are watching this broadcast tonight in the projects, on the corners, I understand. Call you outcast, low down, you can't make it, you're nothing, you're from nobody, subclass, underclass."

He was one of them.

A More Inclusive America: Commentary on Jackson's Democratic National Convention Speeches

In 1984 and 1988, Jackson delivered high-energy, high-volume speeches that got much attention in real time and channeled the moods of the Democratic Party. The general audience became aware of Jackson at the Democratic National Convention in 1984, when he delivered an address introducing black leadership and articulating a social gospel agenda for the Reagan era. At the same time, Jackson had always showed a special interest in economic issues. He liked economics at school, and he earned national recognition as leader of Operation Breadbasket, a premier economic program of King's Southern Christian Leadership Conference. He maintained a focus on economic inequality during the seventies, while advocating black capitalism and flirting with the Nixon administration. All this work and commitment to economic rights and empowerment paid off in 1984 in his profound and articulate critique of Reaganomics. Here Jackson pointed out that in reality, "a rising tide does not raise all boats." The "rising tide" metaphor that had become a mainstay of Republican supply-siders, through Laffer's misappropriation of President Kennedy's remark, was limited to the rich and to the fortunate, but it hurt the poor, which was Jackson's constituency.

As we see, Jackson's addresses at the 1984 and 1988 Democratic National Conventions stand as defining moments of his career. Often mentioned as one of the most gifted and inspiring civil rights speakers of his generation, his addresses confirmed his place as one of the twentieth century's most stirring political speakers, partly because his speeches offered a passionate call for a new kind of America where blacks, Hispanics, and Native Americans would be treated as true equals and where all minorities could be integrated without losing their unique identities. It did not, however, accomplish its immediate goal: Jackson was left at the margin of national politics. His 1984 address, nonetheless, did serve as a manifesto of sorts for issues that he would inject, four years later, into the political discourse.

In his 1988 address, Jackson repeated themes and references of his 1984 address: the civil rights martyrs, America as a rainbow, and the critique of Reaganomics. He added new angles and arguments: a synthetic view of Reaganism, a criticism of the federal bailout of banks and corporations, and a passionate defense of the honor and indispensable role of the poor, the unknown, and the defeated in American society. The Jackson social justice agenda of 1988 included many positions that were at the time "extreme" or "radical" but that have since become mainstream: implementing universal health care, accepting gays and lesbians, raising the minimum wage, appointing women to more positions in the federal government, and addressing the crisis of dysfunction in poorer public schools. "Economic common ground" became a refrain of the Jackson campaigns, including a bailout for farmers and manufacturing plants. His overall vision assumed a primary concern regarding economics for individuals, families, and small businesses rather than for big corporations and financial institutions.

In Atlanta, Jackson transcended the current political environment and diligently shifted between the common ground of reality and the higher ground of moral principles. "If we are principled first," he said, "our politics will fall in place" (Jackson, "Keep Hope Alive").

He revealed an evident interest in moving beyond the civil rights tradition and black politics, stating, "I'm tired of sailing my little boat, far inside the harbor bar. I want to go out where the big ships float, out on the deep where the great ones are" ("Keep Hope Alive"). From these words, it is clear that Jackson would be not satisfied to be seen in terms of identitarian politics, just as it was clear that he would not be invited to provide governance to the national campaign or to the Democratic Party. As a matter of fact, his 1988 address was arguably his last moment in the national spotlight.

Commentators and scholars, such as James R. Hallmark and Felicia R. Steward, have noted that Jackson's 1984 presidential campaign was race-specific and racialized and that the candidate adopted a more universal approach in his second presidential campaign in 1988 to appeal to voters beyond the black community. However, Jackson's two addresses reveal the same inclination toward integration and the same spirit of inclusion. In both speeches, Jackson affirmed his notion of integration, an integration that maintains groups' and minorities' identities, although the narrative in his 1988 address proved more fluid and his tone more convincing. Yet, the two speeches help to understand the gulf between mainstream democrats and Jesse Jackson and his coalition. The gulf was particularly evident in 1988, when Dukakis and Jackson affirmed their conviction that brainpower (the former) and idealism (the latter) could overcome bitter political divisions.

Ultimately, Jackson began his 1984 presidential campaign as a long-shot candidate, an improbable option for president of the United States. Nevertheless, he ended up finishing third in 1984 and second in 1988. At the conclusion of his second campaign, in Atlanta, he thought the leadership of the Democratic Party was not giving him the respect he had earned and the influence and authority that he deserved. Jackson thought he was not taken seriously as a legitimate politician but rather was considered unfit to join the establishment. As a matter of fact, despite two tumultuous and norm-defying campaigns, Jackson remained steadfast to the identities he crafted in his formative decades, being identified permanently with the image of the unapologetic advocate of blackness. For most

Democrats, Jackson was simply declaring a universalism because he had to enlarge his coalition to be politically relevant. The theme of common ground in his 1988 address can be appreciated in this context. Truthfully, he did not work very hard to update his image because the decades that hatched him represent the golden age of the civil rights to which he remained faithfully committed. As much as he might focus on his speech, topics like social justice, Jackson fought for control of the political use of the Civil Rights Era.

Democratic candidates Walter Mondale and Michael Dukakis were crushed by Ronald Reagan in the 1984 election and George H. W. Bush in the 1988 election respectively. Still, Jackson was ahead of his time in the 1980s, articulating problems that indeed persist nowadays. When almost no one discussed sexual-orientation rights, Jackson talked about gays and lesbians. At the height of the Reagan military buildup, he advocated real cuts in Pentagon spending. Jackson also raised issues of economic aristocracy long before the "99 percent" became part of the public vernacular, and he called for fundamental reform—access to healthcare and education, higher minimum wage, the bailout of small businesses and families, ensuring that the rich pay their fair share of taxes—that inspired working people and progressive activists across the country. Reduced to a slogan, this was his Rainbow Coalition, but it was not just an image. Jackson caught a sense that the traditional civil rights message, which conservatives reduced to "affirmative action," had partially run its course. What activist Democrats were looking for was a way to support social and economic justice by accommodating changes going on in society. If the language of Jackson's Rainbow Coalition did not resonate with Obama's 2008 campaign, the idea behind that coalition did.

Of course, in addition to being a political leader, Jackson is also an ordained Baptist minister who regularly preaches in Chicago and in churches across America. Religion played a central role in both his 1984 and 1988 addresses, for he did not hesitate to refer to God or prophets, and he frequently used biblical language and imagery drawn from both the old and the new testaments, injecting religion in his political vision. In 1987, for instance, he was adamant about what comes first in his life: "My religion obligates me to be political, to seek to do God's will and allow the spiritual word to become concrete justice and dwell among us. Religion should use you politically to do public service. Politics should not misuse religion. When the Word becomes flesh and dwells among us, that's called good religion" (qtd. in Henry 37).

This rare combination of religion and politics sets Jackson apart as a politician and as a speaker. His vocation as a minister gave him a rare quality—the ability to connect with his audience in terms of compassion, empathy, and conviction. In his 1984 and 1988 addresses, he rejected the notion of civil religion and recognized the existence of a pluralistic religious society. He even maintained a strict separation between church and state, not advocating faith-driven prescriptions or Christian-based legislations. At the same time, while he recognized his audience as composed of fellow citizens, of fellow Democrats, in his addresses, he seemed to imply that society per se has not been granted an independent salvific quality: remedy comes from the highest, even when it concerns minimum wage or nuclear disarmament. Politicians serve God and a higher ground, and—for himself—Jackson wanted to make God's will, that is, an instrument in God's hands. Religious motivations deserved more authority and held more legitimacy than did his political motivations.

From the vantage point of our times, Jackson's 1984 and 1988 Democratic National Convention addresses are thus a rare combination of Civil Rights Movement revival, stirring religious sentiment, and the prescient vision of the economic struggles of an increasing unequal society. If the Jackson presidential campaigns were not a serious shot at higher office, as some have implied, they remain an injection of the tradition of the Civil Rights Movement into the political discourse. In this context, Jackson's addresses represent a powerful message of inclusion. As a matter of fact, inclusion of the most "dispossessed and disaffected" was the backbone, the core, and the motivation of Jackson's political commitment ("Rainbow Coalition"). On the other side, in his addresses, Jackson introduced new themes and subjects that would become relevant in decades to come. He expanded and enlarged the original narrative of the Civil Right Movement by adding new minorities and issues, dedicating attention to unfamiliar topics, such as bailouts and gays rights. He demonstrated a special concern for economic justice, income, and wealth inequality, and he denounced an unfair distribution of taxes and economic fallouts that resounds still today.

Notes

1. Unattributed citations in this portion are from Jackson, "Rainbow Coalition."

2. Before Jackson, a number of black men and women have run for president but none with serious prospects of winning and a few for purely symbolic reasons: among them were the comedian and writer Dick Gregory and the Black Panther Party leader Eldridge Cleaver in 1968 as well as the Brooklyn congresswoman Shirley Chisholm in 1972.

3. In January 1984, over breakfast at Washington, DC's National Airport, presidential candidate Jesse Jackson uttered those words to Milton Coleman. The week after the airport conversation, fellow *Post* reporter Rick Atkinson talked with Coleman while writing a story on Jackson's relationship with Jewish Americans. Coleman told Atkinson about Jackson's "Hymietown" remarks. On February 13, Atkinson's story ran on the front page of the *Washington Post*, exposing Jackson's statement.

4. Tom Kahn is credited to be the first to frame the notion of "two Americas" in the pages of *New America*, writing, "The technological revolution . . . is creating two Americas—"the affluent society" and the "other America" (4).

5. "Military Keynesianism" refers to the public policy that seeks to increase military spending in order to increase economic growth; "supply side economics" is the macroeconomic theory that suggests that production (supply) underlies economic growth and argues that economic growth can be reached by taxation and fiscal policy that creates incentives to produce goods and services.

6. Unattributed citations in this portion are from Jackson, "Keep Hope Alive."

7. In March 1988, Jackson convincingly won the Michigan primary. It was his first primary victory in a northern industrial state and gave him the status a frontrunner. At that point, Jackson led Dukakis in popular votes and was neck and neck with the Massachusetts governor in delegates. By winning over a quarter of the white vote, Jackson appeared to have broken through with his image as the black presidential candidate.

8. The image of lions and lambs living peacefully in the valley is also part of a Negro spiritual, "Peace in the Valley."

9. This anecdote is provided by Carol Lynn McKibben from Stanford; she is working on a biography of Jesse Jackson and kindly allowed me to quote this episode.

10.	The name, "Kingdom Theory," comes from Jackson's basic assumption that "black people must understand themselves as having the authority of kings and that their dominions are their communities" (Reynolds 428). For a more articulated version of the application of the Kingdom Theory to politics, see Jackson, "David and Goliath."

Works Cited

Cuomo, Mario. "Tale of Two Cities." Democratic National Convention. San Francisco, CA. 17 July 1984.

_____. "We campaign in poetry, but when we're elected we're forced to govern in prose." Yale University, New Haven, CT, 15 Feb. 1985.

Hallmark, James R. "Jesse Jackson's Argumentation as an Explanation of Political Success: A Comparison of Jackson's 1984 and 1988 addresses to the Democratic National Convention." *Western Journal of Speech Communication* 4.1-2 (1992): 118-132.

Henry, Charles. *Jesse Jackson: The Search for Common Ground.* Oakland, CA: Black Scholar P, 1991.

Jackson, Jesse. "David and Goliath." Tendley Baptist Church, Philadelphia, PA. 16 Jan. 1984.

_____. "Keep Hope Alive." Democratic National Convention. Atlanta, GA. 19 July 1988.

_____. "Rainbow Coalition." Democratic National Convention. San Francisco, CA. 18 July 1984.

Kahn, Tom. "Urban League Plan for Middle Class: Preferential Treatment No Answer for Negro Masses—Full Employment Essential." *New America* 16 Feb. 1965.

Kennedy, John F. "Remark in Heber Springs, Arkansas, at the Dedication of Greers Ferry Dam." Heber Springs, Arkansas, 3 Oct. 1963. *The American Presidency Project.* Gerhard Peters & John T. Woolley, 2016. Web. 20 Dec. 2016.

Reynolds, Barbara A. *Jesse Jackson: America's David.* Washington DC: JFJ Associates, 1985.

Rinehart, Daisy. *The Call of the Open Sea.* New York: Witmark & Sons, 1910.

Steward, Felicia R. *The Oratory of Jesse Jackson in Democratic Orators from JFK to Barack Obama 2016.* Ed. Andrew S. Crines, David S. Moon, Robert Lehrman, & Philip Thody. New York: Palgrave Macmillan, 2016. 217-237.

Agency, Activism, and the Black Domestic Worker in Kathryn Stockett's *The Help* and Delores Phillips' *The Darkest Child*

Kaila Philo

During the Reconstruction period in United States history, black people freed under the Emancipation Proclamation and eventually the Fourteenth Amendment sought employment, housing, and education in order to exercise their newfound "freedom." However, most black American families found it difficult to acquire any of these resources, as white employers were not too keen on hiring ex-slaves except under the sharecropping system, especially in the South where, "[a]fter 1865, the largest population of free blacks in America resided" (Dailey xvi). Under this system, blacks were only just barely compensated for their labor, if compensated at all—a condition made all the more common under the newly-minted Jim Crow legislation put into effect. As Jane Dailey notes in *The Age of Jim Crow* (2009), "Jim Crow's power over African Americans came from exclusion" (xiv), particularly exclusion from political, educational, and economic opportunities at upward mobility. Thus, black working-class women entered the workforce as domestic servants, as the American job market scarcely opened itself up to women, let alone black women. This fresh wave of domestic servants prompted for white women a short-lived "utopia," as Susan Tucker calls it. Black domestic servants became normalized in the Deep South, considering so many black women needed the employment and so many white families could afford it. "As late as 1945," Tucker writes, "it required only half as large a family income to employ a servant in the South as it did in other parts of the country; [thus,] the South was long known as a white housewives' utopia" (52).

Two twenty-first-century novels offer us insight into the lives of these women, depicting the experiences of black domestic workers: Kathryn Stockett's *The Help* (2004) and Delores Phillips' *The Darkest Child* (2009). However, there is one important distinction between these two works: Stockett writes from the perspective of a white woman, whereas Phillips writes from that of a black woman. This fundamentally shifts the racial dynamic in the corresponding texts, as Stockett positions the main black women in the narrative—Aibileen Clark and Minny Jackson—as what Patricia Collins calls the stereotypical Mammy figure. In her essay, "Mammies, Matriarchs, and other Controlling Images," Collins explains that there is an unspoken yet universal list of generalized images pertaining to black women. The Mammy, the Jezebel, and the Sapphire—that is, the saintly black mother, the sexualized black harlot, and the sassy black bitch—are the reigning racist cultural conventions intent on painting the destitute, docile black woman as the standard. Such stereotypes are "designed to make racism, sexism, and poverty appear to be natural, normal, and an inevitable part of everyday life" (Collins 77). Barbara Christian further discusses the Mammy in *Black Women Novelists: The Development of a Tradition, 1892–1976* (1980) in which she describes her as:

> black in color as well as race and fat with enormous breasts that are full enough to nourish all the children in the world; her head is perpetually covered with her trademark kerchief to hide the kinky hair that marks her as ugly. Tied to her physical characteristics are her personality traits: she is strong, for she certainly has enough girth, but this strength is used in the service to her white master and as a way of keeping her male counterparts in check; she is kind and loyal, for she is a mother; she is [also] sexless. (12-13)

Based upon these definitions, Aibileen is reminiscent of a modern Mammy, working in white families' homes in Jim Crow-era America, though sporting a wig with straight hair instead. This is evident from the beginning of the novel as *The Help* first introduces Aibileen's perspective centered on the newest child in the white Leefolt household where Aibileen works. Here, she describes Mae Mobley as if she were her own child, literally opening the book with a description that highlights the pride she feels in her position:

> Mae Mobley was born on a early Sunday morning in August, 1960. A church baby we like to call it. Taking care a white babies, that's

what I do, along with all the cooking and the cleaning. I done raised seventeen kids in my lifetime. I know how to get them babies to sleep, stop crying, and go in the toilet bowl before they mamas even get out a bed in the morning. (Stockett 5)

There are clear similarities between *The Help*'s opening paragraph and Christian's description of the Mammy figure. Stockett introduces Aibileen to the reader as a maternal figure despite the fact that she does not yet describe her own child. It is not until seven paragraphs later—after a lengthy recollection of her first days with Mae Mobley—that Aibileen touches upon the loss of her only son, Treelore. Interestingly enough, Treelore is only given one paragraph to Mae Mobley's seven—a detail that prioritizes Aibileen's role as a servant to white families, all the while minimizing her role in her own. Furthermore, Aibileen barely shows any resentment towards her socioeconomic position at all before Eugenia "Skeeter" Phelan enters the narrative. Throughout the novel, Aibileen appears resigned to her current lifestyle, which shows precisely the pitfalls of Stockett's perspective as a wealthy white woman in the white woman's utopia. What Stockett bears witness to is undoubtedly the muted demeanor of a servant conforming to her position in order to survive, as a black maid—especially one in the Deep South circa 1960—is bound to assimilate despite her true feelings regarding her treatment. Failing to fully understand this, however, Stockett and her portrayal of Aibileen perpetuate the myth of the contented slave (or servant) for much of the novel, a tactic employed throughout US history by oppressive white slave owners and later employers in order to legitimize their role in oppression as moral acts.

Delores Phillips, on the other hand, writes from the perspective of a black woman from Bartow County, Georgia, in 1950. Phillips' inadvertent response to Stockett's Aibileen is her character Rozelle Quinn, a jaded domestic servant working for a white family for whom she does not particularly care. This disdain is most evident when instructing the main character and her daughter, Tangy Mae, to replace her: "'I don't care what I do 'round here, it's always the same fifteen dollars. Never mind that I stayed late on Tuesday evening when Mister Frederick's mother came for dinner. Never mind that I walked to the Colonial for flour that Miss Arlisa forgot to pick up. Week in, week out, always the same fifteen dollars'" (Phillips 2). As we see, Phillips' characterization of Rozelle is starkly different from that of Aibileen. She is described as cold, harsh, and violent, not to mention angry yet resigned to her lot in life. While Aibileen is forgiving towards her employers and caring towards their child, Rozelle seems to despise them. For instance, Phillips writes, "'Sign it, Rozelle Quinn,' she said. 'Miss Arlisa probably won't even know who that is. All they know 'round here is Rosie. Rosie do this and Rosie do that'" (2).

Rozelle is, perhaps, the more realistic version of a working-class woman of color with little to no career options at the time. In this sense, Delores Phillips utilizes what bell hooks calls "the oppositional gaze" towards the Mammy figure. As Carolyn West asserts, "This requires us to critically examine, challenge, and ultimately deconstruct these images to reflect more positive and accurate representations" (288). Through the oppositional gaze, Phillips appears more cognizant of the Mammy figure and dismantles it by constructing Rozelle as the anti-Mammy, opting instead to depict the harsh realities for domestic servants and those around them during Jim Crow. In contrast, Stockett, a wealthy white woman writing through a black woman's lens, is either unable or unwilling to decenter white characters such as Skeeter in narratives that have little to do with them and to move beyond stereotypical depictions of blacks. Aibileen pays little attention to her own affairs while devoting more of her time and affection to the Leefolts, despite how coldly Miss Leefolt treats her; Aibileen is thus is the quintessential Mammy figure cemented in the American racial imaginary. Therefore, by juxtaposing these two depictions of black domestic servants, we can discern the chasm between the white gaze and the black bodies under its subjugation.

The Plight of the 54 Percent: The Erasure of Black Motherhood and Childhood

This chasm is first evident in the commentary that each novel offers on motherhood and the real world consequences that black women

---

domestic workers faced when assuming such servile roles. In *The Darkest Child*, for instance, Tangy Mae is forced into domestic servitude by her mother before she is old enough to start the ninth grade. This introduces a conflict in her life, as she has to leave school. "I was in ninth grade, which in itself is miraculous," she recounts, "considering I had never set foot in an eighth-grade classroom. . . . At the age of twelve, my mother's children were expected to drop out of school, get a job, and help support the family" (Phillips 7). This was a common practice during the Jim Crow era, as 54 percent "of black children born into the bottom of the economic distribution" remained in poverty as adults before 1968 (Isaacs). According to Child and Family Policy Fellow Julia B. Isaacs, "Only 13% rise to middle class and only 4% reach the wealthiest fifth of the income distribution." This is starkly different for poor white children, as "31 percent were stuck at the bottom, 25 percent moved to middle class, and 8 percent to the top fifth of the income distribution" (Isaacs). Meanwhile, 45 percent of black children born in the middle class— incomes between 49,000 dollars to 65,000 dollars in 2006 inflation— ended up in the bottom fifth percentile, while only sixteen percent of white children from similar economic backgrounds succumbed to this fate (Isaacs). Thus, black children and white children during Jim Crow came from different socioeconomic backgrounds that often forced black children to enter the workforce early.

There was also a strange divergence in black motherhood during this period because black mothers often undertook the responsibilities of their own children and others'. This is evident in *The Help* when Aibileen claims that she has "raised" seventeen children in her lifetime, a sentiment that feeds into the Mammy dynamic but is not entirely unique to *The Help*. In 1988, Virginia-based writer Susan Tucker published *Telling Memories Among Southern Women— Domestic Workers and Their Employers in the Segregated South* (1988), a collection of interviews from black domestic workers and white employers from Southern homes. In this text, she reveals that white mothers often left their young children at home with "the help," so black servants essentially raised them at this time. This dynamic fostered a docile facade between servant and child while also creating a dangerous dependency for both parties.

In *The Help*, a defining aspect of Skeeter's character is finding out what happened to her childhood maid, Constantine Bates. Constantine was the woman who raised Skeeter and served as her confidante throughout her college years but suddenly disappeared from her life soon after. She is often mentioned throughout the text as a way to define certain habits or pleasant memories Skeeter has. It is soon revealed that Skeeter's mother, Charlotte Phelan, fired Constantine because her daughter, Lulabelle Bates, invited herself to a party Charlotte had thrown for her white friends. When Skeeter learns this, it is too late because Constantine has died of cancer; this news devastates Skeeter and serves as character development for her. Stockett even recalls this towards the end of the novel as closing words to Skeeter's character arc: "'I reckon Constantine would a been real proud a you.' Miss Skeeter smile and I see how *young* she is. After all we written and the hours we spent tired and worried, I ain't seen the girl she still is in a long, long time" (Stockett 195). Constantine, in this context, is less of a character and more of a plot device, propelling Skeeter's narrative forth and driving the overall plot, for it is Constantine that instills Skeeter's appreciation for the help in the first place. This relationship also directly mirrors Aibileen's relationship with Mae Mobley, which is central to Aibileen's character arc. While on the surface these dynamics come off as sweet, there are underlying problematic implications when one compares this relationship to that in *The Darkest Child*.

The matrilineal relationships in *The Help* versus those in *The Darkest Child* show how domestic servitude in this era disrupted mother-daughter relationships in black households while enhancing mother-daughter relationships in white households. The relationship between Rozelle and Tangy Mae is toxic to the point of violence, while Aibileen's relationship with Mae Mobley only serves to boost Mae Mobley's self-esteem and create a happier, safer home for her while giving Aibileen a reason to go on. Skeeter and Constantine's relationship is particularly disheartening considering Constantine's own daughter was alive during their time together, though the reader is offered very little insight into their relationship. Stockett positions Skeeter's dependency on Constantine as the central mother-daughter connection while writing off Constantine's relationship with Lulabelle as a nuisance to the point where Lulabelle even gets her fired.

In this context, in *The Help*, black children are relegated to background characters in their own mothers' stories, as we see in the stories of Treelore and Lulabelle, whereas in *The Darkest Child*, they are not allowed to act as children at all. Both works are therefore vital in communicating the experience of black domestic servants; however, Phillips depicts an experience seldom expressed in post-Reconstruction tales of black workers. Tangy Mae is, at first, withdrawn from school despite her love for learning in order to take on this role as domestic servant, effectively erasing her childhood given the young age she enters the field. Her story inherently calls attention to the unequal access to opportunities that prompts the Civil Rights Movement in the United States, as Tangy Mae will be trapped in the cycle her mother experienced and that seems commonplace in Stockett's work. In *The Help*, after all, the reader is given some insight as to why Aibileen became a maid in the first place when she reveals to Skeeter that she knew she would become a maid ever since she was a little girl: "'Mama was a maid,'" Aibileen explains. "'My granmama was a house slave'" (69). Through these words, it is fair for the reader to assume that Aibileen herself began domestic servitude at a young age, but at the very least, the knowledge of her own fate stole something from her childhood, further limiting her opportunity. This unfortunate dynamic shows what was given up when black women entered this field of work: while white children were always considered children, black children often lost their innocence once they became maids.

Domestic Servants during the Civil Rights Era: Activism Erased and Resurrected

The erasures of black motherhood and childhood, however, are not the only forms of erasure that plague Stockett's work, as she also decentralizes the role that black women played in the activism of the Civil Rights Era. Stockett's *The Help* begins in August 1962, and the reader soon learns that Skeeter has just graduated from the University of Mississippi. In reality, Ole Miss has just admitted its first black student, James Meredith, in September 1962, prompting riots during his arrival that claimed two lives and sent hundreds of wounded to the hospital. This event was the culmination of the tension following the *Brown v. Board of Education* decision that overturned the 1896 *Plessy v. Ferguson*—a ruling that established the separate-but-equal legislation across the United States. Up until Meredith's admittance to Ole Miss, a handful of black students were enrolled in small, whites-only colleges with little to no fuss from the public, but Meredith's enrollment in a large, historic university following an extensive legal battle actualized the new reality of racial integration for many Americans. Still, there is only one mention of James Meredith in *The Help* despite its prominence in the media and cultural conversation of the time, and it is only offered from Skeeter's perspective:

> The television set is on and I glance at it. Pascagoula's standing about five inches away from the screen. I hear the words *Ole Miss* and on the fuzzy screen I see white men in dark suits crowding the camera, sweat running off their bald heads. I come closer and see a Negro man, about my age, standing in the middle of the white men, with Army men behind him. The picture pans back and there is my old administration building . . . I watch the television, riveted. Yet I am neither thrilled nor disappointed by the news that they might let a colored man into Ole Miss, just surprised. Pascagoula, though, is breathing so loud I can hear her. She stands stock-still, not aware I am behind her. (Stockett 41)

Here, a rather pivotal moment in black history, especially for those in Mississippi, is depicted through white eyes. The reader is not given insight as to how Pascagoula feels as she "rushes out of the room, her eyes to the floor" (Stockett 42) after seeing the news report. Rather, she is depicted as just another voiceless domestic servant who serves as the tertiary lens into the black psyche for the reader. As a result, the scene only serves to provide more characterization for Skeeter. Thus, this scene sets up another problematic aspect of Stockett's portrayal of black domestic servants during the Civil Rights Era: they, like Pascagoula, are relegated to passive agents in their own liberation until the end of the text.

Aibileen, the character used to open the novel, is not even present during the interaction, thus Stockett has removed her from a potentially character-building piece of the narrative. This is one of the largest criticisms of the novel: the domestic servants are so far removed from the Civil Rights Movement that they barely seem interested in it when, in reality, black workers were at its core. Historian Premilla Nadasen centers these women in her book *The Untold Story of African-American Women Who Built a Movement* (2015), which details how domestic workers organized at the dawn of the movement. "[Domestic servants] testified, they lobbied, they shared their stories, they wrote codes of conduct and they worked to educate employers," Nadasen tells *Truthout* (qtd. in Karlin). When asked why so few remember the activism of black domestic workers of the '50s and '60s, Nadasen explains that it was because most of these workers did not have the resources or writing skills to document their work. Rather, "[h]istorical narratives are shaped to a large degree by the available archival information. So, those people who kept papers, who wrote memoirs or who had access to media outlets dominate the public record. People with little political clout and limited writing skills are often left out of the narrative" (qtd. in Karlin). This is the case with Aibileen and the other black characters in *The Help*.

Skeeter, on the other hand, who has access to these skills, champions the black maids as the most involved activist in the text, fighting for a cause that has little to do with her to begin with by writing a book based on these maids' experiences. In focusing on these acts as opposed to the roles black domestic workers played in the movement, Stockett effectively perpetuates what is called the *white savior trope* in film and literature. In these genres, a white messianic character saves a lower- or working-class character of color from some form of destitution. This character of color is most often from an urban, rural, or isolated area and proves helpless in fighting his/her own oppression. Despite the inaccuracy of such depictions, it was not until *The Help*'s 2011 film adaptation was released that widespread audiences began to express grievances with various characters' portrayals in the text. For instance, cinema studies scholar Kerry B. Wilson argues that "*The Help* adds to the cinematic trajectory of white savior narratives through its premise of having a single white female protagonist take the responsibility for rescuing her black female supporting characters from racial discrimination" (23). *The Help* serves to perpetuate the "white experience" as the default (Wilson 24) through depicting people of color as helpless to their circumstances without the guidance and leadership of a single white protagonist.

In this sense, readers were not exposed to any of the servants' academic or intellectual abilities, save for a brief mention of Aibileen's bright yet deceased son. The problem, University of Louisville's Trena Easley Armstrong argues, is that Stockett's portrayal of black domestic workers during this time is not particularly new: "Research on black domestic workers is limited and tends to focus on either the oppressive environments in which they worked or the stereotype of the happy benevolent *Mammy*. Both these images reflect strained relationships between the oppressed and the oppressor, and little agency to the black women" (2, italics original). According to Armstrong, these workers were treated as "poor, uneducated, child-like creatures" who were "victims of their own ignorance" (2). This works in contrast with how the black working class sprang into action following the Civil Rights Act of 1964. This is where Delores Phillips' depiction becomes particularly important.

The Darkest Child begins in Pakersfield, Georgia, in 1958, merely four years before *The Help* is set and four years after the Supreme Court reversed the *Plessy v. Ferguson* verdict in *Brown v. Board of Education*. It was not until 1964 that the Civil Rights Act was passed, so both novels are placed in a critical timeframe for black Americans in the South. The authors' approaches to these events, however, vary drastically. While Stockett chooses to focus more on the white families of the Mississippi, Phillips includes the nuances and insights of black domestic workers of the time, centering the narrative around them as opposed to their white counterparts. For example, the main character in *The Darkest Child*, Tangy Mae, is forced to go into domestic servitude at the dawn of her adolescence when her mother, Rozelle Quinn, declares that she is dying. The book focuses completely on their family and their trials as manual laborers or domestic workers, which also includes their involvement in the burgeoning Civil Rights Movement. Phillips introduces the movement through a conversation between Tangy Mae's brother, Sam, and his friend, Junior Fess:

> "Hambone came back from Chicago like he's ready to kill somebody. They're not somebody. They're not going to let him get away with that. We do need change, but he's going about it all wrong. We need to organize like they're doing in other cities, bring in the NAACP. We need to be in agreement on what we're going to do and how we are going to do it. You can't beat a man down with your fists and not expect retaliation but that's just what Hambone thinks he can do. I, for one, think we should solicit help from the outside. We need laws to enforce the law—if you know what I mean. Take Chad Lowe for instance. He's not a sheriff, deputy, or policeman, but he carries a gun and patrols the Negro sections, and we allow it. That's the first thing we need to put a stop to." (Phillips 18)

This passage is in stark contrast with Stockett's portrayal of James Meredith's enrollment to Ole Miss. For one, Phillips grants Junior agency, providing him with the intellectual and spiritual means to attempt a revolution with those he loves. This, plus Tangy Mae's simple love for education and hesitance to leave school to work, resists the societal perception of blacks that both bastardizes and villainizes them, especially black women. In *The Help*, the only black character who appears to care about his education is Aibileen's son, mentioned through a throwaway line as Aibileen briefly recalls his life. Otherwise, a formal education does not play into either Aibileen or Minny's life very much, feeding into this image of the black maid as ignorant and helpless. Most importantly, however, Phillips introduces the ways in which blacks were active in the civil rights struggle, far from the passive observers that Stockett depicts.

Her work is therefore important in challenging what Chimamanda Adichie refers to as "the single story" in American literature—a one-sided depiction of otherwise complex minority experiences that is sometimes "used to dispossess and malign."

Conveying the Black Maid Experience: Psychosocial Trauma Unveiled

One critical—perhaps devastating—difference between how Rozelle Quinn and Aibileen Clark are portrayed as black domestic workers in a post-Jim Crow society below the Mason-Dixon Line is their psychological disposition. Post-slavery racism had perforated employment opportunities for black Americans, while institutional sexism kept women out of the workplace; white women often worked as seamstresses—if they had to work at all—and, by the turn of the twentieth century, black women in America were so restricted in their job prospects that they resorted to domestic work to support their families. In 1890, almost forty percent of all black women worked outside the home in domestic trades, but "[d]uring the 1960s" as economic opportunities further waned, "nearly ninety percent of black women in the South worked as domestic servants" (Armstrong iv). These jobs were exploitative, earning the women low wages, unfavorable working conditions, long hours of work, and no benefits (Tolla 3). This put black women in compromising positions: they were trapped in domestic servitude to survive, and their psychological dispositions suffered because of it.

In *The Help*, Aibileen, indoctrinated in the culture of Jim Crow, is depicted as serene, kindhearted, and resigned to her position in life, though Stockett fails to truly acknowledge this disposition as mandated by a society increasingly violent against black bodies. Thus, one could say that Aibileen is passive to a fault, as depicted later in chapter one when Skeeter and Aibileen converse, or rather, Skeeter speaks to Aibileen and Aibileen responds out of duty. Before this exchange, Aibileen's employer, Miss Hilly, proposes what she calls the "Home Help Sanitation Initiative" in which black domestic workers would be forced to use separate bathrooms in whoever's home they work. Skeeter protests, prompting Miss Hilly to throw Skeeter out of her home, but Aibileen "goes in the kitchen and [doesn't] come out again till [she] hear[s] the door close after Miss Hilly's behind" (Stockett 9). Skeeter then follows Aibileen to apologize for Miss Hilly's bigotry, and the following exchange ensues:

> She shake her head, just a little. "Aibileen, that talk in there Hilly's talk, I mean . . ."
>
> I pick up a coffee cup, start drying it real good with my cloth.
>
> "Do you ever wish you could . . . change things?" she asks.
> And I can't help myself. I look at her head on. 'Cause that's one a the stupidest questions I ever heard. She got a confused, disgusted look on her face, like she done salted her coffee instead a sugared it. I turn back to my washing, so she don't see me rolling my eyes. "Oh no, ma'am, everything's fine." (Stockett 10)

This exchange perfectly encapsulates their positions as active and passive agents in their liberation. Aibileen is the passive agent, complicit in her own oppression by never openly rejecting or resisting her oppressors, while Skeeter, the active agent, immediately mobilizes when Miss Hilly inadvertently threatens Aibileen with an act of cultural violence. Skeeter even experiences an emotional reaction to this violence, while Aibileen appears rather stoic. This seems to be how Aibileen deals with any violence or trauma she experiences, as also depicted earlier in the novel when she mentions her son dying. When positive emotions and experiences are interrupted with the negative, Aibileen simply does not respond. This is a coping mechanism developed from a long history of psychological abuse that results in what sociologist Ruth K. Thompson-Miller calls *segregation stress syndrome* or SSS.

"Preliminary findings indicate that the symptoms of segregation stress syndrome are similar to post-traumatic stress disorder symptoms documented in psychiatric literature," Thompson-Miller writes; however, "segregation stress syndrome differs from PTSD because the traumatic experience was not a one-time occurrence;

it was sustained over time, in African American communities" (iii-iv). On the one hand, Thompson-Miller argues that racial violence that occurred at or around the time of Jim Crow legislation was the culmination of systematic chronic stress, which most often eats away at the subject's psychological well-being. On the other hand, according to the Anxiety and Depression Association of America, emotional numbness and avoidance of traumatic places, people, and activities are also symptoms faced. Though Stockett presents Aibileen as the contented servant, in reality, Aibileen's avoidance of negative experiences should speak to the means by which many African-American people survived during the Jim Crow era. Repressing her true feelings, given her own lack of power, Aibileen may suffer a form of segregation stress syndrome that shapes how she thinks and behaves in predominantly white settings.

Meanwhile, in *The Darkest Child*, Rozelle has become a similar yet significantly harsher woman in part due to her social and economic circumstances. She is generally characterized as cold, Tangy Mae even describing her as a "demon that hibernated beneath her elegant surface" (Phillips 2). Where Aibileen remains passive and kind during her oppressive experience in servitude, one could argue that Rozelle is made controlling and violent, often abusing her own children as her only channel of emotion. One instance in particular that shows this abusive behavior and how deeply it has affected them speaks to the deterioration of Rozelle's psychological well-being that Thompson-Miller finds common among African Americans suffering from SSS. Here, Tangy Mae recounts a lesson she and her siblings learned early in their youth "through a curriculum of intimidation and pain" (13). "'In fact,'" she says, "'we had all been students in that classroom with our mother as our teacher'" (13). In this particularly violent and upsetting scene—scenes the likes of which are wholly absent from *The Help*—Rozelle thrusts an ice pick through her daughter Martha Jean's hand in an attempt to gain control at home when frustrated by her lack of control in a notably prejudicial society.

Rozelle's behavior is quite different from Aibileen's reaction to her condition; however, both narratives speak to the diverse range of behaviors that blacks engaged during the time. The violence presented through such scenes thus shows the very real impact of Jim Crow culture on women like Rozelle, denied the safety and security enjoyed by their white counterparts in a society that still very much perceived of black domestic workers as property. As Thompson-Miller writes, "The possibility that you would be attacked violently was a constant fear for African Americans" (74). To keep their jobs, black domestic workers were often coerced into performing sexual favors for their employers. In fact, it is revealed in the novel that Rozelle was the result of her mother's rape by a white man, a circumstance that may have had lasting and dire consequences on her mental health, leading her to murder her child Tarabelle Quinn later in the novel and eventually forcing her into an insane asylum. While both works have merit in their depictions of the psychological dispositions of black women, the graphic inclusion of such violence in *The Darkest Child* versus the near-exclusion of violence in *The Help* shows how far removed from the realities of black women workers Stockett is. Rozelle Quinn's temperament is heartbreaking but may be the depiction closer to reality for many black mothers of the time, having difficulty coping with the abuse and disenfranchisement they undoubtedly faced.

Conclusion

Ultimately, the dynamic between black woman and white, between oppressed and oppressor, between surrogate mothers and daughters is evident in Stockett and Phillips' differing perspectives. In *The Help*, a black woman's plight from the white perspective may not seem much of a plight at all, for Stockett only sees a shallow interpretation of the domestic servant filtered through the lens of someone in power. One could argue that this is a given considering it is nearly impossible for us all to understand each other's lives despite the biographies we read or write; however, this dynamic is only one example of the much larger, more harmful issue of how black women are portrayed in literature, film, television, etc. The issue is only compounded with works such as *The Help*, now one of the most visible, twenty-first-century depictions of black domestic servants during the Civil Rights Movement, grossing millions of dollars in book sales alone and reaching audiences across the globe through its film adaption, while *The Darkest Child* remains an unsung beacon for those who seek agency. It seems, for some at least, that Stockett has become a defining voice for black domestic workers and their employers as opposed to the workers speaking themselves.

This is by no means an anomaly. The dominant culture controls how marginalized cultures are represented in their media, and if the dominant culture maintains a harmful view of the marginalized, it perpetuates oppressive regimes. For instance, if the American media continues to portray black men as criminals, this image may feed into how others view black men, perpetuating a negative stereotype that often leads to racial profiling. It is therefore important to note that such portrayals have very tangible consequences as to how people are treated in real-world settings. In Stockett's case, she may have ignited sympathy for the workers through *The Help*, but she did not garner respect for these women nor did she inspire many people to read personal accounts from domestic workers themselves—a flaw that makes Phillips' *The Darkest Child* all the more important in presenting that balance of stories needed to combat the pervasive myths that deny African Americans' activism and agency. In the words of Chimamanda Adichie: "Stories matter. Many stories matter. Stories have been used to dispossess and to malign, but stories can also be used to empower and to humanize. Stories can break the dignity of a people, but stories can also repair that broken dignity." It is only through the telling of multiples tales that we can reach a better understanding of these women's lives and their undeniable impact on our society.

Works Cited

Adichie, Chimamanda. "The Danger of a Single Story." *TED*. TedGlobal, July 2009. Online video clip.

Armstrong, Trena Easley. "The Hidden Help: Black Domestic Workers in the Civil Rights Movement." *ThinkIR: The University of Louisville's Institutional Repository* 46 (2012): 1-134.

Collins, Patricia. "Mammies, Matriarchs, and Other Controlling Images." *Black Feminist Thought*. New York: Routledge Classics, 2009. 76-106.

Christian, Barbara. *Black Women Novelists: The Development of a Tradition, 1892–1976*. Westport, CT: Greenwood P, 1980.

Dailey, Jane. *The Age of Jim Crow*. New York: Norton, 2009.

Isaacs, Julia B. "Movin' on Up? The Income Mobility of Black and White Children from the 1960s." *Urban Wire*. Urban Institute, 21 Aug. 2013. Web. 17 Dec. 2016.

Karlin, Mark. "Reclaiming Labor History: How Domestic Workers Resisted Racism in the '60s and '70s." *Truthout*. 18 Oct. 2015.

Levenstein, Lisa. "Revisiting the Roots of 1960s Civil Rights Activism: Class and Gender in 'Up South.'" *The Pennsylvania Magazine of History and Biography* 130.4 (2006): 386-92.

Phillips, Delores. *The Darkest Child*. New York: Soho, 2004.

Stockett, Kathryn. *The Help*. New York: Amy Einhorn, 2009.

Thompson-Miller, Ruth K. *Jim Crow's Legacy: Segregation Stress Syndrome*. Diss. Texas A&M University, 2011.

Tolla, Tsidiso. "Black women's experiences of domestic work: Domestic workers in Mpumalanga." Diss. University of Cape Town, 2013.

Tucker, Susan. *Telling Memories among Southern Women: Domestic Workers and Their Employers in the Segregated South*. Baton Rouge: Louisiana State UP, 1988.

Wallace-Sanders, Kimberly. "The 'Mammification' of a Nation." *Mammy: A Century of Race, Gender, and Southern Memory*. Ann Arbor: U of Michigan, 2008.

West, Carolyn M. "Mammy, Jezebel, Sapphire, and Their Homegirls: Developing an 'Oppositional Gaze' Toward the Images of Black Women." *Lectures on the Psychology of Women*. Ed. Joan C. Chrisler, Carla Golden, & Patricia D. Rozee. 4th ed. Long Grove, IL: Waveland P, 2008. 286-299.

Wilson, Kerry B. "Selling the White Savior Narrative: The Help, Theatrical Previews, and US Movie Audiences." *Mobilized Identities: Mediated Subjectivity and Cultural Crisis in the Neoliberal Era*. Champaign, IL: Common Ground, 2013. 23-41.

Staging MLK in the Age of Colorblindness: *The Good Negro* and *The Mountaintop*

Andrew Sargent

Who was Martin Luther King Jr.? What did he stand for? To most Americans, King will always be the noble advocate of nonviolence who stood on the steps of the Lincoln Memorial in 1963 and proclaimed his "Dream" of a colorblind society. This canonized King, fêted each year with the federal holiday that bears his name, dominates what Renee Romano and Leigh Raiford have called the "consensus memory" (xiv) of the Civil Rights Movement. Yet Tracey Scott Wilson's *The Good Negro* (2009) and Katori Hall's *The Mountaintop* (2009) challenge this safe, saintly, oversimplified version of King and unsettle our conventional ideas of the man and the movement he is credited with leading. Premiering in 2009—just after Barack Obama won the White House and just before Michelle Alexander rechristened our "Age of Colorblindness" (204) the era of a "New Jim Crow" (3)—these plays reexamine King's life and legacy and, in the process, comment on racial contradictions that still roil America nearly fifty years after his death.[1]

Each play takes what might nominally be called a "warts-and-all" approach to staging MLK and centers on a single crisis point in his career. In *The Good Negro*, Wilson considers how the personal shortcomings of King stand-in James Lawrence threaten to sabotage a nascent desegregation campaign in Birmingham, Alabama, in 1962. In *The Mountaintop*, Hall imagines a depressed and exhausted King, who, confined to a Memphis motel room on April 3, 1968— the last night of his life—drinks, smokes, lies, and curses; drafts a speech titled "Why America Is Going to Hell" (5); and propositions a beautiful hotel maid. But what these plays achieve through such humanizing details is not cheap sensationalism. As black women writers resisting what Trudier Harris has called a tendency among many African Americans to "place an aura of protection around heroic figures in their communities" (111), both Wilson and Hall struggled mightily with the politics of their undertaking. Wilson felt "a lot of guilt" about "air[ing] . . . dirty laundry" (Blankenship AR6), while Hall received feedback that she was "a 'confused child' who didn't respect her elders" (Schulman 31).

Wilson and Hall do not expose King's "dirty laundry" to tarnish his legacy; rather, they use it to probe his personal struggles, his overlooked late-career radicalism, and his relationship to the marginalized people his movement sought to liberate. Considering King's womanizing and self-doubt, for example, enables Wilson to suggest how a flawed man was forced, by America's racial hypocrisies and by the needs of a fragile movement, to role-play as a perfect public figure. For Hall, considering an exasperated King at the close of his life prompts us to reckon with King's protests against American capitalism and militarism—critiques typically suppressed in our country's "Dream"-centric observations of the King national holiday.

How exactly, then, do Wilson and Hall stage MLK? In dramatizing King for the theater, both plays draw on historical scholarship that has already sought to tell complex truths about King and the movement.[2] But the plays do not passively reproduce this material; rather they compress and reimagine it. Consider first that in featuring King as a part played by an actor, each play allegorizes the artificiality of King's great-man role. When Wilson's Lawrence confesses, "I can't even remember how I got here" (71) and Hall's King code-switches into a "'King' voice" (12), we glimpse the chasm between the private man and the public figure. Similarly, Hall's focus on King's anger about American involvement in Vietnam and indifference to poverty at home signals that the colorblind integrationist King has become in death is a role he has been cast in by a country stricken with "amnesia about what [he] really stood for" (Romano & Raiford xviii). If, as Michael Eric Dyson puts it, "the best scholarship on King has already warned against smothering him in fable," it is also true that "[s]ometimes poetry" or plays tell "more truth about history" (vii).

Both plays take strategic liberties with the historical record. *The Good Negro* fictionalizes King, creates composite characters, and reorders iconic events, while *The Mountaintop* depicts the actual

King but swerves from naturalism into magical realism, a stylistic analogue of sorts for Hall's contention that King was at once "man" (19) and "angel" (56). Each play also acknowledges the FBI's well-documented harassment of King, with Wilson making it a central motif in her play by using a split stage to juxtapose Lawrence with the two white agents who wiretap him. If the FBI's surveillance allows us to eavesdrop on Lawrence, it also exposes a racial double standard in which Lawrence must conceal his imperfections to avoid destroying his movement, while the vulgar white agents who spy on him are exempted from having to meet such standards at all.

But the plays' most important strategy is to pair King with an unlettered, working-class—and wholly fictional—African-American character whose encounter with the great man forces King to confront his own egotism and class elitism. In *The Good Negro*, this character is Pelzie, husband of the Rosa Parks-like Claudette.[3] Unlike his polished wife, Pelzie embodies the black masses whom the movement purported to liberate but whose lack of "respectability" put them at risk of dismissal by a civil rights elite pressured to focus on "good" Negroes in order to prick white America's conscience. In *The Mountaintop*, this marginal figure is Camae, a beautiful hotel maid who banters with King in an earthy vernacular but who is ultimately revealed to be his angel of death. Camae's presence challenges the historical erasure of black women as pivotal players in the Civil Rights Movement, and, with Pelzie, illustrates how the black grassroots led King as often as he led it.

By granting King a starring role but recognizing the movement's marginal actors, Wilson and Hall anticipate recent work by scholars such as Erica R. Edwards and Robert J. Patterson, who argue that the tendency to privilege a charismatic black male messiah in movement history must be questioned if we are to envision a collective struggle in which many have played, and can play, a crucial part.[4] The plays' emphasis not merely on King but on those around King also places them in intertextual dialogue with the most significant novel on King to date: Charles Johnson's *Dreamer* (1998), which views King through the eyes of a lowly aide and pairs King with a working-class lookalike hired to impersonate the great leader.[5]

Ultimately, this investment in marginalized perspectives may be expressed most powerfully in the plays' authorship. As plays penned by black women, both *The Good Negro* and *The Mountaintop* assert the value of African-American women's voices in defining King's position in the American racial imaginary. That they anticipate by five years Ava DuVernay's *Selma* (2014)—notable as Hollywood's first MLK feature and the rare studio movie directed by an African-American woman—is significant as well. In a sense, Wilson and Hall could be seen as part of a collective of African-American women artists and scholars—whose ranks would include DuVernay, Harris, Edwards, Raiford, and others—who are reassessing how to memorialize a movement in which the contributions of black women were, and are, too often undervalued.

The Good Negro: The Racial Politics of Having to Be Perfect

The Good Negro opens as Claudette Sullivan, a young black mother, is roughly arrested for allowing her four-year-old daughter, Shelly, to use a whites-only restroom at a Birmingham department store where the black toilet is out of order. The arrest, juxtaposed in split scene with Lawrence's sermon to a weary congregation, suggests how King's nonviolent movement paradoxically drew energy from incidents of racist violence: in a sense, the movement *needed* bigoted white cops to brutalize innocent African Americans so that the passions of King's followers could be ignited and the ugly reality of Jim Crow dramatized to a complacent white world. Equally paradoxical is that even as Lawrence will find in Claudette his Rosa Parks-like "good Negro"—one character calls her a "sweet, kind, noble Negro woman who just wanted her daughter to use the bathroom" (Wilson 66)—Lawrence himself is anything but "good." Tortured by self-doubt and stymied by infighting among his advisors, he is also wiretapped by FBI agents who record his trysts with other women in an effort to sabotage the movement.

As the title of Wilson's play implies, it is that tension—between Lawrence's "personal weaknesses" (42) and the "good Negro" standard that a racist society forces his movement to uphold—that forms the play's crux. Wilson explained in 2010 that she chose her title while

> looking at these images of King, and [Ralph] Abernathy, and Andrew Young, and every time you saw them in public, they were impeccably dressed. The image they were projecting to the world was that they were exceptional human beings, so in a way they were saying, "We deserve our rights because we're good." (Goodman Theatre)

Early in the play, Wilson illustrates the pressure that having to be "good" imposes on the movement leaders who must rely on specific black individuals to symbolize to the wider public the oppressiveness of Jim Crow but who struggle to find persons with the requisite polish and pedigree. In one scene, Lawrence and his two closest associates—the Abernathy-esque Henry Evans and the Bayard Rustin-like Bill Rutherford—discuss how earlier desegregation campaigns have failed because the test cases turned out to be, as Henry puts it, one "bad Negro" after another: one woman, Lawrence explains, "had two kids out of wedlock, cursed like a sailor, daddy was drunk. How could we . . . build a movement around her?" (Wilson 18). Accordingly, after Claudette's arrest, Rutherford and Evans must begin the process of what Evans calls "vetting" (8) her so that, as Rutherford puts it, "white people will not be able to find fault with [her] or disparage her character" (17).[6]

The pressure of having to be perfect exhausts and depresses Lawrence. In a poignant exchange late in the play, he confesses that he wishes he could be like "those brothers" he sees "in the pool halls . . . shimmy-shamming up to some honey, smoking and drinking" because, as he puts it, "It's the only time I feel free. Not a Negro then. Just like everybody else. Feels good to be like everybody else" (Wilson 71). This confession suggests that for Lawrence, having to be one of the "good respectable Negroes" instead of being "wild and crazy" (71) has become a straitjacket that constricts his humanity.

As Wilson makes clear throughout *The Good Negro*, this pressure is exacerbated by relentless FBI surveillance. By punctuating scenes with FBI audio recordings of Lawrence and his associates and by using split scenes to position the black civil rights leaders alongside the two white FBI agents who spy on them, Wilson suggests that while both parties speak and behave in ways that would not reflect well on them in public, only the FBI agents can do so with impunity. Consider, for example, the coarse language that the agents—Paul and Steve—use in almost every scene: they refer to Claudette as a "hot piece of ass" (Wilson 12); lace their conversations with "shit" (12, 62), "goddamn" (13, 72, 75), and "fuck" (12, 14, 23, 45, 51, 59, 62, 73, 75); and confess crudely to infidelity. But while the agents' bad behavior mirrors and even exceeds Lawrence's, their power and racial privilege enable them to do anything they want, including prodding an informant to join the Ku Klux Klan and to participate in racist violence that leads directly to the death of Claudette's four-year-old daughter. Meanwhile, Lawrence's own infidelities risk confirming racist stereotypes about sexually insatiable African-American men and bringing down his entire movement. When Paul and Steve compose an anonymous letter to Lawrence that condemns him as "degenerate," "disgusting," and "immoral" (63)—a nod at the real-life letter and sex tape sent by J. Edgar Hoover's FBI to the King residence in 1964—the irony is not lost on the audience that such words could easily describe the agents as well.

This insight is reinforced late in the play, when Lawrence tries to explain to Pelzie why the movement leaders may soon abandon Birmingham: "The whole world is watching. They are waiting for us to fuck it up. They are waiting for us to talk wrong, walk wrong, be wrong, and then they can say, 'See? Look at them niggers. No better than animals. No better. I told you so" (Wilson 81). When Pelzie protests that "[w]hite people don't be talking right or walking right," Lawrence answers pointedly, "No, but they got their rights already" (81). Those in power have the luxury of expressing their full humanity without fear of racial categorization, Wilson implies, while African-American civil rights leaders must uphold an image of perfection in order to counter fictions of black inferiority that segregationists will use to destroy the movement.

"We good enough": Rejecting Respectability

Yet Wilson also invites us to view Lawrence, not racism or the FBI, as the primary author of his own problems. Late in the play, when Lawrence begs his wife Corinne (a Coretta Scott King stand-in), "Don't let that tape destroy us, Corinne. That's what they want. That's why they sent it." Corinne shoots back: "You're destroying us, Jimmy. You! Not anybody else. That's why this movement is all messed up, 'cause you all messed up. Screwing your congregation, rubbing up against everything that moves. Acting just the like coons they say we are" (Wilson 65). Later, she accuses her husband of "put[ting] that child [Shelly] out there just because of that tape" (68). In such moments, Wilson implies that Lawrence is guilty not only of using Jim Crow racism as an excuse for his own unethical behavior but also of failing to realize that his insistence on exploiting a young child—a perfect "good Negro"—to galvanize a freedom rally is arguably a capitulation to the same impossible racial standards that weigh so heavily on him.

Chasing those standards, the play suggests, can only lead to tragedy. Synthesizing the Birmingham Children's Crusade of May 1963 with the Sixteenth Street Baptist Church bombing of September 1963, the play climaxes when Shelly, the "sweet, sweet baby girl [who] was thrown in jail" (Wilson 20), is killed in a retaliatory firebombing after being pressured to speak at a freedom rally.[7] After Shelly's death, Wilson allows Pelzie, who has rejected the movement and hates Lawrence for bedding his wife, to rebuke the great man for caring about Claudette and Shelly not for their inherent worth as human beings but for their instrumental value to the movement:

> Y'all figured 'Dette was good for y'all because she look nice and talk nice. A good Negro woman for all the peoples. That what y'all saw. You ain't know her at all. She a good Negro woman, but not cause y'all say so. And now Shelly. She good for y'all too. 'Cause she just a baby. Can't nobody say 'bout her you ain't talking right or walking right or looking right. 'Cause she just a baby. But y'all ain't know her either. You ain't know 'Dette and you ain't know Shelly. . . . You hear me, Reverend? (Wilson 80)

In delivering this stinging critique of the dehumanizing force of black respectability politics—notably in an un-Lawrence-like vernacular—Pelzie resists the "good Negro" label that the movement leaders have affixed to his wife and daughter. To view a person as "good," Pelzie asserts, is not to "know" him/her. Claudette and Shelly hold value on their own terms, not on the terms that a white supremacist society forces movement leaders—whom Pelzie addresses as "Y'all"—to impose on them. In a sense, the movement's preoccupation with respectability politics meant that in a society that requires African Americans to be scrubbed of all imperfections to qualify as human beings, the only African Americans who could possibly rate as "good Negroes" were children. In the King-led Civil Rights Movement's effort to combat Jim Crow by publicly dramatizing the spectacle of racist violence against morally unimpeachable blacks, Pelzie suggests, the movement inadvertently reinforced the racism that underwrote Jim Crow itself.

In a surprise twist at the end of the play, Pelzie enlists this same logic to convince Lawrence—a man he despises—to remain in Birmingham and continue fighting for black rights. Informed that movement leaders may soon be leaving, Pelzie admonishes Lawrence to "[s]tays here and fight" (Wilson 81) if his slain daughter's humanity is to be honored. Pelzie's powerful rationale: "'Cause we good enough," he tells Lawrence. "We good enough, Reverend" (81). Through Pelzie, Wilson suggests that African Americans deserve their rights not because they adhere to a white-constructed notion of acceptable humanity but because the humanity they already have is sufficient to merit them full equality. Pelzie's words argue that it is the task of the movement to force its own leaders, as well as the society it seeks to transform, to recognize that African Americans—be they a lowly Pelzie or a lofty King—should not have to be "good" but rather "good *enough*" in order to be free.

The Mountaintop: Against King's Deification

In its opening moments, *The Mountaintop* amplifies *The Good Negro*'s attention to unflattering details about King. As the curtain opens on King's drab room in Memphis's Lorraine Motel on the stormy night of April 3, 1968, Hall's stage directions call for a King who is *"[t]ired," "overwrought,"* and *"hoarse"* (5). He urinates (off stage), comments on his smelly feet, drinks, chain-smokes, curses, obsesses over his mustache, lies to his wife on the phone, and makes sexual advances toward Camae, a "mysterious" (4) African-American hotel maid. This blunt picture of King perhaps explains why *The Mountaintop* generated more attention than *The Good Negro*, including a splashy 2011 Broadway run starring Hollywood actors Samuel L. Jackson and Angela Bassett.[8]

Yet embedded in this seemingly tawdry approach is Hall's implication that it is only by engaging with the "human" King, the "radical" King, and the people around King that Hall can wage what Dyson calls a "loving war against [King's] lazy deification" (vii). Consider how Hall intertwines King's urination with evidence of his physical exhaustion and political militancy. Just after King *"loosens his tie. Unbuttons his shirt. Coughs,"* he reads aloud, "Why America is going to Hell" (Hall 5). He then *"goes into the bathroom"* and repeats "Why America is going to Hell" before *"[w]e hear him urinate"* (5). Immediately after he *"flushes the toilet"* and *"walks back into the room,"* King muses aloud, "They really gonna burn me on the cross for that one. 'America, you are too ARROGANT!'" (5). By tethering a King in need of physical relief to the fiery critic of American society that King became in his final years, Hall highlights the physical cost of King's outspokenness; when he *"[c]hecks the phone for bugs"* (6), we glimpse the political costs as well.

Camae's entrance moments later seems similarly aimed at highlighting King's indiscretions: *"stunned by her beauty"* (Hall 7), King propositions Camae within the play's first ten minutes. But again, Hall is pursuing more than salaciousness. While the rapport between King and Camae is charged with sexual energy, it also draws out a folksy King all but absent from *The Good Negro*: as King and Camae flirt, King slips into a down-home vernacular, telling Camae, "I likes you" (12), despite the fact that she ribs "Preacher Kang" for being a "bougie Negro" (27).

Camae's most urgent symbolic role emerges when she dons King's jacket and shoes, stands on his bed, and delivers her own hyper-militant rewrite of King's "going to Hell" speech. "*I got a plan*" (Hall 24), Camae asserts, as she questions the relevance of nonviolent marches. Sermonizing in an animated "'King' voice" (24), Camae bellows, "I'm sick and tired of being sick and tired, and today is the day that I tell you to KILL the white man!" and "We are fighting to sit at the same counter, but *why*, my brothers and sisters? We should build our own counters. . . . The white man ain't got nothin' I want. . . . *Fuck* the white man! I say, FUCK 'em!" (24).

This stunning performance operates on several thematic registers. It expresses a late-'60s brand of black anger, black nationalism, and skepticism toward nonviolence. It suggests that "King" is in part a rhetorical role that can be performed even by society's lowliest members. And, perhaps most important, it dramatizes black women's self-assertion in the movement's patriarchal leadership structure. When Camae first asks King's permission to speak, her wry comment, "*I'm* just a woman. Folk'll never listen to me" (Hall 23), registers that black women were rarely afforded prominent roles in the movement or credited in accounts of the era. As a silenced black woman with the courage to speak truths King cannot, Camae mirrors such figures as voting rights activist Fannie Lou Hamer, who "played a major role in the Civil Rights Movement in Mississippi" and "was a spell-binding orator who spoke from the authority of her experience" but received "no mention . . . in any of King's speeches and writings" (Cone 278). June Jordan faults King for this omission, arguing that "one can find scant indication that Dr. King recognized the indispensable work of black women" in the movement and "no record of his gratitude" for the work of either Hamer or fellow activist Ella Baker (152).[9]

Hall corroborates this chauvinism only a moment later when King compliments Camae's speech but asserts, "*I'm* better. Nobody can make it pretty like me" (27). And when King does attempt to praise Camae, he says, "Not too many maids spouting off well-formed diatribes like that," to which Camae replies in a way that jabs at King's elitism: "What, you thank us po' folk can't talk? You thank we dumb? . . . You thank you always gotta talk for us?" (26-27).

Camae's earthiness, like Pelzie's, also rebukes the good-Negro straitjacket that thrust Rosa Parks into the role of test-symbol for the movement. If, as Danielle McGuire puts it, Parks was transformed into "a symbol of virtuous black womanhood" (100) and "sainted and celebrated for her quiet dignity, prim demeanor, and middle-class propriety, her radicalism all but erased" (107), Camae resists that dubious honor herself. Her status as a literal angel thus becomes highly ironic: at the end of the play, Camae confesses to King that before she became an angel, she worked as a prostitute who, only the night before, was strangled to death by a john in an alley, then selected by God—who is herself a "proud" black woman (Hall 47)—to prepare King for the afterlife.

Even as Camae's speech stages a symbolic moment of black women's power, King's receptive response also reminds us that, by 1968, such anger was, in fact, part of King's *own* makeup. Though King's reputation today rests on his message of nonviolence and agapic love, King had grown increasingly frustrated at America's ongoing poverty, racism, and war-mongering. Indeed, while Camae quickly apologizes that she "just can't control [her] mouth" (Hall 24), she has clearly made King think: "'Fuck the white man'? *(Long heavy beat.)* I likes that," he muses. "I think that'll be the title of my next sermon. Amen! Fuck 'em!" and "Maybe you're right. Maybe the voice of violence is the only voice white folks'll listen to" (25).

King's assent here forces those who would view him only as a gentle integrationist to acknowledge the radical King who was challenged by Black Power; who called the United States government "the greatest purveyor of violence in the world" ("Beyond Vietnam" 143); who encouraged the black man in 1967 to "rise up with an affirmation of his own Olympian manhood" and to "say, 'I'm black and I'm beautiful'" ("Where Do We Go" 246); and whose Poor People's Campaign compelled him to Memphis to support striking black sanitation workers.[10]

Creative Synthesis: Reconciling King's Contradictions

The Mountaintop thus asks us to view King in seemingly contradictory ways: as a nonviolent integrationist and an impassioned radical, a polished icon and a flawed human being, and a leader both irreplaceable and wholly dependent on countless foot soldiers. Such oppositions, the play implies, are essential to a sophisticated understanding of King and to achieving what King himself, inspired by Hegel, called a "creative synthesis of opposites in fruitful harmony" in which "truth is found neither in the thesis nor the antithesis, but in the emergent synthesis which reconciles the two" (*Strength to Love* 1). This synthesis is evident as *The Mountaintop* moves toward its climax, in which Camae, having revealed herself as King's angel of death, helps a fearful King accept his imminent demise. Hall at first presents King as an egotist certain that his death will derail the movement and who must be told by Camae, "It ain't all about you" (Hall 44) and "[Y]ou gone have to pass off that baton, little man" (45). But Camae also concedes that "Many, many will carry [the baton] on, but there will never be another you. You are a once-in-a-lifetime affair" (56).

This balance between revealing and revering King also informs the play's spellbinding conclusion, in which Camae allows King to view images of America's post-1968 future before glimpsing the potential "Promised Land" he will not live to see. Moved by this vision, King exhorts the audience to "[w]alk toward the Promised Land, my America, my sweet America, with this baton I give to you, this baton I shall no longer carry. Because you are the climbers, the new carriers of the cross. I beg you, implore you, don't give in and toss it off" (Hall 62).

While Soyica Diggs Colbert has argued that Hall's "choice to give the King character the final words of the play seem[s] to encourage audiences to focus attention on him" in a way that unfortunately reinforces the received notion of King-centric civil rights leadership (280), it is important to note that this moment of rhetorical grandeur arrives only after Hall has spent the rest of the play dramatizing King's limitations. King's words inspire us only after we have seen him at his most despondent, "*[c]rying his heart out*" and "*dissolv[ing] into the child no one ever saw*" (Hall 52). As Dyson has put it, "Only a King who has descended to the depths of hell and stared at his own mortality can possibly inspire the rest of us to overcome our flaws and failures and rise to our best futures" (x). Moreover, that King's soaring rhetoric speaks to the idea of passing on a "baton"—an image of collectivity rather than individualism—suggests that King's final speech is not so much about King himself as the people who must act on his legacy. In emphasizing the audience's responsibility, Hall echoes June Jordan's hope "that we shall once again begin to build a beloved community *not* looking for a leader but determined to respect and activate the leadership capacities within each of us" (149).

Full Black Humanity

As suggested at the outset, *The Good Negro* and *The Mountaintop* speak not just to the past but to our present moment as well; like other civil rights fictions, they "look through the prism of the Civil Rights Movement in order to assess current crises of political and national progress" (Monteith 216). Both plays close strikingly, for example, with a call for the kind of reenergized civil rights activism that, by 2014, would arguably be embodied by Black Lives Matter. Pelzie's admonition to "stays here and fight" and King's passing of the baton reject the notion that the struggle for racial equality ended with King's death.

Moreover, in opposing the "lazy deification" of King (Dyson vii), Wilson and Hall also challenge the larger dehumanization of African Americans in today's United States. Both plays imply that the Civil Rights Era expectation that African Americans must be "good" in order to qualify as human persists not only in the respectability politics and racial animus that have dogged President Obama but also in the dehumanization of unarmed black victims of police violence that sparked Black Lives Matter.

A society that opts for a whitewashed version of King, for example, is unlikely to allow President Obama—arguably "the apotheosis of the good Negro" (Blankenship)—to be anything but flawless himself. "He's eerily perfect seeming," remarks *Good Negro* director Liesl Tommy, "and that's the only kind of black man that could [have] be[en] elected president" (qtd. in Blankenship). Similarly, a society that requires King or Obama to be "eerily perfect" is unlikely to extend humanity to less "respectable" individuals—Michael Brown, Eric Garner, Trayvon Martin, Freddie Gray, Laquan McDonald, and others—who fail to be "good" in the way that Rosa Parks and Martin Luther King Jr. appeared to be in their civil rights heyday. White America has historically required that its black victims of racism be noble saints; if they fall short of those standards, the nation tends to turn away or blame the dead. For both Wilson and Hall, the society that sands down King's rough edges or radical militancy is a society that succumbs to the pressure King confronted in his own time and that black victims of police brutality face in our own.

In a 2006 *New York Times* interview, Wilson expressed her artistic mantra as "a calling and a mission and a responsibility to show, not so much in a positive or negative light, the humanity, the full humanity, of the African American" (Allen). These plays imply that, by conferring posthumous sainthood on Martin Luther King Jr., we unwittingly engage in a form of dehumanization, one that masquerades as something dignifying or ennobling but that is, in fact, a version of the distortions we practice when we malign the humanity of society's most vulnerable citizens. In staging King for the twenty-first century, *The Good Negro* and *The Mountaintop* strive to capture not just the contradictions of King but the full humanity of the people for whom he fought and died.

Notes

1. *The Good Negro* premiered at the Public Theatre in New York City on March 16, 2009. *The Mountaintop* premiered at Theatre503 in London on June 9, 2009, before moving to New York's Bernard B. Jacobs Theatre in October 2011.

2. Key sources include David Garrow's *Bearing the Cross: Martin Luther King, Jr. and the Southern Christian Leadership Conference* (1986); Taylor Branch's *America in the King Years* trilogy (1988; 1998; 2006); and Diane McWhorter's *Carry Me Home: Birmingham: The Climactic Battle of the Civil Rights Revolution* (2001). Hall's focus on the harried, revolutionary King of 1966–68 also echoes Michael Eric Dyson's *I May Not Get There with You: The True Martin Luther King, Jr.* (2000).

3. Rosa Parks was a forty-two-year-old NAACP activist and department store seamstress when she refused to give up her seat on a public bus in

Montgomery, Alabama, in 1955; her act of defiance sparked the Montgomery Bus Boycott. Though Parks was not the first woman to engage in such civil disobedience, movement leaders concluded that her polished manner and dignified reserve made her an ideal icon for the struggle.

4. See Edwards, *Charisma and the Fictions of Black Leadership* (2012), and Patterson, *Exodus Politics: Civil Rights and Leadership in African American Literature and Culture* (2013).

5. Set in the tumultuous final two years of King's life, *Dreamer* shares with *The Mountaintop* a focus on the radical, exhausted King of 1966–68. The novel is notable for its philosophical depth; Johnson centers his narrative on three characters—King aide Matthew Bishop, King doppelgänger Chaym Smith, and King himself—in order to meditate on the role that society's peripheral players, living in the shadow of a Great Man, might play in shaping the course of history. For a fuller discussion of *Dreamer*, see Harris (83-110).

6. This vetting suggests the actual experience of Claudette Colvin (whose name is echoed by Claudette Sullivan), a black teenager who refused to give up her seat on a Montgomery bus months before Rosa Parks but was passed over as a public symbol because she was seen to lack polish and maturity. See Phillip Hoose, *Claudette Colvin: Twice Toward Justice* (2009).

7. The Birmingham Children's Crusade enlisted hundreds of black youths to march against segregation; the week-long effort revived the flagging Birmingham campaign and provided the movement with instantly iconic images of black children menaced by police dogs and fire hoses. The Sixteenth Street Baptist Church bombing, perpetrated by white supremacists four months later, killed four young African-American girls and is remembered as one of the era's most vicious acts of racial terrorism.

8. In addition to its higher media profile and greater acclaim, *The Mountaintop* has drawn more attention from scholars. In her study of black literary representations of King, Harris devotes a chapter to *The Mountaintop* but never mentions *The Good Negro*; Colbert's article makes a similar omission.

9. For similar readings of the play's emphasis on black women's contributions to the movement, see Harris (123-125) and Colbert (262-264, 272-273). For more on the role of women in the movement, see Jo-Anne Robinson's *The Montgomery Bus Boycott and the Women Who Started It* (1987) and Belinda Robnett's *How Long? How Long? African American Women in the Struggle for Civil Rights* (1997).

10. The Poor People's Campaign (PPC) was a King-led multiracial effort to combat poverty, unemployment, and economic inequality in America in a way that dramatically expanded the scope of the Civil Rights Movement. Begun in late 1967, only months before King's assassination, the PPC culminated in a month-long demonstration in Washington, DC, in the spring of 1968.

Works Cited

Alexander, Michelle. *The New Jim Crow: Mass Incarceration in the Age of Colorblindness*. New York: The New P, 2012.

Allen, Kerri. "In Person: Newark's Brazen Voice." *New York Times* 5 Feb. 2006: NJ4.

Blankenship, Mark. "Civil Rights, and Wrongs, in Alabama." *New York Times* 25 Feb. 2009: AR6.

Channel RBS. "Katori Hall Inspiration Behind *The Mountaintop* Play." *YouTube*. YouTube, Oct. 25, 2011.

Colbert, Soyica Diggs. "Black Leaders at the Crossroads: Unfixing Martin Luther King Jr. in Katori Hall's *The Mountaintop*." *South Atlantic Quarterly* 112.2 (Spring 2013): 261-283.

Cone, James H. *Martin & Malcolm & America: A Dream or a Nightmare*. Maryknoll, NY: Orbis Books, 1991.

Dyson, Michael Eric. Foreword. *The Mountaintop*. By Katori Hall. London: Methuen Drama, 2011. vii-x.

Goodman Theatre. "Making of the Good Negro, The." *YouTube*. YouTube, May 4, 2010.

Hall, Katori. *The Mountaintop*. 2009. London: Methuen Drama, 2011.

Harris, Trudier. *Martin Luther King Jr., Heroism, and African American Literature*. Tuscaloosa: U of Alabama P, 2014.

Jordan, June. "The Mountain and the Man Who Was Not God: An Essay on the Life and Ideas of Dr. Martin Luther King, Jr." *Some of Us Did Not Die: New and Selected Essays of June Jordan*. New York: Perseus Books, 2002. 143-156.

King, Martin Luther, Jr. *Strength to Love*. 1963. Minneapolis, MN: Fortress P, 2010.

_____. "Where Do We Go from Here?" 1967. *A Testament of Hope: The Essential Speeches and Writings of Martin Luther King Jr*. Ed. James M. Washington. New York: HarperCollins, 1991. 245-252.

_____. "Beyond Vietnam." 1967. *A Call to Conscience: The Landmark Speeches of Dr. Martin Luther King Jr*. New York: Grand Central, 2001. 139-164.

McGuire, Danielle. *At the Dark End of the Street: Black Women, Rape, and Resistance—A New History of the Civil Rights Movement, from Rosa Parks to the Rise of Black Power*. New York: Vintage, 2011.

Monteith, Sharon. "Revisiting the 1960s in Contemporary Fiction: Where Do We Go from Here?" *Gender and the Civil Rights Movement*. Ed. Peter J. Ling & Sharon Monteith. New York: Garland, 1999. 215-238.

Romano, Renee C. & Leigh Raiford, eds. *The Civil Rights Movement in American Memory*. Athens: U of Georgia P, 2006.

Schulman, Michael. "King's Speech." *New Yorker* 24 Oct. 2011: 30-37.

Wilson, Tracey Scott. *The Good Negro*. 2009. New York: Dramatists Play Service, Inc., 2010.

What Happens When Death Becomes a Poem?: Understanding the Place of Mourning in Civil Rights Literature

Corrie Claiborne

When Trayvon Martin was killed on February 26, 2012, African Americans in particular entered into a period of public mourning. According to Claudia Rankine, we were once again reminded of that reality of which we needed no reminding: "that the condition of black life is mourning" ("The Condition"). In the intervening years, as we have witnessed Michael Brown, Eric Garner, Sandra Bland, the nine killed in the Charleston shooting, and too many others to mention meet untimely deaths, we began to channel this sorrow into anger and create a new millennial activism that would come to be called the Black Lives Matter Movement. This movement eventually would be centered on battles that the African-American community had fought before: the fight for proper arrests, the right to fair trials, limitation of police force, equal exercise of the Second Amendment, voting rights, and the right to exist as black men, women, and children in public space without fear of discrimination or abuse. Moreover, we came to understand that what Coretta Scott King said is true: "Freedom is never really won, you earn it and win it in every generation" (qtd. in King).

Today, this new millennial activism has been possible in part because of the ways in which protests were made tangible online. In a similar fashion to how the newspaper functioned for Ida B. Wells, social media platforms such as Twitter, Instagram, and Facebook have become a "Red Record"[1] of black suffering, chronicling the abuses that deserved a public, worldwide outcry. However, even though at first glance it appears that much of the fight for freedom only occurs online, people have continued to turn to their music, poetry, nonfiction essays, and other forms of art to process all of the great emotion surrounding this new millennial fight for freedom. In doing so, artists and activists are recognizing that social media can be ephemeral and that the best way to archive all of the multiple ways that people have protested against injustice during the Black Lives Matter Movement is to make sure that this pain is recorded in as many forms as possible. Indeed, the fact that so many have sought to ground their civil rights activism in creative production, especially in literature, speaks to the fact that this literature is key to connecting Black Lives Matter to the long arc of justice that is the Civil Rights Movement.

Because social media platforms retain the right to remove images, videos, and posts, by also creating literature that does not disappear the minute that the march is over, that offers something outside the digital and other than a like or heart button as a response to sentiments or images that people find egregious, Americans have been able to bear witness to all of the emotions that have been raised in this ongoing black struggle. Thus, writers and poets have been able to provide the only true archive of the struggle, as literature is able to live in multiple forms and in multiple spaces, even if controversial. Most importantly, this witnessing, truth-telling, and radical archiving currently happening in civil rights literature has been, at its inception, dialogic—always in conversation with what went on before in earlier African-American life. And it is only through this conversation with earlier time periods and other literatures that African Americans, in particular, have been able to attempt to heal.

Trayvon Martin, Social Media, and the Reimagining of a Movement

For many, the first mention of Trayvon Martin's name was through social media. People were able to share what facts they knew about him: that a young man, armed with only Skittles and a hoodie was walking in his neighborhood, talking on the phone, and attempting to lead a normal black teenage life when he was shot and killed by an armed, self-appointed neighborhood watchman, who assumed that Martin was a criminal. Despite the 911 operator imploring George Zimmerman not to follow and engage Martin, Zimmerman ultimately did follow and engage in a scuffle that ended in Martin's death. Many people, including President Barack Obama, responded to news of the seventeen-year-old's death with the sentiment that they, too, if not for luck, could have been Trayvon Martin. The subsequent outpouring of solidarity extended to people marching in the streets (some as a part of the Million Hoodie March) and posting pictures of themselves in hoodies online to show how they, like Martin, felt hunted. Many people posted both images of themselves and of a young Trayvon Martin simultaneously, as if in some way they became him and were mourning their own deaths. In essence, they were doing what many people did in the poetry of the 1960s and 70s.

For example, immediately upon hearing the news of Trayvon Martin's death, many thought of Jayne Cortez's 1974 poem, "Give Me the Red on the Black of the Bullet (For Claude Reece Jr.)." As this poem is an elegy, it is not difficult to exchange Trayvon Martin's name for the fourteen-year-old Claude Reece Jr., who was killed by police without any evidence of wrongdoing[2]:

> I want the [seventeen years of Trayvon Martin]
> Shot on the [26th day of February]
> Shot in his chest
> Shot by a "wanna be" police officer
> Shot for being black (ll. 7-11)

It was easy to collapse the nearly forty years that separated Trayvon Martin and Claude Reece Jr.'s deaths because so much of what plagues the black community today is tied to the problems of over-policing black youth and the lack of legal protection when someone (especially law enforcement) takes the life of a black child. Black lives have not mattered for a long time in this country, but the same solutions that Cortez was calling for then are the same solutions that we need to turn to now in order to confront the ongoing police and/ or gun violence. Such literature therefore offers a clear call to action, promoting a much-needed change in the racial and cultural landscape of the United States. Indeed, in her poem, Cortez continues:

> Give me the black on the red of the bullet
> i want to make a tornado
> to make an earthquake
> to make a fleet of stilts
> for the blackness of Claude Reece Jr.
> the blackness called dangerous weapon
> called resisting an arrest
> called nigger threat (ll. 12-19)

What is so important in this poem is that Cortez is calling for a radical reimagining that starts with the ground shifting and the landscape moving. The desire to make "an earthquake" (l. 14) and a "tornado" (l. 13) signals that the tradition of violence against black bodies and the racial tension behind it cannot continue. However, among all of the disruption that Cortez is calling for, she is most deliberate in her insistence that the greatest deconstruction needs to happen around the way that we view blackness. The poem reads, "i want to make power / to make power / for the blackness of Claude Reece Jr." (ll. 28-30)—what American society has too often "called pent-up frustration / called unidentified negro / called nigger revolutionary" (ll. 31-33). For Cortez, it is only through reconstructing blackness away from these problematic characterizations or stereotypes that the poet feels that we will be able to make justice.

In response, Tara Betts argues, "As [Cortez] reconsider[s] the losses of [her] slain subjects, [she] offer[s] a sort of catharsis and empowerment for readers experiencing these poems" (7). Indeed, Cortez's poem is as much about her audience's healing as it is about her own, reminding us that the quality that is most a "threat"—our blackness or our black bodies—is the very quality that is going to save the African-American community. "I want the life of the blackness of Claude Reece Jr.," she states (Cortez l. 20). And it is this blackness that she draws from the bullet, and not simply the bullet alone, that will allow Cortez and all women to construct the "warrior masks" that will protect black people (l. 24). This is why many years later #BlackLivesMatter grounded itself in a blackness that could not be replaced with #AllLivesMatter. This magic was and is very specific to the black community.

In "Zimmerman 2012,"[3] a song released by recording artist Cody Chesnutt, we see another example of what Betts identifies as the "gris-gris"[4] in Cortez's work and in African-American literature at large. Here Chestnutt attempted to use his language to force justice when it appeared that George Zimmerman was not going to be prosecuted. The repetition or incantation that Chesnutt uses demonstrates once again how poetry (or song, in this case) can be, as Betts says, both "catharsis and empowerment" (7). Chestnutt declares:

> Zimmerman you're a murderer
> Your guilty heart is pounding // (ll. 1-2)
>
> You killed this kid
> You killed this kid
> Trayvon, Trayvon (ll. 5-7)

The first line of the song delivers the verdict that Chesnutt himself has reached. Immediately touching on the reality that he wants to be remembered above all else, Chestnutt says, "Zimmerman you're a murderer," as this is a song to express anger at the criminal justice system and sadness about the death of another black boy. He also intermittently repeats the names of George Zimmerman and Trayvon Martin but with vastly different tones. The repetition of Zimmerman's name feels like an invective, while Trayvon's name is a litany, a way of offering all of those who were/are hurt by this young man's death a prayer. Chestnutt literally wails Trayvon's name eighteen times and then, at the end of the song, sings it softly, as if to give this child some soft resting place. It is important to note as well that Chesnutt calls Zimmerman only by his last name over and over like a curse and calls Trayvon by his first name, reminding us, by the contrast, that Trayvon is a child and worthy of being seen as such.

Although Keeanga-Yamahatta Taylor and many others correlate the birth of the Black Lives Matter Movement with the death of Michael Brown in Ferguson, Missouri, in August of 2014, it is clear that Trayvon Martin and the literature and music that sprung up around him helped to give shape and momentum to the movement. More specifically, the life and death of Trayvon Martin connected the modern struggle to a Civil Rights Movement that had been ongoing since the work of Ida B. Wells at the turn of the twentieth century. For instance, just as we cannot forget Trayvon Martin, we cannot forget all the men (women and children, too) who were lynched and whom Ida B. Wells catalogued or the many who were killed in the years between the formal Civil Rights Movement of the 1960s and today's Black Lives Matter Movement, like Oscar Grant, Sean Bell, and Amadou Diallo, etc.

The literature produced in response to these losses is therefore vital in linking all of these different strains of American civil rights, even though many young people would like to divorce themselves and Black Lives Matter from the "movement of their grandparents." For example, Taylor states, "The young people of Ferguson had great reverence and respect for the memory of the civil rights movement, but the reality is that its legacy meant little in their everyday lives" (161). Further, she argues that, in fact, the "division between the 'old guard' and the 'new generation' grew as the movement began to take form" (161). Claudia Rankine's *Citizen: An American Lyric* (2014), however, suggests in contrast to Taylor that there is no division between the old pain that African Americans experienced during the height of lynching and the new pain that we are experiencing at the hands of police and wayward white gun owners. In fact, it is only by linking all sorts of pain that Rankine is able to offer a full lyric about the ongoing and so-far-unsuccessful quest by blacks to become full American citizens. In her piece, "In Memory of Trayvon Martin," she speaks about the phenomena of carrying around heartbreak from one pain to another through generations and within families. She writes, "Your hearts are broken. This is not a secret though there are secrets. And as yet I do not understand how my own sorrow has turned into my brother's hearts. The hearts of my brothers are broken" (Rankine, *Citizen* 88).

Initially what Rankine is doing by linking her own heartbreak to the heartbreak of the reader and to the heartbreak of her brothers is illustrating that none of what is happening in Ferguson, Charleston, or elsewhere is new. This heartbreak "is not a secret," she argues (Rankine 88). Everyone's "hearts are broken" and continue to be broken (Rankine, *Citizen* 88). Moreover, immediately following this piece about Trayvon Martin (the text that accompanied a multimedia exhibit) is a picture simply entitled "Public Lynching." The picture does not show who was lynched, and there is no abused black body swinging in the tree; instead, it shows a white mob of women and men pointing up into the tree and posing for the camera. The focus is on the white mob's faces and their guilt. It is evident from the photograph that Rankine does not want to make a spectacle of the dead but to point out that they will not be forgotten and neither will the atrocities that African Americans have suffered throughout American history. However, these ideas will not only stay in our memories because we have photographic evidence (or evidence on social media) but because we also have the stories and the names to go along with the visual record. Like the repetition of the word *heartbreak* within the body of Rankine's poem becomes a form of power and catharsis itself, retelling the narratives of the myriad ways we have dealt with injustice and death also serves to help us mourn properly.

"But Baby, Where are You?": Reconciling Death and Childhood in Literature

As Karla F. C. Holloway states in *Passed On: African American Mourning Stories, A Memorial* (2003), the retelling of previous tragedy in order to process new grief is something that blacks have always done. Moreover, the way that African Americans deal with death is the source, in many instances, of their power. For example, in Elizabeth Alexander's essay "'Can You Be Black and Look at This?' Reading the Rodney King Videos," she concludes that there is something that happens with the re-memory of tortured black bodies that actually creates a revolutionary spirit. Seeing the bloated and abused body of Emmett Till, for instance, spurred Muhammad Ali to become the fighter for justice that he became. In fact, Mamie Till Mobley's decision to have an open casket so that people could see what America had done to her fourteen-year-old son became a rallying cry to many in and outside of the black community, even as the picture of the once happy, smiling, round-faced boy made the world grieve.

This, however, is not always the case. Alexander ends her essay by discussing the mixed-media artwork of Pat Ward Williams in "Accused/Blowtorch/Padlock." Williams' piece displays a *Life* magazine photograph of a lynching once discovered in the woods. Williams includes questions in script that surround the image of the lynched black man, asking specifically how one could just take a picture and not be moved to action. Alexander echoes some of Williams' questions but then adds some of her own, writing:

> Williams's work asks the questions: What do people do with their history of horror? What does it mean to bear witness in the act of watching a retelling? What does it mean to carry cultural memory in the flesh? She shows how to work with images that many would rather forget, and she shows why such images need to be remembered. (94)

Alexander recognizes here, as does the poetry of Cody Chestnut and Claudia Rankine, why trauma needs to be remembered. Indeed, it is only by remembering that people can be moved to act—the main goal of civil rights literature of the past and present.

But what makes the deaths of young African-American boys such as Emmet Till, Trayvon Martin, and Tamir Rice particularly horrific and difficult to remember is that they were children when they were killed, as were the four girls who died in the bombing of the Sixteenth Street Baptist Church in Birmingham in 1963. Both the murders of Emmet Till and of the four girls have often been addressed in literature; however, it has been the deaths of the four girls that have been most often addressed in poetry. For example, the last stanza of Dudley Randall's "Ballad of Birmingham" shows why the death of the girls has had such a particular resonance in civil rights literature and how this tragic event's elegiac treatment is a response to silence within the white community. The poem recounts specifically a mother's pain in losing her child in that bombing and how, in the end, all the African-American community was left with was a question. Randall writes:

She clawed through bits of glass and brick,
Then lifted out a shoe.
"O, here's the shoe my baby wore,
But, baby, where are you?" (ll. 30-33)

By speaking in the voice of the mother, Randall is, in some ways providing a link to many other poets who have also tried to grapple with the unspeakable loss of a child while simultaneously posing the same question that Elizabeth Alexander asks in her essay: "What do people do with their history of horror?" (94). Moreover, the question in the last two lines allows Randall to consider what is left as evidence of the lives of black children. Randall's suggestion is that too often the mother is only left with something insufficient to mark her child's existence, like the shoe mentioned in the poem or a hoodie in Trayvon Martin's case. More importantly, the shoe also reminds us of how often the bodies of black children are treated as objects. For example, the death of Michael Brown in Ferguson was particularly horrifying because his body was left in the street uncovered for hours as "evidence," while his mother was screaming on the sidelines, unable to claim her child. In an act that dehumanized both the mother and her son, we can see the ways in which Brown's remains offered real-time visual proof that black lives did not matter, that they did not have any value. The question, "[B]aby, where are you?" (l. 33) in Randall's work, becomes ultimately a question that not only addresses not being able to physically find one's child but also addresses the different ways in which the dominant white society (viewed here as racist) sees or does not see the lives of the children of black mothers.

This theme is also evident in "American History" by Michael S. Harper, who recounts the impact of the bombing on the collective unconscious of black people and how the different ways of seeing (or not seeing) black lives determine the historical record. Harper's poem also illustrates the dialogic nature of civil rights poetry in that his poem creates a bridge between different eras of the movement by making sure the 1963 bombing is put in conversation with other events that happened to black people all the way back to the Revolutionary War. For example, Harper writes:

> Those four black girls blown up
> in that Alabama church
> remind me of five hundred
> middle passage blacks,
> in a net, under water
> in Charleston harbor
> so redcoats wouldn't find them.
> Can't find what you can't see
> can you? (ll. 1-9)

Like Randall, Harper ends his poem with a question to which he ultimately knows the answer. Harper asks of white America, "Can't find what you can't see / can you?" (l. 9). More pointedly he is directly interrogating with this question why black lives do not matter to white America, quantifying the level to which black lives are devalued in America in this poem by listing the four girls plus the five hundred "middle passage blacks" that he insists again that America refuses to see. Giving these lives a number is important here because it reinforces the fact that the injustices that African Americans experience from the state are not simply a matter of feeling but rather these injustices, like those in Wells' "Red Record," are catalogued in the data and statistics of American history.

Exhibiting Alexander's claim of the power of remembering and retelling in African-American literature, Audre Lorde, in her poem "Power," also provides a record of a child's death and outlines how the ability to discuss it in a poem constitutes the only real power that black women will have. Lorde begins this poem by telling the story not only of a ten-year-old who was killed by the police but also of the black woman on the jury who managed to agree with the rest of the white jurors that the officer should not be convicted. The choice that this black woman makes is framed by Lorde as a choice between poetry (i.e., "power") and the death of black children. Lorde states:

> The difference between poetry and rhetoric
> is being ready to kill
> yourself
> instead of your children (ll. 1-4).

Here Lorde suggests that the black woman juror was willing to let a child die instead of taking the burden onto herself in that "she had lined her own womb with cement / to make a graveyard for our children" (ll. 41-42) by agreeing with the rhetoric of a white supremacist patriarchal system. The black woman's refusal to contradict the assessment of the police shows how easily power can be given over to a racist rhetoric that condones a child's death. As Lorde states, "[T]his policeman said in his own defense/ 'I didn't notice the size nor nothing else/ only the color'" (ll. 25-27). The irony of this testimony is, of course, that it does not show evidence of proper police action but evidence of the egregious racial profiling that inspires the Black Lives Matter Movement. Moreover, the black woman juror's utterance that "they convinced me" (l. 35) seems to directly contradict the work of Lorde's poem. In fact, the black woman's agreement with the eleven white male jurors, Lorde suggests, is not because she saw justice in the white police officer's acquittal but because she was forced to accept their rhetoric. As Lorde states:

> They dragged her 4'10" black Woman's frame
> over the hot coals
> of four centuries of white male approval
> until she let go
> the first real power she ever had. (ll.36-40)

Therefore, Lorde argues that it is only by embracing poetry, rhetoric's opposite, that black people and black women, more specifically, will regain that power back. Otherwise, the cycle of violence continues, as we see today in the rising tension between the police force and members of the African-American community. This is one of the fundamental reasons why civil rights literature today is so important. It not only records these events, preserving them from a historical tradition that too often silences or minimizes the pain that blacks experience, but it also serves as a source of power—the vocalization of a communal spirit of resistance.

Where Do We Go From Here?: Confronting the Police and Black Rage in a Poem

Troubled by the cycle of violence that she witnesses throughout American history, June Jordan in her "Poem on Police Violence" seems to ask the seminal question that has been on the minds of many Black Lives Matter protestors, namely what would happen if police had the very violence visited on them that they seem to time and time again direct at young black people. Her poem represents another arc of Black Lives Matter creative production, serving as a mirror to the American public in order to highlight the fear, pain, and sense of injustices that prompts the protests and demonstrations so prominent in society today. Jordan's poem begins:

> Tell me something
> what you think would happen if
> everytime they kill a black boy
> then we kill a cop
> everytime they kill a black man
> then we kill a cop (ll. 1-6)

The collapsing of the two words *every* and *time* into one word suggests here that what happened to Walter Scott, Michael Brown, Alton Sterling, Philando Castile, Eric Garner, the ten-year-old little boy in Audre Lorde's poem, and Claude Reece Jr. has led to this unending cycle of violence that has no specific time marker. Further, Jordan continues, "I'm saying war is not to understand or rerun / war is to be fought and won" (ll. 27-28). Jordan clearly outlines that what is happening with police in black communities is war—a war with many casualties, a war for power that can be fought and won only if the deaths are marked and mourned, again pointing to the power of modern civil rights poetry.

That climate of war that Jordan alludes to has thus created a culture of fear or rebellion for some, as evidenced by Jericho Brown's haunting tweet on March 20, 2016—"I promise you that if you ever hear of me dead anywhere near a cop, then that cop killed me"—which announced his poem "Bullet Points." As the title suggests, the poem is an attempt to list the casualties of this war and show the ways in which poets are taking back power by reinterpreting black people's engagement with the police. The poem imagines the poet in the place of Sandra Bland, Walter Scott, Freddie Gray Jr., and all the people who mysteriously die in the hands of the police. Brown writes:

> I will not shoot myself
> In the head, and I will not shoot myself
> In the back, and I will not hang myself
> With a trash bag, and if I do,
> I promise you, I will not do it
> in a police car while handcuffed
> or in the jail cell of a town
> I only know the name of
> because I have to drive through it
> to get home. (ll. 1-10)

Lines four through ten seem to specifically reference Sandra Bland, who allegedly hanged herself with a trash bag after being pulled over for a routine traffic violation in a small town that she was just passing through. However, all of the acts of violence, especially the repetition of the word *shoot* in the first two lines, remind us that in terms of keeping a record of this war, many of us do not even begin to know the names of the victims; all we know is that they were "shot," "hanged," or "handcuffed." In fact, the #Sayhername campaign began on Twitter as a way of reinforcing all of the acts of violence against black women that go unnamed. It seems that Brown in mentioning these stories of black death is going to make sure that he would not go unnamed. His declaration, "I promise you that if you hear of me dead anywhere near a cop, then that cop killed me," is his way of preemptively creating his own record.

Furthermore, Brown's personalizing of these black tragedies is really his way of expressing the rage that so many have in the movement, over and over again having to call attention to the random killing of black people, though few seem to be listening. As Brittney Cooper has argued, the problem with public mourning is that it has not felt like it has adequately expressed black rage. Cooper states,

> Every week we are having what my friend Dr. Regina Bradley called #anotherhashtagmemorial. Every week. We are weak. We are tired. Of being punching bags and shooting targets for the police. We are tired of well-meaning white citizens and respectable black ones foreclosing all outlets for rage. We are tired of these people telling us what isn't the answer.

In fact, there are many poets who speak of the pain and the rage outside of poetry because the emotion seems to spill out in other areas. This is why Jericho Brown offered commentary on Twitter but also published his poem elsewhere online. This is also perhaps why Rankine's *Citizen* is not a traditional book of poetry but a collection that links photography, video, art, prose, news reporting, personal memoir, and poetry together. In many ways, their work is an archive of the diverse ways that people have expressed their grief and rage around the killing of black bodies and the Black Lives Matter Movement. The fact that Rankine's poetry collection is not being bound by form, as is true for Jericho Brown and Nikky Finney's works, prevents that "foreclosing" of rage that Cooper railed against.

Nikky Finney in her keynote address entitled "We who Believe in Freedom Cannot Rest," given to the South Carolina Psychiatrists Association on January 29, 2016 in Columbia, South Carolina, seems to be particularly interested in forms of rage and their connection to grief and mental illness. Although much of her talk is prose, Finney has a section of her talk that specifically points to the power of poetry. Here she offers the simple repetition of the name of Tamir Rice, a twelve-year-old who was shot and killed in a park while playing with a toy gun. This poem thus comes as an answer to the questions that Finney asks about Sandra Bland's mother and indeed all the "Mothers of the Movement." Finney asks, "How does

her mother keep going? How do other Black mothers keep going?"
The answer Finney provides is:

Tamir Rice
Tamir Rice
Tamir Rice
Tamir Rice

The fact that Tamir Rice's name is not truly an answer to the question
of how black mothers keep going but a demonstration of strategies
of survival employed using poetry and memory to create a shift in
the society is telling. Finney wants black people to understand that
not only is their psychological health rooted in remembering but
that the solutions to their problems can be found in history as well.
Further, Finney's keynote address shows that sorrow and mourning
cannot be contained only to the time in which the atrocity occurred.
Usually these events do what Cortez addresses in her poem. They
create a "cyclone" and "a tornado" that have effects for generations.
In fact, Finney, in addition to dealing with the deaths of Tamir Rice
and Sandra Bland, mentions one of the greatest events that shifted
black consciousness through grieving and that is "The Weeping
Time," the effects of which she believes still can be felt today. She
writes:

> I want to mention "The Weeping Time," that moment in American
> history that America won't remember, March 2-3, 1859, in Savannah,
> Georgia, when 436 enslaved persons were sold at a racetrack. It was
> the largest sale of enslaved persons in the United States. It was called
> "The Weeping Time" because enslaved Black families were split
> apart, separated, shattered forever. Can so horrific and grief-stricken,
> so cataclysmic a moment in 436 lives spread, with great wings, 150
> years forward, into the psyche and mental health of Black people
> living now who might know nothing of March 2-3, 1859, literally[?]
> (Finney)

The answer to the question that Finney poses is ultimately "yes."
One can hear the effects of history and this event throughout

---

Finney's work and the works of all African Americans who write protest poetry and music. Because African-American literature is dialogic, the past cannot help but inform the present and vice versa. So not only does the Black Lives Matter Movement tap into the earlier Civil Rights Movement to shape its activism, but our view of the civil rights struggle is forever changed by the varied and creative responses to the ongoing nature of black death. By exploring the writers whose poetry invigorated the 1960s, 1970s, and 1980s and comparing them to poets and musical artists of today, we can see the power of the dialogic. To that end, it is easy to see that writing in this new era of civil rights literature is in the hands of those who have managed in the twenty-first century to create testimonial works that become simultaneously a repository for sorrow and a guide for action.

Notes

1. Ida B. Wells' "Red Record: Tabulated Statistics and Alleged Causes of Lynching in the United States" was originally published in 1895 as a pamphlet and later published with her other writings as seen in *Southern Horrors and Other Writings: The Anti-Lynching Campaign of Ida B. Wells, 1892–1900* (1996), edited by Jaqueline Jones-Royster.

2. The edits to Jayne Cortez's poem are mine and originally appeared on my Facebook page and on my blog, *The Living Ain't Easy.*

3. According to *Okayplayer.com*, Chestnutt recorded this song within twenty-four hours of the Million Hoodie March and accompanying the song on the website was a link to the *Change.org* petition that Martin's parents set up calling for the prosecution of George Zimmerman for murder. The petition eventually garnered over two million signatures.

4. In response to Cortez's work, Betts argues that the "repetition of Reece's name happens so often throughout the poem—eleven times—that the incantation of his name is undoubtedly intentional. These ingredients could also be used to form a sort of gris-gris—a pouch that is often blessed and filled with objects to protect the person who wears it or carries it" (7).

Works Cited

Alexander, Elizabeth. "'Can You Be Black and Look at This?' Reading the Rodney King Videos." *Public Culture* 7.1 (1994): 77-94.

Betts, Tara. "'Everytime they kill a black boy. . .': Representations of Police Brutality Against Children in Poems by Audre Lorde, Jayne Cortez, and June Jordan." *Obsidian: Literature in the African Diaspora* 13:2 (2012).

Brown, Jericho. "Bullet Points." *BuzzFeed.* BuzzFeed, Inc., 20 May 2016. Web. 17 Dec. 2016.

Chestnut, Cody. "Zimmerman 2012." *Okayplayer.* Okayplayer.com, 24 Mar. 2012. Web. 17 Dec. 2016.

Cooper, Brittney. "In Defense of Black Rage: Michael Brown, Police, and the American Dream." *Salon.* Salon Media Group, Inc., 12 Aug. 2014. Web. 17 Dec. 2016.

Cortez, Jayne. *Coagulations.* New York: Thunder's Mouth P, 1984.

Finney, Nikky. "We who Believe in Freedom Cannot Rest." South Carolina Psychiatrists Association Keynote Presentation. Columbia, SC. 29 Jan. 2016. *NikkeyFinney.*

Harper, Michael S. "American History." 2000. *Poetry Foundation.* Poetry Foundation. Poetry Foundation, 2016. Web. 17 Dec. 2016.

Holloway, Karla F. C. *Passed On: African American Mourning Stories, A Memorial.* Durham, NC: Duke UP, 2003.

@jerichobrown. "I promise you that if you ever hear of me dead anywhere near a cop, then that cop killed me." 20 Mar. 2016, 12:55 p.m.

Jordan, June. "Poem on Police Violence." *Directed By Desire: The Collected Poems of June Jordan.* Port Townsend, WA: Copper Canyon P, 2005. 272-273.

King, Bernice A. "Echoes From Selma . . . Struggle is a Never Ending Process." *HuffingtonPost.com.* TheHuffingtonPost.com, Inc., 7 Mar. 2015. Web. 17 Dec. 2016.

Lorde, Audre. "Power." 1997. *Poetry Foundation.* Poetry Foundation. Poetry Foundation, 2016. Web. 17 Dec. 2016.

Randall, Dudley "Ballad of Birmingham." 1968. *Poetry Foundation.* Poetry Foundation, 2016. Web. 17 Dec. 2016.

Rankine, Claudia. *Citizen: An American Lyric.* 1st ed. Minneapolis, MN: Graywolf, 2014.

_____. "The Condition of Black Life is One of Mourning." *Charleston Syllabus: Readings on Race, Racism, and Racial Violence.* Eds. Chad Williams, Kidada E. Williams, & Kiesha Blain. Athens: U of Georgia P, 2016. 71-77.

Taylor, Keeanga-Yamahtta. *#BlackLivesMatter to Black Liberation.* Chicago: Haymarket, 2016.

Social Media Meets Social Justice: The Role of the Hashtag in the Contemporary Conversation on Race_____

Deborah F. Kadiri

Because race is a social construct, it informs every sociocultural aspect of life for people of color. When it comes to the black American, the precedent that has been advertised by the dominant society is that black lives are of inferior, if any, value. A long history of enslavement and dehumanization speaks to this fact. The late nineteenth and early twentieth century, for instance, saw the rise of blackface minstrelsy, as white actors caked their faces in black soot and acted in a mocking imitation of African-American song, dance, and speech that reinforced blacks' status as second-class citizens in a post-slavery society. As Eric Lott notes in his article, "Blackface and Blackness: The Minstrel Show in American Culture," "[T] he minstrel show indeed seems a transparently racist curiosity, a form of leisure that, in inventing and ridiculing the slow-witted but irrepressible 'plantation darky' and the foppish 'northern dandy negro,' conveniently rationalized racial oppression . . . [and] took such distortions as authentic" (3). Yet, these stereotypical portrayals, established by the dominant white society, were not new. As Sterling A. Brown notes in his 1933 essay entitled "Negro Character as Seen by White Authors," such stereotypes date back to the days of slavery and the depiction of African-American characters in many white-authored texts. He writes:

> The Negro has met with as great injustice in American literature as he has in American life. The majority of books about Negroes merely stereotype Negro character. . . . It can be said, however, that all of these stereotypes are marked either by exaggeration or omissions; that they all agree in stressing the Negro's divergence from an Anglo-Saxon norm to the flattery of the latter; they could all be used, as they probably are, as justification of racial proscription; they all illustrate dangerous species generalizing from a few particulars recorded by a single observer from a restricted point of view—which is itself

generally dictated by the desire to perpetuate a stereotype. (Brown 180)

Historically, the marginalization of the black community, however, was not restricted to popular culture and the stereotypes that it engendered. As a result, race has remained the one social construct that is responsible for the most recurring causes of national controversy in both virtual and public spaces. The perceived inferiority of blacks has also manifested in violence against black bodies, as evident in February 2012 when a young, unarmed black teenager was shot and killed for reasons that still remain unclear to this day. The murder of Trayvon Martin at the hands of a self-proclaimed neighborhood watchman, who was not held responsible, led many Americans to question the interests of the justice system. In the wake of the trial that ensued, many black Americans came to terms with the harsh reality that their best interest is not a priority of said system—an event that contributed to the development of the #BlackLivesMatter Movement today and its pursuits of the justice long denied blacks.

The nature of contemporary discourse on race is informed by these instances that mark pivotal moments in our history. After all, such instances served as the impetus behind the evolution of discourse associated with the Civil Rights Movement into today's #BlackLivesMatter Movement—a shift that exemplifies the recurring realization that the social construct of race is problematic for people of color. With the passing of time, however, social constructs are often challenged to the point of widespread rejection. This is evident today as the primary perspective of the conversation has shifted from one that previously promoted integration to a fault to one that now focuses on both the positive and negative effects of the differences that undeniably exist between white and black Americans. If, as novelist and playwright Edward Bulwer-Lytton wrote in 1839, "The pen [was] mightier than the sword" (89), as the Internet has become a primary channel through which information is funneled to the public, the power behind the pen has taken on a new form in directing this conversation. As a result, many of the texts that emerge out of our culture do so in conjunction with evolving technologies and the features available through social media platforms. The hashtag, which had its inception on Twitter, has become a particularly influential feature in the dissemination of information and specifically in the facilitation of the national conversation on race.

Historicizing the Hashtag

According to the Oxford English Dictionary (OED), the technical term for the hashtag symbol is *octothorpe*. In his analysis, the Canadian poet Robert Bringhurst points out that the octothorpe is a "traditional symbol for *village*" (Houston). The new terminology is not indicative of a reinvention of this symbol; rather, it simply factors in the discovery of a new function for it. Similarly, the #BlackLivesMatter Movement is not indicative of a reinvention of the Civil Rights Movement; it simply factors in the development of new functions for it. The OED's reference to the hashtag as an organizing center speaks to the practicality of the hashtag as a universal symbol around which communication and engagement can occur. The marriage of the hashtag with today's movement has been prolific for this reason.

The hashtag is also associated with the United Kingdom's symbol for the pound. This implies an overt relationship to the exchange of currency and the mutual ownership that participants in that exchange share. The hashtag is comparable because of the exchange of the currency of thoughts, feelings, facts, and ideas that it propagates. It represents the opportunity to use the agency birthed out of the union of a platform and a voice. This is especially important within the context of challenging the validity of social constructions of race because it takes conversations that may have been occurring within private spaces and projects them directly into the public audience where they cannot be ignored and can actively contribute to the writing of a new narrative for people of color. As Makeba Lavan writes in "The Negro Tweets His Presence: Black Twitter as Social and Political Watchdog," "In the digital age, social media tools like Twitter—a subscriber based micro-blogging site that allows for instantaneous visibility and therefore increased social capital/power—permit the articulation of a diversity of voices as well as new forms of civic participation" (56). The hashtag affords us the social and political capital to participate in this exchange and adds value to these meaning-making and truth-seeking processes.

Hashtags are used on web-based and social media platforms to identify all corresponding activity by a word or phrase that is preceded by the hashtag symbol. Any such word or phrase becomes a searchable link that ties tagged activity to every other occurrence of that particular tag. This allows for the virtual gathering of related content based on keywords. As a result, the hashtag is associated with a contemporary culture of globalization because its reach is not confined by the traditional boundaries and limitations of communication. As long as an Internet connection is available, a hashtag can unite people anywhere in the world over any topic in the world. Its use has become increasingly symbolic because of this nucleic property. Because the hashtag is designed to be used on platforms that were already created to allow and promote limitless dialogue among an unchecked number of participants, its accessibility is universal and its potential is widespread.

However, the facilitation of immediacy is arguably the hashtag's most valuable characteristic, as the hashtag itself evidences a new way of knowing and doing.[1] Virtual spaces are becoming the primary venues for social gatherings because of the eradication of extraneous logistics. There is no need to reserve a space and monitor attendance. There is no maximum occupancy due to fire hazards. There are no time constraints. And most importantly, everyone has an equal opportunity to contribute to the conversation. There is no waiting in line to be heard, and the politics of social hierarchies are rendered virtually irrelevant. These are the main reasons why Twitter discussions are rapidly replacing traditional public forums. The hashtag effortlessly capitalizes on the need for these practical solutions to logistical hindrances that have continuously limited the productivity of conversations on race in the past. It bridges the divide that often separates the rhetorical and real social justice-related content that gives rise to a renewed public focus.

The Hashtag as a New Genre

Access to information regarding the disproportionate number of deaths of people of color at the hands of law enforcers has been a prime example of this. Mainstream media often portrays victims of racial marginalization and stereotyping as criminals based upon past infractions, regardless of whether or not they are related to the incidents of fatality—a trend that reinforces the Brute Negro stereotype of the not so distant past. Old rap sheets, school reports reflecting poor academic records, and unsavory photographs are often the contexts in which the highlight reels of primary media reports frame victims of institutionalized racial profiling. For example, this was the case after two police officers fatally shot Tamir Rice, a twelve-year old boy from Cleveland, Ohio, who was playing with a toy gun. Rather than focusing on Tamir's death, the media focused upon his father's criminal history. Fundamental problems such as these necessitate the development of new genres of civil rights literature and engagement that counter the skewed depictions popularized in today's news. In "The Negro Digs up his Past," Arthur Schomburg points to this need dating back to the twentieth century, asserting that:

> The American Negro must remake his past in order to make his future. Though it is orthodox to think of America as the one country where it is unnecessary to have a past, what is a luxury for the nation as a whole becomes a prime social necessity for the Negro. For him, a group tradition must supply compensation for persecution, and pride of race the antidote for prejudice. History must restore what slavery took away, for it is the social damage of slavery that the present generations must repair and offset. (217)

The use of the hashtag on social media platforms has become the answer to Schomburg's call to counter the flawed portrayals of such victims by generating a new group tradition. As Lavan suggests, "Black Twitter has become a site of counter-narratives and counter-memory, assembling supplementary information that challenges the dominant narrative propagated in traditional media" (57). These counter-narratives are evident in the tweets associated with the top ten Twitter hashtags related to #BlackLivesMatter; #MikeBrown, #Ferguson, #SandraBland, #EricGarner, #BlackTwitter, #Baltimore, #SayHerName, #ICantBreathe, #FreddieGray, and #AllLivesMatter. Because "[t]he most influential users on Black Twitter call attention to prejudice in mainstream narratives . . . while forcing corrective action" (Lavan 57) using the hashtag, it has become a symbol of empowerment that gives the public access to otherwise unknown complexities of these multifaceted narratives. This is the relevance of the hashtag as a new genre within the context of the national conversation on race.

Ultimately, genres create the classification system for artistic composition. Such artistic endeavors typically have some characteristic form or technique. When it comes to literary genres, fiction and nonfiction are two primary categories. There are several subcategories that organize art by layout, style, theme, content, and so on, but the notion of the hashtag as a new genre is one that comes out of the inability to relegate tagged artistry to the confines of any particular preexisting category. The hashtag #BlackLivesMatter, after all, can be used to track events, conversations, photographs, paintings, articles, speeches, blog posts, and tweets that were tagged accordingly. Instead of narrowing down searches in order to arrive at one specific result, the hashtag makes them as expansive as possible but still only yields results that have been marked with the specified tag. Entering #BlackLivesMatter into a Google search will yield results that could be classified as poetry, prose, photographs, and so on—all resources that have helped to provide users context for some of their thoughts regarding race and rhetoric. The hashtag thus serves as a point of entry into networks that have been built around the common purpose of having constructive conversations on these issues that have the potential to lead to the activism that can result in long-term change. This quality makes it a viable candidate for a new genre.

Hashtag Activism and the Pursuit of Social Change

According to Phillip Howard, the principle investigator for the Digital Activism Research Project, "'Hashtag activism is what happens when someone tries to raise public awareness of a political issue using some clever or biting keyword on social media. . . . If your idea—linked to a good hashtag—gains traction you've started a kind of awareness campaign'" (qtd. in Brewster). After the fatal shooting of the unarmed eighteen-year-old Michael Brown in Ferguson, Missouri, community members took to social media with the hashtags #Ferguson and #MikeBrown to not only express their outrage with repeated incidents of police brutality but also to share images and video footage of incidents surrounding the backlash of the tragedy that were not being released to the public through mainstream media and news outlets. With the dramatic increase of direct sources to information, the space that often exists between raw texts and their edited and filtered versions was eliminated, resulting in national outcries for justice.

For many, however, the question of whether or not it is possible to attain concrete and quantifiable evidence of the efficacy of "hashtag activism" remains a concern often raised by those who are hesitant to address such critical social justice issues with contemporary methods. In his article entitled "After Ferguson: Is 'Hashtag Activism' Spurring Policy Changes?," Shaquille Brewster addresses this question by pointing out some of the tangible results that are, in part, due to hashtag activism. Brewster writes,

> After the Ferguson decision, President Obama told peaceful protesters he will personally work with them. Since then, he's requested funding for 50,000 police body cameras, created a task force to get specific recommendations on building trust between communities and law enforcement and invited young leaders to the White House for a meeting in the Oval Office.

Hemly Ordonez, Vice President of Digital Strategy and Mobilization at Fission Strategy, a company that uses digital tools to achieve social change, remarked that this was the first time she had ever seen the president engage with "people who are so close to the ground. . . . . That generally doesn't happen" (qtd. in Brewster). Ordonez, along with many others, acknowledges the direct effects that the utility of social media has in bridging the divide between social change and those who have the ability to expedite it. Without the public outcry surrounding the shooting of Michael Brown, such action may never have occurred.

The #BlackLivesMatter Movement is therefore an invocation of the demand for regard and respect for black lives, black history, black culture, and black people. As the founders of #BlackLivesMatter articulate, this "ideological and political intervention" of an organization exists as "affirmation of Black folks' contributions to this society, our humanity, and our resilience in the face of deadly oppression" ("Black Lives"). The hashtag associated with the movement can be classified as a facilitator of inclusion. Communities have the ability to congregate around a mutual purpose. But like many other social media platforms, by way of its design, Twitter allows for people to communicate under the cloak of anonymity if they so choose. This anonymity arguably promotes an environment in which the sharing and exchange of thoughts and ideas can occur without the prejudices that are associated with visual and audible features of difference.

Some would argue that this same feature eradicates any potential for gatekeeping because those with ulterior or opposing motives and agendas have just as much access to the same tools, tactics, and platforms that are being used to seek social justice and policy reform. There are some instances that have helped to mollify this concern regarding the lack of accountability. For example, on December 20, 2013, Justine Sacco, a former senior director of corporate communications at a leading media and Internet company, tweeted a total of sixty-three characters without suspecting that her life would change so quickly as a result. As she boarded a flight to South Africa, she tweeted: "Going to Africa. Hope I don't get AIDS. Just kidding. I'm white!" As her tweet began to circulate, people took to Twitter to express how distasteful such blatant ignorance and racism was, especially coming from someone working in public relations. The hashtag #HasJustineLandedYet began to trend as Twitter activists sought to educate Sacco about the implications of her thoughtless tweet. Before her plane had even landed, Sacco was no longer employed by IAC.

A similar incident occurred in October of 2015, when Erika Escalante, a twenty-year-old student at Arizona State University, tweeted, "Our inner n*gger came out today," after visiting a cotton field with a friend. Erika deleted her tweet once she realized how much attention it was getting, but it had already gone viral and made its way to her employers. Shortly after, the company she was working for tweeted, "We too find this tweet offensive & we are shocked. This does not reflect our values & culture. The intern is no longer with us" (Isagenix). As a result of these unfortunate instances, many companies have begun to implement mandatory cultural information and sensitivity training for their employees—a step toward correcting these social ills that might not have occurred without the rise of the hashtag as a tool of sociocultural critique. These instances, among others, demonstrate how the hashtag facilitates agency that originates in virtual spaces but intersects with real spaces. Its ability to draw public attention to the inherent mentality of race-based violence within the written word makes the hashtag the perfect propellant for a counterculture that is seeking not only to reactively hold people accountable for blatant racism but to also proactively effect lasting changes regarding the type of treatment that people of color will and will not accept from the dominant society. This relationship between the hashtag and social justice activism is especially relevant to the growing body of academics who are seeking to increase their ability to understand, deconstruct, and skillfully use language across genres in order to have difficult but productive social, political, and cultural conversations.

Some would attribute the ongoing impacts of social media activism to the visibility of the #BlackLivesMatter Movement. After all, the role of the student activist is one that has repeatedly been at the forefront of many recent social justice demonstrations. Gatherings of students in both virtual and real spaces have undeniably resulted in the implementation of actual change. For example, on November 9, 2015, Tim Wolfe, the former president of the University of Missouri, resigned from his duties as a direct result of students relentlessly demanding the removal of a university leader who would not address repeated concerns regarding an environment of racial hostility. #ConcernedStudent1950 is the corresponding hashtag that was trending throughout the ongoing unrest at the university. Concerned Student 1950 is the name of the activist group that emerged out of the tensions of racial hostility at the University of Missouri. This institution admitted its first black student in 1950, and the group's name was multipurposed, as the hashtag tracked the events surrounding the protests for a different kind of equality sixty-five years later.

Movements that celebrate black culture and people by promoting the validity of black life and countering negative stereotypes are also being repurposed as hashtags. The trending tag #BlackExcellence celebrates the greatness and achievements of black people. #BlackGirlMagic celebrates the beauty of black women and girls in opposition to a popular culture that often excludes them from the category of a mainstream beauty standard. Most recently, both of these tags have been tied to images of Simone Biles, Simone Manuel, Michelle Carter, Gabby Douglas, and Ibtihaj Muhammad, some of the women of color who are being called the American heroes of the 2016 Olympics. ABC News tweeted, "#BlackGirlMagic takes spotlight at Olympics," along with an article that calls these women black heroines. Likewise, #IfTheyGunnedMeDown was also a popular hashtag of 2016 that sought to make people aware that the media often portrays people of color in an unforgiving and simply inaccurate light. James Poniewozik, a writer for *TIME* magazine, calls this particular tag:

> a simple, ingenious DIY form of media criticism: direct, powerful, and meaningful on many levels. It [makes] the blunt point that every time a media outlet chooses a picture of someone like [Mike] Brown, it makes a statement. It create[s] identification: so many ordinary people—students, servicemen and women, community volunteers—could be made to look like a public menace with one photo dropped in a particular context. And it ma[kes] a particular racial point: that it's so much easier, given our culture's racial baggage, for a teenager of color to be made to look like a "thug" than [a] white teen showing off for a camera the exact same way.

In each case, the awareness of difference is trending with these hashtags, enabling users to celebrate, validate, and respect difference much more than in the past when racial and cultural differences too often sparked long-term abuse. There can never be enough of this. Now more than ever, discussions on race are being sparked in public and private spaces. These conversations are informing education, society, policy, and even our understanding of the cultural competence of our presidential candidates. Despite some of the discomfort surrounding these discussions, it is important that they occur, not only to raise awareness of their necessity but to also create a counterculture that reinforces affirming representations and emphasizes the talents and achievements that people of color contribute to a culture in which they are undeservedly marginalized.

Still, in light of all this talking, there is the pervasive mentality that conversations on Twitter or elsewhere are often unintentional diversions because while they may illuminate, they do not result in the end goal of achieving change. Sanjay Sharma accentuates this point in her article, "Black Twitter? Racial Hashtags, Networks, and Contagion." Here she argues that there is a widespread misperception "that Black users of Twitter are immersed in trivialities and banal chatter" (Sharma 52), such as the posting of seemingly endless memes as opposed to serious conversation. The problem, however, is that such conversations are simply being oversimplified as insignificant precursors to effective strategizing for action. Within the context of a national conversation on race, as the example of Tim Wolfe's ousting reveals, the hashtag can be a tool for encouraging effective policy reform—often considered the end goal of any strategies to end racism and racial discrimination. For this reason, it is interesting to see lawmakers and politicians also engaging in these conversations as equal participants through the use of the hashtag.

Opposition to the #BlackLivesMatter Movement

The unfamiliarity of the hashtag as a new genre does contribute to the generational divide that widens with the implementation of contemporary methods of communication and engagement. The overarching goals of the leadership of the #BlackLivesMatter

Movement are not much different from those of the leadership of the Black Power and Civil Rights Movements. However, there is a generational divide that highlights the shifts in communication styles through the use of language. Those who participated in civil rights efforts for equality in the past may be justifiably disenfranchised with the way that the #BlackLivesMatter Movement seems to be reestablishing a culture of separate but equal. The notions that we are not all aspiring towards the same things and that we do not all necessarily want to become assimilated and indistinguishable may even be a bit threatening to what was considered the progress of the 1960s. So there is a conscious and intentional generational gap that results from the decision to distance the classic culture from the contemporary counterculture.

In addition to feelings of intimidation associated with the novelty of the marriage of technology and social justice movements, many older activists hold to the idea that non-academic texts are denigrated and cannot be rhetorically dignified. To them, the grandeur and inspiration behind Dr. Martin Luther King Jr.'s 1963 "I Have a Dream" speech is far too powerful to be associated in any way with a tweet confined to the limits of 140 characters. The marching of fingers across keyboards is not comparable to the marching of feet across the bridge at Selma. Hashtags and retweets in virtual spaces are not comparable to the physical gatherings of tangible bodies in the real spaces of churches and at lunch counters. The consensus among some of these thinkers is that there is a kind of irreverence about this ease of access and that the platform of popular culture somehow takes away from the seriousness of purpose.

The rebuttal to this ideology lies in the fact that the contemporary version of the movement is built upon the foundations that were laid in the past. Generations are perpetually being replaced, but many of the same pervasive tensions that resulted in race-based inequalities in the past are still just as prevalent today. These inequalities may present themselves in the forms of microaggressions and racial profiling, but the fact is that they still exist. An old problem that morphs into a more socially acceptable version of itself is not a new problem. The fact that it still remains is evidence that it cannot be solved with an old method, especially since the tools of prejudice and discrimination are evolving as well. The #BlackLivesMatter Movement comes out of this realization. It does not seek to undermine or undervalue past progress or methods; it simply seeks to utilize contemporary tactics to promote access to agency and engagement. By capitalizing on the hashtag's ability to amplify voices, the contemporary movement is employing new methodologies that are pushing an old problem into the public focus once again.

Conclusion

To those who have an acute awareness of the presence of racism in America, the reality is that more often than not, the experiences of their white counterparts cannot be used as a standard or point of equal comparison for black Americans. The concept of racial equality primarily exists in theory alone. The effects of racism are often masked under systems that seek to be overtly politically correct. This is why perpetrators of police brutality are being exonerated under the protection of the legal system. This is why police officers are often not held accountable for the violent executions of black youth. For some, failure to acknowledge race is presented as a potential solution to its challenges when, in reality, it is within this silence that racism is the most prolific. The articulations of the truths regarding these unjust realities are occurring on new platforms because of an awareness of the need to implement new tactics to address old problems. Hashtags have become the rhetorical tactic of choice, seeking to end this silence by transcending these binaries and becoming the unifying center around which conversations that result in change can occur.

In the end, past and current events continue to remind us of the reality that racism is a constant part of this nation's history. Retaliations to some of the countless injustices that confirm this fact have resulted in a revamped movement for cultural and historical awareness that seeks results in the forms of both public awareness and policy changes. This movement is both impassioned and intellectual, but documentation of the ideas and events that take place on either side now emerges on public platforms. Ultimately, the hashtag as a new genre is bridging the gap between public and private spaces and is a symbolic representation of the progress being made by communities that promote the convergence of texts, technologies, and literature on every level of the sociopolitical hierarchy. The hashtag has been the impetus of the #BlackLivesMatter Movement for this reason—a fact indicative of the magnetism of the hashtag. Accessibility to the contemporary texts that are emerging out of our culture and moving the national conversation on race in the direction of productive change therefore legitimize the efficacy of the hashtag as a new genre—a genre that we will continue to engage as we pursue that sense of social justice and equality forever steeped in the American dream.

Notes

1. The unchecked ability to disseminate information on this issue does not come without its weaknesses. Because there is such a wealth of virtual space that allows for dialogue and the exchange of ideas, it is necessary to establish and reinforce legitimacy within the civil rights field now more than ever. The snowball effect of reposts and retweets can complicate damage control when it comes to the spread of misinformation. In this social media-driven culture, the due diligence of verification often goes undone because fictions can appear to be just as persuasive as facts. Buzzwords and phrases that are closely tied to pivotal moments and events can circulate into what is considered common knowledge without even being verified for accuracy. While the hashtag has come to embody the recontextualization of the civil rights struggle using contemporary methods of communication, it is important to be aware that it does not yet have the inherent ability to fact-check what comes after it, which leaves that responsibility up to the viewers and authors of this new genre.

Works Cited

ABC News (@ABC). "#Blackgirlmagic takes spotlight at Olympics." 20 Aug. 2016. 5:05AM.

"Black Lives Matter: Freedom & Justice for All Black Lives." *Black Lives Matter*. #BlackLivesMatter Organization, n.d. Web. 15 Dec. 2016.

Brown, Sterling A. "Negro Character as Seen by White Authors." *The Journal of Negro Education* 2.2 (1933): 179-203.

Brewster, Shaquille. "After Ferguson: Is 'Hashtag Activism' Spurring Policy Changes?" *NBC News*. 12 Dec. 2014.

Bulwer-Lytton, Edward. *Richelieu: or the Conspiracy.* New York: Dodd, Mead and Company, 1896.

Escalante, Erika (@Eri82195). "Our inner n*gger came out today." 25 Oct. 2015. 6:18PM.

Houston, Keith. "The Octothorpe, Part 1 of 2." *Shady Characters.* Shady Characters, 2011.

Isagenix (@isagenix). "We too find this tweet offensive & we are shocked. This does not reflect our values & culture. The intern is no longer with us." 25 Oct. 2015. 11:23PM.

Lavan, Makeba. "The Negro Tweets His Presence: Black Twitter as Social and Political Watchdog." *Modern Language Studies* 45.1 (2015): 56-65.

Lott, Eric. "Blackface and Blackness: The Minstrel Show in American Culture." *Inside the Minstrel Mask: Readings in Nineteenth-Century Blackface Minstrelsy.* Ed. Annemarie Bean, James V. Hatch, & Brooks McNamara. Middletown, CT: Wesleyan UP, 1996. 3-32.

Poniewozik, James. "#IfTheyGunnedMeDown and What Hashtag Activism Does Right." *TIME* 11 Aug. 2014.

Sacco, Justine. (@JustineSacco). "Going to Africa. Hope I don't get AIDS. Just kidding. I'm white!" 20 Dec. 2013. 10:19AM.

Schomburg, Arthur A. "The Negro Digs Up His Past." *Voices from the Harlem Renaissance.* Ed. Nathan Irvin Huggins. New York: Oxford UP, 1995. 217-221.

Shaina411. "Writer/Director Justin Simien Talks 'Dear White People' Gotham Award Nomination." *The Source.* The Northstar Group, 3 Dec. 2014. Web. 15 Dec. 2016.

Sharma, Sanjay. "Black Twitter?: Racial Hashtags, Networks, and Contagion." *new formations: a journal of culture/theory/politics* 78.1 (2013): 46-64.

RESOURCES

Chronology of Civil Rights with an Emphasis on Race ──

1808	Following the Slave Trade Act of 1807 enacted by the British Parliament, the US Congress bans the importation of slaves from Africa.
1831	Nat Turner leads a slave uprising in Southampton County, Virginia. He narrates *The Confessions of Nat Turner* to Thomas R. Gray before his death. During this time, William Lloyd Garrison begins to publish *The Liberator* and Mary Prince's *The History of Mary Prince, a West Indian Slave* becomes the first slave narrative published by a black woman in the United States.
1833	Abolitionist Lydia Maria Child publishes *An Appeal in Favor of That Class of Americans Called Africans.*
1835	Often considered the first black female political writer of her time, Maria W. Stewart publishes a collection of essays and speeches on slavery.
1845	Frederick Douglass publishes *Narrative of the Life of Frederick Douglass, An American Slave.*
1847	Frederick Douglass founds *The North Star* newspaper.
1849	Harriet Tubman escapes from slavery and begins leading slaves to freedom, making her a pioneer of the Underground Railroad. Henry Bibb's *Narrative of the Life of Henry Bibb, an American Slave, Written by Himself* is also published as well as the narratives of Henry "Box" Brown and Josiah Henson.
1851	Sojourner Truth delivers her "Ain't I a Woman?" speech to the Women's Convention in Ohio; it was later published in the *Anti-Slavery Bugle* in 1853.

1852	Harriet Beecher Stowe publishes her infamous novel, *Uncle Tom's Cabin*. Martin R. Delany also publishes *The Condition, Elevation, Emigration, and Destiny of the Colored People of the United States*.
1853	William Wells Brown publishes *Clotel; Or, The President's Daughter*, one of the earliest novels calling attention to the sexual exploitation of female slaves. Solomon Northup also publishes *Twelve Years a Slave*.
1854	Frances Ellen Watkins Harper publishes *Poems on Miscellaneous Subjects*, which scholars often contend started the tradition of black protest poetry.
1857	Congress rules, in the Dred Scott case, that slaves are not American citizens and that Congress itself does not have the right to ban slavery in the states. Frank J. Webb publishes *The Garies and Their Friends*.
1859	John Brown and his followers attempt to launch a slave revolt in Harpers Ferry. Key works include Harriet E. Wilson's *Our Nig; or, Sketches from the Life of a Free Black, in a Two-Story White House, North* and Martin R. Delany's *Blake; or, the Huts of America*.
1861	Under the pseudonym Linda Brent, Harriet Jacobs publishes her slave narrative, *Incidents in the Life of a Slave Girl*. The South also secedes from the Union, marking the beginning of the American Civil War.
1863	President Abraham Lincoln issues the Emancipation Proclamation, declaring the freedom of the slaves held in the Confederate states.
1865	Congress establishes the Freedmen's Bureau in March, just a month before the Confederacy surrenders in April. This time proves quite tumultuous with a radical change in the

American racial landscape marked by the formation of the Ku Klux Klan, the ratification of the Thirteen Amendment, and the rise in black codes intended to restrict the rights of newly-freed blacks.

1868   The Fourteenth Amendment is ratified, granting citizenship to former slaves.

1870   The Fifteenth Amendment is ratified, giving blacks the right to vote.

1877   The Reconstruction era comes to an end in the South, and civil rights for blacks begin to quickly deteriorate.

1881   Booker T. Washington founds the Tuskegee Normal and Industrial Institute.

1892   Anna Julia Cooper publishes *A Voice from the South.*

1896   The National Association of Colored Women is developed, uniting the black women's club movement under figures such as Mary Church Terrell and Anna Julia Cooper. During this time, the US Supreme Court essentially affirms "separate but equal" under *Plessy v. Ferguson*, leading to the Jim Crow era.

1903   W. E. B. Du Bois publishes his seminal work, *The Souls of Black Folk.*

1905   W. E. B. Du Bois founds the Niagara Movement, demanding equality for blacks—a direct protest to the platform of accomodationism he associates with Booker T. Washington and the Atlanta Compromise address.

1909   The National Association for the Advancement of Colored People (NAACP) is founded, becoming one of the most important US civil rights organizations.

1910	The Great Migration begins as masses of African Americans move to the North in search of increasing social and economic opportunities denied them in the South. The NAACP also begins publishing *The Crisis* magazine.
1912	James Weldon Johnson publishes *The Autobiography of an Ex-Colored Man.*
1914	Marcus Garvey founds the Universal Negro Improvement Association (UNIA).
1916	Angelina Weld Grimké publishes her anti-lynching play, *Rachel.*
1918	Alice Dunbar Nelson publishes *Mine Eyes Have Seen.*
1924	In response to the increasing violence against black bodies, Walter White publishes *The Fire in the Flint.*
1925	Alain Locke publishes his groundbreaking anthology, *The New Negro*, calling for a rise in African-American literature to combat the biased (and often stereotypical) account of the black experience.
1930	Georgia Douglas Johnson publishes *Blue-Eyed Black Boy.*
1931	The Scottsboro Nine are indicted on charges of rape, calling attention to the widespread inequities of the American judicial system. George Schuyler publishes *Black No More.*
1935	Mary McLeod Bethune organizes the National Council of Negro Women. Langston Hughes composes his play *Mulatto.*
1938	Richard Wright publishes *Uncle Tom's Children.*
1940	Richard Wright publishes *Native Son.*

1945	Richard Wright publishes *Black Boy*.
1948	President Harry S. Truman issues an executive order, which integrates the United States armed forces.
1952	Ralph Ellison publishes *Invisible Man*.
1954	*Brown v. Board of Education of Topeka, Kansas* renders racial segregation in schools unconstitutional, striking a blow to the *Plessy v. Ferguson* decision.
1955	Emmett Till is murdered in Mississippi. Rosa Parks also refused to give up her seat in an action that sparks the Montgomery Bus Boycott and the desegregation of Montgomery's buses (in 1956). James Baldwin publishes *Notes of a Native Son*.
1957	Martin Luther King Jr., Charles K. Steele, and Fred L. Shuttlesworth found the Southern Christian Leadership Conference (SCLC). In September, Governor Orval Faubus blocks the Little Rock Nine from entering the newly desegregated school until federal troops are forced to intervene.
1959	Lorraine Hansberry publishes her play *A Raisin in the Sun*.
1960	The Greensboro Four begin a sit-in at the segregated lunch counter at Woolworth's and the Student Nonviolent Coordinating Committee (SNCC) is founded. Harper Lee publishes *To Kill a Mockingbird*.
1963	The March on Washington for Jobs and Freedom is punctuated by Martin Luther King Jr.'s infamous "I Have a Dream" speech. Four black girls are also killed during the Sixteenth Street Baptist Church bombing. Key works include James Baldwin's *The Fire Next Time* and Martin Luther King Jr.'s *Why We Can't Wait*.

1964	The Civil Rights Act is passed, helping to curtail a history of racial and gender discrimination in the workplace. The act also establishes the Equal Employment Opportunity Commission (EEOC) to investigate complaints of discrimination. James E. Chaney, Andrew Goodman, and Michael Schwerner are also killed by the KKK for helping to register black voters in the South. Key works include James Baldwin's *Blues for Mister Charlie* as well as Amiri Baraka's *Dutchman* and *The Slave.*
1965	The tumult of the Civil Rights Era continues as Malcolm X is assassinated, state troopers attack demonstrators crossing the Edmund Pettus Bridge, and the Watts riots break out. Congress also passes the Voting Rights Act of 1965 to help increase the black vote, often curtailed by literacy tests and poll taxes. Key works include *The Autobiography of Malcolm X: As Told to Alex Haley* and James Baldwin's short story collection, *Going to Meet the Man.*
1966	Huey Newton and Bobby Seale found the Black Panther Party. Margaret Walker publishes *Jubilee.*
1967	Thurgood Marshall becomes the first black Supreme Court Justice. The Supreme Court also strikes down anti-miscegenation legislation with *Loving v. Virginia.*
1968	Martin Luther King Jr. is assassinated in April, just days before President Lyndon B. Johnson signs the Civil Rights Act of 1968, prohibiting housing discrimination. Shirley Chisholm also becomes the first black female US Representative. Key works include Eldridge Cleaver's *Soul on Ice* and Martin Luther King Jr.'s *Where Do We Go from Here: Chaos or Community?*
1970	Malcolm X publishes a collection of essays and speeches entitled, *By Any Means Necessary.*

1972	The Tuskegee Syphilis Experiment comes to an end after forty years. James Baldwin publishes *No Name in the Street.*
1974	Angela Davis publishes *Angela: An Autobiography.*
1975	Gayl Jones publishes *Corregidora.*
1979	Octavia Butler publishes her neo-slave novel, *Kindred.*
1984	Amiri Baraka publishes *The Autobiography of LeRoi Jones.*
1986	George C. Wolfe publishes *The Colored Museum.*
1987	Toni Morrison publishes *Beloved.*
1992	bell hooks publishes *Black looks: race and representation.*
1998	Daryl Davis publishes *Klan-destine Relationships: A Black Man's Odyssey in the Ku Klux Klan,* covering interviews he conducted with members of the Klan. Kathy A. Perkins and Judith Louise Stephens publish *Strange Fruit: Plays on Lynching by American Women.*
1999	Toni Cade Bambara publishes *These Bones are Not My Child* and Rita Dove publishes *On the Bus with Rosa Parks: Poems.*
2001	Colin Powell becomes the first African-American US secretary of state followed by Condoleezza Rice, who becomes the first black female US secretary of state in 2005.
2008	After defeating rival Sen. John McCain, Barack Obama is elected the first African-American president in US history, marking a supposed shift in the national racial mindset.

2009	Barack Obama is sworn in as the forty-forth president of the United States. In February, the Senate also votes to confirm Eric Holder as the first African-American attorney general.
2010	Michelle Alexander publishes *The New Jim Crow: Mass Incarceration in the Age of Colorblindness*.
2014	In August, Michael Brown is shot and killed by Officer Darren Wilson in Ferguson, Missouri, sparking widespread protests nationwide when the grand jury announces its decision not to indict Wilson. In December, the Staten Island grand jury announces its decision not to indict Officer Daniel Pantaleo in the July death of Eric Garner.
2015	Jason Reynolds and Brendan Kiely publish *All American Boys*, examining the internal conflict of two teens in response to an incident of police brutality.
2016	President Obama signs the Emmett Till Civil Rights Crimes Reauthorization Act of 2016, which allows the Department of Justice and the Federal Bureau of Investigation to reopen unsolved civil rights crimes before 1980.

Chronology of Civil Rights with an Emphasis on Gender____

1784	Judith Sargent Murray publishes her essay, "Desultory Thoughts upon the Utility of Encouraging a Degree of Self-Complacency, Especially in Female Bosoms."
1790	Judith Sargent Murray publishes "On the Equality of the Sexes."
1794	Susanna Rowson publishes the US edition of her novel, *Charlotte Temple.*
1797	Hannah Webster Foster publishes her epistolary novel, *The Coquette.*
1835	Lydia Maria Child publishes *The History of the Condition of Women in Various Ages and Nations.*
1838	Women's rights advocate Sarah Moore Grimké publishes *Letters on the Equality of the Sexes, and the Condition of Woman.*
1845	Margaret Fuller publishes *Woman in the Nineteenth Century.* Other key works published include Samuel May's "The Rights and Condition of Women" and Lydia Maria Child's *Brief History of the Condition of Women in Various Ages and Nations, Volume 2.*
1848	In New York, participants gather at the country's first women's rights convention and adopt the "Declaration of Sentiments," which outlines twelve resolutions for gender equality under the law.
1849	Lucretia Mott publishes her speech, "Discourse on Woman."

1850	The first National Women's Rights Convention is hosted in Massachusetts.
1854	Elizabeth Cady Stanton delivers her "Address to the Legislature of New York," adopted by the State Woman's Rights Convention. Sara Payson Willis also publishes her roman à clef, *Ruth Hall: A Domestic Tale of the Present Time.*
1868	Louisa May Alcott publishes volume one of *Little Women,* completing the work the following year. Elizabeth Cady Stanton also delivers her "The Destructive Male" speech and establishes *The Revolution* newspaper with Susan B. Anthony.
1869	In May, Susan B. Anthony and Elizabeth Cady Stanton help form the National Woman Suffrage Association. In November, the American Woman Suffrage Association forms. Both organizations seek equal voting rights for women.
1870	*Woman's Journal* is founded by Lucy Stone and Henry Browne Blackwell.
1873	After receiving a fine for voting in the 1872 presidential election, Susan B. Anthony delivers her "On Woman's Rights to the Suffrage" speech. Key works published include Ezra Heywood's "Uncivil Liberty: An Essay to Show the Injustice and Impolicy of Ruling Woman Without Her Consent" and Thomas Webster's *Woman: Man's Equal.*
1874	Marie Stevens Case Howland publishes *Papa's Own Girl.*
1875	Critical of Charles Darwin's 1871 *The Descent of Man, and Selection in Relation to Sex*, Antoinette Brown Blackwell publishes *The Sexes Throughout Nature.*

1876	The National Woman Suffrage Association releases its "Declaration of Rights of the Women of the United States."
1881	Thomas Wentworth Higginson publishes *Common Sense About Women*.
1888	Thomas Wentworth Higginson publishes *Women and Men*.
1890	Mary E. Bradley Lane publishes her utopian novel, *Mizora*.
1892	Charlotte Perkins Gilman publishes "The Yellow Wallpaper." Anna Julia Cooper also publishes her black feminist work, *A Voice from the South*.
1893	Colorado becomes the first state in the country to grant women the right to vote; several states follow in the years after. Alice Ilgenfritz Jones and Ella Merchant publish the science fiction novel, *Unveiling a Parallel*.
1894	Kate Chopin publishes her short story, "The Story of an Hour."
1896	The National Association of Colored Women is developed, uniting the black women's club movement under figures such as Mary Church Terrell and Anna Julia Cooper.
1898	Charlotte Perkins Gilman publishes her seminal work, *Women and Economics*.
1899	Kate Chopin publishes *The Awakening*.
1903	The National Women's Trade Union League is established, fighting for better wages and work conditions as women take on expanded roles in the workforce.
1905	Edith Wharton publishes *The House of Mirth*.

1909	Charlotte Perkins Gilman begins to publish her serialized utopian novel, *Herland*.
1911	Charlotte Perkins Gilman publishes *Moving the Mountain*.
1913	Alice Paul and Lucy Burns form the Congressional Union, later renamed the National Women's Party, in order to fight for the right to vote.
1916	The first US birth-control clinic opens, though it is closed ten days later and its founder, Margaret Sanger, is arrested. She opens another clinic in 1923.
1920	The Nineteenth Amendment to the Constitution is signed into law, effectively granting women the right to vote so long denied them.
1921	Continuing her mission, Margaret Sanger founds the American Birth Control League; in 1942, this becomes the Planned Parenthood Federation of America.
1963	The Commission on the Status of Women, established by President John F. Kennedy and chaired by Eleanor Roosevelt, reports widespread gender discrimination in the workplace—an issue that Congress seeks to address, in part, by passing the Equal Pay Act. Betty Friedan publishes *The Feminine Mystique*.
1964	The Civil Rights Act is passed, helping to curtail a history of racial and gender discrimination in the workplace. The act also establishes the Equal Employment Opportunity Commission (EEOC) to investigate complaints of discrimination.
1966	Betty Friedan founds the National Organization for Women (NOW) to end sexual discrimination continuing in the workplace.

1969	Maya Angelou publishes *I Know Why the Caged Bird Sings*.
1972	*Ms. Magazine*, founded by Gloria Steinem, publishes its first issue. The journals *Women's Studies Quarterly* and *Feminist Studies* are also established.
1973	With the *Roe v. Wade* decision, the Supreme Court controversially establishes a woman's right to have an abortion, sparking intense and longstanding debates about a woman's right to choose.
1974	Ntozake Shange stages the first performance of *for colored girls who have considered suicide / when the rainbow is enuf*.
1976	Nebraska enacts the nation's first marital rape law. Maxine Hong Kingston publishes *The Woman Warrior: Memoirs of a Girlhood Among Ghosts*.
1978	The Pregnancy Discrimination Act is passed, banning discrimination against pregnant women in the workplace.
1981	Cherríe Moraga and Gloria E. Anzaldúa publish their feminist anthology, *This Bridge Called My Back: Writings by Radical Women of Color*. bell hooks also publishes *Ain't I a Woman?: black women and feminism*.
1982	Alice Walker publishes her Pulitzer Prize-winning novel, *The Color Purple*. Audre Lorde also publishes *Zami: A New Spelling of My Name*.
1983	Alice Walker publishes *In Search of Our Mothers' Gardens: Womanist Prose*. Joanna Russ also publishes *How to Suppress Women's Writing*.
1984	Audre Lorde publishes a collection of essays and speeches titled, *Sister Outsider*.

1988	Wendy Wasserstein publishes Pulitzer Prize-winning play, *The Heidi Chronicles*.
1989	Alice Walker publishes her novel, *The Temple of My Familiar.*
1990	Naomi Wolf publishes *The Beauty Myth: How Images of Beauty Are Used Against Women.*
1991	The feminist theory journal, *Feminism & Psychology*, is established. Key works published include Donna Haraway's "A Cyborg Manifesto: Science, Technology, and Socialist-Feminism in the Late Twentieth Century" and Susan Faludi's *Backlash: The Undeclared War Against American Women.*
1992	Alice Walker publishes *Possessing the Secret of Joy.*
1994	The Violence Against Women Act works to expand services for the victims of rape and domestic violence while increasing officer training.
1996	Eve Ensler's *The Vagina Monologues* premieres at the Westside Theatre.
1998	Inga Muscio publishes *Cunt: A Declaration of Independence.*
2003	Beverly Guy-Sheftall and Johnnetta B. Cole publish *Gender Talk: The Struggle for Equality in African American Communities.*
2008	Jaclyn Friedman and Jessica Valenti publish their historic collection of essays, *Yes Means Yes!: Visions of Female Sexual Power and a World Without Rape.*
2009	President Obama signs the Lilly Ledbetter Fair Pay Restoration Act, which grants rights to fight pay discrimination. Nicholas Kristof and Sheryl WuDunn

publish *Half the Sky: Turning Oppression into Opportunity for Women Worldwide.*

2016   Effective January 2, women are granted expanded roles in the US armed forces—a decision that challenges a 1994 ruling that prohibited women from serving in combat positions. Officials also reauthorize the Violence Against Women Act in order to combat the history of domestic violence and sex trafficking. These decisions reflect a shift in the national attention to increased women's rights and opportunities, as former Secretary of State Hillary Clinton becomes the first woman to secure the nomination of the Democratic Party and Carla Hayden becomes the first woman and African American to hold the post of Librarian of Congress.

Chronology of Civil Rights with an Emphasis on Sexual Orientation _____

1919	Henry Blake Fuller publishes *Bertram Cope's Year*, often recognized as the first American novel to explore widespread issues of homosexuality.
1924	The earliest known organization for gay rights in the country, the Society for Human Rights, is developed by Henry Gerber in Chicago.
1936	Djuna Barnes publishes her modernist novel *Nightwood*.
1948	Novelist and playwright Gore Vidal publishes *The City and the Pillar*.
1951	Harry Hay forms the Mattachine Society—the first national gay rights organization.
1952	Writing under Claire Morgan, Patricia Highsmith publishes *The Price of Salt*.
1955	The Daughters of Bilitis—the first lesbian-rights organization in the country—is established in San Francisco. Allen Ginsberg composes his poem "Howl," later subjected to an obscenity trial in 1957.
1956	James Baldwin publishes *Giovanni's Room*.
1959	Novelist William S. Burroughs publishes *Naked Lunch*. John Knowles also publishes his infamous coming-of-age novel, *A Separate Peace*.
1961	Illinois becomes the first state in the country to decriminalize homosexual acts, including sodomy, though it takes years for other states to follow.

1963	John Rechy publishes his novel *City of Night.*
1964	Hubert Selby Jr. publishes his novel *Last Exit to Brooklyn*, stirring notable controversy for his depiction of homosexuality and transvestism.
1966	The National Transsexual Counseling Unit—the first American transgender organization—is established in San Francisco.
1968	Mart Crowley's stage play *The Boys in the Band* opens at Theater Four in New York before it is adapted for the screen in 1970.
1969	In June, the three-day Stonewall Riots occur, bringing widespread attention to the gay community's ongoing fight for equal rights.
1970	The first Gay Pride Parade is held in Chicago to remember the Stonewall Riots—an event that now draws hundreds of thousands of spectators and participants each year. Joe Brainard publishes *I Remember*.
1973	Reversing a longstanding tradition, the American Psychiatric Association removes homosexuality from its list of mental disorders. In addition, opposing government intervention in personal sexual affairs, Harvey Milk runs for city supervisor in San Francisco. Key works published include Rita Mae Brown's *Rubyfruit Jungle* and James Purdy's *Narrow Rooms*.
1975	Samuel R. Delany publishes science fiction novel, *Dhalgren*.
1976	Harvey Milk is appointed to the Board of Permit Appeals, which makes him the first openly gay city commissioner in the country.

1977	Charles Silverstein and Edmund White publish *The Joy of Gay Sex: An Intimate Guide for Gay Men to the Pleasures of a Gay Lifestyle*.
1978	In January, Harvey Milk wins an election to the San Francisco Board of Supervisors and supports a successful bill to make sexual orientation discrimination illegal. In November, voters reject Proposition 6 (the Briggs Initiative), which calls for the termination of school employees who publicly support gay rights. In addition, on November 27, Dan White assassinates Milk and San Francisco mayor George Moscone. Key works published include Andrew Holleran's *Dancer from the Dance* and Larry Kramer's controversial work, *Faggots*.
1979	In October, the National March on Washington for Lesbian and Gay Rights occurs in Washington, DC.
1982	Wisconsin becomes the first state in the country to make discrimination against sexual orientation illegal. Key works published include Alice Walker's Pulitzer Prize-winning novel *The Color Purple*, Edmund White's *A Boy's Own Story*, and Harvey Fierstein's *Torch Song Trilogy*.
1984	Berkeley, California, becomes the first city in the country to grant its employees domestic-partnership benefits previously denied them.
1985	Larry Kramer's play *The Normal Heart* premieres in New York.
1987	Bret Easton Ellis publishes *The Rules of Attraction*.
1988	David Henry Hwang's *M. Butterfly* opens on Broadway. Key works published include Edmund White's *The Beautiful*

Room is Empty, Paul Monette's *Borrowed Time: An AIDS Memoir*, and Michael Chabon's *The Mysteries of Pittsburgh.*

1989   Dennis Cooper publishes *Closer.*

1992   Sarah Schulman publishes her novel *Empathy.*

1993   Hoping to end the ban on homosexual service that dated back to World War II, the Clinton Administration implements the controversial "Don't Ask, Don't Tell" policy. Activists, however, criticize the policy, arguing that it ultimately silences gay service people, who are forced into secrecy for fear of being discharged from the military. In April, hundreds of thousands gather for the March on Washington for Lesbian, Gay, and Bi Equal Rights and Liberation, protesting the hostile climate against members of the LGBT community nationwide. Tony Kushner's *Angels in America: A Gay Fantasia on National Themes* debuts on Broadway at the Walter Kerr Theatre. Transgender activist Leslie Feinberg also publishes her novel, *Stone Butch Blues.*

1994   Originally self-published years earlier, E. Lynn Harris re-releases his novel, *Invisible Life*. Mark Merlis also publishes *American Studies*—winner of the Los Angeles Times Book Prize for first fiction.

1995   Howard Cruse publishes his graphic novel, *Stuck Rubber Baby*. In addition, Leroy Aarons publishes *Prayers for Bobby: A Mother's Coming to Terms with the Suicide of Her Gay Son*, and Scott Heim publishes his novel *Mysterious Skin.*

1997   Edmund White publishes the final novel in his trilogy, *The Farewell Symphony*. Annie Proulx also publishes her infamous short story, "Brokeback Mountain," later adapted for the screen in 2005.

1999	Stephen Chbosky publishes *The Perks of Being a Wallflower.*
2000	Offering an alternative to same-sex marriage, Vermont becomes the first state in the country to legalize civil unions for members of the gay and lesbian community; several states follow in the years after. Key works include Michelle Tea's Lambda Literary Award-winning novel, *Valencia*, and Michael Chabon's Pulitzer Prize-winning *The Amazing Adventures of Kavalier & Clay.*
2001	Alexander Chee publishes his debut novel, *Edinburgh*, and Joe Westmoreland publishes *Tramps Like Us*.
2002	Jeffrey Eugenides publishes his Pulitzer Prize-winning novel, *Middlesex*.
2003	In the landmark, *Lawrence v. Texas* decision, the US Supreme Court rules that existing sodomy laws are unconstitutional—a ruling the effectively decriminalizes same-sex sexual activity in the US and its territories.
2004	In May, same-sex marriages become legal in the state of Massachusetts despite strong opposition. Julie Anne Peters publishes her young adult novel *Luna.*
2006	American cartoonist Alison Bechdel publishes her graphic memoir, *Fun Home: A Family Tragicomic*, later adapted as a musical in 2013.
2007	In November, the US House of Representatives approves legislation to guarantee equal workplace rights for members of the LGBT community. Transsexual theorist Julia Serano publishes *Whipping Girl: A Transsexual Woman on Sexism and the Scapegoating of Femininity.*
2008	In May, the California Supreme Court grants same-sex couples the right to marry—a decision quickly overturned in November under the state's Proposition 8. In October,

the Connecticut Supreme Court becomes the second in the country to legalize marriage for same-sex couples. Richard Bruce Nugent's *Gentleman Jigger*, written between 1928 and 1933, is published. In addition, Jaclyn Friedman and Jessica Valenti publish their historic collection of essays entitled, *Yes Means Yes!: Visions of Female Sexual Power and a World Without Rape.*

2009   To improve gay rights across the nation, President Obama not only signs a referendum that allows same-sex partners of federal employees to receive benefits, but he also posthumously awards Harvey Milk the Presidential Medal of Freedom for his efforts to promote equality for the LGBT community.

2010   In December, the US Senate votes to repeal the "Don't Ask, Don' Tell" policy originally enacted in 1993.

2012   Tammy Baldwin becomes the first openly gay politician elected to the US Senate. Barbara Browning publishes *I'm Trying to Reach You.*

2013   In February, more than one hundred Republicans support a brief asking the Supreme Court to legalize same-sex marriage in the United States as a constitutional right. On June 26, the US Supreme Court rules that the 1996 Defense of Marriage Act (DOMA), which strictly defined *marriage* as between a man and a woman, is unconstitutional. Under this ruling, the states themselves must define *marriage.* Manil Suri publishes his novel *The City of Devi.*

2014   Saeed Jones publishes his debut collection of poetry, *Prelude to Bruise.*

2015   In June, through the landmark *Obergefell v. Hodges* case, the US Supreme Court rules that same-sex couples should receive the same legal treatment in marriage as heterosexual couples. In July, the Boy Scouts of America also ends its longstanding ban on gay adult leaders for Scout groups.

2016   The national debate regarding transgender rights erupts. In April, amidst immediate backlash, Target announces policy that allows transgender individuals to use the bathroom facilities matching their gender identities. In May, the Obama Administration follows suit, encouraging public schools nationwide to do the same or risk access to federal funding. The LGBTQ community also takes center stage in June after Omar Mateen shoots forty-nine people and wounds over fifty others at the Pulse gay nightclub in Orlando, Florida.

Selected Works of Civil Rights Literature _____

Because the scope of civil rights literature offered in *Critical Insights: Civil Rights Literature, Past & Present* is so extensive in comparison to past studies, the list of additional works provided below is just a small sample of a large body of literature examining issues of race, gender, and orientation in the United States.

Anthologies

Armstrong, Julie Buckner & Amy Schmidt. *The Civil Rights Reader: American Literature from Jim Crow to Reconciliation.* 2009.

Baraka, Amiri & Larry Neal, eds. *Black Fire: An Anthology of Afro-American Writing.* 1968.

Bergman, David. *Gay American Autobiography: Writings from Whitman to Sedaris.* 2009.

Berlin, Ira, et al., eds. *Remembering Slavery: African Americans Talk about Their Personal Experiences of Slavery and Emancipation.* 1999.

Carson, Clayborn, et al. *The Eyes on the Prize Civil Rights Reader: Documents, Speeches, and Firsthand Accounts from the Black Freedom Struggle.* 1991.

Coleman, Jeffrey L., ed. *Words of Protest, Words of Freedom: Poetry of the American Civil Rights Movement and Era.* 2012.

Daley, James, ed. *Great Speeches on Gay Rights.* 2010.

Jay, Karla & Allen Young, eds. *Out of the Closets: Voices of Gay Liberation.* 1972.

Marable, Manning & Leith Mullings, eds. *Let Nobody Turn Us Around: Voices of Resistance, Reform, and Renewal.* 2000.

Reporting Civil Rights: The Library of America Edition. 2013.

Drama

Baldwin, James. *Blues for Mister Charlie.* 1964.

Baraka, Amiri (LeRoi Jones). *Dutchman.* 1964.

_____. *The Slave.* 1964.

Crothers, Rachel. *A Man's World.* 1910.

Grimké, Angelina Weld. *Rachel.* 1916.

Ensler, Eve. *The Vagina Monologues.* 1996.

Fierstein, Harvey. *Torch Song Trilogy.* 1982.

Hansberry, Lorraine. *A Raisin in the Sun.* 1959.

Kushner, Tony. *Angels in America.* 1993.

Nagy, Phyllis. *Weldon Rising.* 1996.

Wasserstein, Wendy. *The Heidi Chronicles.* 1988.

Wolfe, George C. *The Colored Museum.* 1986.

Nonfiction and Autobiographies

Baldwin, James. *Notes of a Native Son.* 1955.

_____. *The Fire Next Time.* 1963.

Bay, Mia, ed. *The Light of Truth: Writings of an Anti-Lynching Crusader.* 2014.

Black, Jason Edward & Charles E. Morris III, eds. *An Archive of Hope: Harvey Milk's Speeches and Writings.* 2013.

Cleaver, Eldridge. *Soul on Ice.* 1968.

Davis, Angela. *Angela Davis: An Autobiography.* 1974.

Davis, Daryl. *Klan-destine Relationships: A Black Man's Odyssey in the Ku Klux Klan.* 1998.

Du Bois, W. E. B. *The Souls of Black Folk.* 1903.

Emery, Vince, ed. *The Harvey Milk Interviews: In His Own Words.* 2012.

Friedman, Jaclyn & Jessica Valenti, eds. *Yes Means Yes!: Visions of Female Sexual Power & A World Without Rape.* 2008.

Fuller, Margaret. *Woman in the Nineteenth Century.* 1845.

Jacobs, Harriet. *Incidents in the Life of a Slave Girl.* 1861.

Kuklin, Susan. *Beyond Magenta: Transgender Teens Speak Out.* 2014.

Lemert, Charles & Esme Bhan, eds. *The Voice of Anna Juila Cooper: Including* A Voice from the South *and Other Important Essays, Papers, and Letters.* 1998.

Long, Michael G., ed. *Gay is Good: The Life and Letters of Gay Rights Pioneer Franklin Kameny.* 2014.

Lorde, Audre. *Sister Outsider: Essays and Speeches.* 2007.

Muscio, Inga. *Cunt: A Declaration of Independence.* 1998.

Serano, Julia. *Whipping Girl: A Transsexual Woman on Sexism and the Scapegoating of Femininity.* 2009.

Shepard, Judy. *The Meaning of Matthew: My Son's Murder in Laramie, and a World Transformed.* 2009.

Snyder-Hill, Stephen. *Soldier of Change: From the Closet to the Forefront of the Gay Rights Movement.* 2014.

Stanton, Elizabeth Cady, et al. *History of Woman Suffrage.* 1881–1922.

Washington, James M., ed. *A Testament of Hope: The Essential Writings and Speeches of Martin Luther King, Jr.* 1986.

X, Malcom. *By Any Means Necessary.* 1970.

_____. *The Autobiography of Malcolm X: As Told to Alex Haley.* 1965.

Novels

Alcott, Louisa May. *Little Women.* 1868–1869.

Baldwin, James. *Another Country.* 1962.

_____. *Giovanni's Room.* 1956.

Bambara, Toni Cade. *These Bones are Not My Child.* 1999.

Barnes, Djuna. *Nightwood.* 1936.

Burroughs, William S. *Naked Lunch.* 1959.

Butler, Octavia. *Kindred.* 1979.

Ellison, Ralph. *Invisible Man.* 1952.

Fuller, Henry Black. *Bertram Cope's Year.* 1919.

Harper, Frances E. W. *Iola Leroy, or, Shadows Uplifted.* 1892.

Highsmith, Patricia (Claire Morgan). *The Price of Salt.* 1952.

Johnson, James Weldon. *The Autobiography of an Ex-Colored Man.* 1912.

Lee, Harper. *To Kill a Mockingbird.* 1960.

Morrison, Toni. *Beloved.* 1987.

Rowson, Susanna. *Charlotte Temple.* 1794.

Vidal, Gore. *The City and the Pillar.* 1948.

White, Walter. *The Fire in the Flint.* 1924.

Bibliography

Civil Rights Literature with an Emphasis on Race

Armstrong, Julie Buckner, ed. *The Cambridge Companion to American Civil Rights Literature.* New York: Cambridge UP, 2015.

Auger, Philip. *Native Sons in No Man's Land: Rewriting Afro-American Manhood in the Novels of Baldwin, Walker, Wideman, and Gaines.* New York: Garland, 2000.

Byerman, Keith. *Remembering the Past in Contemporary African American Fiction.* Chapel Hill: U of North Carolina P, 2005.

_____. *Fingering the Jagged Grain: Tradition and Form in Recent Black Fiction.* Athens, GA: U of Georgia P, 1985.

Dabbs, James McBride. *Civil Rights in Recent Southern Fiction.* Atlanta: Southern Regional Council, 1969.

Early, Gerald, ed. *Speech and Power: The African-American Essay and Its Cultural Contents from Polemics to Pulpit.* Hopewell, NJ: Ecco P, 1992.

Ernest, John. *Liberation Historiography: African American Writers and the Challenge of History, 1794–1861.* Chapel Hill: U of North Carolina P, 2004.

Fisch, Audrey. *The Cambridge Companion to the African American Slave Narrative.* New York: Cambridge UP, 2007.

Ginsberg, Elaine K. *Passing and the Fictions of Identity.* Durham, NC: Duke UP, 1996.

Graham, Maryemma, ed. *The Cambridge Companion to the African American Novel.* New York: Cambridge UP, 2004.

Gray, Jonathan W. *Civil Rights in the White Literary Imagination: Innocence by Association.* Jackson: UP of Mississippi, 2013.

Glaude, Eddie, Jr. *Is It Nation Time? Contemporary Essays on Black Power and Black Nationalism.* Chicago: U of Chicago P, 2002.

Goldsby, Jacqueline. *Spectacular Secret: Lynching in American Life and Literature.* Chicago: U of Chicago P, 2006.

Mathes, Carter. *Imagine the Sound: Experimental African American Literature after Civil Rights.* Minneapolis: U of Minnesota P, 2015.

McCaskill, Barbara & Caroline Gebhard, eds. *Post-Bellum, Pre-Harlem: African American Literature and Culture, 1877–1919.* New York: New York UP, 2006.

McDowell, Deborah & Arnold Rampersad, eds. *Slavery and the Literary Imagination.* Baltimore, MD: Johns Hopkins UP, 1989.

Metress, Christopher & Harriet Pollack, eds. *Emmett Till in Literary Memory and Imagination.* Baton Rouge: Louisiana State UP, 2008.

Norman, Brian. *Neo-Segregation Narratives: Jim Crow in Post-Civil Rights American Literature.* Athens, GA: U of Georgia P, 2010.

_____. & Piper Kendrix Williams, eds. *Representing Segregation: Toward an Aesthetics of Living Jim Crow, and Other Forms of Racial Division.* Albany, NY: SUNY P, 2010.

Patterson, Robert J. *Exodus Politics: Civil Rights and Leadership in African American Literature and Culture.* Charlottesville: U of Virginia P, 2013.

Rambsy, Howard. *The Black Arts Enterprise and the Production of African American Poetry.* Ann Arbor: U of Michigan P, 2011.

Rushdy, Ashraf H. A. *Remembering Generations: Race and Family in Contemporary African American Fiction.* Chapel Hill: U of North Carolina P, 2001.

Civil Rights with an Emphasis on Gender

Allen, Carol. *Black Women Intellectuals: Strategies of Nation, Family, and Neighborhood in the Works of Pauline Hopkins, Jessie Fauset, and Marita Bonner.* New York: Garland, 1998.

Ammons, Elizabeth. *Conflicting Stories: American Women Writers at the Turn into the Twentieth Century.* New York: Oxford UP, 1991.

Beaulieu, Elizabeth Ann. *Black Women Writers and the American Neo-Slave Narrative: Femininity Unfettered.* Westport, CT: Greenwood P, 1999.

Bell, Roseann P., Bettye J. Parker, & Beverly Guy-Sheftall, eds. *Sturdy Black Bridges: Visions of Black Women in Literature.* Garden City, NY: Anchor/ Doubleday, 1979.

Bobo, Jacqueline. *Black Women as Cultural Readers.* New York: Columbia UP, 1995.

Bragg, Beauty. *Reading Contemporary African American Literature: Black Women's Popular Fiction, Post-Civil Rights Experience, and the African American Canon.* Lanham, MD: Lexington, 2015.

Brown, Julie, ed. *American Women Short Story Writers: A Collection of Critical Essays.* New York: Garland, 2000.

Collins, Patricia Hill. *Black Feminist Thought: Knowledge, Consciousness, and the Politics of Empowerment.* New York: Routledge, 2009.

Dean, Janet. *Unconventional Politics: Nineteenth-Century Women Writers and U.S. Indian Policy.* Amherst: U of Massachusetts P, 2016.

Dubey, Madhu. *Black Women Novelists and the Nationalist Aesthetic.* Bloomington: Indiana UP, 1994.

duCille, Ann. *The Coupling Convention: Sex, Text, and Tradition in Black Women's Fiction.* New York: Oxford UP, 1993.

Fulton, DoVeanna S. *Speaking Power: Black Feminist Orality in Women's Narratives of Slavery.* Albany, NY: SUNY P, 2005.

Graham-Bertolini, Alison. *Vigilante Women in Contemporary American Fiction.* New York: Palgrave Macmillan, 2011.

Hogeland, Lisa Maria. *Feminism and Its Fictions: The Consciousness-Raising Novel and the Women's Liberation Movement.* Philadelphia: U of Pennsylvania P, 1998.

Kilcup, Karen L., ed. *Nineteenth-Century American Women Writers: A Critical Reader.* Malden, MA: Blackwell, 1998.

Martin, Wendy & Sharone Williams. *The Routledge Introduction to American Women Writers.* New York: Routledge, 2016.

McDonald, Robert L., & Linda Rohrer Paige, eds. *Southern Women Playwrights: New Essays in Literary History and Criticism.* Tuscaloosa: U of Alabama P, 2002.

Mitchell, Angelyn & Danielle K. Taylor, eds. *The Cambridge Companion to African American Women's Literature.* New York: Cambridge UP, 2009.

Nunes, Ana. *African American Women Writers' Historical Fiction.* New York: Palgrave Macmillan, 2011.

Patton, Venetria K. *Women in Chains: The Legacy of Slavery in Black Women's Fiction.* Albany, NY: SUNY P, 2000.

Wall, Cheryl. *Worrying the Line: Black Women Writers, Lineage, and Literary Tradition.* Chapel Hill: U of North Carolina P, 2005.

Watts, Emily Stipes. *The Poetry of American Women from 1632 to 1945.* Austin: U of Texas P, 1977.

Civil Rights with an Emphasis on Sexual Orientation

Bergman, David. *Gaiety Transfigured: Gay Self-Representation in American Literature.* Madison: U of Wisconsin P, 1991.

Bibler, Michael P. *Cotton's Queer Relations: Same-Sex Intimacy and the Literature of the Southern Plantation, 1936–1968.* Charlottesville: U of Virginia P, 2009.

Boone, Joseph Allen. *Libidinal Currents: Sexuality and the Shaping of Modernism.* Chicago: U of Chicago P, 1998.

Brookes, Les. *Gay Male Fiction Since Stonewall: Ideology, Conflict, and Aesthetics.* New York: Routledge, 2009.

Corber, Robert J. *Homosexuality in Cold War America: Resistance and the Crisis of Masculinity.* Durham, NC: Duke UP, 1997.

Garber, Linda. *Identity Poetics: Race, Class, and the Lesbian-Feminist Roots of Queer Theory*. New York: Columbia UP, 2001.

Herring, Scott, ed. *The Cambridge Companion to American Gay and Lesbian Literature*. New York: Cambridge UP, 2015.

_____. *Queering the Underworld: Slumming, Literature, and the Undoing of Lesbian and Gay History*. Chicago: U of Chicago P, 2007.

Jarraway, David R. *Going the Distance: Dissident Subjectivity in Modernist American Literature*. Baton Rouge: Louisiana State UP, 2003.

Johnson, E. Patrick & Mae G. Henderson, eds. *Black Queer Studies: A Critical Anthology*. Durham: Duke UP, 2005.

Jones, Norman W. *Gay and Lesbian Historical Fiction: Sexual Mystery and Post-Secular Narrative*. New York: Palgrave Macmillan, 2007.

Jones, Sonya L., ed. *Gay and Lesbian Literature Since World War II: History and Memory*. New York: Routledge, 1998.

Kent, Kathryn R. *Making Girls into Women: American Women's Writing and the Rise of Lesbian Identity*. Durham, NC: Duke UP, 2003.

Leak, Jeffrey. *Racial Myths and Masculinity in African American Literature*. Knoxville: U of Tennessee P, 2005.

Loftin, Craig M., ed. *Letters to ONE: Gay and Lesbian Voices form the 1950s and 1960s*. Albany, NY: SUNY P, 2012.

_____. *Masked Voices: Gay Men and Lesbians in Cold War America*. Albany, NY: SUNY P, 2012.

McRuer, Robert. *The Queer Renaissance: Contemporary American Literature and the Reinvention of Lesbian and Gay Identities*. New York: New York UP, 1997.

Nealon, Christopher. *Foundlings: Lesbian and Gay Historical Emotion before Stonewall*. Durham, NC: Duke UP, 2001.

Schwarz, A. B. Christa. *Gay Voices of the Harlem Renaissance*. Bloomington: Indiana UP, 2003.

Somerville, Siobhan B. *Queering the Color Line: Race and the Invention of Homosexuality in American Culture*. Durham, NC: Duke UP, 2000.

Vogel, Shane. *The Scene of Harlem Cabaret: Race, Sexuality, Performance*. Chicago: U of Chicago P., 2009.

Wolfe, Susan J. & Julia Penelope, eds. *Sexual Practice/Textual Theory: Lesbian Cultural Criticism*. Cambridge, MA: Blackwell, 1993.

About the Editor_____

Christopher Allen Varlack is a lecturer in the Department of English at the University of Maryland, Baltimore County, where he teaches courses in African-American literature, creative writing, composition, and grammar. He earned a PhD from Morgan State University, an MFA in creative writing from the University of Southern Maine's Stonecoast MFA Program, and a BA in communications from Loyola College in Maryland. As a writer and scholar, he is interested in how literature can preserve or reclaim the voices of the past, shedding new light on the struggles and the people who define who we are today. Much of his scholarship thus focuses on antebellum literature as well as literature of the Harlem Renaissance and Civil Rights Era—arguably the most important literary and cultural movements in African-American history.

His recent publications include chapters in volumes such as *Critical Insights: Zora Neale Hurston* (2013), *Critical Insights: The Slave Narrative* (2014), *Critical Insights: Virginia Woolf & 20th Century Women Writers* (2014), and *Baby Boomers and Popular Culture: An Inquiry into America's Most Powerful Generation* (2014). He is also the editor of *Critical Insights: Harlem Renaissance* (2015) and has work forthcoming in *Bury My Heart in a Free Land: Black Women Intellectuals in Modern U.S. History* (2017) as well as the introduction to Fall River Press's new edition of W. E. B. Du Bois's *The Souls of Black Folk.* His current book project focuses on tracing the alternative artistic and intellectual strategies of the rebel sojourner Claude McKay through the seven known novels produced throughout his lifetime.

Contributors _____

Enrico Beltramini teaches at Notre Dame du Namur University, offering courses of business and religion in the Department of Business and Religious Studies respectively. He received his PhD in business from Manchester Business School in 2005 and a PhD in history from the University of London in 2013. His interests include the history of economic inequality in the United States. His work has appeared or is forthcoming in *Guns and Butter: The Economic Ideas of the Civil Rights Leaders (1946–1974)*, *Fire!!! The Multimedia Journal of Black Studies*, *The Journal of Economic Philosophy*, and as chapters in *The Cultural History of Money and Credit: A Global Perspective* as well as *The Economic Civil Rights Movement*.

Corrie Claiborne, Assistant Professor of English and American Literature at Morehouse College, received her BA in English from Syracuse University, an MA in English from the University of Southern Carolina, and a doctorate from Ohio State University. Her essay, "The Bride Price," was published in *Sometimes Rhythm, Sometimes Blues: Young African Americans on Sex, Love, and the Search for Mr. Right* (Seal Press, 2013). In 2010, she partnered with NEH and the South Carolina Humanities Council to deliver a series of lectures about the similarities between the quilts of Gee's Bend, Alabama, and the cultural artifacts of the South Carolina Low Country. Her current book project is an anthology entitled *Landscape, Home, Memory: Framing Gullah Geechee Culture*. She is also the coeditor of a special issue of *Studies in American Culture* called *Redirecting the Gaze: Daughters of the Dust, Black Women's Filmmaking & Black Female Imagery 25 Years Later* (March 2017).

Margaret Cox, Assistant Professor of English at Bristol Community College in Massachusetts, was born in Grenada and moved to New York at the age of five. She earned her MA degree in English from Brooklyn College and her PhD from Indiana University of Pennsylvania. She is the author of *Tales of Women*, a collection of poetry that speaks about the experiences of women throughout the African and Caribbean diasporas. Additional works of her poetry have been featured in the Maple Tree Literary Supplement. Her essay, "Re-Imaging the African Feminine Self," is part of the anthology *Reimaging Gender: African Narratives by Women*. She has also written, "Where the Eagle Perches, Can the Hawk Perch Also?," a chapter of the 2015 *"Things Fall Apart": A Student Companion.*

Carol Bunch Davis, Associate Professor of English in the Department of Liberal Studies at Texas A & M University at Galveston, earned a PhD in English at the University of Southern California. She teaches courses in African-American literature as well as rhetoric, composition, and technical and business writing. Her book, *Prefiguring Postblackness: Cultural Memory, Drama and the African American Freedom Struggle of the 1960s*, was published by the University Press of Mississippi in 2015. She is currently working on another book project, *Time to Live: The Sylvester Outley Story*.

Jessie LaFrance Dunbar, Assistant Professor of African-American and African Diasporic literatures at the University of Alabama at Birmingham, specializes in nineteenth- and twentieth-century African-American literatures, Russian literature and culture, and Afro-Cuban literature and culture. She is the recipient of the Woodrow Wilson Career Enhancement Fellowship. Her current book project, *Democracy, Diaspora, and Disillusionment*, considers the exultation of folk culture in tsarist Russia and its socio-political impact on black émigrés.

Kavon Franklin, Assistant Professor of English at Alabama State University, teaches courses in African-American history and cultural studies, American literature, and creative writing. Her recent works include a publication in the *Pomona Valley Review* and forthcoming articles in *Trespassing Journal* and the *Journal of African-American Studies*.

Hope W. Jackson received her PhD from UNC-Greensboro in cultural studies and currently teaches at North Carolina A & T State University in the English Department. She teaches courses ranging from African-American film and culture to hip-hop discourse. Her dissertation, entitled "Stones of Memory: Narratives of a Black Beach Community," conflates her passion for storytelling with other nuances of black oral tradition, such as folklore, African-American rhetoric, intertextuality, and community pedagogy. Her current research interests include queering gender identity in hip-hop, investigating "superqueerness" in Blaxploitation films, black spaces as sites of resistance, black spectatorship versus the gaze in black film discourse, and narratives in black oral tradition, among others. Her latest publication is a book chapter entitled, "Yes! Black Folks can

Tan Too!" in *Critical Black Studies* (Peter Lang, 2016), edited by Rochelle Brock and Dara Nix-Stevenson.

Deborah F. Kadiri earned her BA in English and her MA in texts, technologies, and literature from the University of Maryland, Baltimore County (UMBC). Her recent research discusses the significance of the rhetorical strategies employed by social justice movements, #BlackLivesMatter in particular. Throughout her time at UMBC, she served as a writing fellow in the Department of English, the writing advisor to the graduate school, and Vice President for External Affairs to the Graduate Student Association. She plans to matriculate into law school and pursue a career in social justice.

Derrick King is a PhD candidate in the English Department at the University of Florida, where he has also taught courses in queer theory, literature, and film. His research interests include American literature, film, critical theory, queer studies, and science fiction. His other publications include essays in the *South Atlantic Review, Extrapolation, Cinephile, and MOSF Journal of Science Fiction.* He has also published a book chapter in an edited volume on the television series *Dollhouse.*

Robert LaRue, Assistant Professor in the Department of English at Moravian College, earned his MA and his PhD in English from the University of Texas at Arlington. Currently, his work attends simultaneously to queer theory's anxiety of the postcolonial and postcolonial studies' anxiety of queerness, with an emphasis on the role of politics in postcolonial queer expressions.

Tasia Milton is a doctoral candidate in English at Rutgers University. Her research focuses on region's impact on gender and sexuality in the production of alternative histories in African-American literature. She has presented her work at the McNeil Center for Early American Studies at the University of Pennsylvania as well as the annual meetings of the American Studies Association and the Modern Language Association.

Sheila Murphy, Lecturer and Writing Program Administrator at the University of Kansas, received her MA and PhD in rhetoric and composition from the University of South Carolina. She has taught rhetoric and writing for several years. Her areas of specialization include feminist peace theories, political discourse, public discourse and violence, and digital humanities and pedagogy.

Kaila Philo is a student in the English program at the University of Maryland, Baltimore County, looking toward one day entering a PhD program in comparative literature. She is the editor of *Purple is to Lavender*, a literary and cultural zine that aims to bring women artists of color from the margin to the center. Hoping to establish herself as a novelist, she has published work in *Mask Magazine*, *The Millions*, *Winter Tangerine*, and *Seven Scribes*.

Mary K. Ryan received her MA in public service from Marquette University and her BA degree in political science from the University of Wisconsin-Milwaukee. She is currently a doctoral student in the Alliance for Social, Political, Ethical, and Cultural Thought program at Virginia Tech, where she teaches in the Department of Political Science. Her dissertation concerns structural racism in the United States. Ryan also has book chapters in the forthcoming volumes, *Spaces of Surveillance: States and Selves* (Palgrave Macmillan) and *The Representation of Poverty in Popular Culture* (McFarland).

Andrew Sargent, Associate Professor of English at West Chester University, teaches courses in African-American, American, and Civil Rights Era literature. His essays and reviews on authors such as Donald Goines, Chester Himes, Amiri Baraka, James Weldon Johnson, and others have appeared or are forthcoming in *MELUS*, *College Literature*, *Great Lives from History: African Americans*, *The St. James Encyclopedia of Popular Culture*, and *MLA Approaches to Teaching Baraka's Dutchman*. He is currently at work on a study of African-American literature and the Civil Rights Movement.

Eric J. Sterling earned his PhD from Indiana University in 1992 and is Distinguished Research Professor of English at Auburn University Montgomery, where he has taught for twenty-two years. He was recently named the Ida Belle Young Professor of English at his university—its top honor—and has published four books as well as six dozen refereed journal articles. He is currently working on a book on the drama of August Wilson.

Leonard A. Steverson, Associate Professor Emeritus of Sociology at South Georgia State College, is currently an adjunct professor of sociology at Flagier College and St. Johns River State College in St. Augustine, Florida. He is the author of *Policing in America: A Reference Handbook,* coauthor of *Giants in Sociology: A Little Guide to the Big Names in Sociological Theory*, and author of several chapters in social-science volumes.

Seretha D. Williams, Professor in the Department of English and Foreign Languages as well as affiliated faculty in the Women's and Gender Studies Program at Augusta University, earned a bachelor's degree in journalism from Northwestern University. She also earned a master's degree and doctorate in comparative literature from the University of Georgia. Williams is a coeditor of the essay collection, *Afterimages of Slavery*, and the author of publications on African and African-American literatures. Currently, Williams' work examines the influence of Margaret Walker on the Black Chicago Renaissance and the Black Arts Movement and situates Walker and those periods within a transnational and transcultural framework. Her earlier research discusses the role of trauma in the novels, autobiographies, and poems of African and African-American authors, such as Chimamanda Ngozi Adichie, Zakes Mda, Langston Hughes, Margaret Walker, and Lalita Tademy.

Gronniosaw, James Albert Ukawsaw 6
Gulf oil spill 58

Hall, Katori xv, 270, 285
Hamer, Fannie Lou 114, 157, 240, 242, 279
Hammon, Briton 6
Hammon, Jupiter xi, 4
Hansberry, Lorraine 120, 327
Harlem Renaissance xxi, xxii, xxxii, 12, 13, 14, 140, 141, 142, 155, 173, 319, 354, 355
Harper, Michael vi, xiii, 123, 133, 137
hashtag, the xvi, 307, 308, 309, 310, 313, 314, 315, 317, 318
hate crime xx, 137, 207, 208, 209, 210, 211, 219
The Help xv, 253, 254, 255, 257, 258, 259, 260, 261, 262, 263, 264, 266, 267, 268, 269
Henderson, Russell 208, 209
Highsmith, Patricia vi, xiv, 174, 184, 185, 187, 189, 339, 349
Hodges, Willis 9
homophobia xiv, xix, 77, 193, 194, 195, 200, 201, 202, 204, 207, 219
Hoover, J. Edgar 275
Howe, Julia Ward xix
Hudson, Winson 157
Hughes, Langston xxxii, 13, 14, 107, 326, 361
Human Rights Campaign (HRC) 210
Hurricane Katrina 55, 56, 57, 58, 63, 65, 66, 69, 153, 154
Hurston, Zora Neale 142, 152, 170, 172, 355

inequality 22, 53, 66, 237, 246, 251, 284, 357
integration 21, 32, 64, 111, 117, 229, 248, 260, 306
invisibility xii, xvi, 27, 55, 56, 58, 62

Jackson, Jesse xv, xxvii, xxix, 237, 238, 248, 251, 252
Jackson, Jimmie Lee 242
Jacobs, Harriet 18, 191, 202, 220, 324
Jefferson, Thomas 5, 15
Jenkins, Anthony 208
Jenkins, David 208
Jezebel, the 254
Jim Crow v, vi, xi, xii, xx, xxi, xxiii, xxxii, 10, 12, 14, 17, 22, 36, 37, 38, 39, 43, 45, 46, 52, 58, 115, 123, 125, 126, 132, 137, 139, 212, 242, 253, 254, 256, 257, 264, 266, 267, 269, 270, 273, 274, 276, 277, 285, 325, 330, 347, 352
Johnson, Andrew 10
Johnson, Charles 272
Johnson, James Weldon 22, 34, 213, 326, 360
Johnson, Lyndon B. 23, 131, 191, 328
Jones, Saeed xiv, 208, 221, 344
Jordan, June 279, 282, 285, 298, 303

Kennedy, John F. xxx, 334
Key, Elizabeth 3
King, Breaion 148, 149, 152
King, Coretta Scott 276, 287
Kingdom Theory 244, 252
King, John 208
King, Martin Luther, Jr. xi, xiii, xiv, xv, xvi, xix, xxx, xxxi, 3, 15, 25, 32, 54, 89, 107, 113, 114, 116, 117, 118, 120, 159, 191, 193, 195, 197, 199, 201, 203,

Riis, Jacob xxix
Robertson, Carole Rosamond 131
Roof, Dylann 171
Rosie the Riveter xxiv
Rule, Jane 175
Russworm, John 7
Rustin, Bayard xiv, 32, 191, 194, 204, 274

Sambo 21, 25, 27, 28, 29, 30, 31, 33
Sanchez, Sonia 142
Sanders, Bernie xxix
Sapphire, the 254
Schomburg, Arthur 309
Schuyler, George xx, xxxiii, 13, 326
Schwerner, Michael 113, 114, 243, 328
segregation xi, xii, xxi, 10, 15, 22, 36, 37, 38, 39, 40, 41, 42, 43, 47, 56, 57, 60, 62, 73, 84, 110, 115, 125, 216, 217, 225, 265, 266, 284, 327
"separate but equal" xi, xxi, 316, 325
sexism 12, 75, 91, 100, 159, 207, 254, 264
sexuality 74, 84, 86, 201, 203, 208, 230, 359
Shange, Ntozake 144, 335
sharecropping xxi, 78, 253
Shepard, Matthew xiv, 207, 208, 209, 210
Shuttlesworth, Fred 15, 197
Sissle, Noble 13
sit-ins 15, 42, 103, 115, 244
Sixteenth Street Baptist Church bombing 132, 137, 276, 284, 327
slave narrative xxi, 5, 6, 33, 323, 324
slavery xii, xx, xxi, 3, 4, 5, 6, 8, 9, 17, 18, 21, 22, 24, 25, 26, 27, 29, 32, 33, 34, 47, 51, 58, 59, 63, 64, 65, 67, 73, 108, 116,

143, 149, 212, 227, 231, 242, 264, 305, 309, 323, 324
social mobility 222, 233, 234
Southern Christian Leadership Conference (SCLC) 327
South Side Writers Group 107
stereotype 152, 191, 213, 262, 268, 305, 306, 309
Sterling, Alton 147, 298
Stevenson, Bryan 17
Stewart, Maria W. Miller 7, 11
stigmatization 195
Stockett, Kathryn xv, 253, 254, 255, 256, 258, 259, 260, 261, 262, 263, 264, 265, 266, 267, 268, 269
Stonewall Inn riots xx
Stowe, Harriet Beecher 51, 324
Student Nonviolent Coordinating Committee (SNCC) 37, 327

Talented Tenth, the 10, 222, 233, 234
Terrell, Mary Church 11, 325, 333
Thurman, Wallace 13
Till, Emmett xiii, 78, 87, 106, 123, 124, 125, 128, 129, 138, 139, 209, 213, 293, 327, 352
Till Mobley, Mamie 293
Toledo, Elizabeth xxviii
Tometi, Opal 147
Toomer, Jean 13, 170
Trotter, William Monroe 11
Truman, Harry 15
Trump, Donald 4, 19
Truth, Sojourner 8, 157, 323
Tubman, Harriet 157, 323
Turner, Nat 7, 9, 30, 323
Tuskegee Institute 10

Uncle Tom 39, 44, 45, 47, 48, 51, 52, 139, 324, 326
United Negro Improvement Association (UNIA) 9
